CABINETMAKERS

To Claudia Weicher,
A colleague who watched
it all happen!
with so much
admiration,

Burt Heff

CABINETMAKERS

STORY OF THE THREE-YEAR BATTLE TO ESTABLISH THE U.S. DEPARTMENT OF EDUCATION

Robert V. Heffernan

Writer's Showcase

San Jose New York Lincoln Shanghai

CABINETMAKERS
Story of the Three-Year Battle to Establish
the U.S. Department of Education

Writer's Showcase
an imprint of iUniverse.com, Inc.

For information address:
iUniverse.com, Inc.
5220 S 16th, Ste. 200
Lincoln, NE 68512
www.iuniverse.com

ISBN: 0-595-15870-6

Printed in the United States of America

Contents

Dedication

I dedicate this book to public service and to public love of public policy.

Bob Heffernan with U.S. Senator Abe Ribicoff.

Foreword

This book took over four years to write, from 1980-1983. At one point, I had in my possession 24 cases of files and documents accumulated throughout the three years of the legislative battle and two years of interviews. Writing the book was the hardest task I have ever undertaken in my very active life.

For more than 15 years, the manuscript has been stored away, waiting for the day when its content could be read by interested people. Thanks to the power of the Internet and the World Wide Web, this important account of American history can finally be made available to all citizens—most importantly, the youth of this country.

Let this book become a lesson to all high school and college students: regardless of whether you come from a wealthy or a poor family, a powerful or an apathetic family, you can, if you have the will and the interest, become involved in the American political and governmental process.

To this day, I continue to be amazed that I was able to serve on the staff of the United States Senate at such an early age, beginning just a year-and-a-half after high school graduation. And I am amazed that I didn't have to be a lawyer to write legislation, to speak publicly, to deal with the White House.

No other book was ever written on the battle to put education in the President's Cabinet, mostly because, I believe, all the other personalities involved fully expected this book would be published and widely distributed. So they held off. I am often asked whether I still believe to this day if the ordeal was worth all the effort, whether elevating education to the Cabinet level had honest merit. I have always believed that, despite the obvious brazen political payoffs made in creating the Department of Education, the effort was more than justified.

I often wondered during the battle if all our talk about lifting up education to the Presidential level would really make education a priority in America. Twenty years of subsequent history have confirmed our predictions: the President of the United States is today dramatically involved in education, education is constantly a major national issue by the political parties, and today the raised consciousness has translated into higher salaries for teachers and, overall, much more attention for our schools.

The U.S. Department of Education has always been targeted for abolition by conservative Republicans. But not even Ronald Reagan, who campaigned to kill the agency, made good on his promise. I believe that every President will realize how powerfully the issue of education resonates with the general public, and that he or she will find much more value in keeping and using the Department, than in abolishing it.

Robert V. Heffernan

P.O. Box 414, Botsford CT 06404

Acknowledgements

My gratitude, first and foremost, goes to Abraham Ribicoff, who turned out to be the most effective teacher in my life. Senator Ribicoff taught all his staff members, by the sheer example of his gracious conduct, how to be a distinguished person in everything you do, how to engender respect and dignity, and—lacking most in today's public service—how to be a statesman. The Senator gave me a precious chance to prove myself, and he will always be my life's mentor.

I am also grateful to the staff of the U.S. Senate Committee on Governmental Affairs, 1975-1980, for hanging on to me all those years when every other intern was allowed only the usual short term of service. Chief Counsel and Staff Director Richard Wegman and Chief Clerk Elizabeth Preast provided constant support and encouragement.

A very special place in my heart is reserved for the star of this book, Marilyn Harris of the Senate Governmental Affairs staff, with whom I shared every day of the legislative battle, every emotional high and low that goes with shepherding a major piece of legislation through the process. Together, we were the team, the engine that passed this bill.

My thanks to all the other persons in this book, in the White House, the agencies and the interest groups. They were all very open in personal interviews that provided critical details long after the bill passed. Almost everyone in this book is an awesome American with intellect and commitment that every citizen should be proud of.

Special thanks to two of my secretaries for retyping the manuscript in the years before computers: Janiffer Baumann and Susan Dunn.

My love and gratitude to my godmother Marceline Barker and her husband Ted for giving me a one-year retreat to finish the book at The Red Inn in Provincetown, Cape Cod.

Lastly, my deepest love to my parents, Roberta and Vincent Heffernan, for their unending support.

THE FIRST TRY

1977-1978

ONE

Cloud of Fate

After some persistent nudging, I finally managed to pin down Marilyn. For me, holding Marilyn Harris to a specific meeting time was never easy.

"Look, Marilyn, we've got to get together sometime today on ED," I half-pleaded. "How about sometime later this afternoon?"

The two of us, and later the whole office, used the term "ED" to mean the Department of Education bill.

Marilyn disliked being pinned down, making hard, irrevocable commitments. A wise Senate staffer never puts words in concrete, for politics is rooted in quicksand.

She knew she had to find time to concentrate, or in her terminology, to *focus* on the ED bill. Already we were nearly two months into the first session of the 95th Congress, and the perennial Ribicoff Department of Education bill had not yet been introduced.

Marilyn gave a long sigh, then flipped through her appointment calendar, probably hoping to be rescued from making hard decisions on the ED bill by another pre-scheduled meeting.

Finally, she caved in. "All right, Bob. 3:00 o'clock in the hearing room, O.K.?"

"Great," I said, patting her on the shoulder to soothe her and show my obvious satisfaction. "See ya then."

*   *   *

We were all very busy that day—February 18, 1977—but happily so. A time of tremendous exhilaration, of renewed senses of purpose and direction.

Jimmy Carter's new presidency was just weeks old, and the entire capital seemed somehow renewed and reinvigorated itself. Everywhere there were new faces and new agendas. It seemed there was so much to do and accomplish, and perhaps not enough time to finish it all. The new Administration energized the whole city.

For us "Old-timers" who were used to dealing with the staid, conservative Administration of Gerald Ford, the change was startling, but welcome. It was a whole new ball game now, a Democratic Congress and a Democratic Administration. The return of one-party rule to Washington. A new era of close executive-congressional cooperation was expected.

We were also very much aware of how important our positions were. The new President came to Washington on a platform of massive reform of the federal government—abolish some agencies, establish others, instill efficiency through reorganization of offices and bureaus, overhaul the civil service and regulatory process. Plain and simple, that was our turf.

There were approximately 25 of us that made up the staff of the Committee on Governmental Affairs, United States Senate. We were young, liberal, and ambitious. We loved politics, and especially the high-stakes politics of Washington.

The Senate had specifically charged the Committee with overseeing the efficient operation and reorganization of the federal government.

Reduced to yeoman terms, we could get into anything the federal government was involved in, and that, of course, was everything.

We were working for a key Senate committee, with new powers and the accompanying public spotlight to match. Our boss, the Committee chairman, Connecticut Democratic Sen. Abe Ribicoff, was perceived as a force to be reckoned with, a distinguished elder statesman with ambitious goals and a right arm for the new White House.

The hustle and bustle around the office that day spoke volumes about our responsibilities. In January, the Committee rushed to confirm Bert Lance as the new director of the Office of Management and Budget (OMB), as other Senate committees rushed to confirm the Carter cabinet appointments in time for the Inauguration. We were well aware that we had direct oversight over OMB and, consequently, over the man everyone was labeling *deputy president.* The Committee was finishing up its consideration of the bill giving the President special authority to reorganize the federal government, a major Carter preoccupation. On the way was the legislation to establish the 12th Cabinet department, the Department of Energy, another bill to set up a consumer protection agency, the ethics-in-government measure, civil service reform proposals, and legislation to reform the federal regulatory apparatus.

All the staffers had many projects to work on, each so busy that there was little time to tell one another the latest scoop. The calendar was jammed with hearings and mark-ups. The mass of incoming phone calls lit up the switchboard like a twinkling Christmas tree. The Xerox machine was so overworked it constantly refused to work. All day long, there were meetings and more meetings. Lobbyists were continually pouring in and out of the office. It was common to see half the staff at work as late as 7:00 at night.

This scene was being repeated all over town. We felt we were an integral part of all the action, important to the Carter people.

*   *   *

I gathered all my ED stuff and walked the few steps from the main office to the hearing room. There was still another half hour or so before our scheduled meeting time. I needed some time to go over my research.

At the large wooden doors, an engraved wood-like vinyl sign caught my eye: "COMMITTEE ON GOVERNMENTAL AFFAIRS HEARING ROOM."

I pulled the big door open with my body weight and was relieved to find no one inside the huge room. In the crowded office buildings on Capitol Hill, finding an empty room is a delight. Our hearing room was a godsend. Sometimes, it was a place where we could escape from the pressures of the legislative process, where there would be some peace and quiet to concentrate squarely on complex materials. Of course, we also knew it as a pressure cooker when used for official functions like hearings or mark-ups.

As Senate hearing rooms go, ours was average in size, somewhat fancy with 25-foot ceilings, massive brass torch-like lamps shooting ineffective light upwards, and walls covered with wood panels. A giant, half-circle dais with American eagles carved in the wood occupied the front third of the room. The dais sat on a special floor elevated a foot higher, obviously for subtly reminding everyone that senators who sit there are the higher authorities. In the well below, a long witness table.

Midway in the room a cluster of tables and chairs rested, normally reserved for members of the press and for witnesses awaiting their turn. The general public was left the latter third, where a meager 50 chairs fit. Even that was probably intentional, for it always looks better on television when a hearing room is jammed with spectators.

Once inside, I spread out my papers and notebooks on one of the long press tables and tried to get organized.

Most of the papers gave sketchy facts on different parts of the old Ribicoff bill that had been introduced and reintroduced biennially since 1965, two years into the Senator's first term. (Nothing ever happened to the bill all the succeeding years.)

We were using last year's old bill as a base to work from. We intended to make a few changes here and there, but basically leave the substance intact. The bill was simple: take all the education functions out of the U.S. Department of Health, Education, and Welfare (HEW), add some education programs from other agencies and departments, provide for a few assistant secretaries and a Cabinet secretary, and *viola*, the blueprint for a *U.S. Department of Education*. On paper, it looked simple enough. But we knew better. If this bill ever went anywhere, it wouldn't look anything like that when Congress finished with it. We'd worry about all that later, but right then, we wanted to get the bill ready so Senator Ribicoff could, within the next few weeks, take it to the Senate floor, file it, and start the massive legislative wheels turning.

I had spent the last month accumulating materials on federal education programs—what they did, where they were located, how much money was in their budgets. Marilyn had asked me to compare the Ribicoff bill with dozens of other Department of Education bills other senators and representatives had introduced. Another memo compared the content of our bill to a study done by a man named Rufus Miles, from Princeton University. Miles laid down a forceful case for taking the "E" out of HEW and went a step further by explaining what other programs should go in or stay out. And, there was a fact sheet I had just finished, listing figures I gathered over the past week from bureaucrats downtown on six different programs that we thought might make a nice addition to the new Cabinet department we were dreaming up.

Shuffling through the scattered papers, I made more notes and changes in the actual language of the bill, then happened to gaze across

the empty room and out the long, tall windows. Outside, it was a typically dreary February day in Washington, the sky darkened with puffy,
dense grey clouds, the temperature in the high 30s.

Little spurts of rain fell sporadically.

With Marilyn nowhere to be seen, my mind lost itself in the hypnot-
ic swirl of the clouds.

*   *   *

Journalism was the field I chose to major in when I headed for
Washington and American University in 1973. The papers and TV stations back home always seemed to have more Washington news than
local news. Like thousands of young Americans, I found myself mysteriously attracted to a city full of newsmakers and important people.

Once in college, it doesn't take students long to discover that one of
the most highly coveted jobs in Washington is a paid internship with
the U.S. Senate or the U.S. House of Representatives. Only a White
House position would rank higher. However, getting one wasn't easy.

There were three ways a Hill internship could be achieved: (1)
through direct political connections where, say, an intern's parents
were big campaign contributors to a senator or representative; (2)
through indirect political connections, where an intern would know
someone who could exert influence in his behalf with a congressper-
son; or (3) through plain luck, being in the right place at the right
time, and being persistent.

For myself, it would have to be number three. My family was totally apolitical. I joined the pack and mailed off some letters to the
Connecticut and Vermont delegations (I was a native of Vermont,
domiciled in Connecticut) expressing interest in a Hill internship.

I was flabbergasted to receive months later a letter from Senator
Ribicoff's administrative assistant: "I think we can probably use you
on our subcommittee staff. I have to forewarn you that the pay is not

very high and the work is very routine at times. If you are still interested, call Marilyn Harris, the chief clerk of our subcommittee...". It was pure luck.

And so, at the age of 18, I became a U.S. Senate staff member. The timing was perfect. When I started my subcommittee internship in September 1974, Senator Ribicoff was coasting to an easy, overwhelming re-election victory for his third six-year term in the Senate. And, as luck would have it, the chairman of the full Committee on Government Operations we were operating under retired. Ribicoff, next in line, became chairman January 1975 and I as a sophomore in college, marched right along with the rest of the staff to claim our prestigious new status: majority staff of a Senate committee.

The job was ideal. Not only did it help financially, but I was building priceless work experience in the midst of undergraduate study.

But where would I go after graduation only three months away? The Senate job would be a hard act to follow. I'd vaguely decided to shoot for a job in the media. Failing that, hopefully they would agree to retain my services at the Senate.

*   *   *

Suddenly, the door swung open and in walked Marilyn at a fast gait, both arms supporting a bundle of files, yellow legal pads, and notebooks. It was 3:10. I smiled.

She gave a long sigh and shook her head. It was her way of acknowledging she was slightly late and had been busy.

"How're you doing, Marilyn?," I asked in an understanding voice.

She forced a smile. "I tell you, if I can just get away from those phones." Of all the people in the office, Marilyn seemed to get the most phone calls.

She plopped down her materials and began sorting things out. Rummaging through her handbag, she couldn't find any pencils and went back to the office to get some. Marilyn rarely wrote with anything but a pencil, probably a tiny facet of her cautious approach to Senate work. Pencil can be erased.

A few moments later, she came striding back into the hearing room with a fistful of freshly-sharpened pencils. We wasted no time in settling down to the task before us. Marilyn carefully looked over my memos and fact sheets, stopping every once in a while to discuss key points.

*   *   *

Marilyn and I made an interesting and effective team. Our skills complemented each other. She excelled in human relations, in soothing egos, in personal bargaining and persuasion, in mediating controversies, and in gently manipulating the human psyche. I was better at writing and expression, at organizing tasks and insisting they be accomplished. It was a vital combination for the course upon which we were about to embark.

Marilyn Ann Harris was then 32 years old. A native of Kansas City, Missouri, she had a BS in education and spent many years as a teacher. She also had an MA in communication. She had been working for Ribicoff for more than three years.

Marilyn blended well into the Washington scene, as if the two were made for each other. She loved the art of socializing. I used to envy her ability to work a reception with grace and easy conversation. Best of all, she used social functions to help with her job. She would remember names of new people and eventually they would become her contacts in Washington offices.

She had a strange kind of kinetic energy that could leave a whole room breathless and charged at times. Yet, she was good at controlling anger.

Both of us thirsted for responsibility and were naturally ambitious and competitive.

Marilyn sensed that the establishment of a United States Department of Education was within the realm of possibility, and she wanted badly to be in on it from the very start. It was going to be her baby, all right. The rest of the staff didn't much care. Most believed the ED bill didn't have an honest-to-goodness chance of making it.

*   *   *

The hearing room was having a therapeutic effect on Marilyn. I could see her blood pressure had come down. We were taking a more leisurely, studious approach in our review.

We had devoted almost half an hour to going over my stuff.

"Marilyn, why don't we take the old bill and go over it page by page?," I asked. She nodded in agreement.

Both of us pulled out our copies of the "old" bill Senator Ribicoff had introduced in September the previous year. Like all the others he had introduced since 1965, this ED bill had died a natural death. In September 1976 Gerald Ford was still President, and a new Cabinet department would be created only over his dead body. But Ribicoff reintroduced his favorite bill anyhow, mainly to signal the Democratic presidential candidate, Jimmy Carter, that he was happy with Carter's pledge to take the "E" out of HEW and make it into a separate department of its own. Should Jimmy Carter enter the White House, Abe Ribicoff was ready and willing to go with the Department of Education idea.

The bill was short, a mere 38 double-spaced pages. Anybody could have picked it up, read it, and understood what it was all about.

"Well, first things first," Marilyn declared, mockingly proud of her first decision. "Change 1976 to 1977," she said, penciling out the "1976" from the bill's title, "Department of Education Act of 1976." We hardly expected the bill could pass that year in time to keep the title, but it was wishful thinking anyway. We weren't even sure the bill would pass by the end of the new, two-year 95th Congress we were in.

Section two contained the "findings and purposes." We read through the seven findings, which spoke in flowery terms of the importance of education to the nation, the bad shape of federal education programs, and therefore the necessity of establishing the department.

"Who in hell wrote all this stuff?," I asked.

Marilyn shrugged her shoulders. "It's been there for years, I guess. I don't think we need to change it."

Next, the officers section. An agency must have a chain of command. Of two things we were sure: the number one honcho would be the Secretary of Education, and the second would be the undersecretary. From there on, the department could be organized in countless ways. The old Ribicoff bill conveniently side—stepped the issue. It simply provided for "four assistant secretaries and a general counsel" who were to "perform such duties and exercise such powers as the Secretary shall prescribe."

"Isn't that a little too vague?," I wondered.

Marilyn frowned, bit her lip, and gently shook her head.

"You know, Bob, I don't want to get into that whole business of parceling out assistant secretaries now," she told me with a notable lack of enthusiasm. Her eyes returned to search the materials for an easy answer.

The silence of the hearing room was becoming more prominent. Outside, the last stages of darkness had begun to settle in. It looked cold and damp, as I took advantage of Marilyn's diversion and glanced out the windows across the room. This being Friday, the Dirksen Senate Office Building was emptying fast as staffers rushed home to get an early start on the weekend.

Marilyn was right. We would have a rough time selling the need for a Department of Education if our bill was as or more bureaucratic than the present set-up at HEW. But on February 18, 1977, we didn't have enough information yet to know exactly what we were doing.

Without comment, Marilyn started writing something on her yellow legal pad. I angled my head to read it from the opposite side of the table:

"legislative affairs
administrative and management policy
evaluation and planning
intergovernmental relations"

"How's that?," she asked.

"You're not going to make a stab at naming the program assistant secretaries?," I inquired. The school lunch, Indian, Head Start people and other special interests would demand it, we knew.

"No, let's wait and see what comes out in the hearings."

"Okay."

Then, skipping over some minor provisions, we prepared to tackle the major section—transfer of functions and agencies. It was here that the anatomy of the new department would be determined. About the only thing we were sure of was that the "E" in HEW would be transferred, that it would make up the core of a separate education department. No one would dispute that. But outside of HEW there were *hundreds* of education programs: school lunch, arts and humanities, Indian education, veterans, labor training, military schools, and so on. They were scattered everywhere. Which should be merged into a new education department?

Each program served a special group, or constituency, and had its ever-present guardian friends in Congress. Moving one could create all kinds of controversy. Establishing a Department of Education was a longshot to begin with. We didn't need to take on any additional aggravation.

Marilyn and I exchanged nervous glances. We could feel ourselves tense up a bit. We weren't exactly sure how to handle this. There were

$20 billion-plus worth of federal education programs, of which we knew little. Two ordinary, unelected staffers making potential billion-dollar decisions.

Spread out on the table were a few papers with the tiny amount of information we had on these programs. Marilyn took a few minutes to look them over one at a time. I sat in silence, biting my thumbnail, also reading, engrossed.

At long last, Marilyn took the copy of the old bill we were marking up and stared for a few minutes at the transfer section, very deep in thought. Then, ever so slowly, she penciled giant "X"s over many of the paragraphs. Head Start...X. Defense schools...X. Indian schools...X. School lunch...X Science education...X. One by one, she crossed out the big programs to be transferred, as if it made her feel better simply to jettison the whole mass.

"What are you DOING?," I demanded.

A moment of silence. She didn't look up.

"You know, I can't put all these programs in the bill, and not know enough about them to defend transferring them, and commit Ribicoff · to supporting their transfer because they're in his bill," she said in a voice that asked for sympathy.

I was at a loss for words. Another long pause, The hearing room silence was almost deafening.

"Oh, Bob, I really don't know." Marilyn tilted her head, supported it with one arm.

"But how can we justify the need for the department and for consolidating ed programs if they're not in our bill?," I asked.

No answer. She started to doodle slowly, drawing little arrows that converged in a center circle, as if envisioning herself in the middle. Another pause.

"Well, I suppose Ribicoff doesn't have to be committed to everything in his bill," she said.

I started thinking fast, hoping to reinforce this small break in her position.

"That's right. You yourself have been telling everybody to work on supporting the *concept* of the department, and not bicker over what should go in or stay out," I argued.

Like Marilyn, I didn't relish the thought of fighting battles to move this or that program. But I could not imagine the new agency not having any "meat" either.

Slowly but surely, she was gaining strength and coming around to leaving the bill intact. Another deep sigh.

We searched each other's eyes for the next move. Suddenly, we broke out laughing.

"Oh hell," she said, turning her pencil upside down. She began erasing her huge "X"s. "I guess we'll have to tell everyone this is a concept bill and we don't have the faintest idea what'll be in the department."

I was relieved. It seemed we needed some sort of game plan for this new department we wanted to create. True, maybe those programs did not belong in an ED. But at least the bill would create much discussion and generate new ideas.

Once that all-important decision had been made, we got brave enough to add additional programs. In went a paragraph transferring the education civil rights functions from HEW. And in went another transferring the National Endowments for the Arts and Humanities, mainly to appease Sen. Claiborne Pell (D-RI), who chaired the subcommittee overseeing education, arts, and humanities.

We hurried through the rest of the bill, which contained most of the "boilerplate" language—the mundane, detailed authorities given every agency to function in their day-to-day duties. We made a few insignificant changes, then finished for the day.

Next week, we would send a clean draft of the bill to the Senate Legislative Counsel for some refinements in the language for legislative neatness. Then, we'd have to send in a memo to Senator Ribicoff to obtain his approval of our decisions. Hopefully, the bill would be introduced formally soon after his sign-off.

*   *   *

Marilyn and I had spent about two hours that bleak February day sprucing up the ED bill for reintroduction and making what we then considered were generally inconsequential decisions on the substance. The idea of a Cabinet Department of Education had not been examined in hearings in Congress for nearly three decades. It had never been considered on the floor of either House or Senate. This was all very preliminary and very subject to change through the strange, deliberative ways of the legislative process. We had no way of knowing what the future would hold in store for this bill.

Yet, unbeknownst to us, a precarious cloud of fate hung over the hearing room that day.

TWO

Early Stirrings

If it weren't for Jack Watson and Don White, we would not have got started on the ED bill as soon as we did. Without having any personal contact, they managed together to get the ball rolling.

*   *   *

A cold Sunday, January 9, 1977. At NBC's studios in upper northwest Washington, Jack Watson was in the hot seat on *Meet the Press*. Watson headed the new President's transition staff.

Much of Washington, D.C. tuned into the program, anxiously awaiting any clues to the fate of certain projects and Carter campaign promises. In just 12 days, Jimmy Carter would be inaugurated the 39th President of the United States.

The press probed Watson from every angle.

He was grilled about the Carter plans for reorganization of federal government. Suddenly, a newsman wondered if Carter lost his enthusiasm for the ED idea.

Watson thought for a quick moment, then replied before a live national television audience, "I have not spoken about that subject with him in the last month or two.

"What we are interested in doing with the Department of HEW is making it work better. Whether or not the creation of a separate Department of Education is the way to do it, as we have surmised or speculated about earlier, I think remains to be seen."

Watson paused, then added, "I think the situation on that question is still fluid."

*   *   *

On the other side of the Potomac River in a far-out Virginia suburb, the word "fluid" stuck in Don White's mind. He was encouraged enough to start making some phone calls the next day.

One person he telephoned was Marilyn Harris. White told her he was trying to drum up support for the Department of Education idea. He had already called the Council of Chief State School Officers, the National School Boards Association, the National PTA, and the National Education Association (NEA). They were all supportive.

To White, "fluid" meant an absence of hard political pressure on the Carter people. He was disappointed the incoming Secretary of Health, Education, and Welfare, Joseph Califano, had said he was not supportive of losing his "E".

Marilyn suggested he and his cohorts try to involve the other principal teacher union, the American Federation of Teachers (AFT) and its president, Albert Shanker. White agreed to try, and added he planned to set up a meeting of key education representatives in Washington to get things moving.

The call ended with White remarking, "(Vice President) Mondale and Riles are close. I think I can get him to talk to Mondale."

Wilson Riles was the Superintendent of Education of the State of California, and Don White was his chief staffer in Washington. Riles was considered one of the outstanding black leaders in America.

In the back of White's mind that day loomed an appealing thought—what a great first Secretary of Education his boss would make. White wanted to take the lead on the issue.

If the Department of Education ever became a reality, President Carter would surely have to give serious consideration to naming the prominent black educator to head it up.

*   *   *

Marilyn could hardly contain her excitement. The groups were starting to mobilize.

We sat in her office for about half an hour looking over the stuff we had and making assignments on researching the gaps. Marilyn piled much of the research on my shoulders.

"How soon do you want this material?," I asked her.

"Oh, I think we ought to get started on the bill as soon as possible," she answered. "How about in a couple of weeks, OK?"

As it turned out, four weeks passed before we had a chance to hold our tete-a-tete in the hearing room.

*   *   *

Jack Watson's little statement provided the first real inkling of the status of the ED promise since the 1976 campaign. An ominous silence on the issue followed the November election. Even when Senator Ribicoff met in December with the President-elect and mentioned the Department of Education bill as being on both their agendas, Carter was noncommittal.

Little by little, the Carter priorities were leaking out, and the Education Department was not among them. The President-elect told the congressional leadership he wanted to concentrate in his first months on simple extension of most programs, on getting special reorganization authority, on development of a national energy policy, on creation of a Cabinet Department of Energy, and on his billion-dollar economic recovery program.

It was obvious that the man who campaigned on reducing the number of federal agencies, and who was proposing to establish a Department of Energy, would find it hard to justify creating another Cabinet department, namely our ED. Or, he would most likely wait until next year, by which time hopefully the public would have forgotten about Energy. After all, it had taken the country 200 years to establish 11 Cabinet departments.

Our Governmental Affairs Committee would be the Senate panel to consider and study both Energy and Education Department bills. We considered it impossible, both politically and logistically, to work on two Cabinet departments at once.

Furthermore, there was an energy crisis. The disarray of federal energy programs exacerbated the crisis. The federal government played a critical role in the energy field, being the chief regulator and overseer. But with education, we would have a hard time conjuring up such a crisis. In contrast to energy, the federal government had only a very limited role in education; the states and local governments were primarily responsible. The need for the Department of Energy was seen as more immediate. ED would have to wait its turn.

When the word came officially from Plains that week the new President intended to transmit legislation to Congress to establish a Department of Energy by February 3, we knew that ED had been definitely pre-empted.

We were determined, however, not to let it fall by the wayside. The Department of Education was a campaign promise, something which could hold Jimmy Carter up to ridicule if not fulfilled. We intended to press for it.

*　　*　　*

James Earl Carter, Jr. announced to the world December 12, 1974 that he was a candidate for the Democratic presidential nomination.

The biggest test for the obscure, one-term former governor of Georgia came almost a year later, in Iowa.

"We now have 1900 agencies and departments in the federal government that I know about," Carter told leaders of Iowa's teachers November 21, 1975. "I intend to cut those down to no more than 200. In Georgia we cut 300 down to 22.

"The only department I would consider creating would be a separate Department of Education."

That commitment helped Carter win the support of most of Iowa's Democrat-affiliated teachers. A short while later, he walked away with a stunning, come-from-nowhere victory in the state's caucuses. Instantly, the unknown former Georgia governor had become a household name and a serious presidential contender.

*　　*　　*

With the arrival of the 1976 presidential election season, the metamorphosis was just about complete. Teacher power had blossomed into a mature political force.

For the first 150 years of the U.S., teachers were viewed and considered themselves as pure academicians, professionals in the field of education. A rigid doctrine pervaded the profession in that period: education and politics do not mix. The politics of funding and supporting the public schools was left to the local boards of education and the state government. Teachers taught children. The line was distinct. A large number of associations and organizations came into existence to enhance the discipline and respectability of the profession, groups centered around the teachers, the administrators, the school boards, the universities, and so on. One of these was the National Education Association.

Beginning with the Great Depression and the Second World War, things began to change. Government at all levels—local, state, and federal—started to take on new roles and new importance. The condition of the public school system was seen as directly affecting the national security and defense. A baby boom increased the construction of schools, education expenditures, and the need for more teachers. The success of the American education system transformed a nation of illiterates into a nation of intellects thirsting for more knowledge and information. The public's already high esteem for educators as individuals further expanded. New media created a new awareness among the people, and they focused more and more attention on government. The state and performance of education in America came under more public scrutiny.

Ever so slowly and cautiously, teachers across the country began to come out of their self-imposed shells. As the schools became centers of social reform and as pressures of change intensified, teachers, not students, were feeling the heat. The politics of education moved from behind closed doors of school boards to front pages of newspapers. Teachers soon saw the need to rally together around common goals and positions to ease the pressures on themselves and their classrooms.

Teachers began supporting and working for pro-education candidates in local races: school board members, mayors, city councilmen. Then, the local education associations organized into statewide associations, and their influence was finding its way to state legislatures and governors. It was only a short time later that the national-level associations cast aside their facade of "professionalism" for more active involvement in the politics of the White House, the Congress, and the federal bureaucracy.

As part of the politicizing process, local-level organizations began to stage work actions, and then full-fledged strikes.

The image of the docile, book-toting teacher had, over a 30-year period, gradually faded. In its place came the activist, socially-concerned, politically-astute educator. In the transition, teachers lost some of the institutional respect they had developed for more than a century-and-a-half. But the quality of the schools and the intellect of the nation improved.

By the early 1970s, teachers had organized political action committees to assist financially pro-education candidates for the U.S. House of Representatives and the U.S. Senate. Once endorsed, a candidate could also count on precious volunteer help with campaign logistics.

Jimmy Carter was a studious observer of this long-running metamorphosis. He knew well how the education system worked and how the politics of education was changing. His campaign literature made explicitly clear his first public office was chairman of the Sumter County, Georgia school board. And, as Governor of Georgia he was involved in education to a great extent.

Soon after making the go decision in 1974 to seek the presidency, Carter targeted the education community for supporting his candidacy. His reasons were obvious.

The teacher network is politically perfect. Teachers are in every town, hamlet, county, city, and state of the union. They are well educated and highly knowledgeable on the issues of the day. They are active in the political system; many hold leadership positions in town and state parties and nearly all are registered to vote. They have more spare time in which to volunteer their assistance in campaign work (especially during the summer months).

Most importantly, the American teacher is still one of the respected members of the community. Teacher unions may not be popular with the general public, but the teacher as an individual still is, trusted and admired by parents. When a teacher works a phone bank for a candidate, chances are his message will at least get a fair hearing. In many cases, his influence will be substantial.

Lastly, teachers vote. In a typical election, their turnout will be higher than any other group. Given that there are an estimated four to five million teachers, their collective ballots could easily determine the outcome of a national election.

In going after the education-teacher vote, Jimmy Carter was a lucky man, a politician in the right place at the right time.

By 1974, the same year Carter declared his presidential ambitions, the biggest and most powerful education organization of them all, the National Education Association (NEA), formally moved to participate in the high-stakes whirl of presidential politics. The decision marked the final phase in the movement of American teachers to the open political realm.

Carter and his staff had many meetings with the NEA leadership in 1974 and 1975, and researched the issues which most concerned the nation's largest teacher union. They found the association had fought over the years for hefty increases in federal education programs' budgets, for school desegregation and civil rights, for collective bargaining for teachers, for women's issues, and for a host of labor—related causes. But of the dozens and dozens of goals near and dear to NEA's heart, one special long-standing desire topped the list far above everything else. So far up, in fact that most NEA leaders thought it was nearly unachievable. It was considered the ultimate goal, and if obtained, would symbolize that the association had transformed itself into perhaps the single most powerful organization in the U.S., that the politicization process had succeeded.

NEA's "impossible dream" was the break-up of HEW and the establishment of a separate United States Department of Education, complete with a Secretary of Education in the President's Cabinet. No higher status could be conferred upon a function in our society.

True, NEA was setting its sights very high, but it was not any different than other well-organized and financed special interests. Businessmen had their Commerce Department, farmers had their Agriculture Department, labor groups had their Labor Department, and the list goes on.

It was clear even to the untrained observer that education in HEW was suffering badly from neglect and from budget and turf battles with its cohabitants—massive health and welfare programs. The low-level U.S. Commissioner of Education rarely met with the President. The whole situation, in NEA's eyes, denigrated the honorable ranking of education in the public view. And, if NEA could do nothing but countenance the status quo, then that spoke volumes about NEA and its rank in Washington, and about teachers and their rank in the nation. All associations must have goals set high enough to rally their troops and justify their continued existence.

Without the support of NEA and its 1,700,000-plus teachers, Jimmy Carter would have to scratch the backing of the education community, an integral part of his election game plan. So, NEA's endorsement was a must.

Carter knew a campaign promise to create an Education Department would not be 100 per cent compatible with another to reduce the number of federal agencies. But dominant energy and economy campaign issues would drown it out. If it did arise, Carter could use it as an example of how the federal government needed reorganizing. HEW was big and out-of-control, so it would be fairly simple to sell the logic of breaking it up. And, he could issue an appeal to the public conscience about how a vital function like education should have a seat at the Cabinet table.

Thus, the creation of a Department of Education would become one of Jimmy Carter's earliest campaign promises, and, some argued, indirectly a key contributor to his becoming President of the United States.

*   *   *

By late June 1976, it was all over for the Democrats. Jimmy Carter had won enough primaries and enough delegates to wrap up the nomination.

Local and state-level teacher affiliates of the NEA worked for Carter in most of the primary states. Their work had a substantial impact.

President Gerald Ford had made no attempts to woo the education vote or to make significant concessions on his dismal education record. It was obvious NEA would give its first presidential endorsement to Carter at its summer convention.

Going through the formalities, NEA President John Ryor once more interviewed Carter June 19 in Atlanta. The Democratic nominee repeated he'd pursue ED "in context of an overall reorganization of government." Right on cue, Carter received the first, historic endorsement of the National Education Association and its political action committee.

A few days later, another strong education supporter came to speak before the NEA conventioneers—Sen. Walter Mondale. A one-time presidential candidate himself with iron ties to the liberal establishment and the Hubert Humphrey wing in Minnesota, Mondale had been consistently supported by the Minnesota teachers in his campaigns.

Mondale told the teachers, "I hope that one of the first things that we do when we get a new President is to read the NEA platform and adopt and create a new Department of Education and put education where it belongs." They cheered. Little did he know, however, that in a few weeks Jimmy Carter would ask his company in the race for the White House, as the next Vice President of the United States. NEA could not have made a better choice itself.

*   *   *

Originally established in 1857 as the "National Teachers Association," NEA remained a nonpartisan, professional organization through the 1950s. Its membership grew at a fast rate. By the 1960s, NEA was touting itself as the largest professional association in the world.

As the association became more involved in state and national political contests, it slowly developed an intricate network. The "UniServe" program put some 1,100 fully staffed NEA satellite offices into operation throughout the states and cities. Each would act as the local or regional conduit or service-station for the national organization, and would provide professional services and guidance to the thousands of locally-based NEA affiliates.

Representative democracy was built into the NEA decision-making process. Teachers at the local level elected their own local presidents. Local teachers were elected by secret ballot as delegates to state and national conventions. Overall policy was set and national leaders were selected by the annual NEA convention, held always during the summer months when schools were closed. The massive convention attendance approached the 10,000 mark every year. So, if the NEA made a decision to support a Department of Education, chances were it accurately reflected the majority sentiment of the nation's teachers.[1]

By the end of 1975, members of local NEA unions were required to belong also to the state and national associations. The rule would guarantee cohesiveness and strength, especially for the national organization, which was already handsomely equipped to argue education's case in the Washington power system. NEA occupied a prime piece of real estate—a modern, 10-story tall office building, symbolically and strategically perched just five blocks straight down 16th Street from the north portico of the White House. More than 250 professional staffers—executives, lobbyists, public relations specialists, and others—were housed there. Its operations were financed by an annual budget in the $45-50 million

---

[1] NEA represents approximately two out of every three teachers in the U.S.

range, most of the funds coming from mandatory dues charged individual teachers. These resources were supplemented by another 1,200 staff and a $150 million congregate budget of state and local NEA affiliates.

As the 1960s and 1970s wore on, NEA's success rate in politics and influence steadily improved. The number of federal education programs tripled during that time, and their budgets zoomed to more than $8 billion in 1976. During the Nixon and Ford Administrations, NEA lobbied Congress to overturn presidential vetoes of education appropriations bills, ending up with a respectable batting average.

In 1972, NEA formed its political action committee, NEA-PAC, to furnish financial assistance to pro-education House and Senate candidates. Of the 184 candidates supported, 140 won election. Not a bad score for the first try. NEA did better in the 1974 congressional elections The coffers of NEA-PAC were fattened to an impressive $225,000, while spending by state, local, and individual members on congressional races was estimated at nearly $2 million. NEA endorsed 282 House candidates, and 229 won. Of its 28 Senate candidates supported, 21 won. That year, NEA could claim anywhere from 4,000-6,000 of its members resided in every congressional district.

The association had played both sides of the aisle, endorsing both Democratic and Republican candidates (definitely more Democrats, though). The movement into presidential politics, however, was a very partisan step—a flat choice between a Democratic or Republican slate. If a revengeful Republican captured the White House, there was the risk many House and Senate Republicans might be more prone to defect from supporting the NEA position on legislation.

The NEA knew it could be swimming in shark-infested waters with its endorsement of Jimmy Carter. So much the association had worked for and had built could go down the drain with one simple endorsement, one election.

The National Education Association tossed the dice. On November 2, 1976, the dice showed snake eyes.

*   *   *

Jimmy Carter won by the skin of his teeth. It wasn't supposed to be that way. He left the Democratic National Convention in August 1976 with an astonishing 20-30 point lead in all major polls. But the lead gradually diminished as the press continued to point out that defining Carter and his positions was difficult.

Fortunately for Carter, his Department of Education promise rarely surfaced. Ford strategists apparently saw little sexiness in the issue and did not want to appear militantly anti-education.

But the lack of debate on ED also had the effect of silencing the proponents, putting the whole notion in cold storage. After winning the NEA endorsement, Carter hardly ever mentioned it again. He had more important things to attend to.

In the end, Carter managed to hang on to his core supporters of disenchanted Democrats and independents. He won with a breathtaking 50.1 per cent of the popular vote—one of the slimmest margins in history.

Victorious politicians fear close margins for a simple reason: groups and/or individuals can claim to have made *the* difference in the election, and the candidate will be expected to forever remember it. The teachers would be no exception.

*   *   *

The week preceding Jack Watson's TV appearance, the new 95th Congress assembled at the Capitol, trying to organize itself for the next two years, select its leaders, and prepare for the coming of Jimmy Carter, his Administration, and its programs.

The House, as expected, easily elected its new Speaker, Thomas "Tip" O'Neill. The Massachusetts Democrat's tough but warm personality and arm-twisting ability was widely expected to be a good omen for Carter, an aid in keeping the often restless House Democrats in line behind their President.

In the Senate, Robert Byrd of West Virginia became the new majority leader. Like O'Neill, he would be a strong leader, a help for Carter. His best talents were in accommodating the wishes and egos of other senators, and in mediating disputes within the upper house. But he could also be particularly vehement at times in staking out and defending positions on issues. Byrd would prove also to be a master at running the floor of the Senate and at the use of its rules.

Senate Republicans unexpectedly elected Howard Baker of Tennessee as their new leader. Baker would be an effective, dynamic critic of the new President. But, like Carter, he was also a moderate southerner with a pragmatic mind who could provide valuable help on many issues.

All in all, things were shaping up nicely on Capitol Hill for the Carter forces. There was hope the campaign promise of a new era in improved Congress-White House cooperation might actually come true.

*   *   *

The Senate began considering Carter's Cabinet nominations.

Exactly one week before Carter's Inauguration, Joseph A. Califano, Jr. sat at the witness table in the second-floor hearing room of the Senate Finance Committee in the new Senate office building.

He was the man Carter had nominated to control the biggest federal agency, the Department of Health, Education, and Welfare. With half the federal budget under HEW's roof, there were hundreds of programs and issues for which Califano would be responsible—national health insurance, social security, drug regulation, abortion, welfare, education, and many others.

But there was one specific issue on which a great deal of skepticism about Califano's views had surfaced—creation of a separate Department of Education. We were nervous about Califano's constant effort to go out of his way to avoid supporting the Carter campaign pledge. Califano was an intelligent man, well-schooled in the bureaucratic ways and tricks of Washington. His opposition could scuttle the whole idea, for the very heart of an Education Department would be the "E" in Califano's HEW.

We could see we were in for a fight.

"I wonder if you would advocate a spin-off of education in a separate department?," a senator asked.

Califano leaned forward and spoke cautiously. "Senator,...quite frankly I would like to look at that issue and ask whether it should be separate or whether it should be part of one larger department for social service."

A slight murmur was heard in the hearing room from some of the education people monitoring the testimony.

"My writing on it is on public record," Califano continued.[2] "I wrote I do not think it was appropriate to add another department directly reporting to the President, that the general thrust of reorganization should be to reduce the number of people reporting to the President of the United States...

"In sum, I would make two points. The American people did not elect Califano, they elected Carter. He said he wanted to look at this.

---

[2] Califano was referring to his book, "A Presidential Nation," published in 1975 by Norton.

"Second, my mind is certainly open on any organizational issue, especially when people like Senator Ribicoff who have served in HEW think it is an important thing to do."

Califano was going out of his way to be noncommittal at his confirmation hearings. He didn't want to do or say anything that would irritate the senators on the committee that would have to approve his nomination.

Coincidentally, Senator Ribicoff sat on the Finance Committee. He and Califano were old friends, going back through the Johnson and Kennedy Administrations in the 1960s. The two had worked together for many liberal Democratic causes.

At the hearing, Ribicoff had taken his seat at the dais to congratulate Califano on his appointment and to give his ritual lecture about the realities of being Secretary of HEW. Ribicoff served in the seat during the first two years of the John F. Kennedy Administration.

"...Many of us feel that HEW is beyond the capacity of one department to handle," the Senator said. "When you understand the complexity and the human beings involved, we are going to have to break it up."

Califano sat back in his chair and grinned slightly.

The Connecticut Senator smiled at his witness. "I know you are going to do your best, and that is all anyone can expect of you...".

*   *   *

Reportedly, there was no great amount of enthusiasm by the Carter people in the selection of Califano. On the plus side, he would bring impeccable qualifications to the job and would be nearly 100 per cent acceptable to the Democratic party and its liberal wing, which was still suspicious of Carter.

It seemed only natural to appoint the talented, ambitious mover-and-shaker who, as the top aide to President Lyndon Johnson, had pioneered the "Great Society" programs into existence as their administrator in the new Carter Cabinet.

But on the minus side, there was some uneasiness among the "Georgia mafia," that close circle of Carter advisors, about the feisty and seemingly independent Italian. Many worried Califano would try to steal the show and upstage the new President in matters concerning HEW, the monument to all the Democratic party had stood for. Others wondered if they could "control" him from the White House. The trouble was, Califano knew much more about the Washington system and its machinations than the Georgians could ever hope to know, having worked within it for more than a decade. He knew the men and women of the media, he knew the Congress inside and out, he knew how agencies can sabotage presidential decisions with which their bureaucrats disagree. Finally, he knew more about running the country from the White House than Jimmy Carter and his advisors, who campaigned as outsiders.

This nervousness stemmed in large measure from Carter's pledge to do away with the Nixonian practices of the past and move toward "Cabinet government." No more would White House staffers boss around members of the President's Cabinet, Carter repeatedly said in the 1976 campaign. The nation would be governed by the President, acting in unison with his Cabinet. Secretaries of the departments would have much broader latitude to run their own agencies and appoint their own people.

The change sounded good, but Washingtonians knew the potential for foul-up was high. The right hand has to be coordinated with the left. A presidential order must be carried out to the letter. And the White House needs to use the agencies and departments to control political situations, such as cutting off federal grants to districts of rebellious congressmen.

The President-elect took a sizable risk in appointing Joe Califano Secretary of Health, Education, and Welfare. But it kept the liberals happy and pleased Vice President Walter Mondale, Califano's biggest booster in the Carter team. The President's advisors knew, though, if anyone could kill the "Cabinet government" concept, it would be Califano.

*   *   *

Meanwhile, our Committee was working on another nomination—that of Bert Lance to be director of the Office of Management and Budget (OMB).

As we saw it, there were four people who could talk with any authority on the Department of Education idea: Carter, Jack Watson, Califano, and Bert Lance.

Lance has been widely touted in the press as the new President's closest personal friend, and many were predicting he would become the "deputy president" in this Administration. OMB was the President's powerful right arm for managing the federal government, clearing forms, rules, and budgets. Carter would also charge the Office with responsibility for his massive reorganization effort.

Lance's views on the ED bill were a complete mystery, although we suspected he would be an instant skeptic, given his conservative background in business and banking. At our Committee hearings on his appointment, the burly Carter strongman spoke in specific terms on just two proposals: the President's reorganization authority and the proposed Department of Energy. He uttered not one word about ED.

We worried a negative Lance position would weigh so heavily with Jimmy Carter that he might abandon his ED pledge.

*   *   *

Jimmy Carter officially assumed the Presidency in a low-key inaugural ceremony Thursday, January 20. Hundreds of thousands of people braved the frigid cold weather outside to witness personally the swearing-in of the new President in the Capitol plaza, and enjoy the long parade down Pennsylvania Avenue to the White House.

The Carters would always be remembered for something they did that day, not said. The First Family got out of their limousines and walked the several miles from Capitol Hill to claim the White House, surprising the nation. It symbolized a new beginning, a delightful common touch.

Forever obsessed with new approached and fresh starts, the American people hoped for Jimmy Carter's success at turning their country around.

*   *   *

Most of Carter's Cabinet was already in place.

Not until the following week, however, was Joseph Califano sworn in as the nation's 12th HEW Secretary.

Califano lost no time moving in to his suite in the HEW building at the foot of Capitol Hill. He brought along an energetic and enthusiastic team to run the mammoth agency, and soon they were working 12-hour days and running their secretaries on two shifts.

He waited less than 24 hours before calling together his first press conference. Califano proclaimed, "With leadership, this place can really fly."

THREE

The Bill's Introduction

Four days after our hearing room drafting session, Marilyn walked into one of the first-floor conference rooms at the NEA building to find a large group of people milling around, making small talk with one another.

It would be her first encounter with all the major elementary and secondary education organizations.

Don White and colleagues had set up the February 22 meeting to try to assemble a core group for supporting the Department of Education. People were there from associations representing state boards of education, school boards, school public relations, secondary school principals, audio visual departments, school administrators, big city schools, PTAs, elementary school principals, vocational educators, and curriculum development. Of course, NEA had staff there, as did its smaller rival, the American Federation of Teachers (AFT).

As the meeting got underway, Marilyn told the group Senator Ribicoff planned on introducing his bill sometime within the next two weeks. Right now, she said, we're in the process of gathering cosponsors. As for scheduling hearings, she didn't know because the Committee was going to be spending much of its time on the Department of Energy bill. But, she said, it was encouraging to see so many education groups together and interested in working for the ED bill.

A total silence fell over the room when the AFT representative, Eugenia Kemble, asked to speak. "The AFT has had a longstanding position in opposition to a Department of Education," she declared with a firm voice, "and we're still opposed. We're worried that a campaign for a separate department would divert attention away from other more important efforts, such as increasing the funding of education programs…".

The awkward silence continued for a brief interval after Kemble finished. No one was really very surprised, yet there was hope AFT might turn around its position and join the rest of the education community in working toward this big goal. The other education lobbyists knew what was going on—AFT was going to try to kill the Department of Education idea just because NEA wanted it badly. The two teacher unions had a history of bitter rivalry. The AFT, they thought, was gambling that it had a reasonable chance of blocking NEA's push for an Education Department, and if it succeeded, the perceived power of NEA would collapse and AFT could win over more teacher locals.

There, right inside the NEA building, the participants sat in the sad realization that this was not going to be an easy fight, that there was no way they could march up Capitol Hill as a unified education community on this issue. The only remaining question was, how hard would the AFT fight the NEA? Time would tell.

White brought the meeting back to reality by simply acknowledging the opposition of AFT and by steering the discussion towards plotting strategy to create the department. It was strange for the pro-ED lobbyists there to discuss a game plan with a confirmed opponent present, but they cautiously plodded along anyhow.

The groups agreed on the need to push the White House. They heeded Marilyn's request and promised to begin making contacts with senators' offices to induce them to add their senator's name as a cosponsor to the Ribicoff bill, and to push for hearings on it.

After much talk, the critical element of the strategy emerged. The best way of pressuring the President to make good on his campaign pledge was to demonstrate broad congressional support. The lobbyists decided it would be best to focus on the Senate, mainly because of the tremendous respect there for Ribicoff, and because the education lobby (particularly NEA) traditionally had more influence with the Senate than the House; it was better organized on a state-wide than on a House-district basis. (Senators are elected in state-wide elections.)

If more than 50 of the 100 U.S. senators cosponsored Ribicoff's bill, the President would in effect be shamed into redeeming his campaign promise. Jimmy Carter could not cite congressional resistance as a reason to back away. They'd worry about the House after the President's decision.

It was a good blueprint, everyone agreed in breaking up their short one-hour meeting. "We're going to win this one!," White predicted.

But one major education group obviously hoped not.

*   *   *

From the start, the American Federation of Teachers had billed itself as a straightforward, upfront labor union. Unlike the NEA, there was never an identity crisis in the AFT. Organized in 1916 with many disgruntled NEA members, the AFT promptly became an affiliate of the old American Federation of Labor (later known as the AFL-CIO), and has stayed there ever since.

The AFT's reputation had been considerably more militant than that of the NEA. It was the first of the two to invoke teacher strikes and collective bargaining. AFT's hardball tactics were successful in winning higher salaries and greater benefits, especially in larger cities with severe urban problems.

In contrast, NEA preferred to depict itself as the *professional* association for teachers, not the labor union.

But, as more big-city school system teachers voted to affiliate with AFT, the NEA too began to seek collective bargaining, seeing a threat to its healthy membership ranks. And as the National Education Association became more progressive, it immersed itself in politics, just as AFT had done all along.

During the 1960s, the rivalry between the two organizations was incredibly intense as they slugged it out for the right to represent local school systems all across the country. NEA's membership gradually increased toward the two million mark. With the baby boom at its peak, the AFT made consistent gains in membership to nearly 450,000 by the 1970s.

AFT had cherished its long alliance with the AFL-CIO, mainly for political reasons. In the big cities, state governments, and federal government, the AFT had political clout because it used AFL-CIO lobbyists to help lobby for education laws and funds.

The NEA, though, saw more value in its independence from the gigantic 13-million member AFL. It could concentrate solely on education, and not be distracted by other higher-ranking labor priorities. When the two teacher unions sought in 1974 to relieve some of the hostility and discuss merging together, the issue of AFL affiliation blocked any agreement.

The AFT was politically weaker than the NEA, but it still wielded a lot of influence. For example, in the 1976 election, AFT's political action committee disbursed more than $60,000 to 94 candidates for House, Senate, and presidential races. Its success rate was 65 per cent in the congressional elections, and its choice for president, Jimmy Carter, won.

AFT's organizational network was nowhere as extensive as NEA's. There were no state affiliates in 15 states. The AFT annual budget of approximately $15 million was only one-third that of NEA and its staff ratio was the same. Little of the AFL's vast resources were funneled to help AFT exclusively.

Yet in spite of all its weaknesses, AFT was a thorn in NEA's side. And, since both had endorsed Carter, there was the strong possibility the President might find himself in the middle of a strenuous tug-of-war between the NEA and the AFT, AFL-CIO. Would AFT President Al Shanker become so desperate as the battle progressed that he would call in all of his political chips and demand a full-court press of the AFL lobbyists? Active opposition of the AFL could erase any chances for a Department of Education.

*   *   *

In the first weeks of March, we were getting closer and closer to finally introducing a bill to establish a U.S. Department of Education.

In the past, that was no big deal. From the early 1900s, more than 130 similar bills had been introduced. Congress had not even taken one from the file drawer since the 1950s.

But this time it was different. Jimmy Carter was the new President, and he had promised to establish one. No other modern American President had made that commitment. Abe Ribicoff, now a powerful Senate committee chairman, was in a super-advantageous position. He chaired the panel that would consider the bill *and* was the only member of Congress to have ever been HEW Secretary. The education lobby had matured into a potent national political force, and education itself had grown to become a major responsibility of the federal government with more than $20 billion of programs.

For the first time in history, the ingredients for success were all present at once.

Preparations for introduction of the bill were time-consuming, but Marilyn and I were making good progress. We spent three full months on research, and then we only scratched the surface. The two of us spent four weeks debating and refining the language of the bill itself, even though we knew it would undergo drastic surgery as it traveled through the legislative process. When we felt secure enough with the language, a memorandum would be written to the Chairman, Senator Ribicoff, explaining the changes in the bill and the strategy behind them. We would have to spend many hours informing other senators' staffs of our intention to introduce the bill, and ask that they check to see if their senators were interested in adding their name as a cosponsor. We'd draft a one-page "Dear Colleague" letter to be circulated to all members of the Senate from Ribicoff asking for support. To accompany the bill's introduction, we'd also have to write a floor statement for the Senator. And, we would alert the press via calls and a release, the latter being coordinated with Ribicoff's press secretary.

One by one, we tackled these tasks.

*   *   *

"COMMITTEE ON GOVERNMENTAL AFFAIRS
United States Senate

MEMORANDUM

March 4, 1977
TO:Senator Ribicoff
FROM:Marilyn
RE:Proposal to Establish a Separate Department of Education

The following includes a brief discussion of the changes made from your Department of Education bill, last introduced September 29, 1976..."

The memo would serve to keep the issue in the forefront of the Senator's mind. Most importantly, it acted as a barometer to make certain we, the staff, were staying within Ribicoff's guidelines.

Senate staffers each day make hundreds of substantive and political decisions independently, and on behalf, of the senator they work for. A senator does not have enough time to involve himself in every detail of the avalanche of legislation. Part of the fine art of being a Senate staffer is knowing how to make the right decisions with general guidance from a senator, taking into account his political philosophy and his political survival.

We were becoming Ribicoff's technicians on the ED bill. He would have confidence in our judgment, because it was based on more thorough research and investigation than he personally could find time for.

With little doubt, the Senator would skim over it, make a check in red pencil at the top, initial "AR", and send it back without comment—his way of giving approval. The decisions we had made were not enough to give him heartburn. They strayed little from his previous bill.

*   *   *

Abraham Alexander Ribicoff. Lawyer, state legislator, municipal judge, U.S. Representative, governor, U.S. Secretary of HEW, U.S. Senator. He was the only American in history to have held all these posts.

His was a perfect rags-to-riches story. Through education and hard work, Ribicoff moved up from poverty to become a lawyer during the Great Depression. In Connecticut, he met up with a man named John Bailey, who grew to become one of the most powerful Democratic politicians in U.S. history. With Bailey's prodding,

Ribicoff won a string of elections, sending him to the state legislature, U.S. House, and the governor's seat.

As governor, he watched and admired the young U.S. Senator from neighboring Massachusetts, John F. Kennedy. Ribicoff worked to advance Kennedy's candidacy for the presidency, and when he won in 1960, Ribicoff practically had his choice of Cabinet chairs.

He chose HEW. He took a strong interest in the education component, but soon discovered the massive health and welfare programs consumed most of his time. A year-and-a-half later, Ribicoff was gone, a man frustrated by the inertia of the bureaucracy and, some said, by diminishing access to President Kennedy. He vowed to break-up HEW and give education Cabinet status all its own.

Ribicoff wanted to be his own man, and ran for U.S. senator from Connecticut in 1962. There, he was recognized immediately for his expertise in federal HEW issues and his knowledge of how the bureaucracy worked. His prestige and power grew as he tackled issues ranging from establishment of the new Departments of Housing and of Transportation to civil rights to international trade to consumer protection.

On assuming the chairmanship of the Government Operations Committee in 1975, the Senator mapped out an active agenda, getting into many previously neglected areas of government reform and management.

He had carved out a role as a true elder statesman and had earned the reputation of eagerly digesting complex issues, daring to take independent stands, and uniquely sensing political trends. The Senator went out of his way to be gracious and fair with colleagues, even enemies. The Ribicoff style was, first and foremost, one of accommodation and compromise. His staff never referred to him as anything other than, "The Senator."

Ribicoff hardly knew Jimmy Carter, but admired his come-from-nowhere feat and agreed with the Georgian's moderate stands on balancing the budget and slimming down the bureaucracy. A few weeks prior to the summer 1976 Democratic convention, the Senator endorsed Carter's nomination, inducing other essential ratification from the party's senior leaders.

In 1977, with the coming of Carter, Ribicoff was at the top of his political career and power. Despite his moodiness and sometimes haughty arrogance, his staff had much respect and affection for the man whose elegance, power, and statesmanship was transforming their young lives into promising futures.

*   *   *

On Monday, March 7, everything seemed to happen all at once. The Senator returned Marilyn's memo to her and indicated no objections to our decisions. That cleared the way for her to set a date for the bill's introduction. She decided on Monday, the 14th, a week later. We had some hustling to do to make the deadline.

A clean copy of our rewritten bill returned from the Senate Legislative Counsel's Office, a battery of astute, nonpartisan lawyers who make sure bills are technically, legally correct. We made still further changes and refinements.

Ribicoff approved Marilyn's "Dear Colleague," and the letter immediately went to all senators.

Marilyn next wrote the floor statement that would be filed with the bill, mainly to educate the public and press on the merits of the legislation. It would be printed in the *Congressional Record* as if delivered personally on the Senate floor. Ribicoff approved it. One copy went to the Senator's press secretary, who would write a press release and distribute it to the national and Connecticut media.

"I am pleased to introduce, along with Senators Magnuson, Humphrey, and Pell and over 20 of my distinguished colleagues, a bill to establish a separate Department of Education," the statement began.

"...Leadership to handle the vast range of educational issues and programs is almost impossible within the Department of HEW because of its immense size," it went on.

"The budget for health and welfare is 18 times as large as the $9.1 billion budget of the Education Division. Yet, the Education Division itself is large enough to constitute a major department...

"...But these reasons are only the 'bureaucratic' side of the picture. American education needs a unified direction. It needs a full-time Secretary of Education who can devote all his or her enthusiasm, imagination, time, and capability to strengthening American education.

"...Hearings have never been held on a proposed Department of Education, and it is my hope that the various components of the bill, including the proposed transfers, would be thoroughly discussed," Ribicoff's statement concluded.[3]

In the Committee office, calls from Senate legislative assistants were starting to come in. Already some 30 senators wanted to have their names printed on the bill as a cosponsor. More would probably call before the 14th, introduction day. No doubt most were initiated by the Washington-based education groups.

That afternoon, Ribicoff's press people had the release stuffed in envelopes and ready to be delivered. It began:

"From Senator Abe Ribicoff (D-Conn.)
Release AM, Monday, March 14, 1977

---

[3] We later discovered several hearings had been held in Congress, but the most recent took place around 1950.

Department of Education

Senator Abe Ribicoff (D-Conn.) today will introduce legislation to create a Department of Education.

The new Department would absorb all the education responsibilities and programs of the Department of Health, Education, and welfare..."

Introducing the bill on Monday, a slow news day, would increase the likelihood of press coverage. The release would travel by messenger to key national and Connecticut reporters in the Capitol press galleries, the National Press Building downtown, and other locations in the city.

*   *   *

Wilson Riles flew to Washington as we were making the final preparations for introducing the ED bill.

"A separate Department would remove education from the bureaucratic jungle in HEW, where the urgent problems of the schools simply do not receive very serious attention," he told a breakfast meeting of California educators Wednesday.

"And most important, it would get education out from under the HEW budget 'cap' which for many years has caused the annual budgets to recommend low figures for education.

"...I ask you to discuss this with your Representatives to urge action during the 95th Congress...We are trying to develop support for Senator Ribicoff's bill."

The California State Superintendent of Education was clearly going to be a big booster. Don White ran off copies of Riles's remarks and distributed them around town.

*   *   *

Everyone was beating up on HEW—for good reason.

HEW was beyond human comprehension: 400 separate programs, 145,000 employees, more than 800 subagencies and offices directly serving 115 million Americans from 5,200 buildings across the country.

Of all organizational entities on earth, HEW's budget was the third largest—surpassed only by the overall budgets of the U.S. government and the Soviet Union. In 1977, it stood at $146 *billion*—nearly half the total federal budget and far above the defense budget. HEW spent money at the rate of $440 million per day, $28,000 per minute, $500 per second. Almost 80 per cent of its budget was *uncontrollable*, forced to rise automatically each year by law to keep up with the population's needs. HEW's *annual increase* in budget alone approached $20 billion.

Social Security consumed three-quarters of HEW's budget and half the staff. The system would serve every living American sometime during his or her lifetime.

Federal health assistance programs accounted for 12¢ of every federal dollar. Medicaid and Medicare cost more than $30 billion annually.

Welfare involved another $12 billion annually. State and local governments were asking Washington to bear the full brunt of welfare costs, so a giant future increase was unavoidable.

And, the price tag on school and student aid programs in HEW's Education Division was rapidly nearing the $10 billion level.

HEW was so vast it required approximately 7,000 officials and $150 million every year just to manage its operations.

Franklin Roosevelt laid the base in 1939 when he asked for and got a "Federal Security Agency." In the FSA, he put the Public Health Service, the young Social Security system, and the U.S. Office of Education (OE), among other agencies. OE was apparently added only to round out the new agency's broad social service mission.

In the intervening years, there had been much support for elevating the FSA to a Cabinet department. Newly installed President Dwight Eisenhower made the idea one of his first proposals. HEW was thus created in 1953. Supporters believed there was an "interrelationship" between health, education, and welfare programs, but were at a loss to demonstrate specific linkages and few ever developed.

The Department's budget started around the $5 billion mark and its staff began at 40,000. HEW symbolized the commitment of the U.S. government to improving the general welfare of its disadvantaged people, and its emergence and increasing visibility helped to set off an irreversible political trend toward more federal involvement in social services.

Through the 1960s, the federal role in education expanded to guaranteeing equal opportunity, calling for billions of dollars more in aid programs. New welfare programs were added as part of President Lyndon Johnson's "Great Society": Medicare, Medicaid, Head Start. And all the while, Social Security benefits soared as more people came onto the system.

Jimmy Carter had a mess to contend with in 1977. Many felt the Department was out of control. Its bureaucrats were too independent. Rules and regulations were becoming a dense jungle for states and localities to wade through. Paperwork and forms flooded the country. The number of offices had grown so large that no one really knew who was responsible for signing off on a decision. The concept of a cohesive HEW whose offices worked together to serve the total individual had vanished.

In the not-too-distant future, HEW would pass the $200 billion level. Members of Congress—liberals, moderates, conservatives alike—began to see that the only plausible solution was major surgery, a total break-up if necessary. Most congressmen, however, respected the toughness of Califano and determination of Carter to reform and overhaul. They would wait and watch how the new Administration handled HEW in its first years.

Early on, it was clear to us that the best reason for taking the "E" out of HEW and establishing a separate Education Department would be HEW itself.

*   *   *

That week in March, Bert Lance and Harrison Wellford met with the President to plan Carter's own reorganization strategy for the federal government as a whole.

Wellford had been named OMB's reorganization chief. The 37-year-old lawyer would head up a huge staff of 100-plus professionals that would concentrate on reviewing every department, agency, and program for possible trimming or abolition. It would be officially called the "President's Reorganization Project," or "PRP" for short. Its officials would fill many floors of the New Executive Office Building across the street from the White House.

Carter approved the plan devised by Lance and Wellford, which called for moving ahead with a few short-term reorganizations that could easily be enacted and give the drive early momentum.

The reorganization drive would take all of Carter's first four-year term. With the limitations imposed by Congress, it appeared there could not be more than four separate reorganization plans submitted by the President in any one year.[4] So, Wellford and Lance would have to pick and choose their priorities carefully.

---

[4] Reorganization plans could rearrange, abolish, or create agencies below the Cabinet level only. Cabinet departments would have to be created or abolished by legislation.

The PRP people were to scour the federal agencies and departments for clues to poorly functioning offices and programs. Soon, PRP would become synonymous with power and arrogance. All over town, bureaucrats feared they might become targets of the President's reorganization squad, that their offices and programs might be abolished, consolidated, or transferred.

The Project would also have its own bureaucracy. Wellford had organized it into six primary divisions: natural resources and energy, economic development, national security and international affairs, general government and regulation, and lastly, human development.

Our Committee, its members and staff, would be working closely in the next four years with Wellford and his PRP gang as they sought our consent to, and input on, their plans. If the President ever decided to go forward with a Department of Education, the PRP would spearhead the effort for him.

*   *   *

Monday, March 14. Senator Ribicoff walked onto the floor of the Senate, carrying in his hands the bulky sheaf of papers Marilyn had given him that morning. He stopped at the central desk in front of the presiding officer, signed the customary "A. Ribicoff" in the upper right corner of the cover page, and without comment handed the papers to the clerk on duty.

Finally, our ED bill had been introduced.

To the Senate officials at the desk, this was just another bill. The enrolling clerk would check it over for conformity to basic Senate rules of style, log it in the Senate's permanent record, and assign a number. From then on, it would be identified as "S.991"—the 991st bill to be introduced in the 95th Congress. The parliamentarian's office would review the substance of the bill to determine which committee it would be officially referred to. While the legislation concerned education, its main purpose was to establish a new agency. So S.991 was referred to Ribicoff's Governmental Affairs Committee, instead of the Human Resources Committee (which had jurisdiction over education policies and programs). The *Congressional Record* clerk would list and publish S.991 with the other seven bills introduced that day in the daily journal. The Government Printing Office would print 1,000 copies in the standard form:

95TH CONGRESS
1ST SESSION

S. 991

IN THE SENATE OF THE UNITED STATES

MARCH 14 (legislative day, FEBRUARY 21), 1977

Mr. RIBICOFF (for himself, Mr. MAGNUSON, Mr. HUMPHREY, Mr. PELL, Mr. NUNN, Mr. ALLEN, Mr. BARTLETT, Mr. BAYH, Mr. BELLMON, Mr. CHILES, Mr. CHURCH, Mr. CLARK, Mr. CRANSTON, Mr. DECONCINI, Mr. DOMENICI, Mr. EAGLETON, Mr. FORD, Mr. HART, Mr. HEINZ, Mr. HOLLINGS, Mr. INOUYE, Mr. JACKSON, Mr. KENNEDY, Mr. McGOVERN, Mr. MATSUNAGA, Mr. MELCHER, Mr. MUSKIE, Mr. PEARSON, Mr. RANDOLPH, Mr. SASSER, Mr. SPARKMAN, Mr. STAFFORD, Mr. STONE, Mr. WEICKER, and Mr. WILLIAMS) introduced the following bill; which was read twice and referred to the Committee on Governmental Affairs

A BILL

To establish a Department of Education, and for other purposes.

1   *Be it enacted by the Senate and House of Representa-*

2   *tives of the United States of America in Congress assembled,*

3   That this Act may be cited as the "Department of Education

4   Act of 1977".

5   FINDINGS AND PURPOSES

6   SEC. 2. The Congress finds that—

7   (1) education is of fundamental importance to the

8   Nation ...

The breakdown of cosponsors was bipartisan: 28 Democrats and seven Republicans. We expected to add many more names in the future, hoping soon to reach that magic halfway number, 50.

Press coverage was skimpy. The wire services sent out small, three-paragraph stories to the country's newspapers. The *Washington Post* put it on the obituary page. To our knowledge, it didn't make TV news.

I had gone to Connecticut for the week and was both surprised and impressed to see the dailies there pick up on the story. "Ribicoff Pushes for Department of Education," was the page two headline in the Danbury *News-Times*. After two-and-a-half years of working for the U.S. Senate, I still marveled at the sensation of traveling anywhere in the country and reading about our work in a local paper or seeing clips on TV.

"His project has amounted to a weighty boulder," syndicated columnist Nick Thimmesch wrote in a dispatch that week. "…But given the public displeasure with the way education is going in the schools these days, and with the billions being spent on education, this might well be Sen. Ribicoff's year to get that boulder to the top of the hill."

FOUR

Posturing

The coincidence was uncanny, but nevertheless there was Joe Califano on NBC's *Meet the Press*—the Sunday following the bill's introduction.

Moderator Bill Monroe pressed him hard on the issue: "Mr. Secretary, during the campaign President Carter spoke out in favor of a separate Department of Education...A good many educators, a good many senators and congressmen believe in that approach. Are you going to oppose that?"

"I was not elected, Mr. Monroe, as President Carter was, and if he wants to press hard for a separate Department of Education, I will do that." Califano was giving the national television audience his standard lingo. "Also, as you know, I have written about this subject...I think that education needs to be more closely related with health and other social services and would prefer to see a department within a department...

"For example, when I was a young student I got my immunization in the school system. That is not done any more today. One of the things we hope to do and the President has asked me to look at is whether or not we can restore that relationship between education and health."[5]

Monroe squeezed his guest for still more. "Have you and President Carter talked since the Inauguration about whether education should be split off?"

"No, not in specific terms. What we have talked about are the first steps, namely to get the programs that are there working as effectively as possible and get them consolidated in one place...". The HEW Secretary was visibly relieved to have another reporter move on to a different issue.

*   *   *

Barely two months into Jimmy Carter's new presidency, Joe Califano's friction with the Georgia gang was getting worse. Squabbles continued over staffing HEW with Carter-approved people and Califano's general independence.

In late March, the story broke that the maverick HEW Secretary had hired a $12,763 chef to cook his meals at HEW. Journalists pointed to the contradiction between the Carter frugality and Califano's perceived "extravagance."

Everyone assumed the story was leaked by a revengeful White House aide. The Georgians privately delighted to see a Washington pro like Califano done in by the system.

---

[5] A few weeks later, Califano announced the Administration would boost aid to the states for immunization by $6 million. Whether intentional or not, the new drive helped underline his assertion that education was tied to the rest of HEW.

After the dust settled, Califano kept his cook and rewrote the job description. But the back-and-forth trickery and maneuvering would continue. A week later, the press reported he had hired also a $43,923-a-year bodyguard.

*   *   *

On Capitol Hill, Congress was busy at work on the early Carter Administration requests. In addition, the Senate was struggling to confirm hundreds of subcabinet appointments.

There were two under Secretary Califano that we would keep a special eye on—assistant secretary of education and U.S. commissioner of education, the two top-ranking education posts in the U.S. government. Both would be demolished if a Department of Education were ever established. Our goal was to replace them with a single, Cabinet Secretary of Education.

The very existence of *two* "chief" positions for education within the same department, HEW, was a major reason for ED. Congress established the "assistant secretary" slot back in 1972 during the Nixon era as a means of elevating education's stature within the HEW pecking order. The U.S. commissioner of education had been the "chief" federal education official since the late 1800s, but was too far down the HEW totem pole to make much of an impact. Congress in its 1972 action left all the program authority with the commissioner, and gave the new assistant secretary not much other than a flashy title. In practice, the two did nothing but feud.

For assistant secretary, the President nominated Mary F. Berry, a prominent, 39-year-old black educator and chancellor of the University of Colorado at Boulder. The main push for Berry's appointment came from the White House, not Califano, although he consented to it after much prodding by the Carter people and several civil rights leaders. Berry prided herself on being independent and outspoken.

Joe Califano wanted, above all, to recruit subcabinet officials for HEW that would be loyal to himself. Consolation came with the appointment of Ernest L. Boyer as commissioner. Boyer, 48, had been chancellor of the giant State University of New York system. He was a no-nonsense-type administrator with a penchant for getting things done, and who also had been accustomed to a great measure of independence and visibility. With Califano's hand-picked man at the real helm of education in HEW, the Secretary would have a firm enough grip on the "E" to overcome any potential problems with Mary Berry.

*   *   *

In the fourth floor hearing room of the Dirksen Senate Office Building, Mary Berry and Ernest Boyer were sharing the witness table before the Human Resources Committee.

"What steps do you see yourself taking toward the creation of a separate department?," the chairman of the education subcommittee, Sen. Claiborne Pell, asked Berry. "I know that the enthusiasm of the Administration has waned with the election…"

For Berry and Boyer, it was a sticky issue. The senators on the committee were determined to use the March 25 confirmation hearing to put in a plug for ED.

"I am sure the President has not forgotten his preelection commitments," she cautiously replied. It would require study, she added.

"I would like to press you a little harder on that," Senator Pell said. "Do you think there will be a separate department before the end of this four-year term?"

Berry chose the safe route. "As Secretary Califano has said, the President made the commitment, and if the President decides still that there will be a department, there will be a department."

Later came Boyer's turn on the ED grill. Pell repeated his question.

"I believe the answer to that lies wholly at the President's discretion, and I have not heard comment regarding that." Boyer said he didn't want to go beyond what the President had said, because to do so would indicate "a preferential direction."

A short while later, the Senate routinely confirmed Berry and Boyer for their new jobs.

*   *   *

In a conference room at the Old Executive Office Building next door to the White House the following week, the ramshackled coalition of education groups were finally being granted an audience by the President's staff. Hearing them out were professionals from the domestic policy staff (DPS), including Beth Abramowitz, who was new to the issue.

Elizabeth Abramowitz, 34, had been on the White House staff for only a week. A soft spoken, cheerful black psychologist with good credentials in education, Abramowitz had been hired to concentrate on education issues for the DPS (which was headed by the President's assistant for domestic affairs, Stuart Eizenstat).

The education lobbyists asked the White House aides what was happening to the Department of Education promise the President made in the campaign. Abramowitz answered that the President wanted to look at ED within his overall administrative plan; that was as far as she could go.

"A three-headed monster would be totally unacceptable to us," one lobbyist said, referring to the HEW Secretary, assistant secretary for education and commissioner of education. ED would be the best solution, he advanced.

Abramowitz proposed that one idea might be to have the Administration set up a high-level task force to study the whole question in more depth for the President. Seizing on that break, the ed people agreed enthusiastically and asked how they could help set things in motion. Abramowitz said she would test out the idea on others at the White House.

After leaving the April 1 meeting, the education lobbyists came away from the White House feeling the ED pledge was still locked in a twilight-zone state.

Beth Abramowitz went back to her office and wrote a memo to her boss, Stu Eizenstat, suggesting the President set up a task force.

*   *   *

Five days later, Jimmy Carter sat at his desk in the Oval Office, all smiles. Standing around him, Bert Lance, Senator Ribicoff, and Rep. Jack Brooks were also grinning broadly. With the stroke of his pen, the new President signed his first major bill giving him special authority to reorganize the federal government. He called it his "most consistent commitment."

The very next day, the President asked Congress to establish a consumer protection agency. The bill would be handled by our Committee and Senator Ribicoff on the Senate side, and by Rep. Brooks and his Gov Ops Committee on the House side. Both were already hard at work on bills to create the Department of Energy.

White House officials released documents listing the first areas to be targeted for reorganization. In a background booklet specially prepared for the press lay the darkest omen. One section had anticipatory questions and answers: "Q: Do you (meaning the Administration) support creation of a Department of Education?

A: *We have not begun the reorganization with preconceived notions. Answers to questions on specific agencies must await further analysis.*"

Two simple sentences. They effectively wiped out a presidential campaign commitment.

*   *   *

At the Committee, Marilyn and I were monitoring all of these goings-on. While the President and Congress worked on higher priority bills, we took advantage of the void to compile background research on ED.

I spent a lot of time digging into the huge $2.5 billion child nutrition/school lunch programs and quickly came to the conclusion they should be switched to a new Education Department. I also looked into where other countries put education in their national government, and discovered the U.S. was one of six out of more than 150 that didn't have a separate ed agency.

We also began considering the costs of our proposed Cabinet department and attempted to work up figures on any savings to improve our sales pitch.

And, we started prepping ourselves to argue against Joe Califano's desire to keep education in HEW and change it to resemble the Defense Department. DOD had a Secretary of Defense sitting over sub-departments of the Army, Navy, and Air Force. Califano wanted to be a Secretary of Human Resources sitting over sub-departments of Health, Education, and Welfare. We found the services still fought and the Secretary of Defense became more powerful. The same would happen in HEW—Califano's seat would get stronger and education's weaker.

Our bill had already initiated some turf moves. Arts and humanities lobbyists began lobbying us and senators to drop the Arts Endowment and Humanities Endowment from transfer to ED. The Graduate School at the Agriculture Department asked out of our plan. And, the National Science Board attacked our suggestion that the science ed programs be moved from the National Science Foundation, because they were "inextricably linked" to science research.

*　　*　　*

Over at HEW, Mary Berry and Ernest Boyer had settled into their new jobs, and their posturing had begun.

Finding what he termed a "cluttered and confusing arrangement" in the Office of Education, the Commissioner of Education, with Califano's approval, slashed the number of offices reporting directly to him. Boyer told reporters his mid-April reorganization "in no way conflicts, supersedes or undermines" future moves towards a separate Department of Education.

The Assistant Secretary for Education used the opportunity to fire off an exceptionally blunt memo to Secretary Califano. "…Unless we get education's house under HEW in order within the next six months, the arguments of those who ask for a new Cabinet Department of Education will strengthen and the President may be compelled to keep the commitments he made in that regard," Berry warned.

She dangled her threatened support for ED before Califano in exchange for a laundry list of things she wanted done to make her job more palatable. Among them: backing her in coordinating all the education programs, involving her more extensively in the budget process, and giving her more say over planning and evaluation of education in HEW. "The internal reorganization announced by OE does not, of course, address these issues," she said.

The Berry memo leaked to the press two weeks later. From the clamor we learned just how loyal Boyer was to Califano and how feisty and independent Berry could be.

*　　*　　*

The Cabinet room was full of cheer and smiles. On one side of the table sat President Carter, Vice President Mondale, Secretary Califano, Stuart Eizenstat, and Beth Abramowitz. On the opposite were the people who helped put them there—NEA President John Ryor, executive director Terry Herndon, and Stan McFarland, chief lobbyist for the teacher organization.

Finally, NEA was having its first face-to-face meeting with Carter since becoming President. The giant teacher union leaders had waited patiently three months for this audience with the President. It was time they got some signals from the top on the projects lining their agenda. It was Wednesday, April 27.

Everyone was congratulating each other. Ryor congratulated the President on his great victory in the November election. "We're very proud to have you in the White House," he said. Carter praised the hard work of NEA in the '76 campaign, and talked of how important they were in sending him to Washington. They reminisced about Mondale's speech the previous July to the NEA convention and the stirring reception he got. It was a genuinely joyful reunion.

Ryor brought the group down to earth. "Mr. President, we're very concerned about what is happening with your campaign commitment to establish the Department of Education." The NEA president looked over at Joe Califano, smiled, and said in a friendly sort of way, we've been hearing Secretary Califano's views on the issue.

The President said he had not changed his position. But, I can't give you a timetable, he told Ryor. We expect to pursue the Department of Education in the context of the overall reorganization effort, he said.

At one end of the table, Beth Abramowitz spilled her coffee on the Cabinet table. In such royal surroundings, everyone pretended not to notice and kept right on talking. It was her first presidential meeting.

Carter motioned to the Vice President, sitting beside him: I'll ask Fritz to head up a task force to look more in-depth at the Department of Education question. The other members would be Stu, Joe, and Bert Lance, he said.

Ryor expressed his approval, and then turned to a few other issues of concern to the teachers, including money for education programs and a national public employees collective bargaining law. They talked another 10 minutes on those matters.

The meeting ended a short while later in the same fashion as it had begun, with each side telling the other how much they looked forward to working with one another.

NEA's leaders could hardly contain their pleasure as they left the White House. Their first meeting, in their view, had been a complete success.

As far as they were concerned, there would be an additional chair added to that Cabinet table after all.

FIVE

Getting Organized

The President's Reorganization Project was off and running, its young, eager-beaver staffers spending the first week of May settling into the New Executive Office Building, a modern, brick high-rise office building across the street and around the corner from the White House.

A collection of talented people, the majority had been detailed from other agencies and departments to work on reorganizations affecting those very agencies. Most had been well-schooled in the workings of the Washington system.

Their offices were spartan and cluttered. No opportunity for interior decoration; they were there to work. As time wore on, the PRP people would be up to their necks in briefing books, fact sheets, research papers, files, and a ceaseless string of meetings.

The energy, excitement, and commitment were understandable. This was a very special mission they were on—a carte blanche to go out in the concrete jungle of Washington and make the U.S. government work better. The sense of power and pride were overwhelming. The PRP staffers knew they were working to fulfill the top priority of the President of the United States.

*   *   *

On the third floor of the NEOB, Patricia Gwaltney was still in the process of hiring staff and putting her office together. A couple of weeks earlier, Harrison Wellford had hired her to head up the 'human resources" organization study. Education would be within her bailiwick at PRP.

Neither Gwaltney nor Wellford thought a Department of Education was a good idea. In fact there were virtually no ED supporters in all of OMB. Even Bert Lance had his serious doubts. During her interview with Wellford, Gwaltney asked the OMB reorganization chief whether the Department of Education would be a top priority. Wellford played it down and noted the President wanted them to start from a clean slate.

A native of Virginia, Pat Gwaltney was 29 years old, an attractive, intelligent woman with a steely constitution. She was primarily an analyst, not a politician. She had worked mostly for Republicans since the early 1970s on the Hill, in HEW and the Commerce Department, and at the Ford White House. She had a master's degree in public administration from Harvard.

The ED issue was on her agenda for eventual study, but during the first week of May she had no idea what would happen to it. There were hundreds of other human services programs she would assign her staff to scrutinize, so her plate was more than full. The challenge of reorganizing all that, plus the obvious power, drew her to the job.

That week, she was focusing entirely on organizing her suite of offices and bringing on board a sizable staff team to work for her. She hired some 10 professionals, whose average age was under 30 and who had worked in various posts in and out of government. Initially, only one or two would concentrate on reorganizing education in the federal government.

Like Gwaltney herself, many members of her crew were skeptical about the Department of Education, no doubt largely because of Gwaltney's own personal misgivings. In their first days at PRP, they expected to be working in the future to convince the President it was a bad idea.

*   *   *

At about the same time, I was donning on my black graduation robe. I had checked out job possibilities in journalism, which weren't good for new grads. But the excitement on Capitol Hill made me want to stay.

I lobbied the professional staff members on the Committee to put in a good word for me with the Committee's chief counsel and staff director, Richard Wegman. Full-time permanent positions for new graduates on the U.S. Senate staff were hard to come by. But, I had nearly three years' experience with the Ribicoff staff to back me up. I knew the Senate inside and out and had become a constant fixture in the Committee office.

Dick Wegman had a reputation in Washington for being a brilliant and effective congressional committee staff director. Behind his warm personality was a dogged loyalty to liberal Democratic principles and a fantastic political mind. A 38-year-old Harvard-educated lawyer, he had worked at the Justice Department and as a legislative assistant to Sen. William Proxmire (D-WI.) before joining up with Ribicoff in 1974, the same year I arrived.

Finally, the third week in May, Dick asked me to stay on. He assigned me to work on the Department of Education bill with Marilyn and do general research for the Committee.

Within a week, I moved out of the college dorms, moved into a comfortable apartment in southwest Washington just off Capitol Hill, and took over a desk and office in the Dirksen Senate Office Building.

I had gone from part-time intern to a full-time, 22-year-old Senate staffer.

*　　*　　*

Art Sheekey used the quiet Friday, May 20 afternoon to pay a few courtesy calls on Capitol Hill. His third week on the President's Reorganization Project staff, Sheekey stopped by to chat with and introduce himself to Marilyn Harris.

His visit was brief, but the two took an instant liking to each other. Sheekey, 38, was a career Office of Education bureaucrat on loan to Pat Gwaltney's operation at the PRP, where his expertise would be put to good use on the education study.

Marilyn listened with keen interest as Art described how Gwaltney was organizing the human services study. Without going into much detail, he also told of some early movement on education in the Administration. Gwaltney, Bert Carp of Mondale's staff, and others from OMB and Mary Berry's staff had been meeting to try to come up with ideas on how to handle the prickly ED problem.

This was our first inside scoop on the secretive PRP.

*　　*　　*

The NEA leaders were so happy with their recent meeting with President Carter they blatted about it to people around town. The education press picked up on the story and soon it was common knowledge.

At the Dupont Circle offices of the rival American Federation of Teachers, they were not amused. NEA's preliminary move called for a countermove.

Senators on our Committee received in May personal letters from AFT President Albert Shanker informing them the teacher's union "has a number of serious reservations" about ED.

"We wonder if a separate department might not divert attention from the fact that the new Administration may oppose adequate funding for education with as much vigor as the old," the letter said.

Shanker borrowed Califano's argument by noting also, "A successful federal education policy cannot be devised and implemented in isolation from the development of health and welfare programs."

The letter was concrete evidence AFT was ready to do battle with NEA, and a stern message to senators this would not be an easy issue.

Shanker was getting increasingly peeved with Jimmy Carter. "The conservatives who thought (Carter) was a liberal are now convinced he's a conservative," he told an AFT conference in May. "And so is everyone else." The President's resistance to spend more money for social programs and his reluctance to endorse a hefty increase in the minimum wage had irritated liberals and labor.

The reports that Carter told NEA he was still for the Department of Education angered Shanker more. "When it comes to prestige or money, this is no time to give away money," he seethed.

*   *   *

By June, the going was getting tougher for the President. The public's support was still strong—66% approval rating in the latest Gallup Poll. But in Washington, the opinion leaders, the press and the Congress were beginning to have doubts about his young presidency.

The Administration stacked one priority on top of another. The Carter people wanted to do too much too fast. Congress was overloaded with a complex energy plan, the Department of Energy bill, economic recovery legislation, the 1978 budget, tax cut bills, consumer agency bill, and the plan to bail out Social Security, to name a few.

The President's problems grabbed the headlines. Inflation continued to worsen. Business groups lobbied hard to defeat the consumer bill. Carter threatened to veto the sacrosanct Labor-HEW appropriation bill, inciting attacks by fellow Democrats. Special interest lobbying ravaged his energy plans. He fought back with verbal attacks on his critics and even Congress.

The President was still in the process of learning to deal with Congress. Not the wheeler-dealer type, he despised the pressure tactics congressmen were used to. Carter's experiment in "Cabinet government" enabled federal agencies to work independently of the White House on bills affecting their own turf. The White House was not keeping track of renegade congressmen; in the absence of retribution, they had little incentive to vote for the President's position.

This President and his crew were captives of the crammed agenda they had created.

Thanks to them, our plate was also heaping at the Committee. The calendar continued to be chock full of hearings and mark-up sessions on the nuclear nonproliferation, consumer protection agency, ethics-in-government bills, and several nominations.

Marilyn persistently, but gently, reminded Dick Wegman it would be nice if the Committee could hold just a couple days of hearings on the ED bill to tighten the screws a little more on the White House. Dick held off, citing all the issues that had to be cleared out of the way first. He had final say (next to Ribicoff) over the scheduling of full Committee hearings and mark-ups. Personally, he did not find the ED bill exciting, and he harbored private doubts about the wisdom of establishing the new department. We had problems of hesitance within our own office.

As May turned into June, Dick's previous estimate of hearings possibly in July turned into September, maybe even October. Marilyn and I were disappointed, but there was still much research and politicking to do.

*　　　*　　　*

The Vice President's "task force" of Bert Lance, Joe Califano, and Stu Eizenstat never formally met altogether at once. Staff handled most of the bargaining and negotiating. Pat Gwaltney represented Lance, OMB and PRP. Califano's top aide, Fred Bohen argued his boss's position. Eizenstat's deputy and Mondale staffer Bert Carp got into the act.

The staffers held a slew of meetings and phone conversations throughout June in an effort to reach some sort of a consensus position. Sometimes, they included staff only, other times one or two of the task force members attended. Eizenstat, Carp, and Mondale met Tuesday, June 7 in the Vice President's office to discuss the situation. On Wednesday, Califano left a budget meeting in the Cabinet Room with Mondale and followed him to his office to plug his view on ED. Documents and papers had circulated among the group for the preceding two weeks.

The President had directed the Vice President to lead his informal task force for good reason. Mondale was the ideal broker on the ED issue. He had become one of Carter's closest advisors, and thus knew how the President thought and what the most agreeable course would be. Being the Vice President, he had rank over everyone else.

---

6 Not only did Mondale work closely with NEA while a U.S. senator, his brother, William, had been a past president of the Minnesota Education Association and was hired by the NEA to help with the 1976 presidential campaign.

Politically, he was close to all the competing interests—the AFT and the AFL-CIO, Joe Califano, and the NEA.[6]

Walter Mondale was rapidly becoming the most valuable, indispensable member of the Carter clan. Jimmy Carter wanted his vice president to be more than the usual docile constitutional figure that attended funerals and not much else. What he got was a vice president who would become a top-notch counselor. Mondale was the solid bridge the Administration had to Democratic elements and to the Washington system. As Jimmy Carter stumbled in his relations with Congress, he called upon former Senator Mondale more often to help straighten things out.

The 49-year-old Minnesotan was a professional politician, the type who rarely misspoke, who rarely lost his temper, who knew the value of working behind-the-scenes, how to be flexible, and when to compromise. He knew well how to use his quick humor.

This President and Vice President were now close personal friends and had a solid working relationship. Carter rarely made a major decision without first bouncing it off his Vice President. Mondale spent most of his time in the special office Carter ordered for him just a few steps down the hall from the Oval Office, not his more ceremonial, far-away suite in the Old Executive Office Building next door.

The President's top advisors, who in past years had been known to mistreat a vice president, respected and protected the new relationship. They were thankful Mondale was a member of their team.

One other person wielded as much influence with the President—Bert Lance. It was only natural that Carter would ask him to serve on the task force with Mondale. The President's Reorganization Project operated within the confines of OMB, which Lance directed.

The predictions of Lance emerging as the "deputy president" were not far off target. Like Mondale, he was around Carter constantly. Carter confided in him. There were stories of the two Georgians spending hours walking and talking together on an isolated Georgia beach.

And in their regular tennis sets, they would often talk more than volley. OMB staffers privately complained Lance was spending more time in the Oval Office than in his own.

Bert Lance literally towered over every agency, office and department of the federal establishment. Agency heads found themselves justifying both their budgets and their very existence to Lance. His philosophy was, "If it ain't broke, don't fix it."

With his strong conservative mindset, Lance would be a good bet to oppose quietly the Department of Education. With his strong Democratic allegiances, Mondale would be a good bet to urge Carter to proceed with an ED bill. Califano, of course, was against it. Stuart Eizenstat was neutral.

Mondale's skills as a mediator would be tested thoroughly.

*　　*　　*

Marilyn and I vaguely knew something was cooking at the White House. But it wasn't until we got phone calls the following Monday, June 13 from our alarmed sources in both the executive mansion and HEW that we realized Califano was making headway in pressing for his "DOD model."

We decided to head off Califano with a letter to Mondale from Ribicoff and key senators. "Dear Mr. Vice President," it began, plugging our stand for taking education out of HEW. "...The bill we have introduced, S.991, now has 45 sponsors.

"As you know, some thought has been given to restructuring HEW internally and modeling it instead after the present structure of the Department of Defense, with its subcabinets and individual secretaries." The letter diplomatically evaded any mention of Califano.

"...Patterning HEW after the DOD subcabinet model would be little more than a simple facelift, and in the end, do much harm to the overall federal education effort," it continued. "Such a reorganization would drastically increase and centralize the HEW Secretary's powers and duties. A secretary of education within HEW would only serve as an administrator—not a policymaker.

"The education functions could even be further buried in unnecessary layers of bureaucracy," the senators said.

Ribicoff signed it after a brief glance, as did Labor-HEW subcommittee chairman Warren Magnuson (D-Wash.) and Sen. Claiborne Pell.

The next day, our sources told us the letter hit the nail on the head—and had arrived just in time.

*   *   *

Marilyn and Art Sheekey talked by phone a week later.

The Vice President would soon be sending a memo to the President on the subject of education reorganization, he told her. The memo would include several options for the President, the PRP staffer said. He didn't reveal any further details.

*   *   *

As Mondale pressed his task force to choose a course of action, the bargaining and pressure became more intense. NEA pushed the Vice President and his staff to announce in favor of a Department of Education as soon as possible. Pat Gwaltney, Harrison Wellford and the President's Reorganization Project wanted to do a five—week study on all the surface options. Califano continued to recommend HEW be maintained in one piece, and if he couldn't have that, then he supported the PRP study, giving him more time to work against the ED idea.

The month-long haggling finally culminated with:

"THE WHITE HOUSE
WASHINGTON

June 22, 1977
MEMORANDUM FOR: THE PRESIDENT

FROM: THE VICE PRESIDENT (initialed 'WFM')
BERT LANCE ('J. McIntyre', 'W. H. Wellford')
JOE CALIFANO ('JACJr.')
STU EIZENSTAT ('Stu')

SUBJECT: Reorganization of Federal Education Activities

"We reached the following conclusions," the memo said.

"…A relatively early decision…is important, in view of mounting congressional and constituency pressures." The memo noted there was much pressure to go ahead with hearings on the Ribicoff bill.

The task force made its recommendation:

"First, a five-week study of overall organizational options for HEW…Members of the task force would take part in the review. At the end of this study, a preliminary round of decisions would be made, including a decision on whether to proceed with a separate Department of Education in some form or to pursue another option.

"Second, following this decision, intensive consultation on detailed options would continue, with a target date to be set by the Reorganization Group." OMB figured it would take another six months.

This approach, the task force joint memo argued, had three advantages. First, it would permit an objective study "*before* affected interest groups become over-committed to their own preferred options." Secondly, if the study recommended the President do something other than create an Education Department, then it would allow the Administration to announce its hard decision and get on with the alternative. Lastly, it would help "decouple" the ED issue from next year's budget decisions and "clear the air", otherwise pressure for the separate department would increase because of budget cutbacks.

The President checked the "recommended" alternative and etched in a big "JC" at the bottom of the page. Carter, in effect, decided not to decide generally on seeking a separate department until sometime in August. All the while, Pat Gwaltney and her PRP team would be conducting their comprehensive "study" on the ED concept for six months. For Califano, the President's decision was a half-victory; he still had a chance to kill ED.

*   *   *

Both Mondale and Califano attached their own personal memos. Mondale's was on top of the whole package. It had the infamous "THE PRESIDENT HAS SEEN" stamped on it.

"Were it not for the reservations expressed by Joe Califano and the OMB Reorganization Group, I would be inclined to recommend a decision now for a separate education department," Mondale told Carter. He had many reasons.

"The NEA and other 'Big Six' education groups (but not the AFT) are convinced that a separate department is the best way to elevate the federal priority for education.[7] We specifically supported that position

---

[7] The "Big Six" included NEA, Council of Chief State School Officers, National School Boards Association, National PTA, American Association of School Administrators, and National Association of State Boards of Education.

and, in part on that basis, received the first NEA endorsement ever given a presidential and vice presidential candidate.

"A separate department is strongly supported by Senator Ribicoff and Senator Pell," the Vice President had written. "Their bill has near-majority cosponsorship in the Senate.

"An extensive Administration review of other options will be seen as a major retreat from our campaign pledge. It will create a serious problem for the NEA leadership who convinced their members to work for us during the campaign.

"Because of budget constraints, there may not be much we can offer education and its advocates, except fulfillment of our campaign pledge for a separate department," Mondale gave as the final reason for supporting ED now.

But, the Vice President said Califano and OMB made a "strong case for careful study."

Carter wrote, "OK...J" on the paper

Califano's personal memo to the President stated upfront, "I do not think the Department of Education is a good idea.

"...The NEA and teacher interests would likely control a Department of Education," he argued. "That conclusion helps explain why the American Federation of Teachers and virtually all college and university presidents oppose such a department. Organized health interests would soon control a Department of Health. The aging constituencies...would eventually take a commanding position in a Department of Income Security...".

What would make the most sense, the Secretary of HEW told the President, is "an umbrella organizational model," like a Department of Human Resources with subcabinet departments, "with a strong central staff to provide *presidential* policy direction."

How would the President back off his campaign promise? The Secretary's "strategy" called for a "quick study of the Education

Department concept" with a subsequent no-go presidential decision that would be made "known promptly."

He warned another reorganization at HEW would be "chaotic."

*   *   *

Thursday afternoon, the next day, leaders of the President's Reorganization Project assembled in the Cabinet Room to brief Carter on the principal areas they had chosen to target for restructuring. Pat Gwaltney sat among them.

When it came Gwaltney's turn, she told Carter she would be working on two projects—the education study and the human services study. She reminded him the task force he had asked Vice President Mondale to chair was hard at work already on the ED issue.

As a result of the meeting, the President approved immediate major reorganization studies of four specific areas: law enforcement, local and community economic development, human services, and administrative services.

Carter appeared personally in the White House press briefing room June 29 to announce the study priorities before a large mass of reporters and TV cameras. "All of us know the (reorganization) task will be a long one," he said. "It's taken long time for these problems to develop."

There was no mention either by the President or in the background materials given to the press of the decision to proceed with the more controversial education study.

Carter left the podium after an eight-minute appearance and turned over discussion of the details to Bert Lance and Harrison Wellford, who held a press conference on-the-spot.

A short way into the conference, a reporter noted "the President earlier said he didn't plan to create any new Cabinet departments. Do you think he is sticking to that or may he change his mind?"

"I have not seen anything in the preliminary discussions about the reorganization that would indicate we would be creating any new Cabinet functions," Lance responded.

"Didn't he promise to separate education?," the reporter followed up.

The OMB Director answered, "There may be ways to deal with that without the creation of another Cabinet position."

Six

The Pressure Builds

Summer in Washington. Almost without fail, the July temperatures soared daily into the 90ºs and often to 100º, the relative humidity never far behind.

While Mother Nature did her duty, the pro-ED people were busy turning up the heat on the Carter Administration. Education groups and Senator Ribicoff could not establish the department without Jimmy Carter's support.

Word slowly leaked out of the plan to proceed with a study, making all of us nervous. If the President was truly committed, why then the need for a study of *options*? The best way to kill something is to study it to death. Studies can consume mountains of time and diffuse the opposition.

We would take no chances. There would be no letting up on the pressure. It was going to be a long, hot, sticky summer.

*   *   *

In Minneapolis, nearly 9,000 teacher delegates assembled at the convention center for the National Education Association's annual convention July 4.

The guest of honor, naturally, was Minnesota favorite son Walter Mondale. "President Carter and I will never forget the role you played in last year's election," Mondale told the teachers. "Today, you have a partner in the White House." The crowd applauded.

Buried deep in Mondale's rhetoric was a vague reference to education reorganization. He called for a "fundamental reform of our federal education effort" that would eliminate "waste and duplication and excess bureaucracy."

But not a single mention of the Department of Education, NEA's dearest project. Only once—at an airport press conference in Minneapolis—did Mondale address the issue. He told reporters there the Carter Administration was making a "high-priority" study of ED. The teachers inside the convention center didn't hear about it until they went home and read their newspapers. NEA officials were mighty upset, and they let the press know about it.

That old happy warrior, Sen. Hubert Humphrey, gave a rousing speech and fired up the teachers.

"I have one bill which is highly controversial, I know, but I personally happen to believe in it," he shouted into the microphone with insistent emotion. "This one bill would reorganize our education efforts, and it would create a Cabinet-level Department of Education."

All 9,000 teachers jumped to their feet and delivered a thundering standing ovation. Humphrey pointedly looked over at Mondale, sitting near the podium, and smiled.

*　　*　　*

Three days later, it was Al Shanker's and the AFT's turn to meet with President Carter and lobby for their projects.

As with the April meeting between the President and NEA, the group sat in the Cabinet Room. The atmosphere was cordial, cool.

The AFT president made a five-minute pitch to Carter for not going ahead with the Department of Education. "We think instead of the schools becoming separate, they ought to become more coordinated with the other activities of government," he said.

Carter responded with a carefully neutral stance. Within my own Administration, he said, people are about evenly divided on the issue. Joe Califano's position, the President told Shanker, is most in line with yours. Carter made no commitments, but left the AFT leaders with the distinct impression he was attaching a low priority to ED. He more or less shrugged off the whole issue. Mondale said hardly anything.

After leaving the meeting, a buoyant Shanker talked with reporters. "I think there is a good chance it will not move ahead," he boasted.

*　　*　　*

Mark Shiffrin sat across from Abe Ribicoff in the Senator's opulent and spacious Russell Senate Building office the following week. The young freelance writer was working on a think piece for *The Washington Post*.

"What is your sense of timing for the bill?," Shiffrin inquired of the Committee chairman.

"We are inundated now," the Senator said. "But it is important to have some hearings this year. I would hope that sometime in September, October we could have a few days of hearings.

"We are serious about it," Ribicoff insisted. "I would prefer that the Administration come out supporting a department (of education). We would have hearings irrespective of what they do."

*　　*　　*

In mid-July, Marilyn and Dick Wegman were called to the White House for a feeling-out session.

Mondale aide Bert Carp wanted to woo the two Ribicoff staffers away from holding hearings. Carp, closely allied with the AFL-CIO and the AFT in the past, feared the ED issue would only pit elements of the Democratic party against each other. A friend of Joe Califano, Carp also agreed reorganizing HEW internally was one way out.

In a White House conference room, Carp explained the study to be undertaken and pledged the President's people would work with the Ribicoff Senate Committee toward a final decision. Pat Gwaltney, Beth Abramowitz, and other Administration officials backed him up.

Marilyn and Dick listened intently. Finally, the Carter officials gently probed the two Ribicoff staffers for their feelings. Dick made clear the Senator stood behind his bill, opposed keeping education in HEW in any form, and had voiced his intention to move ahead with hearings in the near future.

Carp couldn't find any flex in the Senate position.

*   *   *

The teachers' exuberant zest at the July 4 NEA convention pumped some sorely needed adrenaline into the NEA leadership.

Shortly after, NEA chief lobbyist Stan McFarland talked with one of his many lobbyists, Gail Bramblett, about pressing ahead with the Department of Education. "If you want it, I'm going to have to work on it full-time," she told McFarland with typical bluntness. Well, the people upstairs want it, he said, so it's yours. From that day forward, it became Gail's project and would remain so until the very end.

The 27-year-old Georgia native had politics in her blood. Bramblett loved the give-and-take, the dealing and maneuvering in the political world. Her quick mind and strong political sense made her one of NEA's most valuable lobbyists. Gail could be alternately charming and tough when the circumstances demanded it. She sometimes offended people with her outspokenness, but she aggressively represented her teachers. With the arrival of Jimmy Carter and company, her Georgia twang was in vogue.

One of the first things Gail did upon assuming responsibility for NEA's Education Department campaign was call Marilyn Harris and set up a meeting for Monday, July 18. The three of us would, in time, become closely bound to one another as we worked toward the same goal.

Marilyn and I wanted to make sure this was right. "Now, is NEA going to make this a priority?," we asked Gail.

"It's all mine," she said. "I'll be spending every minute of my day on it. We're going after the Cabinet department."

"Good," I said. Marilyn looked over at me and raised her eyebrows. Both of us had broad smiles stretching from ear to ear.

Gail took right over. "All right," she said, "this is what we're going to do in the next week. Stan and John Ryor will be making phone calls to the 'Big Six' and some of the higher ed groups to tell them NEA is going ahead with this and ask their support."

"Second," she continued, "we'll be working with labor to try to drum up support there. We'll be talking to UAW (United Auto workers) and CWA (Communication Workers of America). NEA is close to both of them."

They would also be talking to their contacts on the Hill, she said, asking them to write the President and call Frank Moore (the President's chief lobbyist) urging their support. By putting pressure on the President through Congress, she said, the issue appears politically important. In addition, they would try to talk with some of the House Speaker's staff.

NEA would be generating a big grass roots effort, Gail added, They would be asking their teachers to write the President and remind him of his campaign promise.

*　　*　　*

With the threshold 50-cosponsor mark almost in hand, we launched a blitz the last two weeks of July to nail down the extra six senators to put us over the top, over half the U.S. Senate supporting our bill. Gail Bramblett asked the NEA affiliates in states of senators who had not yet cosponsored to call those senatorial offices. I phoned the senators' legislative assistants to press for a decision to cosponsor from this end.

Slowly, the decisions creeped back out. Five more senators consented to our putting their names on the ED bill. Others wanted to wait for the Administration to take a position.

Finally, on August 2, bingo! The phone rang.

"Bob, this is Jim Bennett with Senator Thurmond. Could you add the Senator's name as a cosponsor to the Department of Education bill?"

"I sure will," I said, keeping my elation under control. "Glad to have you on board."

Cosponsor number 51—Sen. Strom Thurmond (R-S.C.). More than half the United States senators not only supported the ED bill, they had their names engraved on the front cover.

*　　*　　*

Pat Gwaltney found herself, in the first half of July, busy and at the center of much attention.

There was a lot of hot talk about hiring someone under her to spearhead the ED study the President had ordered. The custom in such instances is to recruit a big-name, respected leader in the field to lend prestige and authority to the study. But Califano and his close advisors did not want an individual with enough clout and experience to ram a Department of Education down their throats.

Finally, the parties settled on a compromise candidate: 38-year-old Willis Hawley, a professor-administrator from Duke University. Hawley had headed up an educators-for-Carter-Mondale organization in the 1976 campaign. A devoted, dignified academician, he had little practical, hands-on experience in government and politics—the type the HEW people felt less threatened by.

Hawley went right to work on the mechanics of the study. He spent several weeks drawing up an abstract "study design", much as a university researcher would, and trying to obtain general agreement on how it would be approached.

Meanwhile, his boss, Gwaltney, was involving herself more in the political side of things, dealing with agency heads, the President and Vice President and their staff. Eyes all across the city watched her.

An essential part of Gwaltney's study plan was to touch base with the education groups. She set up the first of a countless number of meetings for Tuesday morning, July 26, in an Old Executive Office Building conference room overlooking the White House lawn. The privileged first guests—NEA staffers, of course.

In addition to herself, Harrison Wellford, and Bill Hawley, Gwaltney had invited Beth Abramowitz and Califano's Fred Bohen to join them. The NEA staff—government relations director Stan McFarland, Gail Bramblett, and Rosalyn Baker (another lobbyist)—arrived and were privately shocked to see Bohen in the room. They knew where he stood.

Gwaltney began her standard lingo. The President has asked us to make a study of the Education Department and all the possible alternatives. We will be meeting with the interest groups, she said. There are several concepts of how federal education programs could be reorganized, she continued, and proceeded to outline some of those, their advantages and drawbacks, it is also possible to keep education within HEW and restructure that department, she noted (to please Bohen), and we would like to hear NEA's views on that. And if a separate Education Department were chosen, should it be broad or narrow?

After listening to approximately 30 minutes' discussion of hypotheticals, Stan McFarland couldn't take it anymore.

"What are we doing talking about *whether* we're going to have a Department of Education?," he all-at-once shouted, his fist pounding the table, his face reddened with anger. "There's no need to talk about *whether* we're going to have a department. The President has already made his decision."

McFarland gestured out the window and towards the White House.

"Now, if anybody in this room wants to walk across the street and tell him he's wrong, go right ahead and do it," he hollered.

The room was tense, silent. A few minutes later, the NEA delegation left and the meeting broke up on that sour note.

The outburst so shocked Gwaltney that she did not return NEA's phone calls for the next month-and-a-half.

NEA could not have made its frustration clearer: To hell with the study—let's get to work establishing a Department of Education.

*   *   *

Marilyn and I hopped a cab that afternoon to the NEA building. Some 30 education lobbyists had gathered to plot more strategy on the bill.

Stan McFarland mentioned vaguely that NEA had met that morning with the OMB reorganization people. They're doing their study, he told the group, but we've got to put more pressure on the President.

McFarland said he hoped the organizations represented in the room would "gear up" their members to write the President and congressmen.

Sam Halperin, director of the Institute for Educational Leadership, tossed out the idea of a "citizen's committee," composed of distinguished American from all walks of life, to support the ED effort. We could get civil rights leaders, businessmen, governors, mayors, educators university presidents, and famous citizens to sign on to such a panel, he said. It wouldn't even have to meet. The committee could be offered as evidence of the broad support in the country for elevating education in the federal government.

Everyone thought it a super idea. The lobbyists made plans to start contacting some big names. NEA offered to coordinate the entire operation.

*   *   *

In the Rose Garden at the White House, a crowd of senators, representatives, and distinguished guests stood in the hot and humid Washington air, listening to the President praise Congress for its speedy enactment of the bill he was about to sign.

Indeed, the Department of Energy Organization Act passed Congress in record time, for a new Cabinet department. It took a mere five months, from the time Carter sent the bill to the Hill to this day, August 4, when he signed it, to create the 12th Cabinet department.

With Senator Ribicoff, Representative Brooks, and others standing behind, a seated Jimmy Carter happily signed the bill to a round of applause.

The 13th Cabinet department—if there was to be one—would not be created as easily, nor as quickly.

*   *   *

But the press was warming up to the oncoming ED battle. And now with DOE out of the way, reporters would spotlight ED as the President's next biggest reorganization fight.

The Washington Star led off with a sympathetic July 19 editorial, "Breaking Up HEW". The paper said, "Mr. Califano likes to have his hands on a lot of handles…but we suspect that even a person of (his) capacity and enthusiasm doesn't have enough hands to keep a handle on the bureaucratic giant that HEW has become."

Syndicated columnist Marianne Means judged, in late July, "the political momentum seems to be against Califano...There is no rational reason for education and health and welfare all being lumped together in the first place."

The Washington Post posted a big headline atop Mark Shiffrin's August 14 analysis: "Promises to Keep: Will Carter Really Create an Education Department?" It was the first real dose of exposure for ED in the newspaper looked up to by opinion leaders and journalists across the country.

"Remember candidate Carter's campaign promise to create a new (ED)?," Shiffrin wrote. "Well, President Carter might prefer that you had a shorter memory." The article's theme had it doubtful the idea would move forward.

"We're going to have a hell of a lot of members who would feel double-crossed," Shiffrin quoted NEA's Stan McFarland.

Secretary Califano, Shiffrin pointed out, is largely responsible for Carter delaying a decision on ED. But Senator Ribicoff's pledge to begin hearings on his bill, Shiffrin said, means the issue will stick in the public realm. "They will serve as an embarrassment if Carter decides to reverse direction and oppose any new department," he wrote.

OMB's study, the *Post* story concluded, enables Carter to put off making a decision on ED until at least the year's end, and maybe longer. "But ultimately," it said, "he will not be able to avoid making a choice, and the evidence indicates that the decision may well turn out to be rooted more in the politics of keeping a presidential promise than in educational logic."

*　　*　　*

Bill Hawley was busy consulting key parties about town for the PRP education study. He wanted to meet with interested Senate staff, so Marilyn set up a meeting for Wednesday, August 17 in the hearing room.

We are looking at a number of models, Hawley began in his hushed voice, such as uplifting the Education Division within HEW, a Department of Education, or possibly even a major restructuring of the Cabinet, which could mean a Department of Human Development or a Department of Education and Training.

Training?, we asked. Combining education with the CETA and job training programs from the Labor Department? (We couldn't believe they would even think of taking on the AFL-CIO and other powerful labor unions.) Hawley confirmed himself. The President often referred to such a consolidation during the campaign, he said.

We presented a united front and talked of nothing other than a Department of Education. We wouldn't consider anything else.

Hawley got our message.

*   *   *

Despite the White House's indecision, we moved forward with our daily research into the programs that would make up our new Department of Education.

I sat through a week of intensive briefings in July by Indian leaders for congressional staff, learning the Bureau of Indian Affairs had failed miserably with its $200 million system of tribal schools and student aid programs, which our bill would transfer to ED. "To Indian people, any change in policy is so threatening," one Indian leader said. "It's going to be very hard to get a consensus."

I delved into the Defense Department's overseas dependents schools, which Ribicoff's bill also proposed for transfer (265 schools in 24 foreign countries, most on military bases). Children of servicemen stationed abroad attended them and they were run by one man in

Washington, no school board. That man, Dr. Anthony Cardinale, told me, "I have many reasons for opposing the transfer. And the (Defense) Department will oppose it also."

"Head Start shouldn't be in a Department of Education or any education structure," Children's Defense Fund lobbyist Harley Frankel told Marilyn in her office August 23. "Head Start is not an education program. It is a comprehensive program including health, nutrition, and social services." We'd already received hundreds of letters from predominantly poor Head Start parents, fearing their successful pre-school program would be overtaken by the powerful public school lobby, which they thought would control the new ED.

National Endowment for the Arts staffers had been hard-at-work for at least two months spreading the word that the agency was in danger of being moved, possibly under an Education Department. We tried swaying several artsy types, but they were adamant. The National Council on the Arts met in Washington the weekend of August 13, its distinguished and famous members lambasting us for having the nerve to propose transferring the Endowment. "It would put the arts dangling at the end of education, and that's just wrong," famed writer Eudora Welty told the presidentially-appointed council.

While researching the normally sour public taste for new bureaucracy, I stumbled onto a new, soon-to-be-released Gallup Poll finding 40 per cent of the American public supporting ED and 45 per cent opposing it. Gallup judged the "sentiment on this issue is fairly evenly divided."

We had to sound out higher education's views on the bill, so Marilyn and I met with Charles Saunders, top lobbyist for the American Council on Education, representing 1,400 colleges and universities. Higher ed was "unimpressed" with the notion of a separate Education Department, he told us. College presidents, already complaining of excessive federal regulation feared ED could resemble a powerful "ministry" of education. Saunders' challenge would be holding his people to neutral ground so that they could play a big role in shaping the bill's language.

Top HEW expert and Princeton University professor Rufus Miles told us in a July 25 private meeting our bill would go nowhere if the Administration opposed it. He believed Hamilton Jordan, the President's chief aide, would have the most pull with Carter on the issue. Yes, Pat Gwaltney and her team would conduct their study, Miles said, but "the political decision is crucial."

* * *

At last—a hearings schedule. Marilyn kept hounding Dick Wegman to set aside some days for the first Committee hearings on the ED bill. Finally, in early August, the two agreed on September 26, 27 28.

Word spread quickly through the education community. Letters poured in, requests to testify from education groups and academics everywhere.

Marilyn and I already had a general idea of who we wanted to lead off in our first hearings. The two of us would determine who got invitations and who didn't. There was still much work ahead in searching for the biggest names and the most eloquent, newsy witnesses.

* * *

"*Teacher*—It's Time for You to Talk to Jimmy Carter," was splashed in big, brazen red letters, tabloid-style, on the front cover of the "NEA Reporter" monthly journal and mailed in August across the country to two million teachers. "It's Time to Tell Him You Want a Cabinet-level Department of Education for Our Nation," it stated forcefully in a slightly smaller black headline. Tell him in your own words. Tell him now."

And they did. Mail flowed into the White House—"thousands" of letters, NEA claimed.

From Capitol Hill, dozens of representatives and senators sent more in July and August. All were instigated by NEA, of course.

Other education organizations were just beginning to prod their members to take up pens and paper. More than 25 state superintendents of education wrote Carter.

The flood of mail would continue through October. White House officials responded with simple acknowledgements, and silence.

Simultaneously, Gail Bramblett and her NEA colleagues had been working the phones all month to line up a grand membership list for the "Citizen's Committee for a Cabinet Department of Education."

They wanted members from all regions of the country. Since the opposing AFT had its primary base in New York, a special effort was made to recruit members from that state. And, since House Government Operations Committee Chairman Jack Brooks was from Texas, Gail looked far and wide for prominent Texans.

In every case, she told her prospective members over and over, "You won't have to do a thing—this is a letterhead operation." NEA would print nice stationery, then use it to write letters to the Hill and the President, and thereby demonstrate to everyone else the "broad" support for ED.

The final list was impressive. Among the notables: Sam Halperin (it was his idea), Wilson Riles, four former U.S. education commissioners, a dozen higher education members including seven university presidents, the mayor of New Haven, CT, two New York state assemblymen, a Texas state representative, the Democratic governor of Oklahoma and the Republican governor of Iowa, five labor unions including the United Auto workers, several respected businessmen, National Urban League, Mexican-American legal defense fund, and Coretta King.

Gail already had in mind her first activity for the ghost committee: use some of its members to open our hearings.

SEVEN

Hearings in the Lance Aftermath

4:40 p.m. Monday afternoon, Labor Day. Deep in thought, I was barreling down the New Jersey Turnpike, heading back to Washington after a relaxing two weeks at home in Connecticut and Vermont.

Suddenly, the music on the car radio stopped dead. I reached to turn up the volume.

"...a bulletin from *ABC News*. Just moments ago Senator Abraham Ribicoff and Senator Charles Percy emerged from a meeting with President Carter at the White House in which they told the President his budget director, Bert Lance, should resign...

I gasped and almost drove off the highway.

"...The two senators said their investigators had found what they termed 'serious new alleged illegalities' concerning Mr. Lance, but they declined to be more specific.

"Speaking to reporters on the White House lawn, Senator Ribicoff said, (Ribicoff's voice) 'I think it would be wiser for Bert Lance to resign. I don't think he can be an effective OMB director pending the outcome of these hearings and investigations. Mr. Lance feels very strongly he has been maligned and wants to tell his side of the story.'"

The radio announcer's voice returned. "Ribicoff chairs the Senate Governmental Affairs Committee and has scheduled hearings on the Lance Affair for later this week…".

Instinctively and irrationally, I stepped on the gas. My heart pounded.

Resign? *Ribicoff said "resign"?* I couldn't believe my ears. A lot can happen in two weeks in Washington, I thought.

*   *   *

Jimmy Carter's closest, dearest, most trusted friend and advisor was in serious trouble, caught up in a sensationalized whirl of daily front-page revelations conveying the air of wrongdoing. And we, the Senate Committee that confirmed and had oversight over the director of the Office of Management and Budget, found ourselves suddenly smack-dab in the middle of it all.

The Lance *Affair,* as reporters began calling it, first surfaced in July over Lance's plans for the long-term sale of his multi-million-dollar stock in the National Bank of Georgia, which he headed prior to joining Carter's Cabinet.

Initially, press and official comment was sympathetic. Of all the Carter crew, Lance had been most successful at winning over Washington and making friends on Capitol Hill. Many felt it wasn't fair that the amiable Georgian should have to suffer big financial losses in order to meet the President's ethical guidelines. "I think we have gone completely ethics happy around this place," exclaimed Sen. John Glenn (D-Ohio).

But then several newspapers and columnists started raising startling charges that Lance had engaged in improper financial dealings during his long banking career.

The stories activated an army of investigators—reporters and federal banking regulators. The media descended in droves upon our Committee. The *Affair* had the potential to become another Watergate-like round of inquiries and intensive press coverage.

Unfortunately for Lance, Washington had gone on vacation for the month of August. No one was in town to make news, virtually guaranteeing heavy coverage of his quagmire. Throughout August, Bert Lance was *the* front-page story.

The first official investigative reports from the Comptroller of the Currency, issued August 18, concluded that Lance's "recurring pattern of shifting bank relationships and personal borrowing raises unresolved questions as to what constitutes acceptable banking practices."

But both the President and Lance thought it would put to rest all the controversy. "Bert, I'm proud of you," Carter told him on national TV.

Instead, the report spawned more questions, deeper investigation, and harsher criticism. The daily stories continued. The White House was losing its grip on the situation.

Jimmy Carter could not afford this first major crisis. He came to Washington partly on a revival of morality and pristine ethics, promising his appointees would adhere to a higher standard.

Lance wasn't a crook, but the American people began to feel that he got special treatment in the buddy-buddy world of big business and banking. The average American couldn't get million-dollar loans and run up hundred-thousand-dollar overdrafts on their checking accounts, as Lance and his family were able to. Calls for Lance's resignation grew.

Senator Ribicoff ordered the Committee staff to conduct their own investigation and to prepare for hearings in September. By Sept. 2, the staff had boiled down all the many charges for the Chairman and Ranking Republican, Percy of Illinois. The laundry list hit the senators like a lead brick. They were the leaders of the Senate Committee that approved this man for that high office and didn't take the time to dig up his backyard.

In their Labor Day meeting with the President, they painted a bleak picture: more hearings and more focused press coverage. In other words, the Lance Affair would go on and on with no end in sight.

*   *   *

In midst of all the turmoil, Lance replied to those senators and representatives who had written the President on ED.

President Carter is "very much aware of the lack of coherence" and the "fragmentation" of federal education programs, and he "places high priority" on acting to correct the situation, Lance wrote in his September 2 letter.

"The President's decision to study this matter does not represent a change in the position he took during the campaign," Lance claimed, but "he reserves the right to decide on an alternative way of reorganizing federal education programs."

The strangely-worded letter would be Lance's final pronouncement on the Department of Education issue. He had other things to be concerned about.

*   *   *

Inside the Committee office, a frantic pace took over the first two weeks of September 1977. Staffers worked the phones to schedule witnesses for the next two weeks of hearings. Reporters hung around, waiting for more news to break. TV newsmen taped their reports outside the office, using the Committee door signs as backdrops. The Capitol police stationed officers around us to control the situation.

Thursday morning, September 8, Chairman Ribicoff gaveled the start of nine exhausting and traumatic days of continuous hearings on the Lance Affair. A slew of witnesses from official Washington and Lance's banking past testified.

Committee staffers dropped whatever they were doing to help out. I took on the task of coordinating the release of hundreds of previously confidential documents to the press. Reporters, lacking sources, continually pumped me for inside details, but I held back.

The stakes heightened as the Public Broadcasting System began gavel-to-gavel TV coverage of the hearings, thereby saturating the issue with more publicity.

The Lance Affair was taking its toll on President Carter. Surveys showed his job approval ratings dropped seven points or more. The public rated his handling of the Lance predicament poorly. A *Newsweek*-Gallup poll found that 67 per cent felt Lance should resign.

Agendas all over Washington were screwed up.

The President and top White House staff devoted much of their time to the save-Lance effort. Hardest hit was OMB, whose leader was preoccupied with his survival. The lack of direction trickled down to the President's Reorganization Project. Pat Gwaltney and her team continued working on the education study, but a certain uneasiness set in. The time was not right to send an interim memo on the Department of Education for a preliminary decision to either Lance or the President. According to the original plan, that was supposed to have been done by the second week in August. Lance's troubles were actually proving to be a blessing of sorts; Gwaltney and Hawley had fallen behind schedule and had not yet written a first draft of the memo.

At the Committee, we canceled hearing on other issues. The entire schedule, packed full of reorganization, government reform projects, and nominations would be delayed by at least a month.

The ED hearings scheduled for September 26-28 were off.

*   *   *

Washington and the nation turned its attention to Lance's climactic September 15 appearance before the Committee.

Inside the hearing room, I counted four TV networks, National Public Radio, eight other TV crews, and some 200 print reporters. This was pack journalism in its purest form.

In the lights at the green felt-covered witness table, Lance delivered his 49-page statement with controlled forcefulness and emphasis. He had waited long for this day in court.

One-by-one, Lance responded and discounted the many charges made against him.

"I did not ask for this fight, but now that I am in it, I am fighting not only for myself and for my family but also for our system," he said emotionally. "…Is it part of our American system that a man can be drummed out of government by a series of false charges, half-truths, misrepresentations, innuendoes, and the like?…"

Afterwards, the Committee began two-and-a-half grueling days of interrogation. Senators pounded Lance with tough, detailed questions.

At the hearings' end, Lance announced, "I shall return to my duties as director of OMB with even a firmer sense of responsibility and dedication." He stepped forward to shake hands with Senator Ribicoff, who sent him off with, "The best of luck to you."

*   *   *

Washington waited anxiously for Lance's next move. President Carter told reporters the hearings had "enhanced" Lance's standing, but he was "keeping an open mind." That weekend, Senators Ribicoff and Percy let it be known their Labor Day recommendation to the President remained unchanged: Lance should still resign.

The end came in a presidential news conference, Wednesday, September 21. Carter took a gulp of air, looked at the throng of reporters, and read a letter from Bert Lance—a letter of resignation.

The President had tears in his eyes. "Bert Lance is my good friend," he said in a wavering voice. "I know him personally, as well as if he were my own brother. I know him without any doubt in my mind or heart to be a good and an honorable man.

"And although I regret his resignation, I do accept it."

In our office, several of us fought back tears—Democratic Senate staffers, working for a leading Democratic senator in the Democratically-controlled Congress, who had just helped (not by choice) to bring down the most powerful advisor to our new Democratic President. The whole putrid affair made us mad.

Jimmy Carter's tremendous popularity with the American people would start slipping from here on out. He would never fully recover from the damage done by the Lance Affair.

*   *   *

All over town, Washingtonians spent the week-after assessing the impact on their programs, projects, or budgets.

Sitting inside the Senate Committee responsible for evicting Lance, Marilyn and I especially had much to worry about. The Carter people knew the Department of Education was Abe Ribicoff's baby and were in no hurry, no mood to give the Committee Chairman anything.

Anger and soreness radiated from the White House. The Georgians blamed the affair on the Washington establishment—the press, the bureaucracy, and the Ribicoff Committee. They came to Washington proudly touting themselves as "outsiders." But now they felt the "insiders" had their revenge, and had purposefully tried to teach the Carterites a lesson or two about dumping on them.

Abe Ribicoff, his aloofness and power, was a prime symbol to them of the establishment—a senator who one moment defended Lance and the next turned around 180° to protect his own hide. They did not consider him a friend. There was so much tension that a near-total blackout of communication between the Carter and Ribicoff people would last almost two months.

During the cooling-off period, the President and his staff would eventually realize they needed Ribicoff more than Ribicoff needed them for piloting Administration initiatives through the Governmental Affairs Committee. And, the Senator was an important force on the Senate Finance Committee where much of Carter's energy, tax, and welfare reform legislation was being considered. They would have to make gestures of conciliation sooner or later to patch things up. But the relationship would be strained.

We had to have the President's support for ED if it was to fly. Would the President hold a grudge against Ribicoff and deny him the vital endorsement of his pet project? Or might Carter cave to the pressure of the NEA and other education groups, support ED, and use it simultaneously as that conciliatory gesture to Ribicoff? No one knew.

Because the President's backing was so important, Marilyn and I worried—along with our colleagues—that the Lance Affair may have weakened Carter significantly. On issues ranging from the economy to energy to foreign policy, Carter's ratings were consistently negative, and that reflected on Capitol Hill where suddenly it seemed all of his major legislative initiatives were in trouble. The President's honeymoon had come to an abrupt end. The Lance Affair made the press and public stop and focus on Carter's weaknesses.

The only consolation we could take in the Lance aftermath was the removal of one (Lance) of the two biggest obstacles to ED (Califano being the other). The President, who had not yet developed a reputation for decisiveness, would probably have found himself in the middle of a sharp dispute among his advisors—Lance and Califano on one side, Mondale, Hamilton Jordan and Stu Eizenstat on the other. Now, Califano would stand alone.

But who would succeed Lance as OMB Director? Would he or she be opposed to ED? Most believed no one could fill Lance's shoes in terms of clout with the President. The general feeling in Washington was that the Vice President's already large role would further expand to fill the gap.

The outlook for the ED bill was chancy and unpredictable. Yet we had gone too far and were too committed to let things ride. Along with the education groups, we decided to keep up the pressure as if the Lance Affair had never happened. Those first hearings were needed now more than ever.

*   *   *

Less than one week after Lance's resignation, Dick Wegman and Marilyn met to go over the Committee's messed-up calendar and straighten it out. Marilyn kept after Dick to set aside two days for ED hearings. The two tentatively blocked out October 12 and 13, contingent upon Senator Ribicoff's approval.

Later that morning, Dick returned from his daily meeting with the Senator. He looked at Marilyn and smiled: "You've got it."

We excitedly sprung into action. We had just two weeks to arrange everything.

The most time-consuming chore would be rounding up witnesses. Ever since March, hearings had been on our minds. We already had a good idea of who would testify.

We decided to have a panel of senators lead-off on the first day, Wednesday, October 12.[8] Following them, a panel of members of the

---

[8] We went through the motions of inviting the two principal Administration officials, HEW Secretary Califano and Acting OMB Director James McIntyre. But they politely declined for lack of presidential direction.

citizens committee that NEA had put together; Gail Bramblett said she'd take care of that. Then, a supportive panel of academic authorities on HEW.

For the second day, Thursday, October 13, we decided to call first a panel of the major education groups to give strong testimony in favor of ED. The second would consist of the former U.S. commissioners of education, mostly supportive also.

Witnesses would address themselves only to the general concept of a Department of Education. For obvious PR and political reasons, we had carefully arranged that most would back the bill. They would stay away from the controversial issues of which programs should go in the new agency.

The two of us split up the phone calls and worked the next week-and-a-half to schedule some 20 witnesses from all across the country.

*   *   *

Bill Hawley called Marilyn Friday, October 7 to ask for the list of witnesses at our hearings. We had by then all but four locked into the two—day schedule.

Hawley admitted to Marilyn the hearings would force his colleagues at PRP, OMB, and the White House to "get going on the Department of Education." The President's reorganization team was restive over the lack of forward momentum on the issue.

That weekend, Hawley finished a first draft of the "preliminary" decision memo to the President. Pat Gwaltney read it through Monday and ordered a total rewrite. She thought it was much too long, too academic, and had little in the way of political assessment. It was not written for a President of the United States. They would spend another month deliberating over, rewriting, and polishing the memo.

Gwaltney and her team had narrowed it all down to three hard options for Carter: (1) a Department of Education similar to the

Ribicoff bill, (2) a broader Department of Education and Human Development that would include human services programs, and (3) strengthening education within HEW.

"We have come to the conclusion that it is not a good idea to have a separate department which isolates education," Gwaltney told Marilyn by phone the day before the hearings. Education should not be isolated from community and family institutions. From that, we inferred she leaned toward the education and human development model.

Marilyn repeated her request for copies of the option papers the PRP staff had prepared. Having them would be extremely helpful in explaining the options to Senator Ribicoff, she said. Gwaltney, ever protective of information and analyses in her office, balked. No decision had been made yet by the President, she noted.

"Well," Marilyn said, "I hope a preliminary decision will be made soon so we don't waste our time moving in different directions."

*   *   *

Large bundles of witness statements arrived Monday and Tuesday.

In between the nonstop phone calls from other senators' staff, press, and lobbyists, Marilyn and I Tuesday put the finishing touches to Ribicoff's opening statement. The Senator read it, made some changes, and added "We need a Department of Education" at the end. We read through the witness statements to develop the best line of questioning for each panel. Ribicoff might use all, some, or none, depending on his mood and curiosity at the time.

"You better get the cameras there," the Senator told Dick that morning. He knew the more press coverage we got, the stronger an effect the hearings would have on the President and his aides. I worked all

Tuesday phoning the major news bureaus in town in an effort to entice them into including ED in their news budgets for the next two days.

*   *   *

About 100 people gathered in the hearing room early Wednesday morning. When I walked in at 9:20 to check on things, there were many faces I did not recognize. It seemed every education-related group in town sent someone to cover the hearing.

A dozen or so reporters sat at two press tables poring over stacks of statements, witness lists, and press releases. There were no TV cameras, no blinding klieg lights, and only a couple still photographers. I was disappointed, but not surprised.

The room hushed as the anteroom door behind the dais swung open and Ribicoff walked in at 9:30 sharp. The Chairman, dressed in a crisp fall suit, sat down at the head of the giant, wooden half-circle dais and started thumbing through the black notebook we prepared for him. Marilyn and I rushed up on the elevated dais floor and took our seats behind Ribicoff.

"Are we ready?," the Senator turned to ask in a whisper.

Marilyn nodded her O.K.

Ribicoff hit his gavel. "The Committee will be in order," he said routinely. "Today's hearing on the creation of a federal Department of Education marks the first time in more than 20 years that congressional committee is actively considering such a proposal," he read into the microphone from his opening statement.

"The Department of Health, Education, and Welfare has been reorganized repeatedly. No amount of in-house reorganization can correct the unmanageability of the nation's largest executive department. To submerge the Education Division's $10 billion worth of programs under the multitude of health and welfare issues is not giving education the importance and national priority it needs.

"We plan to hold further hearings early next year before we begin to mark up the legislation. We will try to secure final passage before the end of this Congress (fall 1978)...".

Several other senators put in special appearances to back the bill.

The first panel—three U.S. senators—came forward to take their seats together at the witness table. After much canvassing, we ended up with Sen. Claiborne Pell, chairman of the education subcommittee, Sen. Henry Bellmon, ranking Republican on the budget committee, and Sen. Pete Domenici, Republican from New Mexico.

Pell testified that in the last decade, as education programs were formed, the education committees in Congress planned them with an eye towards the eventual establishment of an Education Department. The Rhode Island Senator reiterated his view "the arts and humanities be grafted onto the tree of education," although he recognized substantial opposition to the idea.

Oklahoma's Senator Bellmon said creation of ED was "solidly supported" by educators in his state and the nation, but hoped, however, that "restraints upon the growth of bureaucracy are clear."

Domenici, a moderate, focused on the HEW-is-big angle. "...I ask, who do we think about nationally when we speak about a national concern for education? Try as they do, and as dedicated as they are, the secretaries of HEW will not come across."

"I just wanted to highlight the point you make," Ribicoff jumped in. "I have the highest respect and affection for Secretary Califano, but since he has been Secretary, he has not made one major speech or one major statement on education. There is no man busier than the Secretary of HEW..."

(High-ranking White House and HEW sources had called the day before to give us that tidbit and suggest Ribicoff use it at the first hearing.)

In thanking the three senators for their testimony and support, Ribicoff noted, "I think we have a tough road ahead. I know the Administration is looking at this entire problem. I don't know where they're going, but from my point of view I don't think U.S. senators have to wait for a decision by the President.

Marilyn kept nudging me with her foot. It was her silent way of saying, "Ribicoff is sending fantastic signals to the White House."

Three members of the Citizens Committee for a Cabinet Department of Education took their turn at the witness table. "There must be new and clear evidence that the federal government understands that education is the glue of a just and civil society and is willing to commit its authority and resources accordingly," stressed James Farmer of the Coalition of American Public Employees, chairman of the citizens committee. In the move to an Education Department, parent-citizen group leader Carl Marburger saw a chance to increase the "responsiveness" of the federal bureaucracy and establish "clear, open, and real access points for parents, citizens, and students." Maryland county executive Winfield Kelly testified from his local perspective that one federal official should be in control of ed programs.

Senator Ribicoff welcomed the third panel, academic authorities Rufus Miles from Princeton, Stephen Bailey from Harvard (a former American Council on Education executive), and Sam Halperin.

Miles said he supported ED for four reasons. First, education deserves the attention and emphasis that Cabinet status conferred. Second, coordination of education programs can be done far more effectively under an officer with Cabinet rank. Third, a Cabinet Secretary of Education would more strongly articulate the needs of education. And fourth, removing education from HEW would make that "gargantuan" agency slightly more manageable.

"It should be emphasized the type of Department of Education recommended in the bill before you is light-years away from the centralized education ministries of most other nations of the world," Bailey argued in defense of S.991.

Halperin's impressive statement of charts and graphs demonstrated that in budgetary terms, "education is flunking out at HEW." In 1966, education's share of the HEW budget was 11.5 per cent; by 1976 it had dropped to 5.5 per cent. When HEW's proposed 1978 budget moved through OMB clearance, education got cut the most, he showed.

Halperin also discovered that in a period of 12 years, 1965-77, there were 13 different U.S. commissioners of education.

"That is amazing," Ribicoff interrupted him.

"...I do not believe that if the top education official had Cabinet rank, the instability would average less than one year," Halperin replied from the witness table.

Ribicoff asked the three experts if it was true health, education, and welfare were all linked together, as Califano, Shanker, and other opponents had argued.

"This coordination within HEW is simply a figment of the imagination," Miles answered, who was once HEW's director of administration for 12 years.

Satisfied with the first day's positive showing, Ribicoff adjourned at 11:30.

*   *   *

Press coverage of the premiere hearing did not live up to our hopes. There was no mention on TV newscasts. And, the few articles it generated were tucked away deep inside most newspapers.

The *Associated Press* reporter at the hearing quoted Ribicoff on his offhand remark that U.S. senators don't have to wait for the President and his claim that Secretary Califano had not yet made a major speech on education.

Joe Califano saw the AP story in the *Washington Post*. He promptly fired off a letter to his good friend Abe Ribicoff. At the top, he wrote in longhand, "Personal", and underlined it.

"Dear Abe," it began. "I noticed in the paper today that you believed I had made no major speeches on education." Califano enclosed copies of two speeches that we'd never heard of. He signed his letter, "Joe."

We later drafted a letter politely telling the Secretary his speeches, while interesting, were not "major." Ribicoff signed it, "Abe."

*   *   *

As the 10 o'clock starting time approached Thursday morning, October 13, the hearing room gradually filled. I noticed the same faces at the press table, again sifting through piles of testimony. But this morning, there was one TV crew standing by. The President scheduled a press conference for the afternoon, leaving no doubt as to the day's top story.

Several PRP staffers returned to monitor our hearings, as they had done the day before.

Sen. Sam Nunn gaveled the hearing to order. The 39-year-old Georgia conservative Democrat, chairing for Ribicoff, spoke with a smooth, but firm southern accent.

"I know the people of Georgia and the rest of the country are strongly opposed to the proliferation of costly government agencies," he continued. "The creation of a Department of Education, in my view, could actually reduce bureaucracy by eliminating duplication and waste...".

Nunn asked the first panel to come forward, representatives of the "Big Six"—NEA, chief state school officers, state boards of education, PTA, school boards, and school administrators. These associations would become the engines behind the ED bill.

NEA President John Ryor led off, voicing the hope "on behalf of 1.8 million members" that "these hearings will now provide the stimulus to move away from the rhetorical question of whether there should be a Department and focus our attention on what should be included in (it)."

The chiefs and state board members both hammered away at the theme of consolidation of programs and efficiency.

"Far from being an obstacle to the local control of education," a separate department would make possible long-range planning, a coherent federal strategy in education, and clear lines of federal authority, the National PTA president testified.

The school administrators group sent the superintendent of the Toledo, Ohio public school system, set to close its doors for several weeks due to a much-publicized taxpayer revolt in that city against increased property taxes. "There is a real sense of need of leadership for American education," he pleaded to the senators, "...a Cabinet-level post (for) education."

Just then, Senator Ribicoff entered through the anteroom door and sat next to Nunn. He made a special trip from the Finance Committee (which was considering the President's energy program).

Several former U.S. commissioners of education replaced the "Big Six" as the day's final panel. Ribicoff welcomed these respected past kings of the education establishment with an opinion-question.

"Invariably, in looking across this table, every commissioner picked by a President has been of outstanding ability, background, and character," the Senator spoke off-the-cuff. "...Yet from 1965 to 1977, a period of 12 years, there have been 14 different men serving in the Office of Education. It appears to be a revolving door that turns rapidly, which means that there must be something in that office or the HEW organization that leads to great disappointment, great disillusionment, or great frustration.

"Now, I am just curious. From your various personal experiences, what is there about the Commissionership of Education that causes men of such commitment to stay such a short time?," Ribicoff asked.

"I am, I guess, the most recent refugee from the commissioner-ship out of this panel," Utah State Higher Education Commissioner Terrel Bell responded. A Nixon appointee, Bell served from June 1974 through July 1976 in the post. "The Commissioner is an executive level V in the government structure, and in HEW that is one of the lowest forms of human life...," he said. "I did not have the clout in that huge organization...You come to the job and you are soon disillusioned with it.

"Right now," Bell explained, "by the time you get through all of the assistant secretaries (in HEW) and you get the decisions made, and if you win on the Secretary level, then you do not have direct access to OMB and you also do not have the opportunity to appeal to the Oval Office."

Ford Foundation Vice President and Johnson Administration com-missioner (1966-68) Harold Howe agreed. "The commissioner has not always had easy access to the White House," he added, "and I think edu-cation benefits when he does."

"When the Administration at the top level either loses interest in edu-cation or finds other priorities that occupy it more deeply, the Commissioner of Education has very little advocacy in the system," assert-ed Sidney Marland, College Board president and commissioner for two years (1970-71) during the Nixon reign.

In closing, Senator Nunn told the former commissioners their expert-ise would be needed in the future as the bill developed. "I am sure you real-ize, having dealt with the legislative process, that there is no danger of this bill passing and being signed into law tomorrow morning."

*   *   *

Although media coverage of the hearings was light, they did provoke much comment.

A *Hartford Courant* columnist wrote October 16 the hearings showed "Ribicoff tired of waiting for Carter" to move on ED.

The Washington Star editorialized in favor of ED October 18: "To have a Secretary of Education in the Cabinet gives symbolic weight to the nation's concern for an area of dismaying failures…(Young people) can't read, they can't write, they can't make change. They can't turn off the TV."

Syndicated columnist Marianne Means wrote October 20, "The President might be politically wise to go along with Ribicoff on this one," but noted, "Ribicoff is not one of the President's favorites since he led the fight against Bert Lance…".

Carl Rowan, a nationally-known black journalist, commented October 28 on *Post-Newsweek* stations, "Educators think they got a campaign promise from President Carter to create a Department of Education. With an enthusiastic push from the White House, they will get that department. It's long overdue."

*   *   *

To Carter Administration officials, two days of hearings was a strong enough message that Abe Ribicoff was 100 per cent serious about his bill.

"We can see the light at the end of the tunnel," Beth Abramowitz told Marilyn in a phone call from the White House October 17. Drafts of the PRP decision memo are circulating, she said, and an Administration decision one way or the other would come in the weeks ahead.

At the end of October, we still did not have the tiniest indication how the President would come out on the ED issue. But the first hint of the direction his decision might take came from the President's closest advisor—his wife.

In an interview with the *Atlanta Journal and Constitution* published Sunday, October 30, Rosalyn Carter described how she and her husband engaged in policy discussions often, especially during their weekly working luncheons together.

"Last week," she said, "...we talked about education. You know how visible education is in Georgia, and you don't hear much about it now. I wanted to be sure he was doing something about that.

"He told me what he was doing—they are doing a study now for a separate Department of Education, which he had said he would do."

EIGHT

The Presidential Green Light

In the first days of November, the President's Reorganization Project decision memo was just about ready to go to the Oval Office. Pat Gwaltney and her staff polished and refined and rewrote the thick document many times over.

We repeatedly asked them for copies when it was in final form and failing that, we hoped they could at least tell us what PRP's recommendation to the President would be. On both points, Gwaltney and sill Hawley were consistently evasive.

Rosalyn Carter's comments confirmed the signals they had been receiving from the top White House staff that the President was leaning towards taking the "E" out of HEW. The PRP staffers did not know, however, what type of administrative structure the President would decide on or what the timing would be.

At first, a meeting with the President was scheduled for Wednesday, November 2, for all parties to argue their positions. But the President's calendar was jammed tight with receiving foreign dignitaries and prodding a balky Congress on his legislative program.

The Department of Education issue would have to wait for a quieter, less pressing moment.

*   *   *

Joe Califano's men, lobbying hard behind-the-scenes as decision time neared, had been courting one organization in particular: the Catholic Church.

It was the classic strategy of playing the groups off against each other. Relations between the public education lobby (NEA, PTA, school boards, etc.) and the private education community (parochial schools, independent colleges, etc.) were less than cordial. The public school groups fought the idea that the federal government should appropriate precious monies for the support of private schools, especially tuition tax credits.

Comprising nearly 50 million members and 24,000 parishes, the Catholic Church was easily America's largest and a power to be reckoned with. The Church's heavy involvement in local, state, and national politics was no secret.

On Friday, November 11, bishops and Catholic educators met in Washington to take a stand on the issue. For nearly an hour, they extensively debated ED. Some argued that raising education might have merit by giving it more importance in the federal government. Most, pointing to the NEA-Carter relationship, worried the public school lobby would dominate the new department. Many feared "the threat of federal control and encroachment on the private sector."

In the end, the NEA antagonists won out. The bishops decided to renew their half-century-old opposition to ED. It would be up to the Washington-based U.S. Catholic Conference lobbyists to work against the bill and inform the President's staff of their opposition. Soon, priests and parishes across the country would be notified of the official Catholic stand.

For Joe Califano and his people, this was very good news. They now had two powerhouse organizations to back them up—the AFT and the Catholics.

*　　*　　*

Pat Gwaltney and Bill Hawley were noticeably more upbeat that week. They were more open and forthcoming with us. Almost daily we had conversations back and forth.

They had finished their presidential decision memorandum, except for a few minor changes here and there. A draft had been sent to a few agencies and members of the President's task force for review.

"There is a new momentum for a Department of Education," Hawley confided in us Tuesday night, November 15, in a meeting at his office. "The President might want to make a statement in the (January) State of the Union address."

The all-important meeting with the President to go over the various broad options had been rescheduled for Monday, November 28, he said. But he cautioned us that the President might or might not make a firm decision at the meeting.

Gwaltney and Hawley made no secret they would be pushing the Department of Education and Human Development model with the President.

The new optimism pleased Marilyn and I. But the inclination toward a super-broad ED and Human Development model made us nervous. It would be more contentious even than Ribicoff's plan.

*　　*　　*

More good news came the same week. In a November 16 letter to the Tennessee Education Association, Republican Senate leader Howard Baker affirmed his support for the Ribicoff ED bill. The Tennessee teachers, well-organized and active politically, had supported Baker in his campaigns for the Senate.

The cooperation of the minority party leader would come in handy if the bill reached the Senate floor. It also came at a propitious moment, demonstrating bipartisan support to Jimmy Carter.

*   *   *

Thanksgiving week, 1977. With Congress on a one-week recess, Washington was quiet. Like so many others, I took advantage of the holiday to leave town and rest up with the family in Vermont.

President Carter and his family went to Camp David and spent the holiday there.

The November 28 meeting was still on the schedule. Pat Gwaltney and her staff worked feverishly Monday, Tuesday, and Wednesday making last-minute changes in the decision memo which would be sent to Camp David for Carter's perusal over the long weekend.

The PRP staff missed the 3:00 p.m. deadline for sending the memo with the helicopter, so it went by White House car that night to Camp David.

*   *   *

The President's Department of Education decision materials were compiled into a big blue binder notebook. There were memos from aides, the 19-page PRP report, and 87 pages of appendices.

Carter had already seen a short but hard-hitting memo from his top staffer, Hamilton Jordan. The gist of it was, essentially, you made this campaign promise to the teachers and if not fulfilled, you will lose the support of the National Education Association in the next election and on other issues. Jordan argued forcefully for a "go" decision on ED. It would later be credited as a turning point in Carter's decision-making process on this issue.

On top of all the papers in the blue notebook was a memo to the President from acting OMB Director Jim McIntyre marked "CONFIDENTIAL." The 37-year-old Georgian, although much more low-key and lightweight than Bert Lance, had taken over OMB so well that by the end of the year Carter would formally appoint him to Lance's job.

McIntyre summarized the positions he thought the major participants would be taking at the November 28 meeting. "Califano will argue against a separate department and seek approval for undertaking immediate reforms within HEW," he wrote.

McIntyre said the Vice President would probably argue for a narrow separate department and against a broader department "as politically infeasible next year." Stuart Eizenstat's position, he said, "is uncertain at this time."

"OMB will argue that a narrow department makes no functional sense," the OMB director wrote. "We recognize, though, that the substantive case for the broader department is not yet fully worked out, and that the politics will be very hard...We will therefore propose that you reject a narrow department, reaffirm your commitment to a broader concept, authorize some reforms within HEW, and indicate that no overall Administration proposal will be forthcoming until our homework is complete," McIntyre concluded.

*   *   *

The PRP decision memorandum was divided into three main parts: background on the federal role and problems in education, discussion of the three principal structural options, and options for action.

In the background section, the President's Reorganization Project briefed the chief executive on the large federal role in education— 267 programs in 24 federal agencies costing $25 billion in 1977, about 10 per cent of the domestic budget. The programs served six general objectives: promoting equal educational opportunity, improving the relationship between training and work, providing general financial assistance to special populations and institutions, educational research and assessment, operating schools, and promoting cultural development.

"A decentralized and locally controlled education system continues to be seen as a national asset," it told the President, "and while there are strong demands for more federal funds, there is little interest in increased federal control."

The paper sketched out problems faced by American education, such as the drop in SAT scores, declining school enrollments, and a national high school drop out rate of 20 per cent.

"Restructuring federal programs, whether into a new department or within HEW, will not by itself produce constructive change…," the report said. "The federal structure can be important, however, in orienting education toward some concerns rather than others and in determining the level and visibility of federal leadership in education."

HEW's Education Division, the focal point of the federal effort, is "confused and contradictory," the memo claimed.

The second section explained to President Carter the three primary structural alternatives PRP had developed: a "narrowly-based" Department of Education, a "broadly-based Department including education and other human development activities," and a "strengthened" HEW Education Division.

A narrow Department would be "based" on HEW's "E", the report said, and include certain other programs from the National Science Foundation, nutrition education, and civil rights. An asterisk here referenced the Ribicoff ED bill and listed at the bottom of the page the additional programs proposed for transfer therein (Head Start, school lunch, etc.).

Everything was skewed to present the "broadly-based" Department of Education and Human Development in the best light. "It would seek to enable individuals to use and shape better the opportunities society offers," the paper aggrandized. "It would foster a comprehensive state and local service network involving families, schools, and other private and public community institutions...". Candidate programs for such a department included Social Security education aid, Job Corps, and many youth and family welfare services.

Strengthening education within HEW would "preserve possibilities for developing relationships among education, social services, health, and income security programs," the memo said. The third option called for, as expected, consolidating the commissioner and assistant secretary of education posts into a higher-level official in the HEW bureaucracy.

Each of the three options "would probably produce better administrative leadership of programs than the current situation," PRP admitted, but there were advantages and disadvantages to all three.

The narrow department would provide full-time Cabinet leadership and visibility, respond to the campaign pledge, and satisfy "more directly than any other option" the demands of elementary and secondary groups, particularly NEA. However, according to the report, linkages between education and human development would unlikely be considered, expectations of other constituencies for their own departments would be raised, opposition from higher education and child advocacy groups would surface ("though not intensely"), and the number of issues having to be resolved at the Presidential level would increase,

A broad education and human development department would be advantageous because it would improve coordination, encourage rethinking of current priorities, permit greater emphasis on pre-school, postsecondary, lifelong and nonschool learning, and "respond more directly than any other alternative to your campaign pledge."[9] But the paper said such a model "would generate little political backing and much opposition at this time."

Keeping education in HEW and beefing it up there would avoid increasing the number of agencies reporting directly to the President and involve the least disruption. Yet this option, the memo said, would be disadvantageous because it would "disappoint and antagonize the NEA and other elementary and secondary education groups that strongly support Cabinet-level status for education." It would also retain in HEW the "substantial diversity of programs" which put "heavy" demands on the HEW Secretary.

PRP concluded overall that the "narrowly-based" department was the "least attractive alternative," and that the strongest thing going for it is the "enthusiastic" support of the NEA, many education groups and members of Congress.

The education and human development model was "best suited for developing comprehensive approaches to the challenges associated with education," it said. "No one constituency or program would dominate such a department." (The concern over domination of a new Education Department by NEA was the major force behind PRP's advocacy of the broad model.)

HEW's Education Division should be restructured, regardless of whether it stays there or is moved to a separate department, PRP believed. "However, any internal reorganization proposal will have to be reviewed in terms of the political signals," the report warned. (Marilyn

---

[9] The PRP memo repeatedly referred to Carter's early campaign statement that he would consolidate "grant programs, early childhood education, job training,..." etc.

and I felt Califano would use an interim reorganization to clean things up at HEW and thereby block a move later on to ED.)

The President's reorganizers presented him with three options for future action. First, he could announce support for a (narrow) Department of Education and indicate a detailed proposal would be submitted in January or February to Congress in conjunction with the continued Ribicoff hearings. Second, Carter could announce his preference for a broad new education and human development department and do one of two things: direct his staff to develop that proposal, or "defer a final decision on (ED) but note that the broad department seems very promising" and order more study. Califano would be allowed to tinker with his education offices under PRP's eye. Third, the President could announce a decision in favor of retaining education in HEW and strengthening it within.

PRP recommended Carter indicate his preference for the broad department but hold off on sending anything to Capitol Hill until they had time (lots of it) to try it out on the Congress and interest groups.

*   *   *

Joe Califano waited until Saturday, November 26, to send his own 19-page memorandum to the President at Camp David.

"All my experience in government—both as personal staff to a former President and as a Cabinet secretary to you—leads me to urge, in the most forceful way I can, that you reject the narrowly-based separate department on the merits as inimical to the President's policy-making, managerial, and budgetary interests," he wrote Carter.

"As the OMB memorandum indicates, virtually the only reason to create the narrowly-based separate department would be to fulfill a campaign promise and satisfy political demands," he said. "…It is very likely to be dominated by an assertive, nationally organized interest group—the NEA." Califano said it would mean more managers for the

President, "sharply" increase the federal share of education costs, and entail a "24-36 month period of disruption" in the bureaucracy.

"...You need not break your commitment," the HEW Secretary suggested. "You need only decide today that you are not going to keep it by creation of a narrowly-based Department of Education." What Califano was leading up to was simple: reject ED outright, have OMB study the broad model over a long period of time, clean up education within HEW, and toss the education groups a few bones to mollify them over the loss of their ED, especially by increasing education program budgets.

"...This package, plus direct personal contact between high level Administration officials and the NEA leadership may be enough to insure that NEA's criticism is mild," Califano thought.

"Special, in-depth discussions with Senator Ribicoff will be necessary," his memo said.

*   *   *

The 95th Congress returned to Washington Monday, November 28, to wrap up one of the busiest first sessions in memory.

I spent the day driving down from New England, unaware that top officials of the President's Reorganization Project had secured, during the holiday week, a 10:00 a.m. appointment with Senator Ribicoff to get his reaction on the issues that would be discussed with the President that afternoon.[10]

---

[10] We still had not seen the PRP decision to the President.

OMB's Harrison Wellford and Pat Gwaltney joined Marilyn and Dick Wegman in Ribicoff's office. Wellford had, by now, established a good working relationship with the Chairman of the Senate Committee considering his reorganization plans. Ribicoff did not know Gwaltney. Bill Hawley was not there.

There is to be a 2:30 meeting this afternoon with the President on education reorganization, Wellford told Ribicoff. "The President is leaning toward separation (of education)." He added that Carter would be against a narrow, "NEA-based" department.

Ribicoff agreed, but countered, "The chances of getting something broader are limited, and each increment makes it harder to get something in 1978." The Senator suggested an Education Department be set up first and then certain programs added later.

"We've spent the last three weeks talking to the social service constituencies," Wellford said.

"Education would never get off the ground if other things are folded into it," Ribicoff cut in.

Wellford delivered carefully his assessment that many of the transferred programs in the Senator's own bill would be controversial as well.

Gwaltney, sensing trouble, backed up her boss. "Head Start is the most controversial," she said. "We will get opposition to transferring the Arts and Humanities Endowments."

"If you face up to the interest groups that want to leave the Head Start program in HEW, you will win," Ribicoff replied.

The premise for their broader education and human development option, Gwaltney continued, is that the schools are isolated. With declining school enrollments, we now have an opportunity to provide a place for functions other than education, such as nutrition for the elderly in school cafeterias.

Gwaltney explained the HEW Education Division and Office of Human Development Services would form the base of the broader department. It would include programs funded under Title 20 of the

Social Security Act and operated by the states (adoption, day care, family planning, foster care, housing improvement, unmarried services, etc.). Cash assistance, Medicare, Medicaid, and Social Security itself would stay out.

"We need more time to look at this broad option," she told Ribicoff.

"We could probably get a bill in 1978," Wellford joined in, "but we really should have more time because of the need to get the constituency groups behind us."

Ribicoff thought for a moment. The Administration should articulate its position sometime in the spring, he urged. The Senator said he wanted to restart his hearings at the end of March. "We don't want to lose the present momentum," he said.

"While I don't favor a narrow-based Department of Education," Ribicoff said, "I don't want the department bogged down by noneducation programs. Any program placed in the new department must have an education factor."

"Some groups feel that the HEW Education Division isn't going to be enough for a separate department," Wellford reiterated.

"I agree with you," Ribicoff agitatedly replied. "I want a broad department. But I want to keep the welfare areas out."

The Senator added he would also probably take out the Arts and Humanities Endowments.

"Philosophically, we're thinking along the same lines," Ribicoff continued. "The NEA is wrong in wanting a narrow department. I will talk to them and tell them so. Without my support there won't be any new department. I will talk to them."

Wellford and Gwaltney thanked the Senator and left smiling. But they heard only what they wanted to hear from him—the word "broad."

*   *   *

Monday, November 28, 1977 was a cold, wet, dark day in Washington. Outside, the temperature rose only to the low 50°s.

At 2:30 p.m. in the Cabinet Room at the White House, a roaring fireplace helped to take the dampness out of the room. One by one, the powerhouses of the Carter Administration entered and took their seats at the Cabinet table. On the side opposite the President's seat sat Pat Gwaltney, Bill Hawley, Frank Moore, Jim McIntyre, Harrison Wellford, Joe Califano, and Fred Bohen. Facing them were Ham Jordan, economic advisor Charles Schultze, civil service head Alan Campbell, Stu Eizenstat, Presidential assistant Richard Pettigrew, Jack Watson, and the Vice President.

A few minutes after everyone got seated, the President came in and sat in his center seat. Like the others, he brought with him his notebook on the "Reorganization of Federal Education Programs."

As evidenced by the heavyweights in attendance, this would be the most important White House meeting to date on ED. Other than Califano and the OMB-PRP team, few had taken the time over the holiday weekend to read through the mound of memos and background papers. Most came to the meeting cold, not knowing all the details of what OMB was recommending.

The President, however, read through the entire stack at the Camp David retreat, his engineer's mind filled with background and facts on all the issues involved.

Jim McIntyre started off in typical Washington fashion by defining the meeting's purpose, summarizing the issues, and introducing his people. Then he turned it over to Pat Gwaltney.

Gwaltney, following the decision memo, briefly summarized the options OMB-PRP had developed and paraphrased some of the points made therein. She told the quiet group of some trends in education, and why there was a need for some sort of a reorganization. In more detail, she described the three models and ticked off examples of what kinds of programs would be in each one. Gwaltney told the President OMB was asking for a decision to go with one of the options, and PRP would then go back and work out the details.

Carter stopped Gwaltney at times to ask questions. His queries made clear he was well-briefed and understood the subject matter. The decline in SAT/achievement test scores interested him. He talked a lot about his own experiences in education as governor and school board member.

McIntyre reclaimed center stage and began talking about where certain people and groups stood on the ED issue. Just this morning OMB met with Senator Ribicoff, he told everyone, and the Senator favors the whole education and human development package (sic). Ribicoff is more than willing to cooperate with us, the acting OMB director said.

Public opinion favors change, McIntyre told Carter. He cited a recent poll Carter's own pollster, Patrick Caddell, had done that found more than 50 per cent believed establishment of a U.S. Department of Education was a good idea. (The question had been slanted so as to elicit a favorable response.)

Next, Joe Califano made his pitch to the assembled group. He summarized his memo, emphasizing his agreement with OMB that a narrow Department of Education should be ruled out. The HEW Secretary made a number of positive comments in support of the education and human development model.

When Califano finished, there was a long pause. The President asked for the opinions of his other advisors. No one said anything for fear of going first. Carter began calling on people individually. Going around the table, each spoke. It was a thoughtful discussion. Nearly everyone was pro-ED. Charles Schultze questioned the need for a separate department, but he didn't really care. Alan Campbell made some negative comments (he came from higher education) that centered primarily on the technical problems—new positions, personnel ceilings, etc. Stu Eizenstat noted how they had looked at a number of options during the campaign, and recalled how they arrived at the decision to support ED. Bill Hawley said little.

The Vice President chose the emotional, rhetorical route. Mondale said he wanted to see a Department of Education created. Education is important. We never discuss it, he added. Teachers need a voice and a feeling of access. The concerns of children should be represented at the highest levels of government, he continued. They are important to the future of the country.

There was virtually no mention of NEA by anyone.

After Mondale finished, another long silence followed. The President slowly flipped through some of his papers, in thought. He began to speak in a soft voice, his eyes scanning the room and all his staff.

I read the memos over the weekend, he said, and on the basis of all the studies, I'd like to go ahead with a Department of Education. He talked generally about structuring it as broadly as possible.

Then Carter turned to Califano and said, in the meantime, Joe, I'd like you to try to get the education programs working as best you can in HEW, to clean things up over there.

Carter got up and left. The meeting continued on for a few minutes longer and then broke up. It was nearly 4 o'clock. The President had stayed for more than an hour.

*   *   *

Pat Gwaltney and Bill Hawley left the executive mansion like excited young children. After months of hard work, the President of the United States had, they thought, essentially bought their recommendation for a broad new department. The two PRP staffers joyfully recalled back at their office the events of the momentous meeting for the benefit of their 20 or so reorganization aides. In celebration, they had a wine-and-cheese party that afternoon.

Joe Califano returned to his HEW office equally pleased. In a meeting with senior staff the next day, he left his people with the assumption that he presented "Jimmy" his position and the President went for it. The HEW Secretary's strategy was to push for an overly-broad department and an interim reorganization of education in HEW. He left the White House confident he had extracted both.

In reality, Jimmy Carter tried to please all his advisors. And in so doing, confused everyone as to what he had really decided. The President's staff would be spending the next month-and-a-half trying to figure out what the next move would be.

Carter had made no decision on timing. He did not specifically point to one option over another. He did not specifically authorize his HEW Secretary to do a formal restructuring of the Education Division.

About the only sure thing was that the President wanted to make good on his campaign commitment. How and when to do it was one big question mark.

*　　*　　*

Marilyn and I waited anxiously for some word on how the meeting turned out.

Art Sheekey called the next day, Tuesday, privately to brief Marilyn. "There are mixed signals," he said. "Carter didn't go along with OMB and he didn't go along with Califano."

Pat Gwaltney waited until two days later, Wednesday, to fill us in. From the tone of the meeting, she said the President feels strongly about his commitment and remembers it well. He prefers a department as broad as possible. Gwaltney added there was some interest in allowing Califano to make some changes in his "E".

"Stu (Eizenstat), Jim McIntyre and others will have to put heads together," she told Marilyn by phone. "We share the same objectives. Nothing was final."

Beth Abramowitz also called, predicting Califano would try to delay a public announcement on ED by the President as long as he could. The domestic policy staffer urged us to stop any interim legislation that Califano might want. He would almost certainly use it to stop a Department of Education, she warned.

*   *   *

The President's domestic policy chief, Stuart Eizenstat, kept his position on ED a mystery until the November 28 meeting, when he finally voiced support.

"...I am opposed to adding social services to the Department OMB proposes," Eizenstat told Carter in an explanatory memo following Friday.

"I recommend that Jim McIntyre or Secretary Califano testify before Senator Ribicoff's Committee endorsing the *general concept* of a separate Department of Education, not including social services, early next year," he concluded. "...I would recommend against sending up a detailed Administration bill, in view of the long congressional history. I understand this is the position you approved at the (November 28) meeting."

The maneuvering to define the President's position had begun.

*   *   *

The American Federation of Teachers was not sitting on its fanny during all the movement at the White House. The giant AFL-CIO annual convention would be held soon (December 5), and the teachers' union would be working to extract a negative AFL position on ED.

As a courtesy, AFT lobbyist Greg Humphrey called Marilyn to inform her a resolution against the Education Department would be voted on—most likely approved—at the convention.

Humphrey, 31, had been an AFT lobbyist for six years and a lifelong labor organizer. He was well-liked for his unobtrusive, amiable personality, fairness in battle, and ability to stay cool. Marilyn and I got along well with him. We were both sorry he was working against "our" bill; we also knew Greg as an effective lobbyist. For the next two years, we would become chivalrous opponents on the ED issue.

Our efforts to have pro-ED, pro-labor senators talk to AFL-CIO President George Meany were to no avail. At the AFL convention the following week, only AFSCME[11] official William Lucey spoke out against the resolution, largely in response to NEA's prodding. The policy statement was routinely and easily adopted. Nothing could stop it.

One of our big fears had come true—the mighty AFL-CIO now officially opposed the ED bill. How hard it fought against us in the future remained to be seen.

*　　*　　*

Now that the President had indicated his preference for a broad Department of Education, the turf issue became more important.

The arts community had not let up on their pressure to be kept out. Marilyn and I tried to win over National Arts Endowment Chairman Nancy Hanks in a personal meeting, but the strong-willed arts leader easily decimated our arguments. I accepted an invitation to address 75 arts educators on the topic, only to hear them politely tell me, "No one

---

[11] American Federation of State, County, and Municipal Employees

here favors it." Ribicoff had long since written off the transfer. Finally, Senator Pell reluctantly conceded, thereby killing the idea of an education-and-culture department once and for all.

Scientists from all over began writing Ribicoff and the White House hundreds of letters protesting S.991's provision moving science education to ED from the National Science Foundation.

In all serious discussions, Head Start continually surfaced as a prime candidate for transfer. That worried Head Start's most powerful and vocal leader, Marian Wright Edelman, head of the Children's Defense Fund. "It is not clear how children in their schools, families, or communities would feel any positive impact from an education department," she wrote Vice President Mondale December 14. Edelman hoped a decision on ED wouldn't be decided "on the basis of turf, but on what impact it will have on people."

*   *   *

With everyone intent upon leaving town for the upcoming Christmas holiday, Congress adjourned Friday, December 16, not to return for its second session until January 19.

The Carter Administration was falling all over itself to praise its own legislative accomplishments in 1977. At his December 15 news conference, the President cited passage of the economic stimulus package, a strip mining bill, a farm bill, a housing bill, the reorganization authority, the Department of Energy bill, and Social Security legislation.

The press focused instead on the big bills the President failed to get: his massive energy package, welfare reform, and a tax bill, among many others. The biggest foreign policy battle would be fought in the Senate early in 1978 over the Panama Canal treaties.

"I would say that perhaps looking in retrospect, the pace was a little too strong in the first year," the Vice President admitted to reporters a few days earlier.

*　　*　　*

The President's performance was also a topic Sunday, December 18 when Rosalyn Carter appeared on ABC's "Issues and Answers."

The First Lady discussed her life in the White House and defended her husband's work. Again, she mentioned her weekly working lunches with Jimmy. During their last luncheon, she told interviewers, the two talked about the Department of Education issue.

Will the President carry out his campaign promise?, the moderator interjected.

"I'm sure he will," Mrs. Carter responded firmly.

NINE

Now, A Major Bill

Time would be of special significance in 1978. Congress always hankers to adjourn by the end of September, rush home and campaign for reelection in November. The adjournment would be sine die—meaning the end of 95th Congress and the death of all the unfinished bills.

Attention immediately turned in January to the upcoming State of the Union address. NEA badly wanted the President to proclaim his support of ED in the televised speech to Congress. Nearly every day, someone from the government relations office put in a call to the White House staff to apply more pressure for even a slight mention. Normally, the NEA lobbyists worked through Les Francis, himself a former NEA lobbyist and then a member of the President's congressional relations staff. Calls were also made to Hamilton Jordan.

Stuart Eizenstat at first asked Pat Gwaltney only to produce one vague paragraph supporting the Education Department concept for the long, detailed, written State of the Union message which would be sent to Congress shortly after the President's speech. But Gwaltney and her higher-ranking OMB colleagues continually pushed for a sentence or two in the verbal, televised address, where it would have the most impact.

Secretary Califano and his men made many a phone call to White House aides asking that nothing be said. Backing them up was Greg Humphrey of the AFT, who also telephoned the President's staff and put in a negative word.

Drafts of a two-and three-sentence paragraph were flying back and forth like crazy between top Administration officials.

The final decision, however, on the exact content of the President's speech to Congress and the people would be made by the President himself, in close consultation with his speechwriters and his tight inner circle of advisors.

Not even Pat Gwaltney nor the NEA people would know for sure if Carter would say something about ED until he delivered his address at 9:00 p.m., Thursday, January 19.

*   *   *

At the White House, they were still trying to figure out what the President wanted to do on ED.

"It is the Vice President's impression, based on his conversation with the President, that the President wants to 'step back' after the initial endorsement and not become too deeply involved in thrashing out the details of the Department in Congress," Stu Eizenstat wrote in a January 9 memorandum to Hamilton Jordan and the same day, the President read a "confidential" memo from McIntyre entitled, *Next Steps on Education Reorganization*. It directly asked Carter for his decisions.

Choices for a "public reaffirmation" of the campaign commitment included formal announcement in the State of the Union, a special presidential message on education, a statement by Mondale, or a less formal approach as in responding to a reporter's question, the memo said.

"I suggest an informal response to a press question, while we proceed to work with Senator Ribicoff and other members of Congress and the interest groups," McIntyre told the President. Carter checked the "Agree" slot and penned in "VP statement also OK."

The OMB Director asked how the "breadth" of a new department should be described publicly, noting there had been "some disagreement" on this at the November 28 Cabinet Room meeting.

"We advised that you should state your preference for a broad department including education and related human development programs," McIntyre wrote.

Carter checked the "Agree" slot, and wrote next to it, "Be general—not specific—J".

Lastly, how far should HEW proceed with an interim reorganization of its Education Division?, the President was asked. "…The submission of a reorganization plan to the Ribicoff Committee may be confusing and burdensome in light of the legislative proposal for a new department," McIntyre argued. He suggested Califano be allowed to include his changes in other education bills that would be sent to House and Senate education committees.

The President simply checked "Agree."

McIntyre added, at the bottom of the page, "Senator Ribicoff has agreed to postpone his hearings until April so we can develop a joint proposal." (OMB was taking much for granted.)

Despite all the memoranda, the biggest question still had not been answered: When to move ahead?

*   *   *

Ignoring the positive signals coming from the Oval Office, Joe Califano still voiced his opposition to ED in public. The latest came in a wide-ranging interview January 9 with the editors of *U.S. News & World Report*.

"I remain opposed to such a department, but if the President decides to create it, I will do whatever is necessary to help it along," the HEW Secretary said.

*   *   *

"Carter Is Reported Ready to Back Separate Education Department," said a front-page headline in the *New York Times* January 12. "...Officials said the President's announcement would come in his State of the Union message January 19, if not before," the story revealed.

"And they said the President would not specify immediately which agencies and programs he wanted placed in the new department," the article said. "However, Mr. Carter's view was said to be that the new department should handle not only the education functions now in (HEW) but also education activities located elsewhere in the government.

"One official said that the Administration would conduct a year-long study of the government's educational activities before deciding what to put in the new department. Therefore, it is not expected that the President will ask Congress this year to pass legislation creating the department."

*   *   *

No one knew what the hell was actually happening. It was maddening for Marilyn and I those first weeks of January to be on the receiving end of all the crazy, mixed-up signals.

The *New York Times* piece caused us much worry. We had to place great stock in the world's leading newspaper. Yet, that awful notion of another study and the *Times'* conclusion that Carter probably would not press for passage this year left us with the blues. We'd have to start from scratch next year (1979).

"Califano is still fighting us," Art Sheekey told Marilyn in another of their private phone conversations that week. "He's trying to talk the President into not saying anything on the Department."

Gwaltney herself called the next day to send her own signals. The President might say Secretary Califano has been asked to develop an interim proposal, she told Marilyn, and that he would work with Congress for a Department. Gwaltney left Marilyn with the impression that ED was quite a ways down the road and that she supported letting Califano reorganize the "E" in HEW before moving toward separation.

In a stern but diplomatic manner, Marilyn voiced displeasure at the indications that Califano might be allowed fiddle with the HEW structure.

Gwaltney responded politely with nothing more than an "um-hmm."

We would do everything we could to fight Califano on his interim scheme, which had no other purpose than to block the move toward ED. It irritated us that the White House people were still trying to probe us, feel us out on it. If the President wanted an ED anyway, why waste time? Why give Califano his one last chance to destroy it? We could plainly see the Carter clan did not have the guts to stand up to their HEW Secretary.

What we didn't know at the time was that most of the Carter people did indeed share our view. Some, like Harrison Wellford and Bert Carp, wanted to please Califano. But the majority saw Califano's move as self-serving. They gritted their teeth and made their calls to sound us out because they had to. Checking for our reaction was part of the staff work; the option had to be thoroughly investigated.

*   *   *

The news that a presidential announcement on ED might be imminent prompted a stream of preemptive editorial comment from the national press.

Leading the pack was the *New York Times* with, "The High Price of Cheapening the Cabinet."

"...To call it a department and to address its head as 'Secretary' might mean the incumbent sits closer to the salt at Washington dinner parties," the January 16 editorial said. "But it would not alter any real power relationships...The Secretary would have no necessarily greater capacity to summon the President's attention. Indeed, he might have less without a powerful HEW Secretary to turn to for support."

The President's staff and we thought perhaps Albert Shanker and his AFT, based in New York City, or Joe Califano and his public relations aide, (Eileen Shanahan, a former *New York Times* staffer), instigated the editorial at this sensitive moment. We would never really know.

*   *   *

Congress returned to Washington the week of January 16, refreshed and ready to go to work on the second session.

President Carter met Wednesday, one day before his scheduled State of the Union address, with congressional leaders to discuss the agenda for the year ahead and give his priorities. Carter asked that Congress work on a tax reform package, his energy legislation, Panama Canal treaties, civil service reform (to go through our Committee), hospital cost containment, and welfare reform.

He did not mention the Department of Education, leaving doubts in our minds that there would be any mention in his speech.

*   *   *

On the walk to the Senate office building Thursday morning, I noticed the huge television vans and trailers stationed near the Capitol steps that would transmit the State of the Union speech to the people.

As the day progressed, we could discern nothing more about what the President would say in his big speech. NEA lobbyists and PRP staffers knew little more than we did.

The power behind of the State of the Union address is amazing.

Through a simple mention or lack of one, the President can affect the course of events on hundreds of issues and sub-issues. No mention of ED would automatically delay the bill until next year.

A declaration of support would keep its prospects alive for 1978. But we had to be realistic. The President was faced with more weighty issues than taking the "E" out of HEW—like world peace, defense, the economy, etcetera. Psychologically, we tried to prepare ourselves for the worst, for no mention.

By nightfall, snow was falling heavily. About two inches had piled up at the time I left for home. The television network pool had installed a massive bank of super-bright klieg lights outside on the Capitol grounds to add sparkling brightness to the building itself. I stopped to marvel at the picture-postcard scene: the well-lit marble exterior of the Capitol and its dome through dense, descending snowflakes. It was gorgeous.

*   *   *

On my color TV screen, those same images of the beautiful Capitol setting were appearing and being flashed simultaneously to millions of American living rooms.

Then, a team of congressional leaders escorted the President to the rostrum. The applause was noticeably restrained.

"Mr. President, Mr. Speaker, members of the 95th Congress, ladies and gentlemen," Jimmy Carter began. "One year ago tomorrow I walked from here to the White House to take up the duties of President of the United States…".

I could feel myself fidgeting nervously as Carter ticked off many paragraphs of rhetorical puffery and his list of desired projects.

Suddenly, he interjected a new theme. "You have given me the authority I requested to reorganize the federal bureaucracy and I am using it...

"We have made a good start...

"We have brought together parts of 11 government agencies to create the new Department of Energy—and now it's time to take another major step by creating a separate Department of Education."

I fell off my couch onto the carpeted floor below.

The President had consciously added force to those last words and a smile. He got a full eight-second round of applause.

Applause, too! I couldn't believe it.

My phone rang. It was Marilyn. She was as high as I was.

"He said it," I blurted instantly. "My God, Marilyn, he said it"

"Isn't it wonderful," she said, trying to contain her elation. "All right, now we've got lots of work to do. See you in the morning."

"Right," I said firmly, and then hung up. I just could not keep my attention focused on the remaining 15 minutes of the speech. I was in a euphoric daze.

*   *   *

Over at HEW, a glum Secretary Califano had called his top aides together about two hours earlier to inform them the President would announce his support for ED in the speech.

A one-sentence statement was issued to the press by the HEW Secretary: "The President has made his decision, and as I have repeatedly stated, I will work to achieve the President's objectives in this area as in all others."

NEA publicists could hardly restrain their glee. "A Department of Education can do more for American schools than any development in the last 100 years," they wrote in a statement released to reporters.

The AFT reaction was sour. "We think it's a bad idea and it's unfortunate the President is responding to the narrow kinds of thinking that proposed it," one AFT official told the press.

The next morning, Senator Ribicoff called his secretary into his office and personally dictated his own reaction for the press:

"The implementation of the President's stated goals will be important," the statement said. "…I am personally pleased with his endorsement of my proposal to create a separate Department of Education."

*   *   *

They were only 17 words out of a 40-minute speech.

All at once, S.991 became a major bill because the President of the United States had placed it prominently on his agenda. Marilyn and I, and the President's Reorganization Project, would now have to brace ourselves for the coming onslaught. All sorts of interested and affected people and groups would begin to seep out either to influence the train of events or to seek a piece of the action.

The President's announcement also had the largely unwelcome effect of turning loose the nation's editorial writers. In the succeeding six weeks after the State of the Union, we would be hit with a barrage of mostly negative editorial comment, from which we would never recover.

"It would bring a tremendous increase in government red tape and payroll spending," the *Baltimore News-American* said. "The NEA…would be able to get more money from the federal treasury," predicted the *Phoenix Republic*. The Charleston, S.C. *News & Courier* called ED "a labor department for teacher unions."

U.S. News & World Report warned, "Experience leads to the fear that a federal Department of Education would enter our local communities like the Man Who Came to Dinner—a guest to whom, it might be, we could never say 'Good-bye.'"

*   *   *

The Secretary of HEW was getting a little desperate. If he didn't do *something* fast, he would lose one-third of his title and turf, and more than $10 billion worth of programs. He would be embarrassed in the club of old Washington pros.

The last formal card Califano could play was his interim reorganization. The Secretary wanted to reorder education within HEW in the hopes that would buy him more time. We resisted.

The battle came to a head January 25. Harrison Wellford phoned Dick Wegman at 3:00 in the afternoon and said the President had authorized Califano to proceed with interim legislation. Dick replied cautiously there might be objection in the Senate; he would have to check with Senators Pell and Ribicoff and get back to him.

At 3:45, Marilyn rushed into Ribicoff's private chamber and explained the situation. The Senator listened by shaking his head and softly saying, "No, no." Finally, he ended the brief encounter with, "It's thumbs down. Either they want a department or they don't: And you can go ahead and tell that to OMB."

Back at the office, Marilyn talked to Pell's staff and aides to other key senators. Meanwhile, Dick Wegman had talked again with Wellford to apprise him of Ribicoff's flat objections.

Two hours later, the jockeying was over. All the authorizing committees agreed with us; they would oppose an interim reorganization and ask instead the ED bill move quickly. From Capitol Hill, we had engineered unanimous rejection of Califano's plan. It was dead.

*   *   *

Califano appeared a week later before the Senate Labor-HEW appropriations subcommittee to defend his department's budget. Members couldn't resist quizzing him on the President's recent ED announcement.

"That is the Administration's position," Califano told the senators. "I can't change the words in a book I wrote three years ago."

"Will you take some initiative to create a Department of Education or (support) the position the Administration is taking," a senator followed up.

"I think we are looking at a whole variety of initiatives now," the Secretary said from the witness table. "I think my understanding is that the Administration should at least be prepared to testify before Senator Ribicoff's Committee sometime in March or April, whenever it is holding hearings."

"Are you planning to recommend any major changes in the education provisions and structure?," the senator pressed on.

"It depends…," Califano answered. "Now, when you talk about the Department of Education—the biggest aid program in the federal government is the Veterans Administration. So, for it to make sense, you put that program (in). The Ribicoff bill,…would put Head Start in there, the arts and humanities program in there…There is another $16 billion of education programs that would logically go into the Department of Education."

Califano's scheming to stir up the interest groups infuriated the White House and us. Just two days earlier, I personally assured the VFW that we had not the remotest thought of transferring the multi-billion-dollar VA/GI Bill ed programs.

*   *   *

At the President's Reorganization Project, they were all too aware the Department of Education was rapidly moving from the study phase to the political phase.

Pat Gwaltney, Harrison Wellford, and others from PRP-OMB met Monday, February 6 with Bert Carp and Les Francis to discuss next step.

They talked about consulting with the interest groups to dredge up enough support for transferring as many outside programs to ED as possible. They thrashed out ideas on how to get the President, his wife, and top White House aides more personally involved. They agreed special emphasis would have to be placed on getting the House—specifically Chairman Jack Brooks—to begin consideration of a bill in the Government Operations Committee while the Senate considered its version. Otherwise, the year's short, election year session would preclude enactment in 1978.

The discussion was spirited and filled with disagreement, but the group managed to make two final decisions—first, the Carter Administration would not propose its own legislation, working instead with the Ribicoff bill, and second, they would press for enactment in 1978, focusing first on the Senate and then on the House.

*   *   *

"The focus has been changed from human development to education-related programs," Bill Hawley admitted to Marilyn February 9. "The President has decided to call it a *Department of Education*, not education and human development.'"

The PRP team had spent six weeks talking to interest groups around town and were now scaling down their visions accordingly. No one wanted to support their cherished "broad" department and disrupt the intricate turf-power system.

Hawley went down his check list. In the definite "no" column: veterans programs and the Arts Endowment. In the possible "yes" for transfer column: vocational rehabilitation, Indian education, nutrition education, science education, college housing, and youth programs. Still up in the air:

the Humanities Endowment, school lunch, Head Start, and the overseas Defense dependents schools.

PRP had months of work left to do, more analysis and consulting before deciding on their recommendations to the President about the make-up of the new department. The reorganization team would have to gauge the reaction and strength of the interest groups' resistance to moving turf and then render a judgment as to the transfer's chances on Capitol Hill.

But thankfully, in our view, they were not reaching as wide as first indicated. As time passed, PRP would feel more and more heat and would trim its sails to make this fight as digestible for the President as possible.

*   *   *

Ever since the State of the Union address, our appointment books were filled. Everybody was touching base with everybody.

First there were the vocational educators, who met with us to make certain there would be an assistant secretary for "occupational and adult education" in the new department.

Then, the American Federation of Government Employees, representing 3,000 HEW Education Division employees, told us they would lobby for the bill. AFGE was part of the AFL-CIO and would help offset AFT's influence there.

Al Sumberg, portly chief lobbyist for the 75,000-member American Association of University Professors, informed us his group was ready to gear up a "rather substantial lobbying budget" and effort behind ED—precious higher ed support.

Two lobbyists from the Children's Defense Fund stopped by to emphasize their opposition to transferring Head Start.

A delegation of science educators came by to plead that NSF be left alone.

Marilyn and I met with USDA Assistant Secretary Carol Foreman to talk about transferring the school lunch/child nutrition programs to ED. "They are not primarily educational programs," she told us. "They are feeding programs.

Alan Lovesee tried talking us out of moving the Indian schools. The chief counsel for the House Advisory Study Group on Indian Education argued, "The Bureau of Indian Affairs has a pro-Indian bias and experience in running schools. A new Education Department would have no (such) experience."

This was only the beginning. Interest groups would crawl all over us.

*   *   *

Over at the Shoreham Americana Hotel in upper Northwest Washington February 13, I gave my pro-ED spiel to 50 black educators.

"...We expect the Administration will be ready to testify when our hearings resume in mid-March," I told the group.

Marilyn and I began to speak more in public about restarting the ED hearings in March—our way of applying pressure on the Administration to make its decisions quickly. Already one-and-a-half months had passed, leaving little more than seven months to get the bill passed in both House and Senate. The prospects were scary and made us restless.

"It's important to emphasize that the Ribicoff bill is only a *concept bill*, a starting point," I went on. "The Senator is not steadfastly committed to all the transfers in his bill. They are in S.991 to elicit study and comment. Senator Ribicoff wants a broad department. However, he is flexible and open on what should go in it. All of this will be examined in detail at the upcoming hearings.

"As for the future, our hearings, we estimate, will take a minimum of five to eight days to complete. The bill could reach the Senate floor as early as June (I was being optimistic). In the House, Chairman Jack Brooks has not yet announced hearing dates.

"We hope to establish the Department this year," I concluded.

*   *   *

More than 500 students filled the Nashua, N.H. senior high school gymnasium the following Saturday morning, February 18, for a town meeting-type forum with a special guest—Jimmy Carter.

Near the end of the hour-and-a-half session, a student asked, "I would like to know why do you propose to establish a separate Department of Education and would this mean that there would be more federal controls on education in the future?"

"I am not under any circumstances willing to see the federal government have more control over colleges, high schools, grammar schools, kindergartens, or any other aspect of public education or private education in our nation." Carter replied forthrightly.

"The reason for advocating a separate Department of Education has nothing to do with control.

"...When I became President, I was deeply concerned about the quality of education in our country. We spend enormous sums of money. We have in many instances young people who graduate from high school who can't read and write. They know very little about the political structure of our own government.

"And I just feel that there are many ways in which the federal government can work more closely and in harmony with the state, local governments, and private institutions to give education a boost.

"I have spent a half of one per cent of my time since I have been president dealing with education issues. It rarely comes up in my weekly Cabinet meetings. When it does, it involves something concerning the Civil Rights Act or some legal aspect of education.

"...I don't think we will ever have the visibility for education, I don't think we will have the personal involvement of the President and the Secretary at the Cabinet level in education to promote its good points, to correct its deficiencies, as long as we have education buried underneath health and welfare. I just think it needs to be separate."

The students gave the President a round of applause.

Then, Carter added a footnote. "I might say that there has been already introduced in the Senate, in the Government Operations Committee under Senator Ribicoff, a bill that would establish a separate department," he said. "We will not introduce a separate piece of legislation. We will add our support politically from the White House and Administration to the legislation already being considered by the Congress."

TEN

Turf Maneuvers

Up until this point, the debate had been mainly, is it a good idea or bad? That would continue through the passage or defeat of the bill—even beyond.

But the President's endorsement shifted the focus of attention away from the Department of Education itself to its inner workings. With the tremendous resources of the White House behind the bill, a Department of Education could realistically be created. That meant a large number of programs could also be swept up in the momentum of the bill, transferred, and housed within the new ED.

Interest groups could no longer sit back. Suddenly, the threat to them and their programs was imminent. Sometime in the near future, the President would decide on what programs he wanted in his proposed new department. His recommendations would carry great weight with Congress.

If the agriculture types wanted to protect their child nutrition/school lunch programs, the Indians their education services, the military its overseas schools, the scientists their National Science Foundation, and the child advocates their Head Start, ploys would have to begin at once. And these turf maneuvers would concentrate first on heading off the President. Congress would take on abhorrent turf battles only if formally asked by the President.

For the moment, most of the heat was on Pat Gwaltney and Harrison Wellford of the President's Reorganization Project, and on OMB Director Jim McIntyre, who oversaw the entire reorganization effort. They were deep into consultations (Gwaltney and staff especially) with hundreds of affected interest groups, gathering pro-and-con arguments and reading the political situation of every possible program transfer.

Although the President would make the final decision, he would rely heavily on the findings and recommendations of his staff. The Gwaltney-Wellford-McIntyre team would have the primary responsibility for writing the decision memos and making recommendations for or against inclusion in a new Education Department. They were bearing the brunt of the groups' wrath.

That is not to say we were being ignored, however. Senator Ribicoff and his Committee would have much influence on the turf battles, and the interest groups understood that only too well. If a Department of Education was to be created, there would have to be much unity between Ribicoff and Carter. The President had already announced his intention to use the Ribicoff bill, S.991, as his ED vehicle in the Senate. The same people who lobbied Gwaltney and crew would make a point of talking to us, too.

The pace would speed up dramatically. Not only was time running out, but now we would have to engage ourselves in dozens of battles on details of a new Cabinet department blueprint.

*   *   *

Joe Califano, using all angles to stop ED, had long been considered an expert in the politics of turf.

The HEW Secretary appeared February 21 before the House Labor-HEW appropriations subcommittee on his budget requests.

"The President said he'd reach wide," Califano commented on the issue. With reporters scribbling furiously, he proceeded to read from an insignificant and unofficial OMB-PRP list the programs under consideration for transfer: veterans, CETA-job training, DOD schools, Indian schools, the *entire* National Science Foundation, arts and humanities, child nutrition, juvenile delinquency, Head Start, and even the Smithsonian Institution.

This budget hearing resulted in much press coverage. "Califano Lists Agencies Considered for New Education Dept." headlined a *Washington Post* story the next day.

White House aides were furious. In their view, Califano named off all those programs for no other reason than to induce the interest groups into fighting ED. He had no grounds on which to raise the possibility of transferring veterans programs, and he knew it. PRP never seriously considered them. It would have been a kamikaze proposal. The notion was never raised with the President, the Vice President, or with any of the senior White House staff.

Veterans groups were some of the most cohesive, powerful special interests in the nation. Their reaction was swift and acrimonious. "We'd be opposed to adding the VA part," an American Legion official told the *Post*. "We'd fight it very hard. The VA understands veterans' problems." The Disabled American Veterans national commander told reporters any proposal to take anything out of the VA would encounter "massive resistance" from his 550,000-member organization.

*   *   *

The following week, the President, Vice President, and Secretary Califano appeared in the White House press briefing room to present

Carter's new and extensive education program proposals before sending them to Congress.

After Carter's and Mondale's brief appearance, Califano stayed behind to answer reporters' many questions. The last one concerned ED.

"Last week in your testimony before a congressional committee you presented a list of various agencies that were mentioned as possibilities for inclusion in the department," one reporter told Califano. "There have been some who have worked on that list who feel it was misleading and inaccurate. Have you gotten any kind of feedback to that effect and do you regret or wish you hadn't presented that particular list?"

"No," Califano shot back. "…The President has made a decision to go with the department. The objective now is to put together the most meaningful department. The items I indicated in my testimony last week before the House appropriations committee are either items that were in the Ribicoff bill (or) which the President himself mentioned, like job training programs during the campaign…

"And as the President indicated this morning in his own statement, it is time to consolidate as much as we can. I am not unmindful of the political realities.

"Every time you wink at anything in the Veterans Administration there is a tendency of the veterans to spit in your eye. I understand that problem. But I think we have got to look at it…".

Not even the inner chambers of the White House were inviolate from Califano's public ploys.

Days later, outraged White House aides allowed the final word to go out—veterans education programs would never be transferred anywhere.

*   *   *

We had been patiently prodding for weeks, trying to break through the Committee's own crammed schedule of hearings and mark-ups. Finally, Senator Ribicoff approved the scheduling of two days of hearings on ED—for March 20 and 21.

Ribicoff decided on the dates upon seeing a "suggested witness list" we had drawn up. For the first day, we would plan on hearing from the Carter Administration, probably from either OMB Director Jim McIntyre or perhaps the Vice President.[12] In effect, we were imposing a deadline on them to compel quicker decisions on the President's plan.

For the other day, we'd invite state and local officials, higher ed representatives, opposing groups (AFT, the Catholics), and some turf groups.

News of the rescheduled hearings spread fast. Marilyn and I went to work again in a two-week blitz to search out and book witnesses.

*   *   *

I had begun efforts to drum up support for the DOD schools transfer,

"The PTA would definitely favor transferring the Defense schools," its lobbyist, Dave Stratman, told me. He also believed the principal overseas groups would concur. Stratman said he would ask the president of the European Congress of American Parents, Teachers, and Students to initiate supportive letters to Ribicoff and Carter.

The overseas parent groups were active, well-organized, and affiliated with the National PTA. Military parents found it necessary to band together and work for improvements in their sometimes poorly-run and-equipped schools.

---

[12] Vice Presidents have rarely testified before congressional committees. The idea of Mondale being the lead-off witness floated around NEA and the White House for nearly a month. Mondale's appearance would symbolize the high importance attached to ED by the Administration, but was ruled out as too flamboyant and politically risky. It would have underlined too darkly the strong NEA-Carter-Mondale relationship.

I also worked on recruiting support from Senator Nunn, who served on both our Committee and the Armed Services Committee, and was considered by fellow senators a top military expert. In a memo to his staff, I argued the "primary mission of the Defense Department is not education," and there were too many stories of generals and officers trying to influence the curriculum. I also pointed out the overseas elementary and secondary school system, ranking as the nation's 12th largest, were controlled by one man in DOD. I suggested we should look into a school board to make the schools less dictatorial and more responsive to parents. The memo concluded by noting NEA represented most of the overseas teachers and wanted the transfer.

Also, the European PTSA would endorse, I said. Nunn decided to help out.

But from Germany March 9 came a disappointing letter from the European PTSA president expressing "grave doubts."

"...Under the current system, the military community commanders are charged by DOD to provide substantial logistics, transportation, and maintenance support to the community schools...We see no decisive advantage in separating the control of our overseas schools from the Department of Defense," he said.

I immediately called and told an embarrassed Dave Stratman about the letter. "I can see we're going to have to talk with our people overseas," he chuckled.

*   *   *

Some Connecticut school lunch people, in town for the American School Food Service Association annual legislative meeting, met with me March 7 to hear our reasons for moving their programs to ED. ASFSA counted 70,000 school lunch/school breakfast workers among its membership.

USDA has been hostile towards the programs and has catered more to food producer needs instead, I explained to them. The programs are buried four layers deep in the USDA bureaucracy, I continued. If we moved them to a new Education Department, they would be administered by a high-level "assistant secretary for child nutrition." And, these nutrition programs are run through state departments of education and through local education agencies. School lunch is just what it says—*in the schools.* Usually there is more accountability and efficiency when federal, state, and local government structures parallel one another. School lunch should be considered an integral part of the total educational process, I ended my pitch.

"You don't know how many people in ASFSA agree with you," one of the Connecticut people told me.

I was surprised. "Well, why then do your lobbyists say your group will fight hard against the transfer?"

"Don't you understand?," one shot back. "They're all tied into the agriculture lobby. (The ASFSA lobbyists) used to work for the Senate nutrition committee, so they're out to help their friends and protect their contacts over at USDA. Pull the lunch programs out and those guys would be lost".

Later that night at a reception, I repeated my arguments to leaders of the school lunch lobby. Most were very receptive. I was introduced formally to ASFSA lobbyists Ken Schlossberg and Gerry Cassidy, who gave a cold but correct greeting.[13] They set up a private working luncheon with me and the top ASFSA brass the next day.

---

[13] Prior to forming their own consulting/lobbying firm, Schlossberg and Cassidy were staff members of the old Senate Select Committee on Nutrition, which had been chaired by Sen. George McGovern.

At 11:00 a.m. the next morning in the Capital Hilton's presidential suite, we wasted no time in getting down to business. Schlossberg questioned me closely on our intentions with the ED bill.

"Hasn't the President's Reorganization Project discussed this with you?," I asked him.

"Yes," he replied calmly. "We told them we'd oppose it."

Once again, I launched into my case for the transfer. Only this time I practically guaranteed them an "assistant secretary for child nutrition" in ED if the programs were brought over.

As I talked, the group's president walked in and out of the meeting, hardly listening. That disturbed me because she seemed open to my arguments. I wanted badly to win her over, to use her as a wedge against Schlossberg and Cassidy.

The others in the room spoke. Educators have always considered school lunch and school breakfast a luxury, an ancillary service like janitors and nurses, they complained. We're never treated as professionals, as important members of the educational and developmental process, they said.

If nutrition was put in a Department of Education, our budget would be first to get cut, they continued. That negative mentality would dominate the new department because educators would dominate it.

"What has NEA ever done for us?," Schlossberg asked angrily. "Where's NEA when we need help on our bills? They don't testify for nutrition programs or budgets on the Hill. Why all of a sudden do they care so much about helping us out in their department?"

Schlossberg seemed to imply that I was a front-man for NEA.

"Well, maybe it's about time the two of you worked together," I said, trying to conceal my irritation.

The school lunch people didn't respond. I broke the awkward silence by mentioning our upcoming hearings and our desire to have an ASFSA spokesperson there.

"How will the policy (of ASFSA on this issue) be set?," I asked. "Last night I talked to just about every member of your legislative committee and a majority told me they thought it was a good idea," I confronted the small group. "How do they figure into this?"

That visibly upset Schlossberg and Cassidy. Of course, the committee will consider it, Schlossberg tried to recover, but the final decision will probably be made by the executive board. The meeting ended on that uncertain note.

"Schlossberg and Cassidy had better start listening to the members of this association," a Connecticut delegate told me privately downstairs. An effort was underway to fire them and hire another lobbying firm, he said.

Not only had I driven a wedge, but I had also walked into the middle of fierce association infighting.

*   *   *

Harrison Wellford came by the Committee office the next day. He worried that if the President decided to transfer the child nutrition programs to ED, "it might be seen as an attempt to de-emphasize the importance of farming." Jimmy Carter, a farmer himself, wanted a strong farm-agriculture policy. Wellford was warning us OMB-PRP might not recommend the transfer.

Decisions on other transfers in the bill would be forthcoming, the OMB reorg chief told us.

Wellford also let us in on a recent conversation he had with House Government Operations Committee Chairman Jack Brooks, who had not yet announced whether he would move an ED bill out of his Committee. "'We're serious,' we told him," Wellford said. "He also knows the President wants to act on the bill this year." Brooks apparently told Wellford to come back to him when the President had made his specific decisions.

Then Wellford hit us with bad news. The President has been extremely busy, he told us. And Pat Gwaltney's PRP team has been working around the clock on its study of ED details for the President.

"I don't see how we could realistically testify March 20," he said. Wellford asked for a delay.

In the succeeding days, Marilyn and Gwaltney worked out the final date: Friday, April 14. By then, the President would have to decide what he wanted in his new department—no ifs, ands, or buts. White House aides had decided OMB Director Jim McIntyre would be the witness.

With little more than a week before the hearings, the postponement left us with a gaping hole to fill. We did some quick shuffling. The hearings would go on.

*   *   *

Waiting for us in the Committee's conference room upstairs, an hour later, was a delegation from the National Head Start Association.

"We're flatly opposed to moving Head Start anywhere out of HEW," four mothers in the program and their group president told us. They feared NEA might take it over and make it part of the public schools.

Marilyn and I were amazed that so many of these "poor" mothers somehow found enough money to fly to Washington and lobby against the bill. The federal reins on the program were so loose we suspected some of the funds were being diverted to this questionable activity.

One wanted to give her personal feelings. "Before Head Start came along," she began nervously, "my son didn't have a chance to get ahead. He would have started school behind all the others, or he'd have to stay back a lot. I was real worried about him.

"They they started this Head Start program down the street, and I enrolled him. Then, they asked me if I would like to help out. I did, and things haven't been the same since.

"You know, my boy began to read well, and learn, and he was just more interested in learning. I felt useful being with him and helping out all those other young children learn and get a decent meal."

The woman trembled, and talked faster with loud emphasis.

"Today, my boy is doing real well in his schoolwork, and if it wasn't for Head Start, I don't know where he'd be. And now you want to take this and put it someplace else and destroy it.

"What about all those little kids who don't have a chance? How are you going to help THEM?," the woman shouted at us. She broke down and cried, wiping tears from her face. Another mother held her, comforted her. The woman sobbed quietly.

Marilyn and I had been at emotional meetings before, but this went too far. The incident so jolted us we didn't know what to say.

All across the Hill, similar scenes were being repeated. The Head Start community was mounting a swift, massive, emotional offensive against the bill.

*   *   *

It took the Indians some time before they realized ED was a serious initiative. Not until President Carter began actively pushing did they sit up and take notice.

Indian leaders thought it was sufficient that they had told the President's reorganization team of their objections to any transfer of education from the Bureau of Indian Affairs to ED.

"The *Congress* will be doing most of the work on this bill," I chastised them verbally at an informal mid-March pow-wow in Washington. I said we believed the transfer had merit. They looked shell-shocked.

"You must understand," one said emphatically, "there can be no support from the tribes unless they are first consulted ahead of time." An "emergency" meeting of the tribes would be immediately arranged to consider this.

I gave reasons for my personal support of the transfer, the most important being that the extremely grave state of Indian education shows the BIA has been a failure. If all Indian education services were consolidated in ED, we would have to give serious consideration to establishing an assistant secretary for Indian education. (We were giving away assistant secretaries left and right.)

That first meeting had sounded an emergency warhoop. The formidable "moccasin telegraph" system went into action. Indians everywhere would now take sides. The betting was that most would fight us.

*   *   *

The hearing room filled to capacity Monday morning, March 20. We had an expanded complement of press, lobbyists, and public keeping tabs on a presidentially-endorsed bill.

"Like the President, I attach a high priority to the establishment of the Department of Education," Ribicoff told the audience in opening the hearing. "We will be working hard to complete action on the legislation this year."

First up on the witness table, two student groups—Coalition of Independent College and University Students and the newly-merged National Student Association/National Student Lobby—backed the bill and recommended an office of youth and student affairs be specially carved out in the new department's structure. Then, the president of the HEW Education Division employees union said government workers there were constantly confused about who their top boss really was. "Morale throughout the Education Division is at a very low ebb," she concluded.

Ribicoff next called a panel of school lunch representatives that we had quickly thrown together. The official American School Food Service Association witnesses gave "the reasons why we think the (nutrition) programs are best left in USDA, and what we would hope to see should the programs be transferred to a new Department."

Child nutrition programs are tied into USDA, they contended. There is a "close link" to the program distributing surplus farmers' goods to the schools, they believed. USDA, the lead federal agency for nutrition, has expertise in food grading, purchasing, economics, and human nutrition research, they argued.

The ASFSA people recited a list of eight "requirements" their organization felt were "absolutely essential" in a transfer to ED: an assistant secretary, a commitment to expanding the programs, categorical funding, retention of nutrition education, adequate professional staff in ED, maintenance of commodity distribution, a policy in favor of nonprofit school lunch programs, and strict regulation of "competitive foods" (vending machines, contracted food services, etc.).

ASFSA had tried to drive down the middle of the road. To satisfy us and the educators, they left the door open and named their price. To satisfy the agriculture types, they stated a position of favoring the status quo—staying in USDA.

But the Fairfax County, VA. public school lunch director testified in strong support of the move. "Our lunch and breakfast programs are important parts of the child's school day," she said. "We are not a feeding station or dumping ground, nor are we a welfare program. The nutrition, health, and well-being of the nation's children are our concerns."

"If it is all right to have child nutrition programs in a state department of education, what makes it wrong to have it in the federal Department of Education?," Senator Ribicoff asked the panel.

"I don't think we are saying it is wrong," one replied. "We do not oppose the transfer across the board. We want to know what we can expect in a new department."

"So do we," Ribicoff shot back. "That is why we are here."

*   *   *

Four state and local officials sat down at the witness table Tuesday morning.

As I sat behind Senator Ribicoff and juggled a stack of testimony in my lap, I watched the sea of faces in the audience. Two press tables were full, the reporters busily skimming statements and jotting down notes. Aides to witnesses whispered strategy in their ears. Dozens of lobbyists hawkishly monitored every word spoken into the P.A. system.

A New Haven, CT. school official, the Illinois state superintendent of education, a Pennsylvania state legislator, and the Education Commission of the States executive director each supported the bill.

The atmosphere of the hearing room grew tense as the line-up at the witness table changed to ED's two principal opponents—AFT President Albert Shanker and U.S. Catholic Conference Education Secretary Wilfrid Paradis. *Confrontation time.*

Shanker sat expressionless, in coat-and-tie with dark-rimmed glasses and wiry hair. Beside him, Monsignor Paradis, an elderly man dressed in a long black robe and clerical collar, sat erect.

The supreme irony of their joint appearance was not lost on many in the room. In his written statement, Shanker called tuition tax credits, promoted ardently by the Catholics, "the gravest threat to public education we have witnessed in years." Both were clearly discomforted by the other's presence at the same table.

"I am more impressed by the pluses of the present structure (in HEW) than its shortcomings," Shanker began. "…There is a good deal that ought to be preserved…

"I believe that there has been a tendency in public education in America for educators at all levels to isolate themselves," Shanker said. ED would, in his view, "lessen coordination between functions instead of encouraging the cooperation that is necessary." He proposed leaving education in HEW and reorganizing there "on a kind of Pentagon model," essentially Califano's idea.

Shanker noted all the talk about consolidating scattered federal education programs in a separate ED. "...I don't see the Congress going for it because of the struggle that would take place with all the other constituents fighting to keep their particular piece of the action."

The AFT President felt the main reason education groups wanted ED was for more prestige. But, he said, "I believe that a Secretary of a huge department like HEW will always be able to get more time with the President and have more influence than a person who is head of a small department unrelated to other interests."

A nervous Monsignor Paradis started his testimony. "We believe that there is good reason to fear that a new Department of Education will further increase federal interference in both public and private education in areas that rightfully belong to parents and the local community," he read from his statement. Paradis said the Catholic Church "is also disturbed by the continued development, as we see it, of a philosophy of education which runs counter to the nation's traditional acceptance of and respect for pluralism in education...".

Ribicoff couldn't let that go by without comment. "Monsignor, I am assuming you know every senator's record on pluralism," he interjected. "I have a pretty good idea you know mine."

"Yes, I do, Senator," Paradis replied sheepishly.

"I have been consistently an advocate of just what you are saying, whether it is tax credits or programs to assure that every parent would have a right to send a child to a private or parochial school," Ribicoff lectured from his seat.

"So it is an understanding that not all the advocates of this bill agree with your philosophical point of view. My guess is I agree more with you than Mr. Shanker agrees with you," the Senator said.

"On tax credits," Shanker deadpanned. The audience broke out into nervous laughter.

Paradis returned to the security of his written statement. Reading on, he feared the trend against diversity in education "could well be continued and even accelerated if, as we fear, the new department becomes dominated by public school interest groups."

Ribicoff interrupted again. "...I do believe that there isn't one of our 56 cosponsors who would not be insistent that basically education be a local matter and not controlled by the federal government."

"That is very reassuring, Senator," Paradis replied, "but there is a difference between what the legislation's intent is and the way that it actually happens once it gets into operation.

"...I even hate to say this, it would appear to us this proposition is the product of a few well-organized and articulate national lobbying organizations," Paradis suggested.

Later, Ribicoff turned to Shanker's support for organizing HEW like DOD. The Senator noted "the near disappearance from public purview and policymaking of the Secretary of the Army, Navy, or Air Force."

"You want us to testify on whether we should break those up into three separate departments, is that right?," Shanker said sarcastically. "...Seriously, I think it is endless. Why not break up health and welfare as well?"

"As a matter of fact, I think eventually you should," Ribicoff countered.

"Well, I think when the pendulum goes back...there will be a big congressional move to bring departments back together again because they have gotten too far apart with too many Cabinet members," Shanker predicted.

The encounter closed on a conciliatory note. "I am listening to all your testimony, those for and against," Senator Ribicoff told his two adversaries. "That is why we have you here. If we are going to get a bill out, we want to get the best bill we possibly can...".

We breathed a sigh of relief as Ribicoff called the third and final panel of the day—higher education. Although American Council on Education chief lobbyist Charles Saunders talked about his organization's ambivalence, officials of groups representing the community and junior colleges, state higher ed officers, and university professors vigorously endorsed the bill.

"You have all given us a lot to think about," Ribicoff summed up. "…The Committee will stand adjourned until April 14."

*　　*　　*

In just three weeks, the President would decide which programs he wanted in a Department of Education. The turf groups pressed their case.

The proposal to move Head Start "has not been and cannot be substantively justified and is so insensitive politically that I predict it could have disastrous consequences both for the program and the President's already stretched credibility in poor and black communities," Children's Defense Fund leader Marian Wright Edelman wrote in a biting March 21 letter to Harrison Wellford.

"If you do this, I and thousands of poor people in the 1,200 Head Start communities who have sacrificed all these years to keep going…will view your action as a betrayal. We will fight you in every way we can," she vowed to Wellford.

Edelman was out to demonstrate to NEA and the White House the immense political power and cohesion of her national network of Head Start parents.

The National PTA would send an emissary, Ann Kahn, to Germany early April to the annual European PTSA convention, where she would lobby the member group into reversing its knee-jerk opposition to transferring the DOD overseas dependents schools.

Kahn would hand-carry a Senate memorandum from myself to the European group laying down my proposals for improving the school system in ED and for increasing parent participation through a new school board.

"When they hear this, they won't be able to resist," Kahn said confidently. "They've suffered too long under DOD."

A meeting of the nation's Indian tribes and Alaska natives had been arranged for April 10 and 11 in Denver. The topic: ED. I would make the trip there to represent the Committee.

Bureaucrats were joining in the turf maneuvers. USDA's Carol Foreman took the risky step of mailing us copies of a 10-page position paper her office had done criticizing the transfer of her nutrition/school lunch programs. OMB rules forbid agencies from sending such policy evaluations to the Hill without prior approval and screening to insure conformity to Administration policy. Foreman figured it was better to get chewed out by OMB than to lose her turf.

* * *

"It's Protect the Turf, Again, As New Education Dept. Forms," headlined an April 5 Jack Germond/Jules Witcover column in the *Washington Star*.

Not only the education community, but at least seven Cabinet departments were anxiously awaiting the President's decisions, the column pointed out. It also described opposition of interest groups.

"'A lot of these people fear they would be small fish in a big pond dominated by educators,'" Germond-Witcover quoted one White House planner. "'The arguments are never waged on grounds of turf, but that's what it gets down to.

"From all this, it seems clear that unless the Senate moves swiftly, passage this year is a long shot," the columnists deduced. "And it may be that unless Carter goes for a narrower objective, such as simply turning HEW's Education Division into the new department, wrangling within the bureaucracy and the Congress may send the whole idea into oblivion."

ELEVEN

Carter Decides the Specifics

Activity in the offices of the President's Reorganization Project study team was frenzied. The week of April 3 had arrived, and all eyes were fixed on the April 14 hearing we'd scheduled.

Seemingly endless meetings with the interest groups went right down to the wire. Pat Gwaltney and crew wanted to touch base with as many power centers as time allowed. It was important to flush out all the nuances behind every possible transfer to ED. The President should make his decisions on the best information and analysis available.

The White House Congressional liaison staff hurriedly set up appointments with key senators and representatives to sound them out.

The results of all this consultation had to be condensed to a few pages on each issue/transfer in a memorandum for the President—background on a program proposed for transfer, the pros and cons of moving it to ED, and a recommended course of action.

Between Gwaltney, Wellford, McIntyre, Carp, Eizenstat, and the Vice President, the painful jockeying back-and-forth continued daily. Does this program belong in the new department? Would it be too politically damaging? Would moving it hurt the President? Would it hurt the overall ED bill?

When finally finished, the memo would go through one more set of hands—the Cabinet. The departments would be given one last opportunity to comment directly on the PRP recommendations, one last appeal to the President.

Then, the PRP memo, background materials, and comments from White House aides and agency heads would again be compiled into the standard blue binder notebook and delivered to Jimmy Carter.[14] In the meantime, Gwaltney and her people would write a draft statement that would become OMB Director Jim McIntyre's testimony to the Ribicoff Committee. It would be written on the assumption the President would ratify his staff's recommendations, yet could be changed if Carter decided otherwise.

As April 14 approached, the decisions were getting easier to make. On all fronts, opposition to transfers to ED was intense. The safer route was to go with a bare-bones Department of Education, and jettison all those controversial transfers—school lunch, Indian ed, DOD schools, Head Start.

It was a time when Jimmy Carter did not need more controversy. The crammed agenda he had loaded onto Capitol Hill was caving in on him. There were fires everywhere—trouble with the energy bills, Panama Canal treaties, Mideast jet sales package, inflation, and a persistently low public approval rating.

---

[14] All along, Marilyn and I asked repeatedly for copies. Gwaltney was vigilant about protecting the actual documents from outside eyes. We were briefed vaguely on the memo's substance.

"Everything seems to be falling out," Art Sheekey complained to Marilyn in a private talk that week. He and his colleagues on Gwaltney's staff were sad about the toss-it-overboard attitude of top White House staff. The new department would suffer without a meaningful consolidation of education programs, they felt.

In Pat Gwaltney's political judgment, if the President really wanted a Department of Education in 1978, they would have to go with a narrow model. The grand idea of a huge "Department of Education and Human Development" had vanished completely from her mind.

*　　*　　*

On the Sunday night flight to Denver, I was tense and apprehensive.

In Indian country, opposition was growing. The major Indian organizations alerted the tribes that their BIA was under attack. Telegrams had already started to come in to the White House.

Transferring Indian education programs to a new Cabinet department could not have come at a worse time. The Indian community in 1978 was experiencing a revengeful white backlash. Everywhere (especially from the West) white people were openly challenging Indian rights in the courts and in Congress.

They did not trust our motives in improving Indian education. The federal government had a long history of screwing them royally. I thought of myself as just another well-meaning, youthful, idealistic federal official who wanted to make everything right for the Indians.

Yet, little had changed. The white man was still ruining Indian people's lives.

*　　*　　*

After catching a few hours sleep, I woke up Monday, April 10 surprised to find four inches of fresh-fallen snow outside my window at the Denver Airport Hilton. In the distance, the spectacular Rocky Mountains glistened with their early-Spring white covering.

My planned wardrobe for the Indian meetings coincided perfectly with the unexpected weather—casual slacks and pullover sweater. I purposely left my suits and ties in Washington, wanting to appear relaxed, confident, unofficial, and unpretentious.

On the way to breakfast, I noticed many unfamiliar Indian faces milling around in the hotel lobby. The building was filled with Indian leaders for our two-day conference.

Unbeknownst to me, the Bureau of Indian Affairs was playing dirty pool that morning. BIA officials in Washington wanted to whip the tribes' hostility against me and PRP representative Vic Miller. They decided to reproduce 100 copies of the PRP decision memo appendix on the Indian transfer and ship them with one of their men to Denver. (All the PRP memos were confidential, in-house documents for review by agency heads and their staffs only.)

From 10 o'clock to noon, the memo was distributed in a secret, closed-door meeting at the hotel between the BIA official and the tribal leaders. (Formal starting time of our Denver meeting had been set for 1 o'clock.)

The memo noted there existed "no comprehensive federal strategy for Indian education," and tribes have little influence. Support for Indian education is fragmented between BIA and the U.S. Office of Education, with "virtually no coordination" between them, it said.

The transfer to ED would be advantageous, it reasoned, because all federal programs aimed at public school and postsecondary education of Indians would be consolidated.

But, the memo warned, there was the risk ED would not adhere fully to the principles of tribal sovereignty, the federal Indian trust responsibility, and Indian preference in hiring.[15] Also, "any transfer would probably result in significant Indian political opposition, especially by the tribal leaders themselves (who have resisted every major change in recent history, including the Indian Self-Determination Act)."

BIA's strategy worked. The Indians were outraged, particularly by the sentence picturing them as stalwart resistors to change. We had been framed.

When Vic Miller greeted me in the Hilton lobby around noontime, he was hot under the collar. He told me he had just learned that a BIA bureaucrat had flown in from Washington and had given the Indians copies of "my memo" in a clandestine meeting, which they were still holding.

The news shocked me. I could feel my blood pressure rising.

"Well, then, what in hell are we doing here?," I shouted in a whisper to Miller. Then, another thought entered my mind. "Can't the White House control the agencies?"

Miller shrugged in a reaction of futility.

I couldn't believe it. An agency official, here in Denver, engaged in a blatant act of political subversion against the Administration, which had not yet decided its policy on this issue. On every turf issue, we were getting shafted by the very people who should either be supporting us or not doing anything at all. Jimmy Carter had not instilled one ounce of fear in his government.

---

[15] Between 1794 and 1868, the U.S. government signed 118 treaties with Indian tribes agreeing to provide for their well-being through health, education, and other services (the "trust responsibility"), and to recognize the Indian governments as mini-nations within the nation ("tribal sovereignty"). In this century, laws gave Indians preference in hiring for these federal services.

"I've already called Pat (Gwaltney)," Miller said. "I hope they get their asses kicked over at BIA."

*   *   *

Some 75-100 Indian people filled a hotel conference room at about 1:30 that afternoon. Most wore jeans and casual clothing. Some sported Indian jewelry.

The room was silent, solemn. I said hello to a few and tried to make conversation, but the response was decidedly cold and unyielding. Thanks to the BIA, I knew what we were in for.

Patricia Locke rose to the podium and called the meeting to order. The tribal chairmen's association education director informed the audience that most tribal councils were notified of this emergency meeting, and that at least 50 were sending representatives. She asked Peter Campanelli, the BIA man to lead off.

Campanelli, wearing Indian turquoise, talked in a pre-rehearsed tone, as if he had said all this before. "Now, the BIA received the OMB memo on the Department of Education at 5:30. Friday afternoon," he said in a dry, factual voice. "We have been asked to send comments back by the close of business, Monday, today."

"This means that Forrest Gerard (the assistant secretary for Indian affairs and BIA chief) will not have enough time to consult with the tribes," Locke broke in. She was peeved.

Campanelli shook his head. "The OMB memo came as a surprise. The Administration does not now have any articulated policy on Indian affairs. Protective mechanisms must be built in if this is moved. But it is important to first establish an Indian policy. This memo in effect establishes policy."

I noticed Vic Miller had a shaken, disbelieving facial reaction.

"The Secretary (of the Interior) will respond to the memo today," Campanelli summed up, "but I do not know what the nature of the response will be."

Locke then called for the President's Reorganization Project representative. Miller walked nervously to the podium. He knew his head was on a chopping block.

The Interior Department was fully aware of what the PRP was considering months ago, he began. PRP has made a sincere effort to consult the tribes. He outlined at least five meetings and visits made since December.

That's all the audience had to hear. Emotions exploded as comments came hurtling from the floor. One man stood up and read aloud a 1976 Carter campaign statement pledging consultation with Indians on matters affecting them.

"This is another wolf in a sheep's clothing," someone shouted. The audience applauded. Miller stood frozen at the head table, taking it all in.

"This would be detrimental to my treaty," a chief angrily screamed.

"It will take 100 years to iron out problems with the Education Department," another said.

"You should consider transferring OE monies and programs to the BIA," a woman hollered.

Miller was in the hot seat for well over an hour. There was much screaming and anger from the Indians.

Locke eventually moved on to get "the congressional view."

I could feel my heart pounding. Walking to the front of the room, I thought quickly to myself, they don't teach you how to deal with this situation in any political science textbook.

At the podium, I arranged my notes, gazed for an instant out at the highly-charged audience and forced a smile. It was like standing in front of 100 sticks of dynamite with the fuses lit.

I began with deliberate calm and slow enunciation. I explained that I was representing a Senate committee studying this issue, a committee chaired by a man who had always championed the Indian cause, Abe Ribicoff.

"Senator Ribicoff is NOT ramming this down anybody's throat and I deeply resent any such implication," I counterattacked.

I told how S.991 came about, how long our efforts had been ongoing.

"This is a *concept* bill we're talking about. Senator Ribicoff is not now committed to every transfer in his bill. It's there to be studied. He has an open mind.

"We attempted last summer to involve the Indian community in discussions on this bill, only to be shrugged off.

"But just to be sure that every tribe gets a chance to be heard, I will see to it that as soon as I return to Washington, the Committee will send a letter to every tribe requesting official comments."

To my obvious surprise and delight, the room erupted into a round of warm applause. The Indians listened more closely.

We have given this much thought, I told the group. There is a wide range of possibilities—an assistant secretary for Indian education, creation of an all-Indian board of education to govern the BIA schools, legislative language protecting Indian rights.

Several of the previously irate Indians began nodding thoughtfully. "Now that is something I could support," one said.

"Instead of opposing us outright, I want you to take some time, think about our proposals. Sit on it for a while," I said.

"Yeah, we'll sit on it all right," one shouted, drawing an outburst of laughter.

We continued meeting with the Indians that Monday night and all day Tuesday. Emotions cooled and we delved into the more substantive issues and feelings.

A number of people there conceded most Indians are "terrified" of change. They felt that without education, BIA would become a figurehead agency. The Indians made clear their opposition to integration and their desire for separate, distinct programs serving Indians alone. They felt their treaties had made them sovereign people within American society. They wanted "more time to study this."

On the flight back to Washington Wednesday morning, April 12, I did a lot of thinking. Vic Miller and I, inexperienced in the ways of Indian life, had learned something important from the Denver fiasco: Indians were obsessed with what they call "consultation." We thought it meant "let's discuss this." We learned the hard way it meant, "clear everything through us first."

*   *   *

I went from Dulles Airport directly to the hearing room. At 3:30 in the afternoon, Pat Gwaltney and a contingent of aides were briefing some 15 staff reps of our Committee members.

The President still had made no final decisions—two days before the Friday, April 14 hearing—so Gwaltney had little to tell the Senate staffers. All she could do was discuss the possibilities, the programs that PRP had looked at and some of their general findings about moving them to ED.

The big blue binder notebook was not sent to the Oval Office until noon that day. Last-minute refinements, additions, and memos from Cabinet officers held it up.

Carter was hard-pressed for time that week—saving his energy legislation, making speeches, receiving the Romanian president, and lobbying for the Panama treaties.

For the next 48 hours all of us, especially Gwaltney and company, felt like anxious parents outside the maternity ward.

*   *   *

Marilyn and I busied ourselves Thursday with preparations for McIntyre's appearance the next morning and with planning future hearings on the ED bill.

Our strategy called for a fast follow-up. We'd go ahead with a hearing Tuesday, April 18 on the DOD overseas schools and science education transfers. Another was tentatively set for April 27 on Head Start.

All day long we waited impatiently for a phone call from Pat Gwaltney that would tell us the President had made his decisions and an advance copy of McIntyre's statement was on its way. At the New Executive Office Building, Gwaltney and her staff passed the time away Thursday by putting finishing touches to their OMB director's 20-page statement and several charts explaining the structure and statistics on ED.

Throughout the day, Gwaltney kept in constant contact with the President's personal staff. Noon passed, then 3 o'clock, then 5 o'clock. No, the President has not yet reviewed the memo, came the response each time.

Around 6 o'clock, Gwaltney learned the President had left Oval Office for dinner in the family living quarters upstairs. He had not looked at the huge decision memo. Just 16 hours to go before the 10:00 a.m. starting time of our hearing the next morning. The entire PRP staff waited, tense.

Gwaltney let her people go home at approximately 8:30 that night when it became clear to her nothing would happen in the next few hours. She had left her home number with the White House switchboard.

She told her staff to come in early the next morning, by 7:00, "in case there are any changes."

*   *   *

A bright sunrise Friday morning, April 14, cast its spell over the nation's capital. It would be a clear, dry, magnificent spring day. Flowers were out in full bloom around the city.

Jimmy Carter had the reputation of beginning his day at the first call of the rooster. This morning was no exception.

Sitting on his desk was a thick blue notebook. The cover page read, "MEMORANDUM FOR THE PRESIDENT, FROM: James T. McIntyre/Stuart Eizenstat, SUBJECT: Establishing a Cabinet Department of Education."[16]

Around 6 o'clock in the morning, while the rest of the city slept, the President of the United States took his pen and started to read.

*   *   *

"This memorandum requests your decisions on the scope and specific programmatic content of a Cabinet Department of Education," Carter read from the cover page. "Senator Ribicoff will complete hearings on his bill this month in the expectation that committee mark-up, Senate passage, and House action can be accomplished before the Congress adjourns this fall.

"We plan to testify on Senator Ribicoff's bill,…(and) we are expected to take a position on the inclusion in a Department of Education of each program contained in S.991.

"Last November,…you instructed us to undertake a cooperative effort with the Congress to establish a Department of Education. You also indicated your preference for a department that is as broad as possible and not dominated by a single constituency.

---

[16] McIntyre's and Eizenstat's joint signature was a tactical move to present a united front to the President and let him know the issues had been worked through the staffs. When there was a consensus among his staff, Carter usually went along with their recommendations.

"We anticipate Senate passage of a bill this year. Action by the House this year is uncertain, however. Many members of Congress support the concept of establishing a Department of Education, but little consensus exists on what programs should be included in it. The House leadership is especially concerned about any controversy that will lead to disputes among Democrats in this election year.

"If a bill clears the Senate early this summer, House action will be encouraged. After we present our proposal before the Ribicoff Committee, we should have an Administration bill introduced in the House to spur action this year…"

The memo offered two options on the basic range of a new Education Department—"a narrowly-based department which could be broadened later" and "a more broadly-based department that might be expanded still further over time." (The education and human development model received hardly any mention in the memo.)

After describing the pros and cons, the memo said, *"the Office of Management and Budget and the Domestic Policy Staff (DPS) recommend option one, the establishment this year of a relatively small department with a strong core of education programs* (emphasis added)."

"We have considered over the past months a wide range of education-related programs, including training, social services, and research programs. After extensive consultation and analysis, we have concluded that such a broad scope is impractical at this time on both substantive and political grounds…(and) could not pass the Congress in this election year.

The third section—perhaps the most important—proceeded to describe briefly all the programs and asked for a decision from Carter as to whether he wanted them in or out.

For each set of programs, the memo spelled out the primary mission, the nature of the agency's objections, the OMB-PRP response and recommendation, and *what the Ribicoff bill did*. Following that, the standard check-off: "APPROVE_____DISAPPROVE_____"

The President was asked for decisions on 12 program chunks:

• *National Science Foundation science education.* The memo said NSF hadn't committed enough resources to the programs and the transfer would "broaden the focus" of the new department. "OMB AND DPS RECOMMEND INCLUSION..." NSF objected. "RIBICOFF BILL INCLUDES THE ENTIRE NSF EDUCATION DIRECTORATE...".

• *USDA nutrition education.* The memo argued putting it in ED would increase involvement of educators and permit quicker nutrition ed curricula development. "OMB AND DPS RECOMMEND INCLUSION..." USDA objected. "PROGRAM IS NOT INCLUDED IN THE RIBICOFF BILL, BUT COMMITTEE STAFF HAVE INDICATED THAT IT (WILL BE)...".

• *HEW Office for Civil Rights.* At least 75 per cent of OCR's work pertained to education, the memo pointed out. It proposed the new OCR in ED be independent and report directly to the Secretary as a way of warding off adverse tinkering by educators. "OMB AND DPS RECOMMEND INCLUSION OF EDUCATION-RELATED CIVIL RIGHTS RESPONSIBILITIES..." HEW asked a deferral on the decision. "RIBICOFF BILL DOES INCLUDE (THEM)..."

• *Johnson-O'Malley and Continuing Education Programs for Indians.* The Johnson-O'Malley program provided funds to public and tribally-controlled schools for supplementary educational benefits for Indian children. The continuing education programs supported adult education, student college assistance, and junior colleges. The memo saw advantages by consolidating in ED all programs affecting Indians in public schools and in postsecondary institutions. "OMB AND DPS RECOMMEND INCLUSION..." The Bureau of

Indian Affairs objected. "RIBICOFF BILL DOES NOT INCLUDE THESE PROGRAMS."[17]

• *Youth Services Programs.* Included were juvenile justice, runaway youth, and summer/national youth sports. Although attractive, the transfers could attract opposition from interest groups and the programs would have little visibility in ED, the memo said. "OMB AND DPS RECOMMEND THESE...NOT BE INCLUDED AT THIS TIME..." Agencies involved opposed transfer. "RIBICOFF BILL DOES NOT INCLUDE THESE PROGRAMS."

• *Youth Training and Employment Programs.* Under consideration here: Job Corps, summer youth employment, Young Adult Conservation Corps, etc. Transfer would sever links between CETA and other public service employment programs and instigate opposition from labor and minority groups, the memo judged. "OMB AND DPS RECOMMEND THESE...NOT BE INCLUDED AT THIS TIME." Labor Department opposed transfer. "RIBICOFF BILL DOES NOT INCLUDE THESE PROGRAMS."

• *Project Head Start.* Although OMB saw merit in it, the transfer would "stir impassioned opposition" from the Head Start community and civil rights leaders. "OMB AND DPS RECOMMEND THAT HEAD START NOT BE INCLUDED AT THIS TIME BECAUSE IT PROVIDES A RANGE OF HEALTH AND SOCIAL SERVICES THAT ARE BEYOND THE SCOPE OF THE PROPOSED DEPARTMENT."

---

[17] Technically, the memo was right: our bill did not include them. However, our intent was to transfer all of BIA's education responsibilities, reservation schools included.

HEW opposed the transfer. "RIBICOFF BILL INCLUDES PROJECT HEAD START."

• *Department of Defense Dependents Schools.* There would be problems in logistical support, opposition from military personnel, and "likely...excessive intrusion of the new department in the educational process of the schools," the memo said. "OMB AND DPS RECOMMEND THAT THE DOD SCHOOLS NOT BE INCLUDED AT THIS TIME..." DOD opposed transfer. RIBICOFF BILL DOES INCLUDE THE DOD SCHOOLS."

• *National Foundation on the Arts and Humanities.* A transfer might inhibit the Endowments' advocacy role and cause "significant" political opposition. "OMB AND DPS RECOMMEND THAT (THEY) NOT BE INCLUDED..." The two endowments agreed. "RIBICOFF BILL DOES INCLUDE THE ENDOWMENTS."

• *Bureau of Indian Affairs Schools.* Although transfer might be considered in the future, it could also generate opposition from Indians and "run the risk of putting the schools in an agency that does not recognize the trust and other responsibilities," the memo said. "OMB AND DPS RECOMMEND THAT THE BIA SCHOOLS NOT BE INCLUDED AT THIS TIME..." Bureau of Indian Affairs agreed. "RIBICOFF BILL RECOMMENDS INCLUSION..."

• *Telecommunications Demonstration.* "OMB AND DPS RECOMMEND...TRANSFER" of the small, school-based program. The transfer was noncontroversial. "RIBICOFF BILL DOES INCLUDE (IT)..."

• *USDA Child Feeding Programs.* There are few compelling arguments either for or against the transfer, as the programs are not central to the mission of either agency, the memo judged. Transfer could stir considerable political opposition. "OMB AND DPS RECOMMEND THAT THE CHILD NUTRITION PROGRAMS NOT BE INCLUDED AT THIS TIME..." USDA opposed transfer. "RIBICOFF BILL INCLUDES THE FEEDING PROGRAMS."

The final section of the President's memo suggested some "next steps." The first order of business would be to build support for ED. "Immediately after the Ribicoff hearings, we should ask Jack Brooks…and perhaps several other key House members to introduce a bill similar to what we have proposed in the Senate," the memo advised. "If the Senate hearings go well, and Senator Ribicoff reports a bill to the Senate by early May, we believe Jack Brooks can be convinced to open hearings in May or June. This would provide time to pass a House bill this year. We may ask you to talk later this month with the House leadership…".

*　　*　　*

Jim McIntyre had been in his Old Executive Building office just a few minutes before the telephone rang at almost 7:30 a.m. It was the President.

I've gone over the Department of Education memo and made my decisions, Carter told his OMB director. Could you come over? McIntyre left immediately for the Oval Office.

The two men sat together and alone for more than 15 minutes flipping through the voluminous binder notebook and talking. The pages were littered with handwritten presidential notations. Several times, "keep this" appeared. There were also references to "the way we did it in Georgia."

McIntyre was both surprised and pleased at the fortitude displayed by President Carter. As they reviewed the memo, it became clear to him *the President had decided to back the Ribicoff bill.*

Carter reversed many PRP recommendations on program transfers. He asked that Head Start be included, that child nutrition be included, that the Defense schools be transferred, that the Indian schools be moved to ED.

He, himself, had devised his own course: *on the Department of Education issue, follow the lead of Abe Ribicoff.* In these most troubled times for the peanut farmer from Georgia, the President's staff assumed he would want to take the safest path and avoid all the controversy of turf wars. They were wrong. The President had decided to take them all on, except for veterans and labor (on CETA).

*   *   *

Someone from the President's staff secretary's office called Pat Gwaltney at about 7:40 a.m. Your memo on the Department of Education had been looked at by the President and could be picked up now, Gwaltney was told. She instantly sprinted across the street to the White House.

Gwaltney ran into McIntyre in the West Wing hallway as he was returning from his meeting with Carter. We've got some fast work to do, McIntyre told his staff member. They rushed back to the OMB director's office.

Gwaltney and McIntyre spent another 15 minutes discussing the President's decisions and reading his comments on the memo. Carter's decision on the Arts and Humanities Endowments was not clear. He indicated only that he liked conceptually the idea of including them. Knowing what a hot potato it was, Gwaltney convinced McIntyre to call the President and ask for clarification. He did so, warning Carter of the fervent opposition of the arts constituency. Carter decided to leave the Endowments out.

At 8 o'clock, Gwaltney ran back across the street to her suite of offices in the New Executive Office Building. Her staff there hadn't the faintest idea of what would hit them in the next couple of hours.

She jogged ashen-faced through the suite and past her startled staff. Everyone was ordered into her office stat.

"We've got a lot of work to do," Gwaltney nervously told the dozen or so aides crowded into the room. They were all very tired. Some looked as if they had just awakened. They had been working hard all week producing memos and briefing books.

Going page-by-page through the memo, Gwaltney announced the President's decisions. Each time it was a reversal, the staff let out loud moans and groans. There was much disbelief.

Gwaltney quickly ordered staff rewriting assignments. Everyone went running back to their offices and their typewriters to replace negative passages of McIntyre's prepared statement with positive ones. It had to be totally overhauled.

*   *   *

Marilyn and I came in around 8 o'clock that morning. In the event the President happened to make any unexpected turns in the PRP-recommended decisions, we would use the extra time to adjust our materials accordingly.

But there was little doubt in our minds the President would routinely go along with the PRP recommendations. That feeling was reinforced as we glanced at page seven in the morning's *Washington Post*. "New Department of Education to Exclude Major Programs," a story was headlined.

Marilyn phoned Gwaltney's office at 8:30 to find out what was happening. She was put on hold for an excessive amount of time. We exchanged curious reactions.

Finally, one staffer came on the line. "There have been some changes," the person told Marilyn in an out-of-breath voice. "I can't tell you right now what they are, but you'll like them. Somebody will call you back. We're too busy right now."

Marilyn hung up the phone and her mouth dropped wide open. "Something very strange is going on over there," she told me. Our calm gave way to anxiety.

A few minutes later, closer to 9 o'clock, we were talking with Dick Wegman about the bizarre news when the receptionist interrupted us. Dick took an "urgent" call. On the other end of the line, a top

OMB official explained generally that the President had decided to reverse some of PRP-OMB's recommendations. He had made his decisions only this morning. Our people are going to need more time to rewrite McIntyre's statement, the official pleaded. The two negotiated a half-hour delay in the hearing's starting time, to 10:30.

By the time Dick arrived at Senator Ribicoff's office for the daily morning meeting some 10 minutes later, OMB Director McIntyre had called to inform the Senator of the turn of events. Ribicoff became highly pleased at learning the President would be backing his bill—with almost everything in it.

But we still did not know the details. Marilyn and I felt helpless.

The hearing room was already beginning to fill up with lobbyists, spectators, and press. They knew nothing whatsoever of the frantic behind-the-scenes activity.

*   *   *

At 9:30, Pat Gwaltney trotted back across Pennsylvania Avenue to brief her boss, Jim McIntyre, on the revised statement he would deliver and on the many arguments supporting the program transfers.

By 10:15, the rewritten statement had been final-typed.

McIntyre and Gwaltney left in the OMB director's chauffeured car at 10:20 for our hearing in the Dirksen Senate Office Building. Considering the heavy downtown traffic at that hour, they were running very late, holding up a Senate committee.

*   *   *

Not since the Lance Affair had I seen our hearing room so packed. People lined up even against the back wall, three rows deep. More spilled out into the hallway, where two police guards tried to maintain order. More than 200 lobbyists, journalists, and bureaucrats had come to hear the President's wishes for the location of federal education programs.

The turnout wowed Marilyn and I upon entering the stuffed chamber at 10:15. From the mass of humanity, I could see familiar faces—Head Start lobbyists, a delegation of Indians, school lunch people, NEA staffers.

The lobbyists in the audience were especially nervous. They had expected a 10 o'clock hearing. The absence of the usual stack of testimony plus the half-hour delay meant something was up. Most turf lobbyists first came relaxed to the hearing, expecting McIntyre to say the President had endorsed PRP's recommendations for leaving their programs out of ED.

The drama heightened as a rumor swept the hearing room audience that the President had opted for a broad Department of Education. Reporters and lobbyists pressed through the crowd to ask Marilyn and I for details. We refused comment.

Senator Ribicoff arrived at 10:25, followed by our ranking Republican, Senator Percy. Percy's presence was an important signal that he was interested in this bill for positive reasons. Suddenly, at 10:35, the room fell so silent you could hear a bill drop to the floor. The Capitol police were clearing a path for the OMB director and Pat Gwaltney. They had difficulty walking through the crowd.

Ribicoff whacked his gavel as McIntyre and Gwaltney took their seats at the witness table. "We welcome you today, Mr. McIntyre." Ribicoff's voice boomed through the hushed room.

Senator Percy commented, "We look forward with great interest to what you are going to say because it was impossible to get a copy of your testimony even at 10:30 when you were scheduled to be here," Percy smiled at McIntyre. The audience laughed.

"By the way, do you have more than one copy of your testimony?," Senator Ribicoff asked humorously, holding the statement up in the air.

(Gwaltney had given her copy to the Chairman.) The room erupted into laughter once more.

"The ink is still a little wet...," McIntyre responded.

"I would like to indulge the Chairman and Senator Percy to go through my statement in detail this morning because I think it is important that all of the statement be read," McIntyre said into his microphone. The crowd quieted and listened.

"...We propose today that we and the Congress work together to establish a Department of Education this year," the OMB director continued.

...I am especially pleased to testify this morning since we share a common view of the essential components of the department," he read, looking directly up at Ribicoff. "The nucleus of the new department is the entire $13 billion education division of the present HEW...

"In addition, we agree that the following programs should be included in a new Department of Education: certain science education programs of the National Science Foundation, HUD's college housing program, the U.S. Department of Agriculture Graduate School, education-related activities of HEW's Office for Civil Rights,...HEW's Project Head Start, USDA's child nutrition programs, the Department of the Interior's BIA schools, Department of Defense's overseas dependents schools, and HEW telecommunications demonstration program.

"Let me comment further on these programs..."

When McIntyre ticked off one-by-one the programs slated for transfer, the audience reaction was animated. A Head Start lobbyist wildly shook his head "no." Some child nutrition advocates sighed and buried their heads in their hands. The Indians in the room looked angry. The shock all around was deep.

Marilyn and I had smiles so wide we looked down at our laps in embarrassment. The President of the United States had backed—almost completely—the major bill we were working on. We couldn't help but feel an overwhelming sense of personal accomplishment.

The OMB director briefly commented on each of the President's desired transfers. On Head Start, for example, McIntyre said "this Administration is fully committed to maintaining and strengthening (its) characteristics...by building in safeguards." Including the child nutrition programs, he said, "will represent a clear federal statement that the responsibility of education for the nation's children does not stop at the classroom but extends to all services provided by the schools." In proposing the Indian education transfer, McIntyre pledged the new ED "will uphold the trust relationship." He recommended that both BIA and DOD school systems be gradually phased into ED "to insure an orderly transition." The option of transferring the Arts and Humanities Endowments "should be reserved for future consideration," he suggested to the Committee. McIntyre added it would be "premature" to include job training and youth services.

"Thank you very much, Mr. McIntyre," Ribicoff said with more than a routine tone. "I want to take this opportunity to commend the President...I must confess that during the pulling and hauling I had considerable doubt about the follow through, but it becomes apparent the President has opted for a strong Department of Education...

"As a matter of fact, I had a lot of questions I was going to ask you that I don't have to ask now," Ribicoff ribbed his witness sparking a round of laughter.

"Great", McIntyre replied.

"I was all set for a big debate," the Chairman continued. "Now I have just commendation." He shifted to the serious side.

"Of course, many of the suggestions are controversial. There is no question that the special-interest groups are going to make themselves heard. We will give them an opportunity to come in now that you have given us the Administration's blueprint...and express their point of view."

"I can pledge to you the full support of the minority in moving this forward very rapidly," Senator Percy told Ribicoff.

*   *   *

Not a single person had left the hearing room until Senator Ribicoff banged his adjourning gavel at noon. The hearing was that monumental.

Marilyn and I had problems fending off the crush of reporters and lobbyists up at the dais. We simply couldn't talk to them all.

A dozen journalists held Ribicoff hostage at his seat, throwing out rapid-fire questions to the pleased-as-punch Senator. "They've gone along with our whole plan," Ribicoff boasted.

He was pressed for more details on timing. "If the Administration is enthusiastic, and it seems that they are, and if the Senate passes it early enough and comfortably enough, I think the impetus will be there for the House to go along," the Senator forecast.

*   *   *

Several times during the hearing, my mind drifted back to that February 1977 meeting Marilyn and I had together in the then-deserted hearing room.

Cold chills swept my body as I realized the two of us were really responsible for what had happened this day. The President had just decided to back the Ribicoff bill, a document which we had drawn up.

We had, in effect, made the President's decisions year earlier.

I shuddered as I remembered how Marilyn at one point had taken all those billion-dollar programs out of the bill, and how we went through painful deliberations before deciding to put them back in. Then I recalled those mysterious, swirling clouds outside the hearing room that dreary February afternoon—*clouds of fate.* Fourteen months later, the President of the United States would endorse a bill that we, two Senate staffers, routinely and unsuspectingly had written.

TWELVE

Turf Wars

The looming question was, why did Jimmy Carter reject the unanimous advice of his advisors that he should go with a smaller, less controversial ED?

If he really felt the need for a broad Education Department, there was no shortage of programs to pick from—job training, veterans, etc. Yet the President stuck only to those programs in the Ribicoff bill.

Carter obviously wanted to ride Ribicoff's coattails, to please the Connecticut Senator as much as possible. He needed Ribicoff's cooperation and support for many reasons. The President had many reorganization plans and civil service reform to clear through Ribicoff's Committee. And, he needed Ribicoff's support for his Mideast plane sales package.

Almost seven months had passed since Bert Lance resigned. Jimmy Carter had yet to make a major peace offering to Abe Ribicoff.

And, there was that Carter commitment to the National Education Association hanging over his head.

Come Friday morning, April 14, Carter had powerful incentives to follow Ribicoff's lead on the ED issue. To him, the most important parts of the long decision memo were not the pros-and-cons on the transfers—they were the sentences that spelled out what Ribicoff's bill did.

The President naturally assumed Ribicoff would carry the ball on ED. The Senator would steer the bill through the Senate, and from there the House would need a little push. That course meant the least amount of work and involvement by the inundated President.

But, did Carter have to decide the specifics? His domestic policy advisor, Stu Eizenstat, repeatedly argued for only endorsing the concept and letting Congress fight out the turf wars. The President could have gotten away with that. Instead, he decided yes-no on every program transfer in the memo.

At no place in the decision memorandum was the President informed of our formal stance—S.991 is a *concept bill,* and Senator Ribicoff is not committed to each and every transfer in his bill. True, we were privately hoping Carter would go with a broader department, but we would take what we could get.

The President thus decided to disrupt political turf when he didn't absolutely have to. He decided to back the specific program transfers in S.991 on the false assumption Ribicoff wanted everything in his bill.

When Carter decided to back Ribicoff's bill, he inadvertently locked Ribicoff into supporting the Senator's own bill. In the sometimes screwy world of politics, Carter had actually made Ribicoff's decisions for him, in much the same way Ribicoff's bill framed Carter's decisions.

Senator Ribicoff was overjoyed at the hearing not so much because the President had opted for a broad department, but because of the thrill of victory in a surprise, sweeping presidential endorsement of his bill.

OMB and the President's Reorganization Project staffers were happy with the President's decisions, even though their recommendations were reversed. The broadest department made the most sense and would be good insurance against NEA domination, they fervently believed.

The President's men and women saw his decisions as building a strong Department of Education—a bold, masterful stroke of decisiveness that would inject much energy and forward momentum in the lagging spirit behind ED. Instantly, they began drafting a bill with intentions of persuading House Government Operations Committee Chairman Jack Brooks to introduce it and move it in the House. Carter's decisions sent a signal to Brooks that ED had fully graduated to his priority list. Now, Brooks would have to face up to the issue and make his own moves.

*   *   *

Carter's get-tough mood stretched over into the weekend. He summoned his staff and Cabinet to Camp David to evaluate his Administration's standing.

The President hit up his staff for leaks about Cabinet members and for overloading the agenda. Later, he criticized the Cabinet secretaries for disloyalty to his policies. Top aide Hamilton Jordan rebuked the Cabinet for not rewarding or punishing congressmen and interest groups when they supported or opposed Carter bills.

Carter closed the "summit" by pledging to be tougher and "meaner" in the future. Whether his teamplayers backed his new ED decisions taking away their turf would be a real test.

*   *   *

Walking down the Dirksen Senate Office Building corridor early Tuesday morning, April 18, one colleague after another asked, "Have you seen the *Post* this morning? You're not going to like it."

At the top of the day's editorial page was the heading, "A Department of Education?"

"…We think it is a bad idea," the nation's most politically powerful newspaper said.

The paper worried that "one of the principal risks of creating a separate education department is that it will become a creature of its clientele…Much more probably, it would be the National Education Association, the organization of teachers and school administrators who already exert a great deal of influence on education policy in Washington. In a way, this would be giving them their own department."

We had our own analysis of why the *Washington Post* went the way it did. First, we believed the higher echelons of the editorial staff distrusted and disliked the NEA and its motives. It was a case of one Washington powerhouse jealously upbraiding another.

Our second, and more from-the-gut feeling, was that Joe Califano was responsible for the editorial. Whether rational or not, we couldn't turn our eyes away from the fact that the HEW Secretary was a good friend of *Post* editors Ben Bradlee and Meg Greenfield, that he served as counsel to the *Post* in the early 1970s. Indeed, arguments used in the editorial closely paralleled Califano's.

We knew the fallout of negative editorial comment from both the *New York Times* and the *Washington Post* would be devastating and infectious. With these two liberal pillars of American journalism against us, hundreds of other newspapers would follow suit.

*   *   *

Reaction of the turf groups to the President's decisions to transfer their programs was swift, touching off two months of vicious battles. The special interests would mount sweeping, no-holds-barred public and covert campaigns to pressure Congress into blocking Carter's plans.

We all felt under siege. Now, the Ribicoff people and the Carter people were united behind S.991 and its transfers. We would be working · closely together day and night, as one team, to fend off the turfers.

Pat Gwaltney was nervous that the President's own political appointees might not fully and sincerely support his decisions in testifying before our Committee or in lobbying congressmen. She expected many would act in public as if they were being forced to carry out the Administration positions. Few would exert themselves beyond the minimal efforts requested by OMB-PRP. The bureaucracy would foil, frustrate, and obstruct.

The battlefield had shifted to the Senate and our Committee.

Marilyn and I would be feeling the brunt of the fighting.

*   *   *

Tuesday morning, April 18, the turf hearings were off and running. We had scheduled two panels: one for the DOD overseas schools, the other for NSF science education.

At the witness table, I.M. Greenberg and Anthony Cardinale from the Pentagon had somber, waxen expressions. The military almost never willingly gave up turf.

"The Department of Defense supports this transfer and will work with the President's Reorganization Project and with the Congress to insure that the transfer of functions to the new Department is made smoothly," Greenberg read from his intentionally brief and weak statement.

A deputy assistant secretary, Greenberg had been sent under White House orders to tout the Administration line. Neither he nor Dr. Cardinale, the man most directly in charge of the schools, personally supported the move.

Sitting beside Cardinale was one of his chief adversaries, the executive director of the NEA-affiliated Overseas Education Association representing nearly all of the 9,000 overseas teachers. The union leader said he couldn't "overemphasize our gratification" on hearing the President's support for the transfer. The overseas teachers disliked the strong military influence in their schools.

At the same time in Berchtesgaden, West Germany, there was much confusion at the PTA convention. On one side, the military types and the AFT representatives argued against moving the DOD schools to ED. On the other side, National PTA's Ann Kahn, NEA officials, and my memo pushed for the transfer.

News flashed through the American military global communications network the day before that the President had asked Congress to include the schools in his new ED. The Commander-in-Chief had made his decision.

At the convention, Kahn's effort and the President's decision pushed the parent group into the support column. The prospects for pulling off the transfer were excellent; all primary interests were now in favor.

*   *   *

The scientists still wanted out.

Marilyn searched everywhere across the country for advocates of transferring science education from the National Science Foundation, but came up empty-handed.

At the April 18 Committee hearing, only a deputy to the President's science advisor testified in favor, but it was widely known he sided more with the science community on this issue than with the President.

"I do not think (we) are under any illusions about some of the disadvantages, because we are talking about $56 million worth of highly specialized programs in science education that have had a very good track record at NSF," he told the senators. "...We are talking about this small and somewhat unique program going into a very large department."

Yet, the Carter official acknowledged the programs for training science teachers and developing science curricula would get broader and wider implementation at ED than at NSF, particularly through the public schools. His statement amazed us for its lukewarmness.

*　　*　　*

Alarm spread through the child nutrition and agriculture groups, who would come together to fight the school lunch transfer.

All 18 members of the Senate Agriculture Committee hurriedly signed on to a joint letter to Senator Ribicoff right after the April 14 hearing laying down in no uncertain terms their opposition. "I do not intend to sit idly by and let this happen," Ag Committee Chairman Herman Talmadge (D-GA.) warned in a *Congressional Record* statement.

NEA and its allies were fighting to hold on to the nutrition transfer (along with everything else). The chief state school officers and the National PTA alerted their members to write and visit senators backing the move.

We had a serious political problem, though, on our Committee. Our top Republican, Senator Percy, had served as the ranking member on the then-defunct Senate nutrition committee. Agriculture lobbyists, who had retained their close relationship to Percy, asked the Illinois senator for help. He in turn requested formally that we schedule an additional day of hearings solely on the nutrition issue. It would become a field day for the nutrition people to denounce the transfer.

The Monday, May 8 hearing had us uptight. We had no control whatsoever over it. Marilyn & I sat behind Percy, who took over the chairman's seat, but all we did was listen. Percy's staff had arranged most of the hearing.

Percy called the first panel of witnesses—a supportive panel we'd arranged. The Iowa state education chief testified that transferring child nutrition would reduce burdensome federal requirements. New York City's school lunch director felt USDA had "no real knowledge of school organization."

Five consumer representatives then took their seats at the witness table and proceeded to blast the transfer. The Children's Foundation president told of a to-be-released study entitled, "I Would Rather Go to Hell Than Run a School Breakfast Program." The phrase came from a local school official. A Community Nutrition Institute official said the transfer would diminish funding and "jeopardize" the relationship between basic research and child nutrition.

Percy's staff allowed ASFSA lobbyists Ken Schlossberg and Gerry Cassidy a highly unusual second chance to bring *two* more school lunch people to Washington and stress the group's now "unalterable" opposition.

USDA Assistant Secretary Carol Foreman's testimony was a charade. Everyone knew that she was vehemently opposed to losing her turf, and that she was testifying for it only because she had to support the President. Percy would take advantage of her awkward situation.

"The Department of Agriculture supports President Carter's proposal…," she read from her statement.

"Was there a divided opinion within the Department of Agriculture?," Percy probed her.

Foreman shifted in her seat, showing the tension. "…Well, sir, I suspect that there are none of us who like to give up a piece of our turf…".

"…But in the initial recommendations that you made, did you recommend that these programs be transferred to the Department of Education…?," the Senator pushed harder.

"We did not recommend a transfer."

The Republican Senator wanted to know if Foreman's support "is based upon the fact that the President made a decision and, therefore, it is your duty as a member of the Administration to support that decision in the best way you can?"

"Yes, sir, that is true...," Foreman conceded.

Finally, Percy let her off the hook with a wry smile. "I understand the difficult position it puts you in."

Foreman simply nodded, got up and left.

Ending the hearing, four producer group representatives solidly opposed the transfer. The farm bureau, milk producers, egg producers, and cattlemen all agreed on the need to keep USDA in one piece. Their major concern, however, was that the new ED might try to dump the program distributing surplus commodities to schools, thereby eliminating a valuable market for farmers' goods.

From the moment the agriculture/nutrition lobbyists left the hearing room, they would not cease in their struggle to axe the transfer from the bill. They drummed up publicity. They got other senators to write Ribicoff and the President criticizing the proposal. And, they worked their contacts in the 15 states represented by senators on the Committee.

By mid-June, they had constructed a semi-formal coalition of consumer and producer groups with a panicky name—"SAVE SCHOOL LUNCH!...A Nutrition Coalition Dedicated to Children."

We were locked in a serious clash with the agriculture sphere, about which we knew little. Publicly, my lingo to the press was that the Committee would come under intense pressure from both sides on the transfer and that we expected amendments would be offered both in Committee and on the Senate floor to extract it from the bill. If we won in Committee, it would be by a hair's margin. Our opponents told the press they would "get enough support" in Committee.

A letter from Senator Percy June 23 confirmed for us what we expected all along: "During the Committee's mark-up of S.991,...I intend to offer an amendment to strike the proposed transfer of USDA's child nutrition programs."

*　　*　　*

The Head Start community was traumatized. "This is the most crucial mailgram that your legislative committee has ever sent you," the National Head Start Association wired its troops April 17. "Head Start is in serious trouble…the most disastrous and potentially dangerous position in which (it) has ever been placed. Immediate action is absolutely necessary. Thousands of letters, phone calls and telegrams must now flood the congressional offices if Head Start is to survive…You must write now no matter how many previous letters you have sent on this issue…"

Marilyn worked two, sometimes three, phone lines at once the succeeding two weeks in a frantic nationwide search for positive witnesses on the transfer. We'd scheduled a hearing for April 27.

Her luck was poor. Of those few who supported the move, only a couple were willing to stick their heads out publicly before a U.S. Senate committee and risk incurring the wrath of their peers.

The intensity of feelings against the transfer impressed us. We began to admit to each other behind closed doors that Head Start might become the first we would lose.

"The question of whether the program should be administered by a Department of Education or a Department of Health and Welfare is certainly a difficult one for the Committee to consider," Sen. H. John Heinz (R-Pa.) told the filled hearing room April 27. Marilyn and I sat uneasily behind him. We had tried desperately to find a Democratic senator to chair the hearing, but had to settle on Heinz, the only one who had an opening in his schedule and who supported ED.

Leading off at the witness table, respected and prominent black legislators Sen. Edward Brooke (R-MA.) and Rep. Shirley Chisholm

(D-N.Y.) angrily denounced the transfer. Chishoim called it "a forerunner to public school control of all Head Start programs."

Jim Parham came next. The deputy assistant secretary for human development in HEW directly oversaw the program. He was not pleased in the least at having been chosen the HEW official to defend the President's position. No one at HEW wanted to do it.

"President Carter has expressed his desire that those strengths of the Head Start program should be safeguarded," he began slowly and dryly. "...A detailed statement on these reassurances will be forthcoming."

Whereupon, Parham proceeded to spend nearly half an hour giving factual background on the program: over six million children had been served...400,000 per year...with nearly 50,000 staff and 125,000 volunteers...half the children were black...25 per cent white...15 per cent Spanish-speaking...receiving education, nutrition, health, social, handicapped services. He offered no reasons for making the transfer to ED.

"Thank you, Mr. Parham," Senator Heinz said, shaking his head in bewilderment as the bureaucrat finished.

"...Let me simply ask you, though," Heinz continued. "Do you favor or oppose transferring this very important program to the Department of Education? From your testimony it is impossible to determine how you feel about that...".

"It is very seldom that I think anyone desires to give up a popular program that brings great satisfaction," Parham replied meekly.

The hearing room was dead silent.

"There are frankly legitimate concerns on the part of people who have nurtured and developed Head Start," Parham went on.

"...The Administration's position, our position, is to support the President's proposal."

"Mr. Parham," Senator Heinz responded, "I hope you won't think it amiss if I characterize what you have just said as about the most lukewarm, half-hearted statement in support of the Administration proposal I have ever heard from someone who is part of that Administration."

Parham apologized.

"Just so I understand you, do you support this proposal by the President?," Heinz inquired.

"I support the proposal by the President, Mr. Chairman." Parham looked as though a major confession had been tortured out of him.

In the back of the room, some Head Start lobbyists struggled to hide laughter. The President's Reorganization Project staffers in the audience were shocked, embarrassed, and angry.[18]

The HEW official's pathetic performance was the perfect set-up for the third panel: Marian Edelman and several colleagues spearheading the lobbying drive against the transfer.

"...The issue before this Committee today is children, not politics," charged the Children's Defense Fund leader.

Edelman ridiculed the Administration's wish that Head Start's parental involvement and health-nutrition services serve as a model for other federal education programs. "This assumes that a $600 million program will create the bureaucratic leverage to reform a $17 billion department supporting a $90 billion public education system. Such hopes only reflect a naive theorizing divorced from political and educational realities, both in Washington and in communities throughout the country.

"...I am so tired of the little the poor have been given over to salvage and reform everybody else...".

---

[18] A transcript of Parham's testimony, underlined in red, landed on the President's desk a few days later. Carter was reportedly very upset, especially after having spent a weekend at Camp David dressing down his Cabinet for not forcefully advocating his positions.

She concluded angrily, "If the President made a last-minute judgment on this issue based on inadequate information, the Congress should not support it."

One of her colleagues expressed the fear that "Head Start may become a hiring program for unemployed teachers rather than a developmental program for economically disadvantaged children."

Marian Edelman, pleased with the punch her appearance packed, left the room with a raised clenched fist in salute to her chief lobbyist Harley Frankel, who sat in the audience.

On the final panel were three witnesses brave enough to back the transfer. Continuity between pre-school and public school education was important, they agreed. Head Start "will survive anywhere it is," one remarked.

Two weeks later, we began behind-the-scenes discussions with our allies on dropping Head Start. It was fast becoming too much of a liability. Thousands of letters in opposition poured daily into Hill offices. Two senators—Heinz and Cranston—had decided to draw up amendments to our bill that would delete the provision, and senators tripped all over themselves in the rush to sign on.

Our own boss was having reservations. Senator Ribicoff met with a large delegation of Head Start mothers from Connecticut. Their forceful views impressed him so much that he knew then and there the transfer would be unattainable.

No one dared take on Marian Edelman and her united, vocal network of Head Start mothers and civil rights groups.

Harrison Wellford sent a memo to the OMB director June 12. At the top, it was marked "ADMINISTRATIVELY CONFIDENTIAL."

"No senator on the Governmental Affairs Committee publicly supports the inclusion of Head Start; at least eight senators are opposed," Wellford told Jim McIntyre.

"...In the House, Jack Brooks, due largely to local political considerations, will not introduce or support a bill that includes Head

Start," the memo continued. "The Black Caucus, which has three members on (Brooks's) Government Operations Committee, adamantly opposes the transfer..."

Wellford suggested to McIntyre that he "ask the Vice President to talk with Marian Edelman and indicate that we will not push the Head Start transfer. The Vice President should ask for their support of the Department."

At 1 o'clock that afternoon, Senator Ribicoff met with McIntyre and before the OMB director could say anything, he urged that the Administration find a way out of the Head Start problem. The Senator wanted the issue disposed of before Committee mark-up.

The Head Start community had its moles inside the Administration and on Capitol Hill. They knew—with sheer delight—that they had won a big victory, that we had decided privately to buckle under their pressure. But that did not stop them from fighting on with more force. More Head Start parents and workers continued traveling to Washington and lobbying members of Congress. Mail started arriving in bags.

It was going too far and we were being made to look like thirsty villains. The Head Start community had its political motives in this fight, too. Head Starters weren't battling us solely for the kids; they wanted to put NEA in its place.

*   *   *

House Indian expert Alan Lovesee and I talked over lunch the Monday following the April 14 hearing. "You're going to take a lot of flack on this one," he warned.

The National Tribal Chairman's Association wrote Senator Ribicoff April 20 expressing "strong objection and alarm" at the Indian transfer.

Our secretaries were working furiously at their typewriters, banging out nearly 400 official Committee letters to tribes asking comments on the proposed transfer—the letters I had promised in Denver.

The Bureau of Indian Affairs' pranks in Denver still had me boiling. I phoned Assistant Secretary for Indian Affairs Forrest Gerard and chewed him out.

"We did nothing out of the ordinary," he replied. "My people did nothing wrong or improper."

"Well, I'll tell you it (clandestinely passing out the PRP memo) was done quite obviously to set up the Indians against me and the PRP guy, and I resent your ploys." My anger swelled fast. Gerard switched to a cooler voice and tone, one that asked for understanding. He explained that he disagreed with the President's decision and that most Indian people opposed it also. The credibility of the BIA, himself, and the President had been destroyed by this one move, he said.

We scheduled a hearing on the Indian transfer for May 16. Gerard, himself an Indian, dared the President's staffers to let him testify. He would assuredly speak his mind, taunting them afterwards to fire him. The White House was inclined to send the Interior Department's second-ranking officer, Undersecretary James Joseph, who would more reliably defend the President's decision.

Again, to the dismay of the President's staff, we decided to ask a Republican, Sen. Ted Stevens of Alaska, to chair the hearing. Stevens supported the ED bill, and the sometimes loud and combative Alaskan had built a reputation as a defender of native American causes. But there was the risk he might be persuaded by the Indians to oppose the transfer, even though some Alaska native groups had told us they would support the move.

I confess I was trying to steer Stevens in my direction in favor of the transfer. "Indian education programs are fragmented between two different federal agencies ($500 million worth, split evenly between BIA and OE)," began a memo I sent him listing reasons for the transfer.

"...The condition of Indian education is poor, and continues to progress at a snail's pace in BIA...The tribes still have little influence over the education of their children...There is no high-ranking official in the federal government who speaks for Indian education...The issue of what will happen to the BIA often clouds the issue of which agency could provide better education for Indian students...". I added that special Indian civil rights could be protected in the bill.

It seemed most of the nation's 250 tribes wanted to testify. We had been courting particularly the Navajos, and indications were that the tribe would support the transfer with conditions. With more than 150,000 members, the Navajo tribe was by far the largest. Almost half of all students in BIA schools were Navajo.

By 6 o'clock Monday night May 15, we had received only five of the 14 statements that would be delivered at the next day's hearing, The Indians were not complying well with the Committee's rule that prepared statements be delivered to us 48 hours in advance.

I sensed something strange was going on. A source informed me by phone that nearly all the Indian representatives invited to testify had spent the afternoon secretly caucusing at the Skyline Inn, just off Capitol Hill. Our Indian opponents worked over our Indian supporters, striving to hammer out a consensus position against the transfer.

I was madder than hell. "Damn it, we want a diversity of views. That's how I set up the hearing," I complained to my source.

At the hearing the next morning, Administration officials led off. Interior Undersecretary Joseph assured Senator Stevens the transfer was not intended to change "in any way" Indians' special relationship with the U.S. government. He recommended a phased, three-year transfer, "which allows time for working closely with tribes, Indian organizations, and parents." U.S. Office of Education Deputy Commissioner Gerald Gipp testified the transfer would mean "more efficient management", "less confusion," and being able to expend "more energy" on Indian education. Stevens listened sympathetically.

Then the National Tribal Chairmen's Association., National Congress of American Indians, and National Indian Education Association. came to the witness table to express their "total opposition."

"...We are extremely critical of the way the BIA has administered Indian education," the NCAI rep told Stevens. But, "...moving 8,000 or 10,000 BIA employees over to another department is not going to have one single effect on that program," he ranted. "You are taking those same people over there, the people that are causing the problem."

Lionel Bordeaux, brawny, pig-tailed president of the Indian education group, used a "little legend" for his testimony.

"I think it contains a more that basically relates to what we are talking about here," he tried to justify himself to Senator Stevens. The mostly Indian audience listened with full attention.

"There is an old Sioux legend that my grandfather told me long ago. The story goes that a sparrow decided to fly south for the winter. Unfortunately, it got too cold and he waited too long. Finally, after much thought and deliberation, and very reluctantly, he started his southward journey. Ice began to form on his wings. He came crashing down in a barnyard nearly frozen. The sparrow thought it was the end.

"A cow came along and crapped on the sparrow. The sparrow definitely thought it was the end. Lo and behold, the manure warmed him, brought him back to life. Warm and happy, he began to chirp. He began to sing.

"A cat in the area heard the chirping sounds, investigated, cleared away the manure, found the chirping bird, and promptly ate him.

"Three lessons are contained in this particular story. The first lesson: Not everyone who craps on you is necessarily your enemy. Second, Not everyone who takes crap off you is necessarily your friend, and third, most importantly, if you are warm and happy in a pile of crap, you would do well to keep your damn mouth shut. Thank you."

The hearing room exploded into belly-aching laughter.

"That is a great story," Senator Stevens praised Bordeaux, some three minutes later once the laughter had died down. The Indian educator had blown away his opposition with a single joke.

"I understand your positions," Stevens continued. "I think that you have got a real point that you should oppose this transfer until the details of it are delineated and you have an opportunity to consult...I don't think this is going in the right direction...".

The Indians in the well below smiled. I cringed. Stevens was going their way.

The Indian leaders left the witness table, confident they had won over the Senator.

Following them, a third panel consisting of NEA's "First American Caucus", Coalition of Indian-controlled School Boards, and American Indian Higher Education Consortium. The NEA rep, a Cherokee, delivered a strong defense of the transfer. Her appearance was counter-productive; everyone understood NEA's motive in having one of its own there to argue for keeping the ED bill intact. The Indian school boards and higher ed reps opposed the bill.

Finally, members of six different Indian tribes lined up across the witness table. The effect of the previous day's pre-hearing conference showed most here. The Mississippi Choctaws' statement went from previously supportive to neutral. They wanted language in the bill protecting Indian rights. If that was done, the Navajos agreed, "we will be less hesitant to support the transfer." The 19 Pueblo tribes stuck to their position of support for the bill and transfer "with conditions." Those included specific language reaffirming the trust obligation, an assistant secretary, a "National Indian Education Policy Board," and increased funding. The Montana Northern Cheyenne tribe went from supportive to opposed. The Minnesota Chippewas and the Affiliated Tribes of Northwest Indians believed the new ED would lack "sensitivity" to Indian educational needs.

Most left the three-hour hearing determined to fight the transfer all the way.

Hundreds of tribes and organizations wrote in response to Senator Ribicoff's April letter soliciting comment. Less than a fifth supported the transfer. The Lac Courte Oreilles of Wisconsin called our bill "a disguised measure to dismantle the BIA." The Colorado River Indian tribes wrote "it is not a new department that is needed, but implementation of the promises, goals, objectives that have been expressed in the past."

By June, I decided we had consulted enough. I knew backwards, forwards, inside and out the positions of the Indians. In mid-month, I reviewed with relevant Hill staff the long list of changes we were prepared to incorporate in the bill to make the BIA transfer more acceptable to Indian people.

Letters went out again to all tribes announcing those changes: establish an office for Indian education headed by an assistant secretary, phase into ED the BIA schools over three years, retain existing eligibility requirements, and include specific language in the bill continuing the trust responsibility, Indian preference in hiring, and self-determination. A hefty list of concessions.

Days later, the Navajo Nation chairman wrote Senator Ribicoff. "…We cannot risk dismantling the BIA, as inadequate as it is, for shaky promises of something better," he said in a change-of-mind. "…In short, we must oppose S.991 because, like so many offers made to Indian people in the past, it seems to promise much, but could cost us our (rights)…". The other tribes had turned around our largest supporter.

*   *   *

Most interest groups wanted out of ED. But by the first of May, one surprised us by asking to be included—the handicapped/rehabilitation lobby.

In 1978, more than $600 million was budgeted for the Bureau of Education for the Handicapped in the U.S. Office of Education, and nearly $1 billion for the Rehabilitation Services Administration, housed within the Office for Human Development Services in HEW. The handicapped community badly wanted the two efforts merged into one comprehensive agency.

The handicapped wanted to demonstrate their ability to become fully functioning, contributing members of society. They did not like RSA's association with welfare programs in HEW. In ED, they saw an opportunity for reversing that dependent image. Most states operated the rehab programs through their education agencies.

But the politics within the Carter Administration resisted the move. For one thing, the President himself disagreed. While Governor of Georgia, Carter had reorganized the voc rehab programs and shuffled them into the state human resources agency. He had personal interest and knowledge in the issue. For another, Secretary Califano, already being asked to relinquish much of his turf, wasn't the least bit excited about losing a billion dollars in voc rehab.

Handicapped groups were nevertheless undeterred. Tired of fighting to keep programs in the bill, we were happy to accept a huge chunk of turf that truly wanted to be part of our new department.

*   *   *

By Friday, May 12, the reorganization team needed more direction from the President.

"(Senate Majority Leader) Byrd is optimistic about passage of the Ribicoff bill, but Speaker O'Neill indicated that House passage this year is unlikely," OMB Director Jim McIntyre told Carter by memo.

"In my view, although it will be difficult, favorable action by the House in the short time remaining in this session is possible if the

White House undertakes a strong advocacy effort in the Congress," McIntyre said.

Congressional leaders were planning an October 1 adjournment.

"We need your guidance on how strong a push should be made, since this decision will have significant implications for the allocation of your time…"

McIntyre's main concern was the House of Representatives. "As you know, there is not a contingent in the House strongly advocating the creation of a Department of Education," he reminded the President. "…The inclusion in our proposal of several controversial programs, especially Head Start and child nutrition, seems to curb the enthusiasm of some members who otherwise support the…Department. House members will probably take no initiative until we indicate clearly, through the introduction and strong advocacy of an Administration bill, whether this is a high priority."

The President signed off on McIntyre's recommendation: "press forward for enactment this year."

Terry Straub called Marilyn Friday afternoon and told her the news. The charming, 32-year-old PRP congressional liaison director, a native of Indianapolis, had managed the Carter campaign in Indiana and was now managing the political fate of a host of reorganization measures on Capitol Hill, spending more time on ED.

"The key is (Jack) Brooks," he said. Straub felt that if the House Government Operations Committee Chairman could be persuaded to push the bill, then he in turn could work on Tip O'Neill.

"McIntyre has to talk to Brooks…But he is less than enthusiastic about the Department of Education. Jack Brooks and the Speaker are a problem," Straub concluded.

If something didn't happen in the House soon, everything would go down the drain.

*   *   *

The tenth hearing, set for Wednesday, May 17, would feature Jim McIntyre to round out his earlier, sparse testimony.

Still unresolved was the standing request of three Republican senators that HEW Secretary Joe Califano testify. The issue went all the way to the President, who personally ordered Califano only to send a statement, saving both the Secretary and Carter political embarrassment.

HEW Undersecretary Hale Champion came to the Committee hearing in Califano's place, and brought along Califano's meticulously-worded letter. "I...support the *President* in *his* belief that a Department of Education can help the nation meet its educational challenges (emphasis added)," it said. Nowhere in the letter did Califano say directly, "I support the Department of Education." Califano even left his signature to the autopen machine.

"We do not believe HEW is unmanageable," Champion stressed to Ribicoff (who thought the opposite). "We do believe education has the size, scope, and character to deserve its own place in the Cabinet."

James McIntyre, Harrison Wellford, and Pat Gwaltney sat together with Champion at the witness table in the well.

Head Start was very much on the senators' minds. "Why is there such strong objection by the Head Start people?," Senator Ribicoff asked the OMB director.

"I think that the fear of any change is a natural inclination of any individual," McIntyre responded. "...We do not propose and we do not anticipate that the community-based programs will be absorbed by the schools, as some people fear. We want Head Start to be an innovative model for other programs..."

Ohio Democratic Sen. John Glenn, perched next to Ribicoff at the dais, said his mind had changed after "doing some reading the last few days...I thought it was basically pre-kindergarten. That is not it. It is a parent-involvement-type thing, nutrition, getting the children to learn some skills...It is one area of government which is a bright, shining example of how things should work. I hope we are not about to kill the thing off."

"Is it true that you originally advised against inclusion of Head Start in the new Department of Education?," Senator Percy asked McIntyre.

"Senator, I really think that my personal recommendation to the President is like your staff recommendation to you...," McIntyre irritably answered.

Ribicoff turned to the child nutrition issue. With the entire agriculture committee against him, the Senator suggested to the OMB director that he look for compromises.

"I think that before we mark this up, again you ought to sit down with (Agriculture Secretary) Bergland for an overall discussion of all the nuances," Ribicoff insisted. "...I don't personally see how it is going to hurt the farmer. It might hurt the bureaucracy, the Department of Agriculture. But certainly the children are going to eat food whether it is under the jurisdiction of the Department of Education or the Department of Agriculture."

Meanwhile, Sen. John Danforth (R-MO.) had casually strolled into the hearing and asked a simple question that few had given much thought to. "Mr. Champion, do you think that this new department would improve the education of kids?"

"...It improves the federal role in education," Champion replied. "...But it is not farfetched to say that to improve federal performance would be of assistance to the people trying to provide better education at the state and local levels."

Several minutes later, the hearing broke up. Ten days of hearings—a healthy number for any bill—left us exhausted. But we had to focus our minds now on a future Committee mark-up of S.991, and fighting the turf battles to their miserable end. Things would have to move fast. We were running out of time.

*　　*　　*

The month of June saw a lot of hard logistical and raw political work done.

The battery of lawyers at the President's Reorganization Project were working diligently on their draft of an ED bill, with intentions of handing it to House Committee Chairman Jack Brooks for introduction.

Pat Gwaltney and her staff met the first week of June with Brooks's chief Committee staffers to discuss the issues. Gingerly, Gwaltney offered to furnish a copy of her draft bill. To her relief, Brooks's people seemed open to reviewing it. Over the next few weeks, the two sides met frequently, bargaining their way to a single version.

Jack Brooks, however, had not yet offered to do anything. He and his staff knew that ED was one of the President's top ten priorities, and he had become one of Carter's strongest allies on the Hill. The White House had made the issue more palatable for him by backing off Head Start. But, whether and when he would move the President's bill, nobody knew.

The President had not yet personally asked Brooks for his help. Carter was probably the only one who could get to him. Top White House officials were thinking of a way for Carter to woo Brooks. There was the possibility of a direct Oval Office meeting. Or, there was some thought of tieing in the end-of-the-month political trip Carter would make to the southwest. For months, a ceremony dedicating the federal building in Brooks's hometown, Beaumont, Texas, to the Congressman had been planned. Perhaps the President could stop off in Beaumont. No final decisions had been made.

Lobbying and P.R. never ceased. I flew to Connecticut June 8 to address, along with White House assistant Beth Abramowitz, the university professors' group at Yale. The American Association of University professors had backed ED since 1974 and were proving to be very helpful in pushing the bill, dispelling the notion that higher ed wasn't excited about ED. AAUP's Washington lobbyist, Al Sumberg, was taking an out-front position and worked daily with us.

Early the next morning, five NEA lobbyists worked over the 15 senators' staffers who dropped by for coffee and Danish—"How's your senator on child nutrition?"; "The Indian teachers are solidly behind the BIA transfer"; "NEA is the exclusive representative of the overseas teachers"; "No, we don't want to 'take over' Head Start."

NEA made plans to bring to Washington in June at least two teachers each from states of senators on the Committee to lobby for the bill.

The teachers were briefed on the 17 Committee senators' current positions on the bill and on the three transfers most important to NEA: child nutrition, Head Start, and Indian education.

NEA considered as "swing votes" on nutrition Sen. John Heinz, Tennessee Democrat James Sasser, Florida Democrat Lawton Chiles, and Missouri Democrat Thomas Eagleton (who chaired the agriculture appropriations subcommittee).

For the Indian transfer, NEA targeted Washington Democrat Henry Jackson and Senator Stevens.

All senators had been subjected to "intense lobbying" on the Head Start issue, NEA warned its teacher-lobbyists.

A delegation of Connecticut NEA teachers met with Ribicoff in his Washington office to firm him up on his own bill. They extracted a commitment from him to support the nutrition and Indian transfers. But on Head Start, Ribicoff told his constituents he felt it was "all but lost."

Marilyn and I, meanwhile, were up to our ears in the nitty-gritty of legislative drafting. The first, nearly complete version of the PRP ED bill was given us June 12. From then on, we worked every day revising and rewriting draft after draft of the bill.

Although we were using the PRP bill as a base, ours would look slightly different when we finished it. We reworked their findings and purposes section. The PRP version provided for 14 unnamed principal officers to govern the new department; we specifically named the assistant secretaries—for civil rights, Indian education, child nutrition, etc. We wrote into our drafts more protections for the various groups, for example, preserving Indian preference and rights of the overseas teachers to continue using DOD commissaries and hospitals. There were other differences.

Marilyn and I had a new partner in this aspect of the process—Susan McNally, a fresh, young lawyer in the Senate Legislative Counsel's office. McNally eagerly took on the massive project of helping us overhaul and redraft the PRP bill for our purposes. For the next year-and-a-half, she would become the Senate's principal legal expert on the ED bill, learning and stumbling with us as we went along. McNally redrafted the bill nearly ten times through the days of June and early July.

We were under pressure to move fast and schedule a mark-up. But the Committee calendar would not open until after the July 4 recess.

*   *   *

Hundreds of people were in town for the annual meeting of the Day Care and Child Development Council of America. I had been asked to receive more than 50 in the hearing room June 23. Most were black and Hispanic women.

I managed to get out just a few sentences on the bill before the verbal shrapnel flew at me.

"All this is gonna do is put our Head Start centers in the public schools," one irate woman bellowed. Her colleagues nodded affirmatively, emphatically. "Teachers don't care one damn bit about us parents. All they want is their lousy 9-to-5 job and collect their paychecks, and out the door they go.

"You guys here in Washington don't know what in hell you're doing," another roared. "You start up a good program like Head Start and then you try to kill it."

It was the same old scene. Head Start mothers getting so emotional they broke down, making me out to be the cause of all their misery.

I sat and listened to it all for a full hour, too exhausted to fight back anymore, a victim of battle fatigue. I prayed the turf wars would not go on much longer.

THIRTEEN

The Committees Act

Out on the tarmac at Andrews Air Force Base in suburban Maryland, Air Force One was fueled, stocked, and ready-to-go.

Friday, June 23. The President would begin a three-day swing through the vast State of Texas.

White House operatives had arranged for several meetings and events. The President would attend a Democratic fund-raiser in Houston, visit major Texas cities, and review a military demonstration at Fort Hood. It was a political trip in every sense of the term.

Dozens clambered aboard the majestic blue-and-white Boeing 707: an army of Carter aides, Democratic Party Chairman John White, and five members of the Texas congressional delegation.

One seat had been saved for Rep. Jack Brooks.

White House staffers decided to include a stop in Beaumont, Brooks's hometown. The President would take time out to make a special appearance at dedication ceremonies naming a federal building there after Brooks. The 56-year-old Congressman was flattered.

Jimmy Carter had come to find the House Government Operations Committee Chairman immensely helpful, especially in moving his reorganization legislation. The two had become good friends.

In his cabin on board the presidential plane, Carter took a few minutes to quickly skim a memo from Frank Moore outlining the President's proposal on ED, the reasons for it, the politics involved, and how Brooks could politically benefit by moving it through his Committee, which he ruled with an iron hand.

Then, Carter called Brooks to his cabin and proceeded softly to ask "Jack" for his help. How could Brooks, captive aboard the President's plane, refuse the plea from his Democratic President?

Saturday morning, thousands turned out in Beaumont to hear and see the President at the newly-named "Jack Brooks Federal Office Building." Carter gave the crowd his standard anti-inflation lingo, and also spent much time praising Brooks to his constituents.

Five days later, back in Washington, Brooks introduced H.R. 13343, "A Bill to Establish a Department of Education." A press release issued from Brooks's office said the Chairman would begin hearings in mid-July.

*   *   *

It took six months, but Jimmy Carter had finally used his key to unlock the main door blocking ED. Jack Brooks's commitment now enabled ED to at least have the appearance of possibly becoming a reality. Without his help, the bill was dead.

The question now was, could Brooks get the bill passed in the U.S. House of Representatives in the short time remaining? At most, he had six weeks to stage his hearings, hold his mark-up, and send the bill to the House floor. Brooks would have to do in six weeks what we had done in 18 months.

And, to make things a little more complicated, bills on the House side are almost always reviewed through subcommittees first. Brooks's ED bill was immediately referred to a subcommittee he chaired— Legislation and National Security.[19] The subcommittee would hold the hearings and its mark-ups, then send its approved version on to the full Committee for more marking-up.

As if there weren't enough hurdles, the House also required every bill to obtain a *rule*, specifying how the bill could be amended and how much time would be spent debating it on the House floor. So, once the bill had cleared Brooks's Committee, it would go to another, the House Rules Committee. ED would have to be on the Speaker's agenda if it were cleared through Rules, and that was another problem altogether.

Compared with our Committee, the reception ED would receive in the House GovOps Committee would be on the darker side of night-and-day. Most House lawmakers saw the whole thing simply in terms of a President making a raw payoff to the NEA. Instead of focusing on the unmanageability of HEW, many House members would choose to accentuate the "ED-is-more-bureaucracy" angle, figuring they would earn brownie points with voters.

Brooks's Committee itself was nowhere near as harmonious as Ribicoff's. Strongly opposing liberal and conservative factions constantly grinded away at each other, usually erupting into highly partisan Democrat vs. Republican contests. Democrats outnumbered Republicans, 29-14. Brooks was a tough, entrenched, fiercely loyal

---

[19] Committee chairmen decide whether a certain bill is referred to a certain subcommittee. Since Brooks had made a commitment to the President, he would refer the bill to no other subcommittee than his own, staying in full control of it from start to finish.

Democrat, a committee chairman who expected consistent loyalty from his Democrats. He was normally able to corral his Dems behind him on issues and procedural votes, often infuriating the Republicans. Brooks sometimes took a perverse pleasure in aggravating Republicans. He was a true political sportsman.

A preliminary analysis by the White House staff and NEA indicated the bill would be voted out of the House Committee. ED proponents were relaxed, assuming that Brooks, strong as he was would maneuver to overcome obstacles and get the bill out. But the AFT influence was more pervasive here, touching at least eight Democrats. In addition, most Republicans were staunch conservatives who were not eager to give Jimmy Carter anything. NEA had helped just four of the Committee Republican members in the last election, including, importantly, the Ranking Republican, Frank Horton of Rochester, N.Y.

Perhaps the bill Brooks introduced was the best evidence of hard times to come. Only two other reps cosponsored it. Three out of 435 U.S. Representatives.

In an effort to take some of the heat off, Brooks himself decided to drop Head Start from the bill. By doing that, it became a *Brooks* bill, not a Carter bill, for the President had not officially backed off from his desire to transfer the program. Otherwise, the bill resembled in every way that which Gwaltney and her PRP lawyers had spent the last month drafting.

Now that Brooks had given "go" orders to his staff, there was all-out cooperation between them, PRP, and NEA. The three groups worked daily together in a crash effort to schedule witnesses and hearings.

*   *   *

Marilyn and I kept asking for a mark-up date. Senator Ribicoff kept putting us off, citing all his other commitments, appointments, and duties.

Ribicoff finally relented and approved dates for our first Committee mark-ups: July 11 and 13. Much work remained to be done—finalizing the bill, coordinating other senators' amendments, briefing the senators' staff, preparing background papers on everything for the senator...

*   *   *

Mark-up. In Washington, the term connotes an event at the core of the legislative process: a formal meeting of a congressional committee to actually mark up—revise, rewrite, and rework, then approve or reject—a bill.

Marilyn and I had been through countless mark-ups before on other issues. Senators would debate and vote on the general issues and sub-issues, leaving details to be worked out by their staffs. Much of the sessions' actions would be choreographed beforehand; we would know which senators would offer which amendments, and which ones would speak out.

In two separate meetings with senators' staff prior to the first, July 11, mark-up, we learned a number of senators planned either to offer formal amendments or to discuss specific issues in the public forum. Several staffers put us on notice that if Chairman Ribicoff did not move first to strike the Head Start transfer, he would be overrun by other members' eagerness to do so. By now, everyone knew Senator Percy would offer an amendment to axe child nutrition/school lunch. Senator Stevens' aides warned us their boss might ask the Committee to vote on deleting the Indian transfer. Conservative Republican Sen. William Roth had his staff draw up several amendments to preserve local control of education and cut back the bureaucracy. Sen. Muriel Humphrey (D-MI.) had decided she would offer an amendment to transfer the vocational rehabilitation programs to ED.[20] So far, no one objected to the DOD schools transfer.

Not until late Friday afternoon, July 8—just three days before our first scheduled mark-up—did we finally finish redrafting S.991 and send it to the Government Printing Office. The bill Senator Ribicoff introduced in March 1977 had 40 pages. Our revised version had stretched to more than 70.

*　　*　　*

Our arms numb from lifting massive bundles of files, briefing books, and papers, Marilyn and I entered the hearing room at 9:55, Tuesday morning, July 11. We passed the guards at the main door and saw that the room was packed to capacity. Senator Ribicoff arrived promptly at 10:00.

In mark-ups, several tables were grouped together in the pit below the dais to form a giant square table, large enough to accommodate the 16 Committee members. The Chairman and Ranking Republican sat at one end of the table. Democrats sat to Ribicoff's right; Republicans to Percy's left. Senators' aides formed a human wall around the table.

Marilyn and I would sit beside the Chairman, constantly whispering in his ear and coaching him with responses and talking points. Behind

---

[20] Mrs. Humphrey was in the sixth month of filling out the term of her deceased husband, Hubert.

us, Susan McNally from the legislative counsel's office would prompt us on technicalities, as needed.

Harrison Wellford, Pat Gwaltney, and many PRP staffers filled the first row of audience seats. A group of NEA lobbyists sat nearby. I recognized the faces of dozens of turf lobbyists. Journalists from the *Washington Post*, *New York Times*, wire services, and education press had come to cover our historic first mark-up. The hearing room was one big social; the chatter was deafening.

Ribicoff whacked his gavel with a bang, bringing quick silence and lobbyists scurrying for their seats. A working quorum of five senators were finally in the room—the Chairman, Percy, Jacob Javits (R-N.Y.), James Sasser (D-TN.), and Humphrey. It was close to 11 o'clock.

"...Much time, thought, and hard work has gone into this bill," Ribicoff read from his opening statement. "The Committee devoted 10 days of hearings to the legislation. Nearly 100 individuals in the field of education have testified. The Administration spent more than a year studying the need for the department and the various transfers...

"I am pleased that Chairman Jack Brooks of the House Government Operations Committee has introduced legislation to create a Department of Education. The House Committee will begin hearings next week...

Without so much as drawing a breath, Ribicoff said, "I want to bring up the question of Head Start.

"I know all of you here have heard from the many parents and people concerned about the transfer...I do feel the Head Start program has worked well in the past and is working well now...I recommend that we do not include Head Start in our bill..."

Other senators expressed agreement with Ribicoff's comments. The motion to drop Head Start passed "without objection." It was gone in five minutes.

Muriel Humphrey offered her amendment to transfer the HEW vocational rehabilitation programs. She argued the move would prevent the "reorientation of (voc rehab) along a welfare line."

Both Ribicoff and Percy spoke in favor. Ribicoff called on Harrison Wellford to give the Administration's view. Knowing VR was lost to ED, Wellford talked listlessly about the programs involving a broad range of social and medical services distant from the education functions of the new ED. But, the Committee passed the amendment without objection.

As the senators discussed a minor amendment, Sen. Ted Stevens rushed in through the anteroom door with aides trailing behind.

"Ted, you always have interesting things to say," Ribicoff smiled and spoke across the table to his Alaskan colleague. The two seldom agreed politically, but respected each other and were friends.

"Mr. Chairman, as you know, I conducted the hearing on the BIA transfer, and all but one group appearing from the organized Indian community opposed the transfer," Stevens said in his loud public voice. He listed the groups and tribes one-by-one.

"One reason for their opposition is that the governing bodies of the Indian tribes were not consulted," he continued. "They will only support such a move when they have seen the track record of the new Department and are assured that the trust responsibility will be maintained...".

The other five senators listened impassively, many rubbing their chins and staring at the ornate ceiling of the hearing room.

Marilyn asked me quickly to write down the Indian groups supporting the transfer. We handed it to Ribicoff.

"I would say that we know of several Indian tribes and organizations that support this," Ribicoff spoke into his microphone. "The Pueblos, the Choctaw Nation, they all approve of the transfer.

"In the past, the BIA has been consistently indifferent to the health and education of Indians," Senator Ribicoff spoke off-the-cuff. "When I was Secretary of HEW, we transferred the health program from BIA to HEW in 1961 and that led to a significant increase in improvement of health care for the Indians."

"...Dropout rates exceed 50 per cent for elementary and secondary students, 75 per cent for postsecondary students," he read from a statement I gave him.

The Chairman called on Harrison Wellford to join in the defense. Wellford stood up from his seat in the audience and told the senators the President "believes strongly Indian education programs should be in one place."

"The transfer should only be made if the recognized Indian spokesmen can agree to it," Stevens insisted. "If my amendment is not adopted, I and other senators will try to amend it on the floor.

"The Indians at this time are doing better in education throughout the U.S. because they are controlling their own schools for the first time," he appealed to the Committee members.

I noticed many Indian faces in the audience anxiously watching the mark-up proceedings. Most of those present were against us.

Ribicoff abruptly cut off the debate. "The question is on the Stevens amendment, and the clerk will call the roll...". My heart pounded. I figured we would win, but I wasn't 100 per cent certain.

For three tense minutes, the votes of the 16 senators were tallied, one-by-one. Several absent senators voted by proxy.

Stevens lost, 7-3. The Committee would recommend to the full Senate that Indian education be consolidated in ED. I breathed a loud sigh and slumped down in my chair as the Chairman gaveled the first mark-up to adjournment.

The Alaskan Senator walked out of the hearing room in a huff, vowing to win his case on the Senate floor. Indian leaders in the hearing room were equally incensed and revengeful. Groups of them cornered, in the hallway outside, some of the Democratic senators who voted with us, demanding to know why they did.

* * *

Clearly, the momentum on the Indian transfer was with us. The day following our mark-up, the Americans for Indian Opportunity board met in Albuquerque, N.M. and voted 14-7 in favor of the transfer, largely on Ribicoff's strong urgings to LaDonna Harris.

Meanwhile, Sen. James Abourezk (D-S.D.) had approached Ribicoff on the Senate floor to chat about the Indian issue. Ribicoff told him how deeply he felt the transfer should be made, and that impressed Abourezk, chairman of the Senate Indian Committee. Abourezk had always defended and sided with the Indians, but this time he was personally inclined to agree with Ribicoff.

Bills such as ours were raising Indian emotions. That very week, more than 2,000 Indians were arriving in Washington, the end of their widely-publicized "Longest Walk" campaign to protest bills on Capitol Hill that they felt would diminish the unique federal responsibilities to tribes. S.991 was one.

Several met with Ribicoff, Marilyn, and I in the Senator's grand office three days later. Patricia Locke (she arranged the Denver meeting) was there, as was the Minnesota Chippewa chief, an Alaskan native, and three others. The atmosphere was cold and stiff.

Each of the Indians spoke five minutes on the hazards of the transfer, using the same old arguments. Ribicoff listened patiently.

"Indian education isn't going to be drowned in the Department of Education," the Senator tried to assure them. "The bill will guarantee Indians certain things…"

"You're not listening to us," Locke gestured angrily to Ribicoff. "We want one agency for Indian people. This bill will destroy the trust responsibility. Indian people do not want this…"

She was on the verge of all-out shouting and screaming. The tone of the meeting turned rapidly acrimonious.

"We know you're concerned about Indian children and want to do the best," one Indian said soothingly.

"Well, you tell us what you want in the bill and we'll change it," Ribicoff offered. "If it's deficient, let us know. We'll change it."

By this time, Locke and two fellow Indians were steaming mad, up from their seats, and heading for the door.

"White man making decisions for Indian people," Locke hollered at Senator Ribicoff as she stormed out into the quiet hallway.

Two of the more cool-headed Indians stood up and apologized to the Senator, who was upset enough that he didn't respond.

Once the whole gang had left, Marilyn and I stayed behind to console Ribicoff. Gripping the back of his chair, the Senator stood and complained bitterly, "It's the BIA. They've stirred them all up."

"You don't know how right you are," I told him in a subdued and truly sad voice.

*   *   *

Our attention turned immediately to the next mark-up, set for Friday, July 14.

The big battle would be over child nutrition/school lunch. By our preliminary head counts, we knew the vote would be breathtakingly close. NEA was leaning hard on certain senators, badly wanting to keep alive claims of consolidation in this reorganization. For me and Gail Bramblett, it became personal thing, a hard-fought battle between us and American School Food Service Association. lobbyists Schlossberg and Cassidy, whom we still perceived as watching out for their own interests.

By late Thursday afternoon, the situation was perilous: Senator Percy's staff and the ASFSA lobbyists had lined up six hard votes for the amendment to drop the transfer. Two other senators were leaning their way. Percy needed nine votes to defeat us, assuming all 16 members were present. On our side, we could count only four hard votes for the transfer, with another four—Glenn, Sasser, Charles Mathias (R-MD.), Heinz—still undecided. NEA affiliates in those states were calling on-the-hour to the four undecideds. I also asked the state school superintendents and the state PTAs to apply some pressure.

The Carter Administration desperately wanted Committee approval of the nutrition transfer. At about 6:30 Thursday night, a PRP staffer called to tell us a decision had been made to compromise at the last possible minute and, hopefully, win over those precious few undecideds. According to the plan, Senator Ribicoff would offer an amendment to insure that full responsibility for funding, acquiring, and distributing agricultural commodities to the schools would remain in USDA, while the bulk of nutrition funding would go to Education. PRP gambled this proposal would give the undecided senators an out, an opportunity to say, "I believe this meets the basic objections of the farmers," and then vote for the transfer.

Yet, for it to succeed, the plan would have to be kept secret and sprung upon the Committee first thing in the morning. The undecided senators would be secretly briefed on the compromise, and hopefully their vote secured.

Given our shaky political situation, we agreed to the plan without hesitation.

*   *   *

The hearing room was no less crowded at 10 o'clock Friday morning, but many faces had changed. This morning, lobbyists from agriculture, consumer, nutrition, and child advocacy groups filled it. The head count on nutrition looked better. Senators Glenn and Mathias sent over their proxies that morning—against the Percy amendment and in support of the transfer. That still left Sasser and Heinz.

Immediately upon arriving at 10:20, Senator Percy played the role of lobbyist himself. He made a special point of collaring Heinz and arguing his case. As Percy left, I heard Heinz say, "I'll think about it."

Finally, at 11:05, Ribicoff gaveled the mark-up to order.

Percy began the discussion. The Illinois Republican talked nearly 20 minutes in support of his amendment. He claimed that nutrition is not a high priority in the nation's schools, and that it is "not the primary function of education." The transfer would also jeopardize funding and pull the programs away from USDA nutrition research and expertise, he argued.

"Although the Administration has pledged its continued support for the commodities aspect of these programs, this guarantee may become more dominated by educators...," Percy charged.

Marilyn and I exchanged nervous glances. That line in Percy's statement showed us neither he nor his staff knew anything about our secret strategy.

"Gentlemen, let me respond to Senator Percy," Ribicoff cut in. The Chairman argued that the transfer would "create a uniform administrative chain between the federal, state, and local agencies" and "allow for more administrative simplification."

"And lastly, the surplus commodity program will not be affected by the transfer," Ribicoff continued.

"...I received a letter this morning from OMB Director McIntyre who...suggests that S.991 be amended to retain the responsibility for obtaining commodity funding in the Department of Agriculture...

"So I move that the bill be modified in accordance with the Administration's suggestion...," Ribicoff said.

Percy's eyebrows raised.

Senator Heinz asked to speak. "I have felt some concerns that the transfer would have done some violence to our commodities program," he said cautiously. "...The change that you suggest on behalf of the Administration addresses that concern," he gestured toward the Chairman. "For that reason, while I have previously been inclined to support Senator Percy, with that change I will not support my good (Republican) colleague from Illinois...".

"I would like to respond to this change," Percy said with teeth gritted. He was irate. "I think that the Office of Management and Budget is in this case being more political, frankly, than is good management," the normally restrained Senator yelled out. His face turned bright red, his fist banged the table, and his angry eyes looked directly at Harrison Wellford.

Wellford shifted back and forth in his seat, embarrassed by Percy's attack. This was not good for the Carter official who needed Percy's cooperation to pass the President's reorganization plans.

"...Just to sort of take care of the farmers on one side by assuring them they are going to get theirs is really failing to respond to all the testimony we had," Percy roared on. "The bulk of the testimony was not from farmers, those just interested in commodity programs. The bulk...was from nutritionists, from home economists, from people who are in a position...".

While he railed on, one of Senator Sasser's staffers tiptoed in the room past all the spectators up to Dick Wegman, who sat with Marilyn and I. He handed Dick a hand-written proxy, on yellow legal paper, from the Tennessee Democrat in opposition to Percy's amendment. We had eight senators in our column.

Gail Bramblett had a worried look on her face. I got up, maneuvered through the crowd, and whispered in her ear the good news. She instantly covered her mouth with her hand to muffle her joyful scream.

"I think, if there is no further comment, the clerk will call the roll on the Percy amendment," Ribicoff said in stopping the debate. The whole room tensed up.

The chief clerk called out the names. The votes see-sawed back-and-forth. The clerk, at the end, announced the result was eight against the amendment, six for.

"I understand we have two on the way down," Percy protested.

"Even if the two voted with Senator Percy it doesn't count," Chairman Ribicoff ruled.[22] "So the amendment is defeated."

I leaned back in my chair, tilted my head back, and inhaled a deep breath of air. We had won the nutrition transfer in Committee.

Ribicoff immediately offered an amendment to keep surplus commodity funding and distribution with USDA, and it passed without objection.

In all the noisy clamor following adjournment, one Senate agriculture committee aide pointedly told Gail Bramblett, "You're the best goddamn lobbyist I've ever seen here, but I'm going to beat you." Indeed, the ASFSA, agriculture, and nutrition lobbyists made plans then and there for introducing a similar amendment on the Senate floor.

*   *   *

The mark-up stage wasn't quite finished, though.

Conservative Republican Sen. William Roth of Delaware asked for one more session to offer his amendments on preserving local control of education—and busing. The Committee met again July 18.

---

[22] The two remaining senators voted by proxy with Percy, resulting in an 8-8 tie. Percy needed a majority vote to drop the transfer.

"We don't intend that control of education will be taken out of localities and the states," Ribicoff told his colleagues. The senators agreed. Roth's amendment inserting language in the bill to that effect passed unanimously.

The anti-busing amendment was another matter. We could not afford embroiling the Department of Education in that hot controversy. Even the conservative southern senators on the Committee joined Ribicoff in persuading Roth to withdraw his proposal.

At long last, Ribicoff proudly announced, "Gentlemen, I move we report out the Department of Education bill. The clerk call the roll."

An emotional milestone for us, Marilyn and I listened to the call. One senator after another repeated the same precious word—"aye." The Committee vote was unanimous.

*　　*　　*

"In a victory for President Carter, the Senate Governmental Affairs Committee voted unanimously yesterday to create a new Department of Education with about 24,000 employees and an annual budget of $18 billion," the *Washington Post* reported the following morning.[23]

"The bill's chief sponsor, Committee Chairman Abraham A. Ribicoff (D-Conn.) smiled broadly during the 14-to-0 vote but warned that only 'a few short months' remain to push the bill through the Senate and House before the 95th Congress adjourns.

---

[23] The figures were the sum totals of the work force and budgets of existing programs.

"When the measure goes to the Senate floor, American Indian and agricultural interests will try to strip the new Department of its control over Indian education programs and child nutrition programs...

The turf battles had narrowed down to just two—nutrition and Indian education—and had shifted away from the Committee to the full Senate and House Committee. The two groups were busy plotting new strategy to block the transfers.

In New Orleans that week, the American School Food Service Association. held its annual convention. Lobbyists Ken Schlossberg and Gerry Cassidy pushed through a resolution strongly condemning our Committee's action.

Senator Percy's staff worked energetically to round up cosponsors for his yet-to-be-filed amendment on the Senate floor.

Indians began a two-pronged effort to lobby all U.S. senators and the House GovOps Committee. In the Senate, they would work with Senator Stevens and his staff to drum up support for his floor amendment striking the transfer from our bill. "I shall oppose the transfer until the concerns of the Indian people have been met," Stevens vowed in a Senate floor speech.

*   *   *

As the Committee voted to report out the ED bill, House and Senate leaders were meeting to draw up their agenda for the 10 weeks remaining in the congressional session.

On the "must" list: 13 regular appropriations bills, 56 reauthorizations for expiring programs, and an additional eight top priority measures that included hospital cost containment, civil service reform, labor law reform, and Humphrey-Hawkins full employment bill.

Then there was the "special interest" list—those bills the President wanted but were assigned a lower priority. There rested the Department of Education.

Our delay in moving the bill to the Senate floor was the principal reason. Already, July was half over. We still had the bill to polish and a report to write. Seeing all that remained to be done, the congressional leadership decided ED would be a long shot.

*   *   *

Marilyn and I sat down at our typewriters Saturday morning, July 22, and began the onerous job of writing the Committee report on S.991.

Committees of the Congress are required, when they send bills on to the full House or Senate, to file a *report* explaining the bill, its provisions, its purposes, its costs, and its complete text as agreed on by the Committee. The report is also used to justify the bill, a formal sales brochure, and to set forth the Committee's intent.

Intent is most important. Often, it is said House and Senate committee reports have the "force of law." They comprise an additional, more extensive set of directions to the bureaucrats who will implement the laws. And, courts often look to committee reports for guidance in their rulings as to whether Congress intended certain things to happen or not happen in enacting a statute.

So far as we could determine, no records existed of previous committee reports on a Department of Education bill. Ours would be the first; we would be cutting new ground. The task to us was truly monumental. All the knowledge and data we had accumulated in the past year-and-a-half would be synthesized into a readable, 150-page text.

We would spend more than a week writing and rewriting the report. Marilyn and I spent as many as 10 hours each day writing and consulting each other.

The first draft went routinely to Senator Ribicoff. To our complete surprise, he read it. More than that, the Senator went through it with a red pencil.

Ribicoff took special interest in the section I had written on "The Need for a Department of Education." Generally, his editing toned down some of my rhetoric. He had an eagle eye for any passages that could be remotely construed as asserting federal control or dominance in education.

Before he went to the Senate floor with the bill, Ribicoff wanted to know all the nuances and have the facts and arguments straight in his mind. He was also well aware that if the other 99 U.S. senators made any preparations at all for floor debate, they would likely first read the Committee report.

*　　*　　*

"DEPARTMENT OF EDUCATION ORGANIZATION ACT OF
1978

REPORT
of the
COMMITTEE ON GOVERNMENTAL AFFAIRS
UNITED STATES SENATE

to accompany
S.991

TO ESTABLISH A DEPARTMENT OF EDUCATION AND
FOR OTHER PURPOSES"

...the report began.

"The Committee...to which was referred the bill S.991...recommends that the bill, as amended, do pass."

The first section stated the "Purposes" of the bill, "...to make the federal education effort more effective and coordinated," etc.

I had divided the "Need" section into five parts. First, "education is important to the nation," where I wrote that "Democracy depends for its very existence on a highly educated citizenry. And because the people are involved in decision-making at all levels of government in the United States, education is and should be of vital concern to federal, state, and local governments." Second, "the troubled state of American education" discussed the prevalent problems, such as declining SAT scores, etc. Third, an indictment of HEW. "...The Committee finds that the overall mission of HEW has changed so substantially since its formation 25 years ago that education is almost out-of-place in that Department." Another "need" reason was the "scattered, fragmented federal education effort." The report noted there were 300 programs in 40 agencies. S.991, it said, "will achieve a significant amount of consolidation," transferring more than 170 programs to ED. The last part talked about the "importance of Cabinet status for education." "...Cabinet officers carry weight in Washington. They can bring problems to light easily."

In the report's third section, I traced the 125-year history of the bill. It began with Congress's 1867 passage of a bill creating a "non-Cabinet" Department of Education as part of Reconstruction following the Civil War, a tiny agency that existed only a year, later demoted to a bureau and placed in the Interior Department. President Calvin Coolidge, in a 1923 message to Congress, considered education "a fundamental requirement of national activity which is worthy of a separate department and a place in the Cabinet." Meanwhile, the bureau became an "Office of Education," and was transferred to the Federal Security Agency when established in 1939 by President Franklin Roosevelt. It stayed there until 1953, when it became the "E" in HEW, created through an Eisenhower reorganization plan. The federal education effort grew from $400 million then to more than $10 billion today, prompting more interest in ED. Senator Ribicoff attracted much attention on introducing his first bill in January

1965. Democratic presidential candidate George McGovern supported ED in his 1972 campaign. And then, in 1976, Jimmy Carter's rise to the presidency.

After that came a lengthy portion entitled "Areas of Discussion." Functions of various offices were specifically laid out. Each of the major transfers were discussed extensively and justified.

In terms of legal impact, perhaps the most important part was the "Section-by—Section Analysis." Here, we wrote what we thought each section of the bill said and what we wanted it to do. For example, in the principal officers section, I slipped in a sentence stating "the Committee's belief that Indian tribes must be involved in the selection" of the assistant secretary for Indian education. And, the report recommended the Secretary of Education look into setting up boards of education to govern the DOD and BIA schools.

As required, the Congressional Budget Office estimated the cost of the bill. CBO calculated it would go from $3.3 million in ED's first year to $11.1 million in its fourth year.

Following that, the text of the approved bill as reported was presented, along with the changes in existing law.

On the Senate floor August 9, Senator Ribicoff filed the report. S.991, "as reported," was instantly placed on the official calendar, ready to be taken up by the full United States Senate.

*   *   *

As we labored on the report, and as PRP and NEA staff concentrated on the House Committee, Senator Percy's staff was finding it remarkably easy in persuading senators to cosponsor the draft amendment to drop child nutrition on the Senate floor.

Percy filed his amendment August 1 with the Senate bill clerk. *There were 48 cosponsors!* We were caught totally off guard. Neither

NEA nor PRP had done any lobbying to offset the agriculture/nutrition groups' work.

The next day, Percy added two more names to his list, bringing the total to 51—more than half the Senate. In the following week, four more senators cosponsored the amendment.

We had lost the school lunch transfer. Percy's men skillfully took advantage of our distractions. They felt tricked and out-maneuvered at our mark-up. Now, they had their revenge.

*   *   *

All the while, across Capitol Hill, House Government Operations Committee staffers were working around-the-clock organizing hearings. The Department of Education had become a harried, two-track effort.

At 10:00 a.m., Monday morning, July 17, Chairman Jack Brooks, cigar in hand, gaveled the first subcommittee hearing to order. Brooks sat in his highback swivel chair at his special podium, towering top and center over the many other representatives who filled seats at the long, elevated, two-tiered wooden dais stretching from one side of the House hearing room to the other. A giant American eagle bas-relief, taken from the United States seal, projected from the back wall behind the audience.

"We are anxious to work with you in seeing that H.R. 13343 is reported at the earliest opportunity so that the new Department may become a reality in the 95th Congress," lead-off witness NEA President John Ryor told Brooks from the witness table several feet below.

"Does an expansion of the number of Cabinet officers bother you?," Rep. Benjamin Rosenthal, New York City Democrat, asked the NEA leader. Rosenthal's district was entirely AFT territory, and he would become a staunch opponent of ED.

Ryor noted Congress had recently established Departments for Transportation and Energy. "Surely education is as important a function to this national government...

House members seemed obsessed with the federal control of education issue. The PTA, school boards, and state chiefs discounted it. The chiefs' witness argued there was "a greater threat" in education being spread around 40 agencies than by "focusing that responsibility in one place." Illinois Republican Rep. Tom Corcoran suggested the control issue was "the major roadblock to passage." Higher ed lobbyist Charles Saunders asked the subcommittee to insert "explicit language" prohibiting federal control in the bill.

By the second day of House hearings, July 20, the lack of enthusiasm was manifest. It was an election year, and a jammed congressional agenda was keeping the congressmen bottled up in Washington more than they could stand. And now, as they saw it, the President decided at the last minute to slip in one more big bill, one more excruciating headache.

Supporters were tired and huffy. "Everybody so far supports the department but doesn't want his program included," complained Ranking Republican Frank Horton (N.Y.) "…If you pick it to pieces, it is not going to be effective, so why then create the new department?"

Opponents were ready to pounce. Arch-conservative Illinois Republican John Erlenborn hit up the "political decisions of rewarding one interest group" with a Cabinet department. "…(It) would signal an ever-expanding and deepening (federal) role in educational decision-making…," he charged. The six-term Congressman was a tenacious, natural enemy of the education lobby, one who felt Washington should stay out of education.

Brooks's hearing room was full of Indians. "The rapidity with which this legislation is being pushed through Congress is frightening to tribes," one testified. "We have spent 100 years sensitizing (BIA)," Patricia Locke asserted on behalf of the tribal chiefs. "…We can't take another 100 years to sensitize a new department."

Closing the day, a panel of academics denounced the NSF science education transfer.

On the third day, July 31, civil rights groups went before Brooks's subcommittee to warn the new ED might resist "aggressive" civil rights enforcement. They demanded the new office and assistant secretary for civil rights be insulated from political pressures and be directly accountable to Congress (To lower the heat, NEA was lobbying House Committee members to accept their demands.)

Handicapped groups tried to sell the Reps on transferring vocational rehabilitation programs. Their leader, Dr. Frank Bowe, delivered his own statement, despite his deafness. "Rehabilitation basically is an education-related activity," he said. His impressive testimony turned many congressmen around.

AFL-CIO chief lobbyist Andrew Biemiller made a special Capitol Hill appearance to oppose the Brooks bill. Unable to stop the ED steamroller in the Senate, the AFT and AFL had decided their best chance to kill the bill was in the House. "We see no compelling need for this proposal," he said. Biemiller's appearance worried us, for the more the huge labor organization got into this battle, the harder it would be to pass the bill.

"It is great to be fighting shoulder to shoulder with you for a change," Erlenborn said, grinning ear to ear. There were chuckles in the audience. The AFL considered the Republican one of the most anti-labor members of Congress.

A collection of agriculture and nutrition groups filled the witness table, including many of the same faces we had seen on the Senate side. They attacked the Ribicoff Committee compromise to leave surplus commodity distribution in USDA. "Now the schools would be faced with a split jurisdiction," one claimed. "What kind of coordination is that?" Another noted Ribicoff exempted Head Start because it was working well in its present location. "We think the same logic applies to the child nutrition programs," the witness said.

That afternoon, NEA teachers roamed the House office buildings' hallways to reinforce support and lobby. Just two more days of hearings remained, and Brooks would hold a "quick" mark-up session shortly after, that was the plan. The NEA effort wasn't extensive. Through the hearings, confidence was abundant. Everyone assumed Jack Brooks and his people had everything under control, that he would get out a bill with most transfers intact.

Brooks's Committee came back the following morning, the first day of August, for its fourth hearing.

Rep. Shirley Chisholm, the first witness, voiced her intention to "forcefully and vociferously" oppose ED. This came as no surprise, considering the black Rep's New York City district was entirely AFT country. "While others may choose to debate this issue in terms of lofty and admirable ideals…," she spoke loudly into her microphone, "I find it extremely difficult to disassociate formation of this department from its onerous political origins." Audible groans came from the audience. People knew her political motivations.

The rest of the day, a stream of Carter Administration officials showed up to back the bill and the transfers within.

Transition costs would be absorbed through "existing program resources," OMB Director Jim McIntyre assured a skeptical, cost-conscious panel. He predicted management efficiencies would result from consolidation in the long run. "The Department of Education will not substantially increase federal personnel," he claimed, and would have fewer supergrade positions than any other Cabinet department.[24]

---

[24] Supergrade positions were those in the top three levels of the civil service (GS 16-18), reserved for administrative personnel and program directors.

"Now, Mr. McIntyre, we have developed a new love affair in the hearings," Brooks said later with a straight face. "The Bureau of Indian Affairs now is deeply appreciated, widely respected and loved by the American Indians in this country and I have always thought they previously had some minor differences."

Snickers came from the audience. McIntyre smiled. Brooks freely used humor and ribbing in running his Committee.

"They were fighting like the Turks and the Greeks for about 200 years," he went on, "but we find in this bill we have brought them together...

"Despite that love affair..., do you feel it is essential that we transfer Indian education to the Department of Education?"

"Yes I do," McIntyre curtly responded. "...I will be glad to elaborate."

"It is not necessary," Brooks told him. The audience laughed.

John Erlenborn waited eagerly to question McIntyre. "I think one of the campaign promises the President made that found the most responsive chord across the United States was his promise to reduce, reduce the size of this overwhelming federal government," the Republican boomed from the dais. "...Instead we are creating new department, new agencies, new functions...".

McIntyre made clear ED was also a campaign pledge. "Apparently people approved that. He was elected."

Erlenborn continued his attack with other Carter appointees. He said Secretary Califano deserved "team player of the year award" for publicly backing "this rotten idea" when he really opposed it.

"He has fully supported it and not as a rotten idea," HEW Undersecretary Hale Champion retorted abruptly. On this score, Erlenborn was right, but Champion resented his partisan manipulation of the "rotten" situation both he and Califano were in.

Erlenborn replayed the same line with USDA Assistant Secretary Carol Foreman, Interior Undersecretary James Joseph, and Defense Department official I.M. Greenberg over the transfer of their turf.

More opposition witnesses queued up before the House subcommittee in its last hearing, August 2.

The U.S. Catholic Conference reiterated its concern that an Education Department would intrude into local and state policymaking.

Greg Humphrey represented the AFT. "What you have got is a bunch of organizations who bang together some testimony as best they can with relatively short notice, coming up here and ranting on you," the lobbyist contended. "…I do not think you have had any real examination of the issues involved in a federal department…".

Humphrey tried shooting down the notion that AFT opposed the bill simply because NEA supported it. "We achieved and arrived at this position long before the current battle between the organizations was exacerbated…," he said.

A short while later, Brooks adjourned his express hearings and informed the audience, "We will continue meeting tomorrow morning at 9 o'clock." With time running out, the House Chairman was taking his ED bill directly to the mark-up stage.

*   *   *

It was 9:07 a.m., Thursday, August 3 when Jack Brooks whacked his gavel. You could tell he was in a hurry, all businesslike and efficient. In a few minutes, he pushed a reorganization plan through the subcommittee mark-up to clear the way for ED.

Brooks was up against a critical deadline. The Speaker of the House, Tip O'Neill, warned all committee chairmen that bills reported after Friday, August 11 would not be considered on the House floor before the early October adjournment.

The audience seats in the extra-wide hearing room were filled with lobbyists and staff. PRP's dapper congressional chief, Terry Straub, socialized with subcommittee members.

Sitting behind Brooks were his two top Committee aides, Bill Jones and Elmer Henderson. Jones, 38, the Committee's chief counsel, was a native Texan and had worked many years for Brooks. Henderson, 65, was a mild-mannered black man with long experience in Washington.

"There has to be an overwhelming, clear-cut case for the need for creating a new agency," Rep. Rosenthal told the crowd, and the proponents had demonstrated "an abysmal failure of proof" that ED was needed.

"This has been a hurry-up proposition," Ranking Republican Frank Horton complained. "But I do support the concept." Horton's support was vital in moving the bill. NEA had supported him in past elections.

Brooks introduced several minor amendments for consideration.

Rosenthal offered an amendment giving the Office for Civil Rights all the powers demanded by the civil rights groups.

"We're giving new substantive authority?," Horton asked.

"Exactly," Rosenthal replied. "…It's what we're doing by the creation of the Department of Education. No sense in pussy-footing around…".

Rosenthal's amendment was adopted by voice vote. NEA and the White House hoped it would at least buy neutrality from the rights groups on ED.

That unsubstantiated feeling of many House members that somehow ED would expand federal control or authority over education got a boost the following Sunday in a strategically-timed *Washington Post* analysis.

---

[25] So strong were Epstein's feelings that at one point during the 1978 ED debate he informally lobbied his friend, House committee member Rep. Henry Waxman (D-Cal.) during a lunch they had together. Waxman voted against the ED bill at every opportunity.

The headline said it all: "Uncle Sam's Growing Clout in the Classroom/Creating a New Department is a Backdoor Way to Establish a U.S. Responsibility for Education Itself."

Co-author *Post* writer Noel Epstein had intense, negative vibes about ED and was partly the driving force behind the paper's opposition to it.[25] The article was also written by education specialist David Brenneman of the Brookings institution.

They argued that with "virtually no public debate," ED had "the potential to transform the way education is governed in the United States."

"…This, it must be emphasized, does not mean that a Cabinet-level department would be designed to lead to federal 'control' of education," Epstein/Brenneman reasoned in the article. "…The question is how much federal influence there should be over education, how much say in education priorities, in standards, and in other education decisions. This can be determined in many ways—where Washington puts its money and where it withholds funds, what requirements come with the money…". That influence had "burgeoned in the past decade."

They believed a new ED would become a stronger tool in future political pressure to increase this "influence."

But, their basic theme was faulty. The establishment of a Cabinet department does not, in itself, mean new federal policies, authorities or powers are created. The Cabinet secretary is limited in the exercise of authority by the laws he administers—laws which are enacted by Congress and agreed to by the President.

We aimed to have one federal education leader who would have to account for federal education programs—a tool for better controlling and defining the federal role in education. We believed a Cabinet secretary of education, operating from a new base of strength *within the Washington power system*, would have more clout to approach another administrator on his turf and point out conflicting or duplicating, rules, regulations, and paperwork.

Epstein/Brenneman's article grossly overinflated what we feared all along might rear its ugly head—the false issue of a U.S. Department of Education somehow tearing apart the nation's proud tradition of local-ly-controlled schools.

*   *   *

Gail Bramblett had spent all the next day making the rounds in the House office buildings. At 5:00 that afternoon, she stopped by Rep. Corcoran's office to chat about the ED mark-up the next morning.

"Have you seen all the amendments for tomorrow?," Corcoran's staffer asked the NEA lobbyist.

"What amendments?," she asked. Gail could feel the color drain from her face. *Amendments?*

Aghast, she ran out of the office to a nearby Longworth Office Building open-air telephone booth. Frantically, she dialed her NEA government relations office, hoping to catch her superiors before they left for home. The phone rang and rang. No one answered. NEA's leaders would spend a quiet night at home, assuming Jack Brooks had everything under control. The Carter and NEA people had total confidence in Brooks. Perhaps too much confidence.

All was not well in his Committee and subcommittee. There were probably enough votes to get the bill out of committee, but counts on the individual transfers were sketchy and worrisome. In preliminary readings, there were many negative votes on school lunch, DOD schools, and Indian education. The *Post* article spurred ED opponents on to doing whatever they could to delay reporting the bill. The situation called for more work.

Mad and frustrated, Gail took the phone receiver and threw it in the air. The House had adjourned for the day, her colleagues were gone. On the verge of tears, she went home.

*   *   *

At 9:45 Tuesday morning, the temperature outside had already passed the 80° mark and was headed for the mid-90°s, the typical Washington summer humidity stifling.

Inside the House Committee hearing room, things were getting equally hot and sticky. Jack Brooks had just the remaining four days to push the ED bill through both his subcommittee and full Committee and still meet the Speaker's deadline.

Immediately after gaveling the August 8 subcommittee mark-up session to order, Brooks brought up the Indian transfer. Rosenthal proposed an amendment deleting it entirely.

A voice vote was taken. "In the opinion of the chair," Brooks spoke slowly, looking at the members to his right, then his left, "the ayes have it and the amendment is agreed to."

I buried my head in my hands. Brooks had just let go the Indian transfer as if it were a hot potato.

Hardly fazed, the Chairman moved on to Florida Democrat Don Fuqua's amendment to drop the nutrition/school lunch transfer. Bypassing debate, Brooks went directly into his vote-call routine. "In the opinion of the chair, the ayes have it and the amendment is agreed to." He said it all so quickly he hardly drew a breath.

I sat in the audience with my mouth dropped wide open, trying to comprehend it all. Brooks had obviously calculated that the only way to move the ED bill as expeditiously as possible to the House floor was to discard all the controversial provisions. In ten minutes' time, Brooks surrendered what we spent months trying to attain and hang onto.

Next, Erlenborn offered an amendment to strike the entire DOD schools transfer. "…There is a clear and present danger if we put a Department of Education in the business of operating schools," he argued. Brooks refuted Erlenborn's arguments, believing ED would be in a better position to keep up with education and the professional development of teachers.

"The question is on the adoption of the amendment by Mr. Erlenborn...," Brooks cut off the debate. The Chairman ruled the noes had it, and the amendment was defeated.

I was relieved.

Rep. Tom Corcoran proposed including a provision prohibiting federal control of education.

"The gentleman is making a sincere effort...," Erlenborn commented, "but no matter how well-intentioned, he will not be successful." He quoted at length from Sunday's *Washington Post* piece.

The subcommittee adopted Corcoran's prohibition by voice vote.

Fuqua offered an amendment deleting the NSF science education transfer. He also served as the second-ranking Democrat on the House Science and Technology Committee. It was adopted on a show of hands, 5-2.

This is really getting out of hand, I worried. Three major transfers—science education, Indian education, and child nutrition—cut from the House bill.

Corcoran proposed that the Labor Department's youth and job training programs be transferred. Our blood pressure elevated, knowing if adopted, the amendment could easily kill the bill. Brooks called for a vote. "Apparently, the noes have it," he ruled. Erlenborn demanded a roll call vote. All the Democratic members were joined by Republican Horton in voting against the Corcoran amendment, 7-2.

Erlenborn wanted to tamper some more with the bill. He offered an amendment striking the Intergovernmental Advisory Council on Education, labeling it "the national school board." A PRP invention, the Council would consist of state and local officials and could only advise the Secretary. He again demanded a roll call vote and was the only member voting for it.

The vocational rehabilitation groups persuaded Corcoran to offer the amendment consolidating handicapped programs. "Secretary Califano feels very strongly that it should be there (in HEW)," Brooks responded, waving in his hand a letter from Califano. Using his proxies, Brooks pulled off a defeat of the voc rehab transfer, 6-3. Only Republicans voted for it.

Finally, at almost noontime, the subcommittee was ready to vote on sending the bill to the full Committee. The clerk called out the 11 names. Only three were recorded against the bill—Rosenthal, John Conyers (D-MI.), and Erlenborn.

Brooks's staff made immediate preparations for an early morning full Committee mark-up the next day. If the subcommittee was any indication, the ED bill was in for rough times.

*　　*　　*

More than 30 U.S. Representatives filtered into the House GovOps hearing room shortly after 9 o'clock, Wednesday morning, August 9. The Committee had 43 members, a motley group of liberals, moderates, and conservatives from wealthy, blue-collar, rural and urban areas. They included a host of colorful and sometimes loud personalities in competition with each other.

Brooks began by noting the new version of his bill approved by the subcommittee did not transfer Head Start, Indian education, child nutrition, nor science education. "Even without these programs the new Department will be of considerable size: $13.5 billion and 15,000 employees, making it one of the major departments," he said.

The Committee then went into a filibuster state. Opponents forced verbatim reading of the entire bill by the chief clerk. We also expected they would try to amend it to death. Their objective: stall until well past the Speaker's deadline of Friday, August 11.

Our detractors picked apart the bill word-by-word. They spent almost an entire day on the purely rhetorical "Findings and Purposes" section, demanding time-consuming roll call votes on every innocuous little amendment. Armed with his pile of proxies, Brooks fought them off.

"...You can look at this language, and here is the congressional intent: the federal government is going to be leading education, going to be deciding how educational systems will be designed," Erlenborn preached to the members. That was the point of most amendments.

That afternoon, Brooks started throwing out the hot stuff again. He offered an amendment dropping most of the "findings" section. "The language was never intended to expand the federal government's role in education," he told the audience. The Committee adopted the amendment with a chorus of "ayes."

Hours later, the Committee clerk proceeded to read aloud the bill's second title. A Democrat asked that it be considered as read.

"I object," New York conservative Republican Rep. John Wydler said flatly and loudly.

The reading went on for a long while—ten pages' worth. Erlenborn then offered an amendment to delete the section establishing an office to administer the DOD overseas schools.

"...The Administration felt that the children would be better off if they had the Department of Education running their schools instead of the colonels and generals," Brooks argued against Erlenborn.

Erlenborn pointed out that overseas military bases were "total integrated communities" where DOD also provided food, medical care, and postal service.

The roll call vote was close. In the end, 19 members voted against Erlenborn, 17 for. The Illinois Republican managed to pick up nine Democratic votes, but he still lost.

At 4:20 p.m., Brooks called it quits for the day. Under the Chairman's orders, the sleepy-eyed House Committee came right back in at 9:15 the next morning, Thursday, August 10.

South Carolina Democrat John Jenrette first off brought up his amendment transferring the voc rehab program—the same language tried earlier in subcommittee and defeated. Jenrette wanted to punish Califano for the HEW Secretary's campaign against smoking and criticism of tobacco price supports.

Brooks again noted Califano's opposition.

Wydler couldn't resist joshing Brooks on this one. "Up to this point, we have been hearing various groups who want to get out of this proposed department...Now we have a group who apparently wants to get in...You want to keep them out," he motioned to the Chairman. "Why not let them in?"

Brooks called for a voice vote. "In the opinion of the chair, the ayes have it," he announced. After some lobbying by the handicapped groups and NEA, Brooks relented and let it pass.

Nevertheless, Wydler asked for a roll call vote—an embarrassingly obvious harassment.

"A roll call is requested by the distinguished, able, and perceptive gentleman from New York, Mr. Wydler," Brooks fumed.

The voc rehab amendment passed, 29-9. Jenrette flashed a satisfied smile.

A sixth grader could have easily deduced by now the bill was slipping from Brooks's control. The next move proved that. Rep. Corcoran, in a surprise motion, asked to reconsider the vote on Erlenborn's DOD schools amendment. It was clear Erlenborn had lobbied and turned around enough of his colleagues to win a second try at dropping "his" DOD schools.

The clerk called the roll. The room was hushed. Everyone knew it would be close. The vote to reconsider was 20-18, with nine Democrats joining the Republicans in supporting Erlenborn. Among them were a few surprises: Cardiss Collins, a black Rep from Chicago, Connecticut's Toby Moffett, John Jenrette, New Jersey's Andy Maguire, and Barbara Jordan, a respected black Texan.

Jack Brooks sensed he was in serious trouble. "…The people opposed to this (transfer) are opposed to the bill. They are trying to torpedo it. They would be for any amendment you could dream up in your wildest imagination, and this is the simple fact.

"…The Defense Department spends $127 billion, and this is $350 million, a mere drop in the bucket to (DOD). They are not vitally concerned with education. Everybody knows that." Brooks was about as insistent and emotional as he ever got. His appeal was a message to his Democrats that he wanted this vote and this transfer. It was an appeal for loyalty.

As he listened, Toby Moffett sat up in his chair with a quizzical expression on his face. Moffett was no friend of the military establishment. Brooks's point that DOD was not interested in children of military families struck a responsive chord in Moffett's mind. He leaned over and discussed the issue with his good friend Rep. Andy Maguire, another liberal.

Moffett announced he'd switch his vote. He decried federal bureaucrats: "I think it might be good for people who are making education policy to get out and be able to run programs."

Erlenborn grinned, masking his displeasure at losing Moffett.

Another roll call vote was ordered, this time on the amendment to delete the DOD schools office. The hearing room was edgy. Throughout, the margin stayed even. Moffett voted no and his friend Maguire sided with him. Then, the clerk announced, 20 ayes, 21 noes. Moffett had made the one-vote difference possible, turning a sure win into a bare defeat for Erlenborn.

Later, a move by conservatives to take out of the bill the expanded authorities of the Office for Civil Rights was rejected, 29-5. Erlenborn tried convincing the Committee the Labor Department's job training programs (CETA, etc.) should be transferred, but was defeated, 25-6.

Due to House floor debate on a tax bill, Brooks had to recess at one o'clock that afternoon. The Committee could not reconvene again until Monday morning.

The ED bill would miss the Speaker's deadline.

Erlenborn was full of smiles as he got up from his seat. His strategy was working. "Delays May Doom Carter's Proposed Education Agency," headlined a *Washington Post* story the next morning. "...With enough delay, it might be too late for the leadership to schedule the bill for floor action," the story said.

Already, nearly 70 other bills were stacked up, waiting for Rules Committee approval. Only seven weeks remained before final congressional adjournment.

*   *   *

Marilyn and I passed the time away working on the mass of briefing and background papers, speeches, arguments and counter-arguments that would be needed on the Senate floor. We would have to wait until Senator Byrd, the majority leader, called up the bill.

Monitoring the House Committee proceedings persuaded me the best defense was preparation and covering bases. I decided I'd talk with as many Senate education legislative assistants as time allowed. Going down the list of 100 senators, I began making phone calls and personal visits, extolling the virtues of the bill and its transfers. I made many friends in the process, and also learned what our opponents were planning to do to us on the Senate floor. I spotted problem senators in advance and was able to warn NEA and the Carter people to do something about them.

Marilyn negotiated with those senators who planned to amend the bill the time they would need on the floor for debate. Carefully and fairly worked-out time agreements were essential to clearing a bill for Senate floor action, to preventing a filibuster, and to controlling the debate.

*　　*　　*

In more humid, hot surroundings, the tired House Committee Monday morning stumbled into its hearing room in the spacious, modern Rayburn Office Building.

ED supporters and fence-sitters had a letter from the Vice President waiting for them when they arrived at work. "Creating a Department of Education this year is an important priority of our Administration," it reminded them.

The Chairman opened his mark-up renewing once more his request that the bill be considered as read.

"I object, Mr. Chairman," Erlenborn said, then immediately again proposed an amendment to axe the Intergovernmental Advisory Council on Education. He lost on a roll call vote, 23-9.

Conservatives wanted the bill amended to establish an office to which Indian programs would be transferred. Their capricious motives were self-evident. Most of Brooks's Democrats helped to defeat the amendment, 18-12.

The Committee debated for 20 minutes an Erlenborn amendment striking a mundane membership requirement for the intergovernmental council. Adding insult to injury, Erlenborn demanded a roll call vote, losing 24-9.

There were more whimsical amendments. Brooks couldn't stand it. "Why don't we just accept the amendment and not talk about it anymore," he griped to one opponent.

The Committee managed to move on to the bill's third title, the transfers portion. The Clerk began to read it. Brooks interrupted, asking unanimous consent that it be considered as read and open for amendment.

A chorus of conservatives shouted, "Objection."

As the clerk continued reading, a round of frustrated sighs could be heard in the room.

At noon, a weary Jack Brooks called it the end of another tiring day, and ordered his members back the following morning. One thing was clear: he was prepared to stay with the bill for as long as it took to report it out.

9:18 Tuesday morning, August 15, Brooks smacked his gavel hard, bringing order to his hearing room. *The sixth mark-up.*

"I ask unanimous consent that the bill be considered as read...," the Chairman bellowed.

"I object, Mr. Chairman," Erlenborn said with pleasure. It appeared the stalling tactics would continue. Erlenborn still had a pile of amendments to gut the bill wherever he could. One would strike the transfer of the international education program, which should have routinely gone to ED.

"I think that this would do no basic harm to the legislation and I would see no objection to it," Brooks said, tossing out yet another program to mollify his opponent.

A Republican offered another amendment that would transfer Indian education to ED. (The previous amendment set up an Indian office.) Members tired of voting over and over on the same issues. The Committee decided, 19-14, against the Indian amendment. Indian education would stay out of the House bill.

Erlenborn proposed an amendment dropping the DOD schools transfer. (Last time, his amendment would have cut out the office.)

"Mr. Chairman, this amendment has been offered before," an irritated Frank Horton complained. "...We have had it amply debated on two or three occasions, both in subcommittee and the full Committee...I move the previous question."

It was highly unusual for a Ranking Republican to challenge one of his own party on a procedural question, but tempers were flaring.

Erlenborn demanded a roll call vote. This time he lost more votes—24-16. The DOD schools were safely in the bill.

More votes followed on keeping various programs in or out. The Committee finally finished with the transfer title.

"Title four," Brooks stated. "The clerk will read."

Suddenly, Erlenborn interrupted. "Mr. Chairman, I ask that this title be considered as read and open for amendment."

"Without objection," Brooks smiled.

Erlenborn must have figured he had stalled long enough, or his antics were going so far they might cause irreparable damage to his personal relationships with other Committee members.

A major blockage out of the way, the Committee considered and disposed of several boilerplate amendments quickly.

Rep. Robert Walker, conservative Pennsylvania Republican and avowed ED opponent offered an amendment prohibiting the Secretary of Education from using quotas in affirmative action programs, a touchy civil rights issue. Walker demanded a roll call vote, and was turned back, 25-9.

Brooks later received consent to dispense with the formal reading of the remaining titles.

California Republican Rep. Paul McCloskey had an amendment requiring that before ED came into existence, OMB certify that the actual costs and personnel be less than that of those functions and offices going into ED. The amendment was squashed, 23-15.

McCloskey offered a motion to recommit the bill to the Committee, a last effort to prevent it from being reported to the full House. "To set up a Cabinet office is inherently to suggest that the federal government will be making policy decisions in education," he argued.

Brooks said education problems were so serious they warranted attention and visibility from the President's Cabinet. "I will guarantee you that if you had three little children, like I do, you would know it was serious," he told his colleagues.

On a roll call vote, the McCloskey motion lost, 28-9.

"Mr. Chairman, I move that the Committee report the bill to the House with the recommendation that it do pass," Horton said.

Relieved sighs swept through the crowd as the Committee roll was called for the last time. We anxiously listened to the vote.

The clerk announced the result: 27 votes for ED, 15 against. Four Republicans voted for the bill; seven Democrats cast ballots against. A good strong vote. We were very happy.

The feisty, balding Chairman Brooks took his cigar out of his mouth and smiled. He had gone through holy hell for his President.

FOURTEEN

Staying Alive

The next move was up to the Speaker.

Would Tip O'Neill make an exception to his deadline and ask the House Rules Committee to clear ED? Would he then bring the bill to the House floor, pushing aside other important bills in the rush to adjourn by October 1?

"The Administration wants a bill. The Speaker wants a bill. A bill will get to the floor," Jack Brooks proclaimed to reporters shortly after mark-up.

The Chairman might have been a little too confident. O'Neill was highly responsive to two constituencies that wanted ED dead: the AFL-CIO and the Catholics. Joe Califano was a good friend. The growing controversy made him leery of expending precious time and clout on the issue. Most of the House's 435 members did not want to have to deal with it during an election year.

A weighty factor would be how hard Jimmy Carter leaned on Tip O'Neill. The Speaker would wait for the definitive signal from the White

House. But Carter was still juggling many projects—natural gas, civil service reform, tax bills—which the Speaker was steering.

At some point in the next few weeks, the President's lobbyists would probably approach the Speaker, his staff, or both, and say, "The President would very much appreciate the Rules Committee clearing the Department of Education bill...". Rules was the Speaker's clearinghouse.

Even if the Speaker relented and Rules considered ED, there was still no guarantee the Committee would vote affirmatively to send it to the floor. Education groups had all but ignored the panel. NEA sent August 17 an alert notice to its state affiliates asking "urgent action" in lobbying the 16 Rules Committee members. Gail Bramblett expressed some worry about Rules, but seemed to feel Tip O'Neill was "key." Only four or five Rules Committee members were considered hard-core NEA supporters. And, NEA's relations with the Speaker were less than pristine.

Everything was put on hold Friday, August 18, as the House adjourned for three weeks of rest and campaigning. President Carter and his family headed for the Idaho wilderness.

The U.S. Senate, meanwhile, continued in session. We were told to be ready to bring up S.991 "at a moment's notice."

*   *   *

In little more than a week, Jack Brooks rushed to file his Committee report. It covered just 32 pages—the briefest report on a major bill I had ever seen.

The report semi-apologized for the bare-bones department it proposed, but said, "Even so, the Department of Education will be a major unit of the executive branch in size, budget, and responsibility." The "justification" for the new agency was contained in six short paragraphs.

Many Committee members filed additional and dissenting views. Rep John Erlenborn was joined by 10 colleagues in attacking the DOD schools transfer (ED would "view the DOD dependents as laboratory mice"). Five Democrats signed on to a critical statement, convinced that "congressional authority to create Cabinet-level departments should be exercised with careful restraint and only after an overwhelming show of necessity." Rep. Leo Ryan (D-CA.) called it the "worst bill...a hasty, ill-conceived, and poorly-executed attempt at consolidation that will not function." Erlenborn and seven other Republicans submitted a bitterly partisan statement charging the bill was "a political payoff in every sense of the word."

*   *   *

NEA lobbyists spent the last two weeks of August walking the halls of the Senate office buildings. They held special meetings with Senate Republican leaders, and received support for expeditious consideration of the Ribicoff bill. They also visited more than 40 other senators and their staffs, asking support for the bill and for the Indian education transfer.

Meanwhile, PRP staffer Decker Anstrom was burning his shoe leather in Senate hallways. The 27-year-old assistant to Pat Gwaltney had a sharp political mind and cool demeanor. Over a four-week period, he met with every legislative assistant covering the bill for each senator, dropping a pile of background and advocacy papers on their desks.

The major education groups sent one last round of letters supporting S.991 to the senators, including a final one from NEA's "citizen's committee."

I continued behind-the-scenes lobbying of senators and staff on the Indian issue, Marilyn on the science transfer. We were developing, for introduction by Sen. Pete Domenici (R-NM), an amendment to S.991 adding more protections for Indian rights. Science educators mounted a modest campaign against the NSF transfer. Marilyn worried that Sen. Ted Kennedy might propose an amendment to delete it from the bill, but the health and scientific research subcommittee chairman had opposed every other transfer and no doubt felt some ambivalence about chewing at it more.

The giant child nutrition/school lunch transfer was, by now, an embarrassing goner. Six more senators cosponsored the Percy amendment, bringing the total to 61.

The Senate, tired from working long days in the Washington heat, recessed for a week-and-a-half. Senators would return right after Labor Day and work furiously to meet their planned early-October adjournment.

The President cut short his vacation and returned to Washington August 30. There was much work left to be done in preparation for Congress's return. And, as if the man from Georgia hadn't already buried himself deep in too many projects and bills, he would take precious time out for one of the most risky gambles of his Presidency—a summit between himself, Egypt's President Anwar Sadat, and Israel's Prime Minister Menachem Begin. The three world leaders met at Camp David September 5 and settled down to long and arduous negotiations.

At union-sponsored Labor Day picnics around the nation September 4, NEA members approached U.S. representatives and senators to ask their support for House and Senate ED bills. NEA Washington lobbyists spent the succeeding days talking with House Rules Committee staff about scheduling the Brooks bill.

September 1978 *would be the busiest month Washington had ever seen.*

*   *   *

Early Thursday afternoon, September 7, one of Sen. Robert Byrd's floor staffers called our office. "We're hoping to bring up the ED bill shortly." A temporary gap in the Senate schedule cropped up.

Marilyn and I instantly alerted White House and PRP aides, NEA and fellow Senate staffers. Breathlessly, we gathered together our arm-bursting stacks of black notebooks, files, background papers, speeches, etc., and sprinted for the Capitol building.

Hurrying into the Senate Reception Room, we saw many NEA and PRP staff already there. Dozens of lobbyists, concerned with other bills, filled the ornate room with chatter.

Marilyn plunked down her materials, ran to the entrance of the cloakrooms, signed for her temporary floor pass, and trotted carefully past senators to the Senate floor. She had to find one of Byrd's lieutenants to learn the scoop. Simultaneously, PRP's Decker Anstrom manned phones and discussed the situation with White House lobbyists in the unmarked Vice President's office, off the north end of the Reception Room.

In the 15-20 minutes since that first call, Democratic and Republican floor aides had been negotiating in a side room. The Majority Leader had already forced the Senate onto a "multi-track" system, meaning several bills were being considered on the floor, one or more of them set aside to accommodate problems in senators' schedules. Republican staffers resisted adding yet another bill.

Bill Hildenbrand was the biggest stumbling block. "I've got all these holds," the 56-year-old chief Republican floor assistant bristled. Hildenbrand was tough and acerbic, the kind of man a minority party needs to keep the majority in check.

"What holds?" Byrd's and Carter's people wanted to know which senators objected to immediate Senate consideration of ED, and why.

Hildenbrand was vague. Some (Republican) senators are still drafting amendments, he told the Democratic staffers. He tossed out names: "I think Helms has a couple, and Schmitt has a few...".

Byrd's men figured Hildenbrand was simply stalling, and that surprised them because both Republican leaders, Howard Baker and Ted Stevens, favored the ED bill. They weren't sure of Hildenbrand's real motives.

Senator Stevens had not yet returned from Alaska. His amendment to drop the Indian transfer would be the most controversial. Hildenbrand seized on that as the primary reason for not bringing up the ED bill. His resistance was adamant, especially because Stevens was the Republican whip.

Senator Byrd was told the gory details. The serious-minded West Virginian knew the odds were against him and the ED bill. He also knew the President wanted the bill, and the Speaker of the House would not even *consider* scheduling the House bill for floor action unless and until the Senate had passed its version. In addition, Abe Ribicoff was a good and loyal friend to whom he owed much.

There really wasn't time in the jammed Senate schedule, but Robert Byrd had decided he would make the time. Come hell or high water, the U.S. Senate would pass a Department of Education bill before adjourning *sine die.*

Mostly in deference to Stevens, with whom he had to deal on scheduling other remaining major issues, Byrd agreed to wait and try again the following week. But the Majority Leader had sent crystal-clear signals to the Republicans that the bill would be brought up.

Back in the Reception Room, we all gathered in a tight semicircle to discuss the news. Marilyn and I were let down; we'd been fired and primed to hit the Senate floor weeks ago. We had learned one thing, however; the Republicans needed more work. NEA made plans immediately to gear up constituent pressure on them.

* * *

A week later, Gail Bramblett phoned Marilyn from the House Rules Committee. There was urgency in her voice. "We're in trouble over here...".

After weeks of pushing, the Brooks ED bill was scheduled Thursday, September 14. But the Speaker did nothing more than get Rules to consider it. Tip O'Neill didn't lean on any of the 11 Democrats on the panel to approve the rule.

Going in to the small, chandeliered, third-floor Capitol hearing room Thursday afternoon, the NEA lobbyist was alarmed. For the first time, an AFL-CIO lobbyist worked over members asking their vote against granting a rule for the ED bill. The U.S. Catholic Conference also lobbied hard. AFT lobbyists were there, too. Like hungry wolves, they had waited for our most vulnerable crossing. A negative vote in Rules this late in the game would kill us.

Indeed, a quick head count showed the bill was in jeopardy: four hard votes against, six votes in favor. But five Rules Committee members would not commit themselves one way or the other: Florida Democrat Claude Pepper, Illinois Democrat Morgan Murphy, Louisiana Democrat Gillis Long, Massachusetts Democrat Joe Moakley, and Tennessee Republican James Quillen. Each was under tremendous pressure to vote against ED.

Marilyn and I raced across the Capitol plaza and up to the Rules Committee room. Inside, the small, oblong room was packed and stuffy. We met up with Gail and White House lobbyist Terry Straub, and sat together to watch the proceedings. Only members of the House could testify before the Rules Committee. First off, Jack Brooks and GovOps Committee Ranking Republican Frank Horton took the witness seats to ask approval of the rule. They were followed by a string of opposing members: Erlenborn, Dan Quayle (R-IN.), McCloskey, Walker, and others. There was discussion about the political motives of the President, and questions about expanding the federal role in education. Many representatives wondered why the bill could not be delayed until 1979, when Congress would not be so rushed and debate could be more "thorough."

The testimony and questions went on for nearly two hours. Members and lobbyists strolled constantly in and out of the hearing room. During the proceedings, the politicking outside was hot and heavy. At one point, Gail and another NEA lobbyist met in an adjoining room with Rep. James Quillen. Several minutes later, Gail came back and sat beside me.

"Did you get him?," I asked anxiously.

"Yes," she smiled. "He told us to make the check out to 'Quillen for Congress.'"

My mouth dropped wide open. I didn't know if she was joking.

Earlier, she met with Quillen and asked his support for the rule and for ED. "You want me to do something for you," the Tennessean shot back at her, "why don't you do something for me." Republicans in that state envied the extensive assistance NEA had been giving Sen. Howard Baker in his re-election campaign.

NEA has a set procedure for endorsing candidates, Gail explained to Quillen, and we couldn't back you on-the-spot. She said she would see what she could do. She placed a call to the Tennessee Education Association. "I'll take care of it," the TEA executive director told her. He called Quillen, and the congressman a short while later told NEA's Washington lobbyists he would vote for the rule.

Claude Pepper was coming around. Although his district had more AFT than NEA teachers and a large Catholic population, the 78-year-old Florida Democrat was being tugged in the opposite direction by Rep. Mary Rose Oakar (a close personal friend of Marilyn) and by the White House. Rosalyn Carter was scheduled to go soon to a fundraiser for the veteran politician in Florida, but White House aides hinted a "no" vote might darken those prospects.

The Catholics had Morgan Murphy's ear. The four-term Congressman's ward in Chicago was heavily Catholic. The windy city's

Catholic chieftain, Cardinal John Patrick Cody, reportedly asked he oppose the bill and the rule. Murphy was slipping away from us.

Joe Moakley held out the longest. The three-term Bostonian had AFL-CIO and Catholic people crawling all over him. Boston teachers were AFT-affiliated. Terry Straub asked the Speaker's staff for help from the top; Moakley would respond to an appeal from the dean of his state's congressional delegation. O'Neill talked to him.

The Speaker's staff also talked to Gillis Long, who was being pressured to vote negatively by Louisiana's AFT and AFL leaders.

The behind-the-scenes pulling-and-tugging continued up to the last minute. The Rules Committee Chairman gave everyone in the room a 20-minute advance warning on the vote. Lobbyists jumped up to fetch members and corral them back for the big decision, which could have been decided alone by attendance, or lack of it.

At last, the roll was called. The Committee voted 9-5 to clear the ED bill for House floor action. We had picked up Pepper, Long, Moakley, and Quillen. Murphy voted no.

Only a last-minute lobbying blitz by the White House and NEA saved the bill from total disaster.

*   *   *

The next day, Friday, we were called to the Senate floor at one o'clock.

Marilyn and I gathered our stacks of papers and notebooks and jogged to the Capitol, our adrenaline, blood pressure, and nerves hyped.

We dropped our papers in the crowded Senate Reception Room and headed for the floor.

Senator Ribicoff strolled from the cloakrooms and stopped us. "There's a problem," he said with a slight smile. "It seems Stevens objects to bringing up the bill today. From what I can gather, he doesn't want to offer his Indian amendment because there are a number of senators who are out of town."

Gail Bramblett and her NEA colleagues were mad. Gail thought Senator Stevens was holding off as a way of forcing NEA's capitulation on Indian education. Also, other Republican senators still had "holds" on the bill. Gail interpreted that to mean Republican floor staff chief Bill Hildenbrand was still up to his old tricks.

NEA and White House staff spent more than an hour trying to break the deadlock, to find out whether those "holds" really did exist. Hildenbrand refused to talk with them.

Senate passage was supposed to have been easy. The second false alarm made us wonder whether we would win our fierce struggle against the clock.

*   *   *

Saturday morning, I escaped to a friend's cabin in West Virginia and spent the day relaxing and chopping wood.

Marilyn and I worked together all day Sunday preparing for the Senate floor consideration that we *hoped* might come the following week.

The nation's capital continued waiting for word from Camp David, where the Mideast summit had gone into its 12th day. Sunday night, the three leaders flew together by helicopter to the White House at a late hour. In a televised East Room ceremony, Carter stunned the world by announcing Sadat and Begin had agreed to a framework for peace in the Middle East. No one else in modern history had been able to penetrate the concrete wall separating Egypt and Israel.

Jimmy Carter, who had trouble hitting it off as President, suddenly became "competent" and up-to-the-job. His miraculous feat sharply boosted his political stock.

For much of Monday, the Senate continued hacking away at the natural gas act, one of the President's major energy bills. Bills concerning taxes, full employment policy, hospital cost containment, and reauthorization of programs remained to be acted on.

The Senate was convening daily at 10:00 a.m. and recessing often well past dinner time. Late evening sessions through September were common. Old timers remarked that in the history of the Congress, they had seldom seen such frenzied activity and long hours. So many bills would be passed; so many would die.

We spent the day making further refinements in our papers and floor materials. We had no idea when we would be called to the floor again. It could have been any day.

*　　*　　*

Tuesday morning, September 19, 1978. My phone rang at 11:15. "We're on the floor in 15 minutes!," an excited Marilyn blurted out. "Meet you at the elevator."

Nervously, I piled my files and fled down the Dirksen Building hallway, through the subway to the Capitol.

The two of us dashed through the Senate's Reception Room directly to the cloakrooms' front desk, flashing only a jittery smile to our team-players who had already congregated outside.

The cloakroom gatekeeper recognized us. "Department of Education?," they asked. We nodded. "Sign here. They're waiting for you."

In my nervous excitement, I scrawled my signature, clipped on the peach-colored floor pass to the lapel of my jacket, and walked briskly through the quiet cloakrooms.

Gently, both of us swung open the wood and glass doors leading into the Senate chamber. A quick glance showed only five or six senators on the floor.

Ribicoff was already in the well at the desk reserved for senators managing a bill. Next to him stood Robert Byrd. Steps away, Ted Stevens stood at the Republicans' primary well desk.

As Byrd spoke to the presiding officer, Marilyn and I tiptoed to the seats in the well next to Ribicoff and silently arranged our materials.

"Madam President, I now ask unanimous consent that the Senate…proceed to the consideration of Calendar Order No. 1000, S.991, the Department of Education Organization Act…".[26]

I noticed the Majority Leader's styled, coiffed, silver grey hair and the light suit he wore. The West Virginian appeared confident and in control of the proceedings. I found myself looking up to him.

"Is there objection to the request of the Senator from West Virginia?," the presiding officer inquired. No response. "Without objection, it is so ordered."

The bill was officially before the Senate.

"The bill will be stated by title," Senator Allen said in a formal voice from the high-back leather chair up on the elevated center podium.

A Senate clerk sitting at the desk just below the presiding officer flipped on his microphone and pronounced, "A bill, S.991, to establish a Department of Education, and for other purposes."

"Madam President, I ask unanimous consent that the following staffers of the Committee on Governmental Affairs be permitted to remain on the Senate floor during the consideration and votes on S.991: Dick Wegman, Marilyn Harris, Bob Heffernan…," Ribicoff read from a long list we put in his hands.

I spent a partially dazed moment taking in the scene. Some 20 feet above and surrounding us, a hundred hushed spectators gazed down from the visitors' galleries. I could tell many were struggling to recognize famous senators. Directly overhead the President's chair, news

---

[26] Alabama's Sen. Maryon Allen sat in the Senate President's chair. The Constitution assigns the Vice President the post of President of the Senate. But Vice Presidents, busy with other duties, preside only in exceptional circumstances. Democratic senators (members of the majority party) took turns presiding over the Senate hours at a time.

reporters sat peering down at us from rows of wood counters in the press galleries. Embedded in the massive, high, suspended ceiling, brightly-lit glass panes fashioned in the shape of a huge American eagle spewed soft light throughout the cavernous chamber.

The Senate chamber was paneled in rich-looking wood. Rows of 100 small desks lined up neatly on a slightly terraced floor descending down to a well, encircling the presiding officer's seat and its surrounding long desks/counters. Columns of marble framed the President's seat. Plainclothed guards were stationed at each of the five main entrances to the Senate floor.

On both sides of the center well, teams of youthful pages sat on the light blue carpeting, waiting for orders from senators and staff. Senate staffers sat in dark brown couches, pushed up against both corners in back of the chamber.

Dressed in a pressed, brown suit with a designer shirt and gold cuff-links, Ribicoff looked like an old pro, a distinguished member of the Senate club.

"Madam President, for the first time in the history of this body, we are considering legislation to create a separate, Cabinet-level Department of Education," the Senator read from the lengthy opening statement I had written.

"...More than 60 senators—Democrats, Republicans, moderates, liberals, conservatives—have sponsored this legislation. This is not, by any means, a partisan issue.

"...I wish to thank Senator Percy, the ranking minority member of the Governmental Affairs Committee, for his support...".

By now, Percy had arrived with his staff and sat across the aisle from us. Through every minute on the floor, we would make certain either Percy or another supportive Republican was there managing the Republican side, and helping us out wherever possible.

Ribicoff continued for ten minutes reading the statement to an empty Senate chamber. Back in the Senate office buildings, senators and staff listened to the proceedings via a small green speaker box. Occasionally, a senator would stroll in, chat with other senators and staff, or sit at his desk and meditate.

Muriel Humphrey wandered about, offering senators handfuls of M&Ms, which they joyfully gulped down.

To the kid from New England, this was overwhelming. It's hard to sit on the U.S. Senate floor and not feel privileged, or reflect on the momentous debates that reverberated within its walls, and how the course of history was changed and set often through actions decided by sometimes dramatic votes.

"...Federal education programs are too important to be mismanaged or smothered in bureaucracy," Senator Ribicoff read on. He had pinned on a microphone, wired to the desk below.

"We need a Department of Education, and I urge my colleagues to support this measure."

As Ribicoff talked, a clerk with a portable stenotype machine stood nearby, recording his every word for posterity, for the *Congressional Record*.

"Madam President, I suggest the absence of a quorum," Senator Stevens addressed the chair.

"The clerk will call the roll."

Instantly, buzzers sounded throughout the Senate complex, notifying senators of a quorum call on the floor. "Mr. Abourezk...Mrs. Allen...Mr. Anderson,...," a desk clerk routinely called out to the deserted chamber.

Senators, however, would ignore the call. Stevens asked for the quorum call to temporarily lay aside the proceedings, a stalling-for-time tactic.

I had been running back and forth between our desk on the floor and the phones outside in the cloakrooms. While Marilyn stayed with Ribicoff on the floor, I phoned aides in an effort to arrange for certain senators to come to the floor and offer their amendments. Some

were out of the office, at committee meetings, or otherwise indis-
posed to make a quick trip to the floor. Floor managers' staff spend
much of their time coaxing senators, trying to keep things moving on
the floor.

New Mexico Republican Sen. Pete Domenici agreed to come to the
floor and propose the amendment we drew up adding more protections for Indian rights. A respected moderate, Domenici represented
the state with the second largest concentration of Indians in the
country. The Senator rescinded the quorum call and addressed the
chamber in support of the Indian transfer. He noted "Indian people
are split on the issue," and claimed "this amendment addresses the
concerns expressed by Indian tribes and organizations."

Ribicoff and Domenici then read from a script I had written that further clarified our intentions in the transfer, known in Senate parlance as
a *colloquy*.

Barry Goldwater, hearing the Indian debate in his office, came to the
floor and joined in. The 70-year-old conservative and veteran senator,
up to this point, had not involved himself in the ED issue. But he came
from another heavily populated Indian state, Arizona.

Goldwater admitted BIA's handling of education had been "dismal."
He served notice he would vote against ED (no surprise to us), against
the Indian transfer, but for the Domenici amendment because "it is
worth a try."

Senator Stevens returned to the floor. "I shall not oppose the amendment of the Senator from New Mexico, but I want to make clear that it
does not obviate the need for my amendment," he announced. The
Alaska Republican made a deal with Ribicoff that a vote on his amendment would be held off until the following week.

Our political motives behind Domenici's amendment was to make
the Indian transfer more palatable to wavering senators. Stevens could
have called for a roll call vote and turned it into a test vote on his
amendment to strike the entire Indian transfer.

The debate shifted to the BIA transfer itself.

I got Senate Indian Committee Chairman Jim Abourezk to appear on the floor. He gave a stirring defense of the transfer. "…Anytime that anybody says 'We are going to abolish the BIA' or one of its functions, the Indians are the first to rush to their defense.

"The reason is, I think, that the Indians feel the BIA is all they really have. They are pretty vulnerable…

"Anytime the Bureau of Indian Affairs and its very practiced bureaucrats see a threat to their survival, to their jobs, they run to the tribes and say, 'This is tantamount to termination,'" Abourezk continued.

"The word 'termination' to Indians is a word like 'extermination' to Jews…That is the design. That is deliberate."

The South Dakotan's speech was terrific. He was calling a spade a spade.

"…The best thing that can happen…is to transfer education out of the Bureau of Indian Affairs and the hopeless state in which it is found in that agency," the Senator boomed.

Goldwater had sat patiently at his desk listening to Abourezk. He jumped to his feet with a response. "…As bad as the BIA has been,…I have seen disastrous results to education under HEW (which is) under the complete domination of the National Education Association…".

Domenici, tired of the overly-long debate on his little amendment, moved its adoption. The Senate adopted it by simple voice vote.

Senator Stevens stood at his desk a few steps away. We settled back in our seats, in anticipation of a lengthy statement from the Alaskan. It seemed awkward to me to go through the Indian debate one day and hold the vote on another, probably sometime next week. But the Senate works its schedule around its members.

"I know the defects of the BIA…The Indians themselves have been forceful in their criticism of the BIA operations. But to be categorical and to be concise and candid about criticism does not mean they seek to do away with the entity that now is showing responsiveness to their needs," Stevens spoke emphatically.

...The whole point of self-determination is to allow the decisions affecting Indians to be made in the tribal council rooms and not in Washington, D.C.," the second-ranking Republican argued. "Congress jeopardizes that commitment if we allow this transfer against the expressed wishes of the Indian people...".

Domenici stayed around to rebut Stevens. "A decision to leave Indian education within the BIA assumes that the BIA will improve upon its record," he said. "I do not agree with that assumption." Domenici said his amendment put into place adequate safeguards, and the Pueblo Indians in his state were "anxious to try the transfer."

During the debate, Senator Ribicoff was a bit agitated. "Those poor Indians," he confided softly to Marilyn and I. "Nobody wants to try anything new, something that might work."

Even as we talked, Indian leaders roamed the halls of the Senate, lobbying for the Stevens amendment. Many waited for a decision from Ted Kennedy, who had involved himself in the Indian cause during the late 1960s. Liberals usually followed the Indians' position, but if Kennedy supported the transfer, many would find it easier to follow their conscience.

Ribicoff rose to deliver the statement I'd prepared against the Stevens amendment. "The BIA's performance record is a national disgrace," he read. "...How can we expect an agency predominantly concerned with natural resources and land management to have the expertise and ability to improve Indian education?"

The statement revealed the BIA spent $2,000 more per student than the national average, and $1,000 more than the DOD schools scattered worldwide. Ribicoff concluded later, "I hope the Stevens amendment is defeated."

Ribicoff's Republican counterpart, Charles Percy, also spoke against his minority leader's position.

At 1:30 p.m., managers of the natural gas bill asserted their privilege to reclaim the floor. The Senate set the ED bill aside. Marilyn and

I gathered together our papers and left the floor to make way for incoming energy staffers.

We didn't know when we would return.

*   *   *

Out in the Reception Room, the bevy of education and Carter Administration lobbyists sat down together in a corner and concocted plans for getting ED back to the floor ASAP. Using phones in the unmarked Vice President's Capitol office, the lobbyists spoke with senators' staff in an effort to clear the way for considering the bill later that afternoon.

There were problems. Bill Hildenbrand continued to insist that senators still had "holds"—including the Senate's arch-conservative, Jesse Helms, who had been ill and hospitalized. The Majority Leader sent word that time agreements with these and other senators were being negotiated, and that it was risky to proceed without them.

Fed up with Hildenbrand's invention of all sorts of "holds," NEA asked for and got an appointment with the minority leader first thing Wednesday morning, September 20. Tennessee Education Association's executive director flew to Washington on the spur of the moment to attend.

The NEA officials met Howard Baker in his Capitol office. With NEA's help, the top-ranking Republican appeared an easy bet for re-election in November.

Gail Bramblett began the meeting by stressing how much NEA wanted to complete action on the ED bill this year. She also told Senator Baker NEA was interested in insuring that it wasn't perceived as a strictly Democratic bill, that Jimmy Carter did not get all the credit.

But, there seems constantly to be a big problem in getting up the bill on the floor, she complained. "We keep hearing there are holds on the bill, but we can't seem to find out whose holds they are."

Baker frowned and said he didn't know of any holds on the bill. "Let me check with Bill Hildenbrand." The Senator picked up the phone and called the Republican floor staff head to his office. Moments later, Hildenbrand walked in, visibly shaken at the sight of NEA lobbyists in his boss's suite. Baker explained to his staffer NEA was upset at the difficulty in scheduling the Department of Education bill. He asked Hildenbrand if there were any official holds. Hildenbrand answered that there were some "recently," but he would have to "go back and check."

*   *   *

Marilyn and I rushed over to the Senate floor at 10 o'clock Wednesday morning. For some fresh air, we walked the outside route, under the giant trees and through the Capitol's beautifully landscaped grounds. The flag was being hoisted over the Senate side of the Capitol, indicating the Senate was just going into session.

The cloakroom guards, knowing us on sight now, rushed us through clearance for the Senate floor, indicating we were on for sure.

Inside the Senate chamber, we saw Byrd standing by his desk. Only a handful of senators were present.

With our arms juggling heavy bundles of notebooks and files, we quietly walked around the rows of desks to the couches in the far right corner. The ever-vigilant guards motioned to Marilyn and I to sit down. I began to realize their real duty was to make sure staffers did not look like senators on the floor. We were forbidden to stop anywhere on the floor and talk, standing up—except when in conference with a senator.

Soon the Senate finished its "morning business" routine of assorted statements, prayer, approval of the journal, etc. "Mr. President, I ask unanimous consent, now within the framework of the unanimous-consent agreement on the natural gas bill, that the Senate resume consideration of S.991," Byrd addressed the chair.

There was no objection. We were on again.

Byrd, looking around for a floor manager and not seeing one, suggested the absence of a quorum. Marilyn and I transported our papers down to the managing desk in the well.

"Good morning," she told Byrd. "Senator Chiles will be managing the bill, and we understand he's on his way." The Florida Democrat had agreed to fill in for Ribicoff, who had other commitments.

The Majority leader simply nodded.

I took advantage of the pause to search out some Republican staffers and try to clear certain amendments with them. Just as I swung open the door to a Republican cloakroom at the back of the chamber, I saw Bill Hildenbrand in heated conversation with someone else.

"I'd like to take those fuckers at NEA and—," he stopped short, on seeing me.

I walked out post haste, both embarrassed and amused.

Meanwhile, Chiles trudged into the chamber, ready to begin the proceedings.

Senate leaders allowed the ED bill to return to the floor that morning with the understanding only noncontroversial amendments would be gotten out of the way.

First came school lunch/child nutrition. "On behalf of Senator Ribicoff, I request that the Percy amendment be accepted by unanimous consent," Chiles said, looking up at the presiding officer.

And so it was. My mind quickly flashed back to all the battles with the school lunch people and with fiercely turf-protective agriculture lobbyists. Now, we were relinquishing it without a fight.

Chiles then proposed, for Muriel Humphrey, her amendment to rename HEW once the "E" was removed. She wanted to drop the term "welfare." After weeks of negotiations, all parties finally settled on *Department of Health and Human Services*. The amendment was considered and passed in less than one minute. Millions of Americans had become familiar with "HEW." If the ED bill passed, thousands of buildings, papers, rules, regulations, and contracts would suddenly sport "HHS" instead.

Chiles moved right along to another amendment, this one on behalf of Senator Roth. The Delaware Republican proposed a new section installing a ceiling on the number of staff employed by the new department. In the interests of governmental efficiency, we readily agreed to it. We also used it as a trade-off; Roth would be less inclined to offer an anti-busing amendment.

Byrd reentered the chamber with a white piece of paper in hand, a draft time agreement on the bill and remaining amendments that his staff had worked out with the Republicans. The document limited debate on remaining amendments and the bill to so many minutes per proposal, per side. The agreement was adopted.

Lacking further business, ED went off the floor at 12:51 until further notice.

*   *   *

"We have arrived at a critical juncture regarding the Department of Education bill," OMB Director Jim McIntyre told the President's chief lobbyist, Frank Moore, in a memo delivered late that afternoon.

"The House Rules Committee has granted a rule and the House leadership has indicated that it is willing to schedule the bill for floor consideration as soon as the Senate acts...

"In a meeting with Tip Wednesday afternoon, Byrd told the Speaker that he will 'pass the bill next (week)'. Tip now understands the ball is in his court.

"In short, enactment this year is now possible, with the help of your staff...I believe you should contact Speaker O'Neill as soon as possible to reaffirm the Administration's interest in the bill and to ask him to attempt to find time for the bill on the House floor...".

Congress was tightening the vise on Jimmy Carter. At most, there were three weeks left before *sine die* adjournment, translating into less than 20 days of legislative session. The President, still riding high on the crest of popularity and prestige following the Camp David summit, was beginning to realize now that his biggest problem in getting all of his priority bills passed was not Congress, but instead time. His advisors and Cabinet were coming to the same conclusion: many major bills would not make it through the logjam.

Soon, Carter would have to assess the situation, decide which bills would fall into his "must" category, and then figure out a way to break the bad news to groups behind the jettisoned bills. There would be political heat to take either way. Administration officials began posturing frantically, working to convince the chief executive he should intercede with the congressional leadership for saving "their" own special bills.

On ED, Carter was willing to wait-and-see. During a question-and-answer session with editors Friday, September 22 in the Cabinet Room and in an Aliquippa, Pa. town meeting Saturday, the President carried on his promotion of the bill.

"It may not pass this year; I hope it will," he told the town meeting. "But if it doesn't, then I'll be pursuing it again next year."

***

The weekly Whip Notice circulated that weekend to Democratic Senate offices warned of the busy week ahead. The Senate leadership's first priority was to complete action on the natural gas bill. Listed also alongside other priorities was "S.991, Department of Education (complete consideration of)."

"As we approach the hoped-for adjournment date of October 14, the leadership reminds senators that late sessions may be expected daily and Saturday sessions are definite," the notice said.

From this, we gathered our bill probably would not be reactivated on the floor until mid-week.

The last-minute lobbying escalated. Conservative Sen. Harrison Schmitt (R-N.M.) would offer amendments to block the DOD overseas schools and NSF science education transfers. Education groups bombarded the Senate with mail and phone calls against Schmitt's proposals.

I had high hopes we would beat Stevens on the Indian amendment, but the vote counts told us more work had to be done. I counted 39 votes against Stevens, 23 for, and 38 undecided. I could see the liberals were holding off, caught between the Indian's position, Senator Abourezk's strong stand for the transfer, and Ted Kennedy's indecision.

On the bill itself, we were in fine shape. Our day-to-day canvass of the Senate showed, if all senators were present, 70 votes for ED, 9 against, and 12 undecided.

AFT lobbyists were nowhere to be seen; they wrote off the Senate and instead worked the House, where they knew much less effort could kill the bill.

*   *   *

NEA set out to move the ED bill to the House floor. The teacher union asked for and got a chance to push its case in a high-powered meeting with the Speaker Wednesday, September 27.

On arriving in the Speaker's off-limits, second-floor Capitol conference room, NEA President John Ryor and execs Terry Herndon and Stan McFarland were surprised to see Jack Brooks standing off to one side. Curiously, this was their *first* private tete-a-tete with both O'Neill and Brooks on the subject.

The Speaker ambled on in and plunked down his large frame into one of the chairs. White House lobbyists Terry Straub and Bill Cable sat discreetly in the sidelines.

283 / Robert V. Heffernan

Ryor had his pitch all planned mentally. He had brought with him a confidential, preliminary vote count on the House, showing ED would pass easily (238 in favor, 39 leaning in favor, 69 opposed, 16 leaning against, 50 undecided, 23 unknown).

The NEA President started by thanking the Speaker for the meeting. "This is a priority for America's teachers." He had good words for Jack Brooks, and intimated NEA would be helping him in his race for re-election.

Ryor uttered just three sentences before Brooks cut him off.

"I don't want your—endorsements," he hollered at the shocked NEA officials. "I don't want your—money. I won't take your—money...".

Everyone in the room was aghast. Tip O'Neill's jaw dropped open. The House Chairman's outburst struck like a bolt of lightning. Brooks went on and on.

"...The Speaker here has been good to you, but you're screwing around the Speaker...Your goddamn teachers are crawling all over us...".

When Brooks finally ended his diatribe, there was a stunned silence. No one knew what to say.

"Look, Congressman," Herndon broke in, "we didn't come here to antagonize you or the Speaker. You're our friends...".

Another long pause. At last, the Speaker, in a soft, husky voice, told the NEA leaders across the table, "Well, we'll do the best we can to bring the bill up."

Shaken, the NEA people got up and left. It was an understandably short meeting.

Days passed before NEA figured out Brooks. They later learned he was trying to curry the Speaker's favor, because he had badly crossed O'Neill on another bill.

Brooks also had a gripe with NEA. The Texas State Teachers Association, NEA's state affiliate, opposed Brooks's good friend, incumbent Democratic Gov. Dolph Briscoe, in his primary race. Briscoe lost.[27]

The Texas teachers had always supported Brooks in his campaigns, but they were seldom a driving force. Not until the ED bill surfaced did they start to take more interest in him and assist him. NEA political operatives made plans to contribute money and manpower.

Ryor and his team were doubly depressed about their stormy meeting because they also considered it their one chance to sway the Speaker and save the bill.

NEA had difficulty getting through to O'Neill. Only the executive director of their Massachusetts state affiliate was on good terms with him. They felt frustrated and certain that Tip O'Neill did not understand them—the potential political power of their organization, nor the meaning of their difficult entry into presidential politics. NEA was an up-and-coming political force in American labor, and the Speaker was slow to realize it and reward them accordingly.

*   *   *

The beauty of the nation's capital came out in bright, clear 70° weather Thursday, September 28.

---

[27] In November, the NEA-supported Democrat went on to lose the gubernatorial race to conservative Republican Bill Clements.

The Senate met at 9:30 a.m. Marilyn and I stayed close to our offices, making final refinements in our materials, expecting to be called to the floor at any moment.

The call came at 3:30. We rushed to the Senate floor.

Inside the Senate chamber, Ribicoff sat waiting patiently while Robert Byrd moved minor bills and resolutions out of the way. Senator Schmitt also stood by.

At 4 o'clock, Byrd had the Senate resume debate on the bill. "It is my hope that the Senate will complete action on this bill today," Byrd intoned. "Therefore, I would anticipate a fairly lengthy session today and several roll call votes. I hope both cloakrooms will announce (this) to senators…". The Majority Leader had decided to hold the Senate late into the night until it had finished our bill.

As we got settled, Schmitt called up his amendment on DOD schools, charging it would be "prohibitive" for the new ED to duplicate logistical services the Pentagon provided the overseas schools. "It is foolish to believe that the bureaucracies of two Cabinet agencies will cooperate to prevent duplication," the Republican Senator said, his voice amplified throughout the chamber.

The chair recognized Ribicoff. "Mr. President, I rise to oppose the amendment…" His statement repeated all the arguments in our report, plus inserted in the *Congressional Record* a series of articles by the *Army Times* entitled, "Dependents Schools in Europe: A Disorganized System in Danger of Flunking."

"Mr. President, I will move at the proper time to table the amendment," Ribicoff announced. "I ask for the yeas and nays on the motion to table."

"…the yeas and nays are ordered," the chair ruled.

We had settled on a strategy of *tabling* most amendments, in the hope that we would pick up votes of senators who would feel more comfortable tabling an amendment—officially setting it aside—rather than having to record their position on the issue itself.

As Schmitt rambled on, I ran out to the cloakroom phones to summon Sen. Sam Nunn to the floor. The Georgia Democrat later told fellow senators "the Department of Defense and the Armed Services Committee do not give these schools the attention they deserve."

Nunn also noted, "This is probably the only transfer in this bill that is fully supported by all affected parties."

Schmitt spoke in vain a few minutes more, making a last effort to convince the Senate his amendment was right.

"Mr. President, I move to table the amendment," Ribicoff said.

"...The question is on agreeing to the motion...," the chair announced. "The yeas and nays have been ordered and the clerk will call the roll."

The first vote on our bill began. Immediately, bells rung throughout the Capitol and Senate office buildings, telling senators they had 15 minutes in which to come to the floor. "Mr. Abourezk...Mrs. Allen...Mr. Anderson...," the desk clerk shouted above the bell ringing.

I was certain we would beat Schmitt on this amendment. Anxiously, I waited to see how high the margin would be.

For the first ten minutes, only a handful of senators registered their vote. The floor was quiet. Senators chatted to each other in small clumps.

At a table in the well next to the main desk, Democratic floor staffers jotted down a general, simple description of the issue. Other staffers would surreptitiously hold the paper in their hands, as if looking down at it, and stand at the entrances to the chamber. When a senator walked through the door, he would often stop and glance down at it, then go and vote intelligently.

"RIBICOFF MOTION TO TABLE SCHMITT AMENDMENT DELETING DOD DEPENDENTS SCHOOLS TRANSFER. COMMITTEE POSITION: YES VOTE," the paper said.

Suddenly, four bells rung loudly, bringing a senatorial stampede—the five-minute warning. Wave after wave of United States senators came strolling through the doors. The clerk broke out of his alphabetized routine, calling a senator's name whenever he saw a raised hand.

We were winning big. I could see most cosponsors of the bill following Ribicoff's position. Even some of the undecideds about the bill voted with us.

The mass of senators grew larger, congregating on the floor talking loudly. The clerk struggled to recognize ones who had to vote.

Ribicoff was kept busy in conversation with dozens of his colleagues.

"Well, what do we have here, Abe?," Sen. George McGovern asked him.

"Oh, it's a Schmitt amendment that I'm tabling. Vote 'aye'," our boss ordered kindly.

McGovern smiled and so voted.

"Are there any other senators who wish to be recorded?" The presiding officer banged his gavel in an unsuccessful attempt to restore order to the stately body. The clerks rechecked their addition several times, then presented the tally sheet to the chair.

"On this vote, the ayes are 65, the nays are 23, and the amendment is laid on the table...".

I felt great, having worked hard on keeping the DOD schools in the bill. Victories over the military were hard to come by.

Senator Stevens offered his Indian amendment for a final decision. Everyone tensed up, knowing this would be the biggest battle in the ED bill.

"...The Chairman (Ribicoff), I am sure, will say there has been consultation. Yes we sent them questionnaires," Stevens spoke in emotional, emphatic tones. "He will say and others will say there are important Indian people who support the bill and oppose my amendment. That is true.

"But the overwhelming majority...pleaded with me...I urge the Senate to listen to them..., their plea to Congress not to do this...without their consent."

I was worried. We were going into the vote with two significant factors against us. First, Senator Abourezk was out of town. We could have used the Indian Committee Chairman on the floor, twisting arms during the vote. Second, and most depressing, Stevens' aides were distributing copies of a statement by Ted Kennedy supporting the amendment. At the last possible minute, Kennedy came out with a low blow to the ED bill; he had opposed every major transfer.

I rushed to the phones in a desperate attempt to summon pro-transfer Indian-state senators to the floor and help us. Senator Domenici arrived in minutes.

Ribicoff delivered another closing statement against Stevens, then yielded control of his time on the amendment to Domenici, on the theory that it looked better to offset Stevens with another Republican, Indian-state senator.

"My Indian people are saying, 'So long as you protect certain rights that are ours,...we cannot lose,'" Domenici asserted on behalf of the Pueblos in his state. The New Mexico Republican seldom argued with such feeling and strength.

"...I fail to see the risk...It is not working now...".

The chair announced all time had expired. Sen. Barry Goldwater asked unanimous consent to proceed for 30 seconds more.

"I do not want the Senator from New Mexico to think I am defending the BIA," Goldwater said, looking at Domenici. "If you want to introduce an amendment to do away with the BIA, I will support it...".

"...It would have no more support from the Indian people than the transfer proposal before us has," Domenici heatedly retorted.

"All time has expired." The presiding officer banged the gavel. "The question is on agreeing to the amendment of the Senator of Alaska...". Again, a chorus of bells announced another 15-minute roll call vote.

This time, we decided to allow an up-or-down vote, instead of tabling the amendment. It would be close and we needed every vote. Many Republicans, we learned, automatically voted "no" on Democratic motions to table Republican amendments.

My blood pressure jumped 20 points. I wanted to run around the Senate floor and grab every senatorial arm I could, but there would not be enough time and it would be a tad improper. Marilyn and I stood, somewhat helpless, next to Ribicoff in the well.

Outside in the Reception Room, Carter and NEA lobbyists did grab arms, pulling senators aside for a few seconds of persuasion. Indians were there too. Looking up in the galleries, I could see more Indians. No doubt many of them had come to watch us squirm.

Senator Ribicoff, sensing our tenuous position, latched onto a few colleagues and gave a quick hard-sell. Domenici worked the Republican side, getting in a few words here and there.

Stevens too was collaring senators. He was cashing in all his chips on this one. Even his staff worked the floor, pulling many Republican senators aside. On seeing that, I decided what-the-hell and talked to some Democrats.

The five-minute warning sounded. Senators were everywhere. Our situation was critical. Many Democrats voted with Stevens—actually, with *Kennedy*: Brooke, Bumpers, Durkin, Ford, Hart, Inouye, Nelson, Packwood, Sarbanes, Stafford, Stone...

Mississippi's James Eastland voted "aye."

"Senator," I gasped, "you voted wrong"

The retiring, 74-year-old patrician Democrat slowly pulled a cigar out of his sour face and approached me in all the confusion in the well.

"What's that?"

"The Mississippi Choctaws *support* the transfer. They *oppose* the amendment!"

Eastland turned around and consulted some colleagues. Mysteriously he left, not changing his vote.

Senator Sasser voted "aye." I couldn't believe my ears. A member of our Committee, Sasser opposed Stevens in the mark-up.

I saw Sasser's staffer out of the corner of my eye, walking fast towards a cloakroom door to escape before Marilyn or I came running.

I caught him.

"Your senator voted with Stevens!," I exclaimed, out-of-breath.

He was indignant. "Look, it's not my fault you didn't do your homework. You should have talked to him."

I threw my hands up in the air, forgetting for the moment I was on the floor of the United States Senate. Then, I ran back to our desk in the well. It was chaotic; we were clinging onto senators at every opportunity.

Alaska Democrat Mike Gravel approached us. "Shall I vote my politics or my conscience?"

"Oh, your conscience, your conscience," Marilyn and I begged in unison. Frantically, I leafed through my Indian notebook and pulled out a sheet listing the Alaskan native organizations and villages supporting the transfer. Gravel, often at odds with Stevens, seemed surprised at some of the names. He stood, thinking.

On the other side of the aisle, Stevens and Domenici were lobbying furiously. Republicans Dole and Griffin each heard a pitch from Stevens and his staff; both voted "aye."

Across the room, Connecticut Republican Lowell Weicker walked through the doors. Stevens floor staffer Susan Alvarado stopped and pointed a finger at him: "Vote yes or I'll never play tennis with you again." Weicker voted "aye."

Iowa Democrat Dick Clark voted "aye." Ribicoff went after him. "No, no, Dick. This is an up-or-down vote. I'm not tabling this one."

Clark switched his vote to "no."

The clock stopped. "Are there any other senators who wish to be recorded?," the chair asked. For five minutes, there were last-minute changes and switches.

Gravel raised his hand: "Mr. President?" He whispered to us, "My conscience."

"Mr. Gravel," the clerk shouted through the crowd of senators.

"No," he responded loudly.

Seeing the tally, Majority Whip Alan Cranston asked to switch his vote—from "no" to "aye."

Robert Byrd stood in the well, watching his floor people count the votes. Seeing that his wouldn't decide the issue, he also told the clerk, "Aye." The Majority Leader bought some good will insurance with the Assistant Minority Leader, Stevens.

Finally, the bad news: "On this vote, the yeas are 47, the nays 39, and the amendment is adopted."

Stevens had won. Indian education would never be in ED.

I slumped back in my seat, very close to crying. Marilyn was saddened. "Well, you can't win them all," Ribicoff consoled us. "We put up our best fight and they won fair and square."

Senator Schmitt recouped the floor and began talking to the chamber about his next amendment to drop the NSF science education transfer.

I was hardly aware Schmitt was even talking. But the Senate schedule allows no time for mourning.

"Look on the bright side," Marilyn tried to be cheerful. "At least this improves our chances for passing the House. Now, we just might get our Department after all." True, the major difference between Brooks's and Ribicoff's bills had been eliminated.

Marilyn went over to congratulate Stevens' staff, one of her typically gracious gestures. I would do so soon also, for despite my feelings, I still respected Senator Stevens and his staff.

Meanwhile, Ted Kennedy walked over to me. "This is my statement on the science education matter," he told me in his thick Bostonian accent. "Would you see that it gets included in the *Record* during the debate on Schmitt's amendment?"

"Certainly, Senator."

As Kennedy walked away, I felt someone tugging at my arm. Sitting beside me, our student researcher Jon Greenblatt with his jaw dropped open. "Do you know who you just talked to?," he asked.

"Yes, Senator Kennedy." I was too numb to feel swayed by the glamorous, Camelot-like presence of the Senator from Massachusetts.

"Oh, Jesus," Jon laughed in amazement.

Kennedy returned to chat with Ribicoff. Up in the galleries, a hundred high school students were "ooing" and "aahing" and pointing.

"Look, Abe, about that Indian thing...". Kennedy was surprisingly sympathetic almost to the point of being apologetic.

In the background, Senator Schmitt droned on in defense of his science education amendment.

"...Well, your brother and I worked together to put Indian health in HEW and that worked so well that the Indians are getting as good medical care today as we're getting in the rest of the country," Ribicoff explained. "I mean, what is the BIA going to do for the Indians?"

"Yeah...yeah...," Kennedy repeated, shaking his head affirmatively. "I know...I know...". Moments later, their confidential talk ended, Kennedy raised his arms slightly: "Well, what could I do? The Indians were after me to oppose it...".

Ribicoff solemnly shook his head. From one politician to another, he understood.

"...The transfer of science education programs from the National Science Foundation will not meet the goal of improving science education in this Senator's opinion," Schmitt told a rapidly emptying, distracted Senate chamber. "...The science community is strongly opposed to the proposed transfer." He repeated earlier arguments that science education and research were interrelated.

Ribicoff rose and rebutted Schmitt, reading from a paper Marilyn wrote. Our Senator argued the Education Department should be involved in science ed.

Kennedy's statement cleared the way for Schmitt's amendment to be voted down. As health and scientific research subcommittee chairman, Kennedy could have raised a big stink, but he had already done enough damage to the ED bill. Kennedy supported, instead, keeping the NSF transfer in the bill until the conference between House and Senate to work out differences, and then dropping it there in exchange for something else, thereby giving Senate conferees a trading tool.

Kennedy's political philosophy was simple: always satisfy every constituency. In ED he kept the Head Start, Indian, and science groups happy by opposing their transfers, and he kept NEA happy by cosponsoring Ribicoff's ED bill.

Outside, darkness had settled on Washington. High atop the Capitol dome, the bright beacon light told the city the Senate was still at work. Marilyn, Ribicoff, and I were anchored on the floor until the bill passed.

A string of senators stopped by our desk during the science debate with a standard, amusing question: "Do you think I have time to run over to the Monocle and eat dinner?" They did not want to miss the next vote while dining at the familiar, nearby Senate watering hole.

Several senators briefly interrupted the floor proceedings for a prearranged colloquy with Ribicoff on state-local control of education. Marilyn had written most of the script. She couldn't have constructed a stronger legislative history. "...A Department of Education...will not in any way lead to federal control or dominance of education," Ribicoff read into the *Record*. The feds should have no control over local formulation of policies choice of curricula, school administration, and program content, he said. The colloquy would guide courts and the Department in future decisions.

Schmitt closed debate on the science amendment. Ribicoff moved to table his amendment, and the Senate bells tolled yet again, signaling a 15-minute vote.

Everyone knew Schmitt was going through the motions; someone had to play the loyal opponent. He would lose badly again, but he didn't seem to care much. Final passage was near, and then all could go home.

Dozens of senators checked with us. "How do I vote?," asked North Dakota Democrat Quentin Burdick. "I'm counting on you to keep me in line," New Hampshire Democrat John Durkin deadpanned to us.

Finance Committee Chairman Russell Long trotted down the floor terraces. "What's this, Abe?"

"Oh, it's a Schmitt amendment that I'm tabling," Ribicoff answered, downplaying its worthiness.

"Oh, *shit*," Long puckered his face, and promptly voted "aye."

Ribicoff smiled.

It was getting late, past 8 o'clock. We worried that some senators would get restless and go home for the night. We wanted a good count on final passage. Ribicoff yawned as he sat waiting for the vote to end.

The Senate chamber was filled with a piercing roar from 80 chatty senators as the final votes were tallied. Schmitt lost again, 62-23. Absent were 15 senators.

Sen. S.I. Hayakawa (R-CA.) proposed an amendment wiping out the language of S.991 and requiring instead a study on whether an Education Department should be established.

"…All I know is that from more than 40 years in government, the only way to kill something is create another study," Ribicoff later responded. He moved to table Hayakawa's amendment, repeating the routine of a roll call vote.

We watched anxiously as senators recorded their positions on this test vote of the Senate's sentiment on ED. The result: 70 yeas, 14 nays, and 16 absentees.

Schmitt later reclaimed the floor and resumed his carping against the bill. "We have largely had our say," he admitted. Our opponent delivered a wandering, closing summation. "…I am afraid, Mr. President, every parent will regret our actions if they lose more and more controls over the lives of their children to the federal government...".

Senators with their hands in their pockets paced impatiently on the floor, waiting for the final vote. "How much longer are we gonna stick around here, Abe?," was the typical question.

Finally, it came time to vote.

"Mr. President, a parliamentary inquiry," Ribicoff addressed the chair.

"The Senator will state it."

"The vote now is on final passage?"

"The Senator is correct."

A loud chorus of "*Vote! Vote!*" erupted from the senators standing around.

"The bill having been read the third time, the question is, Shall it pass?," the presiding officer announced.

As the buzzers sounded their official call, we beaming, relieved. It was 9:35 p.m.

"Mr. Abourezk...Mrs. Allen...Mr. Anderson...Mr. Baker...," the clerk called out.

Senator Schmitt came over and extended his hand to Ribicoff. "Congratulations, Abe, for your sake."

"Well, well, you've waited a long time for this vote," a smiling George McGovern complimented Ribicoff. "What's it been, 15 years?"

"A long time," Ribicoff laughed.

I took a deep breath, stretched, and looked up around the galleries. Mostly staff and senators' wives sat there; few of the general public stayed so late. Some 15 reporters sat at the long counters in the press galleries, waiting to record the final outcome and then rush to file their stories.

10 minutes passed, and the bells rang out once more. More senators crowded into the well.

The floor staff's notices said: "FINAL PASSAGE. S.991, DEPARTMENT OF EDUCATION BILL. COMMITTEE POSITION: YES."

We watched the vote excitedly. There were a few surprises.

Sen. William Proxmire (D-WI.), the Senate's efficiency-in-government nut, voted no (his staff held out hope for a yes vote). On the plus side: Robert Dole (R-KS.) (convinced by Percy to support the bill upon deletion of child nutrition), Robert Griffin (R-MI.) (up for re-election in a tough race), and Richard Schweiker (R-Pa.) (a one-time Ronald Reagan running mate).

Nevada Republican Paul Laxalt, a conservative, walked in and raised his right hand. The clerk called his name. "NO THANK YOU," he cried out with obvious disgust. No great loss there, I thought.

At last, the presiding officer announced the final count. "On this vote, the yeas are 72, the nays are 11, and the bill, as amended, is passed."

Marilyn and I hugged each other. Ribicoff congratulated each of us with a warm handshake.

The Senate had sent its message to the House—move this bill!

FIFTEEN

The President Kills It

The unpitying clock radio came on loudly Friday morning. Peering one-eyed from my pillow, I could make out "7:30." My body wanted badly to go back to sleep.

"…At the top of the news this morning—the world's Catholics are stunned today by the loss of their newly ordained leader, Pope John Paul…"

The radio announcer's voice brought me to an immediate sit-up in bed.

"…The Pope died in his sleep last night. First reports from the Vatican say he was stricken by a heart attack. John Paul served as the holy father for only about a month…".

I dropped back into bed, burying my head in the pillow, snickering at the shocking news. "Don't believe it," I muttered to myself. "Work two years, night and day, on a Cabinet department, finally pass it, and the *Pope* of all people bumps us off page one."

A Catholic myself, I found the new Pope's death saddening. *But now?*

The major national recognition that we craved, like most Washington professionals, would be pre-empted by the rush of world events,

* * *

"President Carter's plan for a department of education was passed by the Senate last night 72 to 11," the *Washington Post* announced in a short story on page three.

"…The bill now goes to the House, where a similar measure is awaiting floor action.

"Some House opponents reportedly are hoping to stall House passage past the adjournment of Congress or delay it long enough so that a House-Senate conference could not be completed…".

From the White House, officials released a presidential statement "welcoming" the Senate action. Carter publicly thanked Byrd and Ribicoff and urged the House to "act promptly on this measure."

* * *

Word circulated Friday through the House Democratic cloakrooms that the leadership might that day bring up the resolution granting a rule to Brooks's ED bill. The time was ripe, coming on the heels of a decisive Senate vote. The Speaker would honor his commitment.

Rep. Leo Ryan rushed to the floor, determined to block it. Puzzling his Democratic party leaders, Ryan began objecting to routine unanimous consent motions. Then, the Californian began demanding quorum calls. Applying still more heat, he pushed for roll call votes on minor motions and bills. Generally, he was making a total nuisance of himself, wasting precious time on silliness.

There was a quick huddle on the House floor. Majority Leader Jim Wright and Whip John Brademas asked Ryan what the problem was.

Ryan insisted the ED rule resolution be pulled off the day's agenda; that was his price.

The leadership backed down, and ED was temporarily laid aside.

*   *   *

Monday, October 2. Only 10 days left in the 95th Congress.

NEA officials raced to save the bill. Telegrams went out to every House member from the teachers union, stressing the need for each of the representatives' help in getting the bill before the House for a vote. Other education groups did likewise. NEA convinced civil rights leader Coretta Scott King and National Urban League President Vernon Jordan to lend their names to another round of telegrams.

AFT-backed liberals and black members of the House were fighting hard against the Brooks bill. AFT showed it could raise hell in the House.

A rag-tag band of opposing House members had formed. Democrats Rosenthal, Chisholm, Conyers, and Ryan joined with Republicans (normally their antagonists) Erlenborn, Arlan Stangeland (Minn.), Clarence Brown (Ohio), Quayle, and Walker in working against ED. Staffers of these Reps came together Monday morning and settled on a strategy of filibuster by amendment. Quayle submitted 12, Walker filed 24 more. There would be many others. Each proposed transferring every imaginable program. No amendment was too bizarre in the rush to bury the bill.

*   *   *

The 26-member House Republican Policy Committee met the next day, Tuesday, to consider a motion recommending that the House's 144 Republicans oppose the bill.

NEA lobbyists made some fast calls and visits. Numerous Republican senators who voted for Ribicoff's bill were asked to speak with House GOP colleagues in their state delegations.

At the closed-door meeting, Walker and Erlenborn spoke against the bill, predictably touting the partisan line that Jimmy Carter was only paying off a campaign debt. But NEA had lined up some forceful voices that offset them. Most importantly, House Minority Leader John Rhodes said he would support the bill. (The Arizona Education Association. had struggled to maintain a decent working relationship with him.) Rhodes was hardly enthusiastic, but at least he sent positive signals to his followers. James Quillen, Tom Corcoran, John Anderson, and Frank Horton also spoke in favor.

A vote was taken, and the motion was defeated with votes to spare. The bipartisan facade would stay, for the time being.

*   *   *

Wednesday, October 4. Traditionally, the busiest day of the week in the U.S. House of Representatives.

House Democratic leaders again placed the ED rule on the day's agenda. Rep. Robert Walker, watching the floor like a hawk, jumped to his feet early in the day and objected to a normally routine unanimous consent request that the reading of an unrelated conference report be dispensed with. The House reading clerk, consuming much time, laboriously read the 50-page report aloud.

Majority Whip Brademas set about negotiating with Walker, only to learn his price: pull ED off the schedule.

AFT head lobbyist Greg Humphrey had already gone to respected Wisconsin Democrat David Obey and asked his help. Obey paid a visit to the Speaker. Unless ED is dropped from the agenda, he told O'Neill, we'll tie the House up in knots.

The Speaker had also received earlier a call from AFL-CIO lobbyist Andrew Biemiller, who told him, in essence, if we get this on the skids, we don't expect you to rescue it.

Meanwhile, Rep. Clarence Brown introduced four amendments to the Brooks ED bill. Erlenborn filed another 33 amendments, Quayle 26 more, Walker 29 others, and Ryan five more on top of those. Most had capricious intents.

Neither John Brademas nor Jim Wright nor even Tip O'Neill had trouble understanding mathematics. In their avowed mission to filibuster, the ED opponents could be expected to draw out debate on each of their amendments to the 10 minutes allowed by the rule, *plus* demand a roll call vote, taking 15 minutes more of precious floor time. The equation was scary: more than 100 amendments multiplied by a half-hour equaled at least 50 hours of floor debate. And that didn't include general debate on the bill and related motions.

Brademas agreed right then and there to drop ED from the House schedule.

*   *   *

"President Carter's plan for a separate new Education Department was put in jeopardy yesterday when House leaders agreed to delay a vote on the measure until next week," the *Associated Press* reported the following day.

"The House calendar for that week already is crowded with such priority legislation as natural gas pricing and other energy bills, tax cut legislation, and a vote to override President Carter's promised veto of a public works bill.

"Frankly, looking at it from that standpoint, I seriously doubt if we can get it done," House Majority Leader Jim Wright (D-TX.) said of the education bill. "…As a procedural matter, it seems unlikely that we could even get to it…"

*   *   *

NEA bigwigs rushed to Capitol Hill, belatedly mounting a full court press. Many Association officials had been concentrating on other education bills. ED had been left largely to a single lobbyist— Gail Bramblett.

Head lobbyist Stan McFarland applied pressure to John Brademas, who already was caught between the kettle and the stove.

"Pull your people off me," Brademas raged at McFarland in a Capitol hallway, then stalked away, fuming.

Early Thursday morning, October 5, Arizona Education Association. officials joined NEA lobbyists in a meeting with John Rhodes to shore up his support and ask help. Later, a few minutes after the 10:00 a.m. convening time of the full House, Rhodes rose on the floor. "I think this is important legislation and hope that the majority leadership will schedule it for consideration by the House before adjournment of the 95th Congress."

Rhodes and other "supportive" Republicans took sheer delight in publicly backing the bill while watching it sink under the Democrats at the helm.

Nearing desperation, NEA threw together a breakfast meeting Friday morning, October 6, and invited a half-dozen members of Congress who favored the cause. In a quiet, out-of-the-way Rayburn House Office Building conference room, the congressmen told the NEA people, in their judgment, it was too late to rescue the bill. Stan McFarland was particularly irate and frustrated, realizing tardily that if NEA lost this bill, the crap would fall on his head. All along, the top NEA management had laid back, confident in the leadership of Jack Brooks and White House lobbyists. Now, with the roof caving in all around, they were coming to the sad realization that more help should have been given to Gail Bramblett, and more attention should have been paid to the House.

NEA-Washington flashed a legislative alert through its vast national network, calling for all members, local and state affiliates to keep up pressure on House members.

But the raised hopes were dashed as the agenda for Congress's last week was released. Altogether, some 61 bills remained to be acted on. ED was on the list, in the "Thursday, Friday, and Saturday" category, and fourth from the bottom.

*   *   *

As if adding more straws to the camel's back, Reps. Quayle and Walker filed 20 more amendments Thursday and Friday. Among them: school prayer and busing, two of the most controversial issues ever to come before Congress.

*   *   *

"We've got momentum," Hamilton Jordan proudly boasted to the Washington press corps. One-by-one, Congress was disposing of the President's priority bills, and the Georgians stood a good chance to end their first two years with respectable legislative achievements. Energy, tax, budget, employment bills were progressing well.

Jimmy Carter and his men were gradually becoming more skilled at utilizing control over the federal government. They were beginning to twist arms and threaten and punish, and everything else it takes for a successful President to push a balky Congress in his direction. The Camp David summit had helped induce more Democrats to line up, behind the President.

But only the President could save ED now.

The House would meet just five more days. 61 bills in five days?

The President *had* to pick his priorities. One week before, black leaders converged at the White House, pressuring Carter to designate the Humphrey-Hawkins "full employment" bill a "must." The President relented and the bill was scheduled.

He could have done the same with ED. The bill, like others, lay at his mercy. It was not dead, only dormant. With the mere utterance of a few words, Carter could resurrect it. He could lean on the Speaker.

The President's men kept a close eye on the situation. OMB, PRP, and other staff argued within the top ranks of the White House for finishing off the bill. Next year might be more difficult. There would undoubtedly be more conservatives elected in November.

ED would be exposed as a major Carter priority without the benefit of being overshadowed by other heavies—energy, taxes, Panama, etc. They were so close, and the thought of fighting the battles all over again...

Top aides Ham Jordan, Stu Eizenstat, and Frank Moore would assess the bills remaining, their political situation, the President's political situation, and the minutes still on the clock. The decision, however, would ultimately be Carter's, hashed out over the long Columbus Day weekend.

*   *   *

Washington Post editors were experts in political timing.

"As time grows short and the end of the session approaches,...there is one prominent bill that Congress can dump overboard with a clear conscience, and that is the defective and divisive attempt to establish a new Department of Education," the paper began its lead editorial, Sunday, October 8.

"The bill is the inspiration of the National Education Association, an organization that has much the same relation to the public schools that the plumbers union has to the plumbing business…"

Someone at the *Post* did not like the NEA.

Lo and behold, William Raspberry had written an op-ed column on the very same subject, the very same day. ED would "bring the federal government, willy-nilly, headlong into national education policy," he said. "…Delaying consideration of the measure until the next term would give us time to argue the proposal on its true merits—not just the nebulous promises of its supporters."

*   *   *

Tuesday, October 10. Washington paused for 30 minutes at 4 o'clock in the afternoon, glued to TVs and radios.

In my Room 3214 Dirksen Building suite, I listened to a radio—apprehensive, tense.

Reporters jammed the Old Executive Office Building auditorium for Jimmy Carter's 38th press conference. Their chatter stopped when the President walked through the side door and stepped out into the blinding television lights.

Four days to go before Congress adjourned.

"I have a brief statement to make to begin with…", Carter spoke into the triad of microphones.

All around the city, people with bills hanging in suspension held their breath.

"As all of you know, we are approaching the end of the 95th congressional session with a great deal of work still to be done," the President led off. "We are searching for a fair tax bill…The Senate…will take up the full employment (Humphrey-Hawkins) legislation…The most important bill left in the House is on energy…". Carter reiterated *four times* that the natural gas bill was his "most important priority."

Impatiently, I strained to hear reporters' questions. Halfway through, television newsman Daniel Schorr sought recognition and Carter called on him. His question brought me up out of my chair.

"How high a priority do you still set on the creation of a Department of Education, first at this session of Congress, and if it doesn't happen at this session, then the next one?"

"I have advocated and have worked hard this year for the establishment of an independent Department of Education," Carter said, glancing around the room. "I don't think that education in our country has gotten an adequate hearing in my own Administration or previous ones because it has been part of HEW, with health and welfare the dominant portions of that department.

"I think at this point, it is unlikely that the bill will pass this year. The Senate did pass the bill. The House was not able or willing to take it up. But I still have it as an important goal of mine to establish this department."

My face instantly flushed red and hot. All at once, the primitive feelings of anger, hurt, and frustration fused within me.

"I think it is important that a more efficient delivery of educational opportunity to children in our country be achieved," Carter continued. "I think the primary control of the schools, obviously, ought to be at the local and state level, but I think it will make it more effective."

Caught up in my emotions, I didn't hear the remaining 10 minutes of the press conference.

The President of the United States had just signed the death certificate on his own bill!

Over and over, I repeated aloud, "I don't believe it," "I can't believe it."

Suddenly, I remembered Marilyn had not been told the news. I tore off down the hallway and ran past startled secretaries into her office. Talking on the phone, Marilyn took one look at my face and abruptly ended her conversation.

"Oh God, what's wrong?"

"Oh, nothing," I screamed. "Just the President has killed our bill, that's all." I recounted his statements, best I could remember under the circumstances.

"Jesus, with friends like him, who needs enemies?," I cried pacing back and forth, gesturing in the general direction of White House.

By now, we had made a scene. Other Committee staffers and lawyers gathered round to listen in. Marilyn and I became depressed.

"What do we do now?," I asked in a calmer voice.

Marilyn silently shook her head. Her eyes watered as she sat in a daze. Our colleagues quietly left us to mourn.

*   *   *

Incensed NEA officials punched in the phone numbers of numerous White House aides and threw a royal fit. The Carter people who had worked on ED were heavyhearted, sorrowful. It was part of their job to listen and console angry interest groups.

But why did the President have to say anything other than he *supported* the bill and *hoped* it would pass this year? He could have left the door open, but instead slammed it tight. What incentive did Speaker O'Neill have now to bring up the bill? Carter's staff conceded their boss could have handled it differently.

The President had made a big boo-boo.

Hastily, the White House staff wrote a compensating note and had it personally delivered the next morning:

"To Speaker Tip O'Neill

"The creation of a separate Department of Education is one of my priorities for the 95th Congress.

"...We believe that a large majority of members of the House support (it). I appreciate your scheduling this bill for floor action this week. I ask that you bring up the bill on Thursday and complete action that day if at all possible.

Thank you for all of your help.
With warmest personal regards,
Sincerely,
JIMMY CARTER"

The letter was blatantly cosmetic and an embarrassing way of covering ass. The President's people made it public.

The damage, though, had already been done. The letter would have no effect on Tip O'Neill. The only way now ED could be considered in the House was if work progressed so rapidly on other bills that a hole would open in the schedule.

*   *   *

We spent the week putting up a positive front—a Department of Education bill would pass in the future, but we really weren't sure.

Capitol Hill was awash in activity. Hallways jammed with last-minute lobbying. White House and agency limousines parked everywhere. Police struggling to control the flow of people. The House and Senate came in earlier in the morning and stayed in session later at night. Lawmakers and the staffs were drained, irritable, pushed to their limits. Congressmen had one thing on their minds: get out of Washington.

Bills were being chucked left and right. So long as there was the tiniest glimmer of hope, the champions of ED would work to save it.

At NEA, Stan McFarland floated the idea of Jack Brooks and other cosponsors sending a "Dear Colleague" letter urging action on the bill. Gail Bramblett blurted back, "It's time to start mending fences and get commitments for next year, otherwise we'll just make Brooks mad."

Going on the theory that anything would help, Marilyn and I spent Friday, October 13 writing and obtaining signatures for a letter to the President. "We urge you to do whatever is necessary to assure final House action on the legislation this Congress," it said. "In the event the bill is not passed, we plan to introduce similar legislation immediately upon the beginning of the 96th Congress…". The letter was signed by Abe Ribicoff, Warren Magnuson, and Claiborne Pell—the Senate's education heavies.

"It'll be on his desk first thing tomorrow morning," White House lobbyist Dan Tate assured me at 9:30 Friday night in the packed Senate Reception Room,

But the day's *Wall Street Journal* included ED among "the list of bills that won't pass." The latest House agenda had been slimmed down considerably, to some 30 bills. However, ED was still at the bottom.

Both House and Senate prolonged their sessions late into the night. If the congressional leadership had its way, the two bodies would stay in session continuously throughout the weekend without stop until the "must" bills had been passed.

*   *   *

By the time I walked across the Capitol plaza at 9:30 Saturday morning on the way to the office, the House and Senate had convened and the whole place was buzzing in commotion.

We would maintain a long and painful vigil throughout the final hours of the 95th Congress. Top NEA lobbyists constantly strolled around the House floor entrances. White House aides, especially Terry Straub, didn't leave the Hill.

I sauntered between the two chambers, sitting in on the proceedings, talking with colleagues.

Bills' fates were being decided expeditiously. Civil service reform: passed. Humphrey-Hawkins: passed. Energy: passed. Labor-HEW appropriations: passed. Tax cut: passed. Tuition tax credits: died. A filibuster on the natural gas bill was holding up the Senate.

Without fail, every few minutes I stayed in touch with members of our ED team and with the "tapes." House and Senate cloakrooms regularly record the latest floor situation and information, which could be heard by calling special phone numbers. Each time, ED was listed on the agenda, but still near the bottom.

Too jittery to think about sleeping, I spent all Saturday night at the Capitol. In the Senate, I saw tempers flare over the natural gas filibuster. In the House, members debated several bills. Down on the floor, I could see that many had not shaved. Some dozed off; others suppressed yawns. Many ties were undone.

Rep. Robert Walker seemed cemented to the House floor. The Pennsylvania Republican didn't leave for fear that the leadership might call up the ED bill in his absence. I stared at his grayhaired head from the galleries above, wondering why is he so obsessed with killing ED?

By Sunday morning, Congress had been in session for nearly 24 hours straight. It seemed odd seeing so much activity so early on a Sunday morning—like a normal workday.

Two dozen major bills either had been passed or were close to completion. House and Senate leaders announced that once action had been finished on both energy and tax bills, Congress would close up and go home.

Like a loyal and loving father committed to his sick child, I called the House recording every ten minutes for an update on ED's condition. The last one I heard said, "...At 6:46 p.m., Sunday, October 15, 1978, the U.S. House of Representatives adjourned *sine die*...". It had been a 37-hour marathon weekend.

ED was dead.

*   *   *

Late that night, I jogged for an hour around the dimly-lit Mall that stretches from the Capitol to the Washington Monument, then slumped onto a stiff wooden park bench near the foot of the Capitol.

A lot of pent-up frustration had to be worked out of my body. I sat deep in thought, reflecting on where I'd been and on where I'd be going.

Another lonely jogger approached; the muffled sound of his sneakers beating against the crushed rock brought me back to reality. He stopped for a second, panting, and looked at me. "You're not supposed to stop," he chided me with a smile, and then disappeared into the darkness.

I watched him leave, then turned slowly to look at the bright, ivory Capitol dome framed by the cold, star lit sky.

You're not supposed to stop!

THE SECOND TRY

1979

SIXTEEN

An Attempted Resurrection

Where did we go wrong? Marilyn and I mulled over the question for weeks after. We concluded several different factors contributed to ED's death.

Time was our number one enemy. Had there been just two more weeks in the session, the bill might have passed. Part of the blame could be put on the President. We were ready to proceed back in the fall of 1977. But Carter's decisions were delayed and delayed until April 1978. He dallied much too long—until June—before leaning on Jack Brooks.

Fighting turf wars consumed far too much time. Here again, if the President had backed a narrow Department, the matter might have moved more quickly. Yet the need for consolidation of federal education programs was our best argument. Politically, we had at least to make the effort to pull together as many programs as we could.

NEA and White House aides didn't learn until September that they were taking the House for granted. But they had many diversions and abundant confidence in Brooks. The President failed, once deciding to

315

pursue ED, to commit the necessary personal backing and resources of his office. The NEA leadership was equally guilty of this.

Indeed, the lack of high-level leadership cost us dearly. No one individual was responsible for spearheading the ED drive for the President. And it hurt that the key member of Carter's Cabinet, Joseph Califano, lobbied against the bill.

Marilyn and I made our mistakes, to be sure. Perhaps we could have moved our hearings and reports faster. Perhaps Senator Ribicoff could have been a little more enthusiastic about his own bill. But we had few apologies to make—*we passed our bill.*

1977 and 1978 had been a learning process for all of us. We would use that painful experience in going forward to 1979.

*   *   *

Would it, could it be revived? That was largely up to the President.

Although nasty turf issues had been decided, there was no guarantee moving the bill in 1979 would be any easier. The next time around, Carter and Mondale would have to roll up their sleeves and involve themselves more deeply in the bill's political aspects. Jack Brooks would want to see a stronger presidential push.

Beth Abramowitz called Marilyn and revealed the President had met with Jim McIntyre Monday after Congress's adjournment. Without going into much detail, Carter told his OMB director he wanted to put ED near the top of his list in '79.

All that week, we heard rumors that either Carter or Mondale would make a definitive statement soon. It came on a campaign swing through Huntington, West Virginia October 20, when the Vice President told NEA teachers there, "I am happy to say today that President Garter will go back to Congress and ask for a separate Education Department. He will press for its passage, and we'll have a signing ceremony in the Rose Garden before the 96th Congress adjourns."

* * *

Journalists said their phones rang the Monday following adjournment from AFT staffers who were anxious to be credited with the defeat of ED. A true-to-life David-and-Goliath story. Small AFT taking on giant NEA and bloodying its nose.

Greatly encouraged by their "victory," AFT officials set about planning new strategy for winning again in 1979. AFT lobbyist Greg Humphrey, Catholic Conference lobbyists Frank Monihan and Jim Robinson, and AFL-CIO lobbyist Ken Peterson lunched together at the chic Chez Camille restaurant in mid-October. The foursome expected Republicans in the 96th Congress would be far more partisan, with the 1980 presidential election closing in. The lobbyists would continually hammer away at the notion that ED was being sought only for Jimmy Carter's re-election campaign, solidifying Republicans against the bill.

A numerical goal was set: to defeat ED, the lobbyists figured they would need 120 Republican and 100 Democratic votes in the House. Again next year, they would make the House of Representatives the primary battlefield.

* * *

On Capitol Hill, it was beautifully peaceful. No bills to worry about, no senators, no representatives, people on vacation, hallways and cafeterias clear. Tired and emotionally depleted, I took off almost the whole month of November and headed for the serenity of New England.

It was one of those rare times when Washington was not the focus of attention. The nation attuned itself to the November 7 elections. President Carter and Vice President Mondale crisscrossed the country plugging

Democratic candidates. Washingtonians anxiously followed every detail of the off-year elections; the results would impact on their projects.

The 1978 races for congressional seats would in no way be seen as a referendum on establishing a Department of Education. In only a handful was the issue debated at length. But there would be many new faces and changes in the House and Senate committees' membership that would influence the fate of our bill.

As usual, NEA increased its involvement in the campaigns. NEA's first qualification was support for ED, although the union did back a few incumbents who opposed it yet had otherwise good education records.

As returns poured in, it became obvious Republicans were going to increase their minority proportions in both houses of Congress.[28]

Conservative Republicans ousted five prominent Senate Democrats— Haskell of Colorado, Clark of Iowa, Hathaway of Maine, Anderson of Minnesota, and McIntyre of New Hampshire. Each supported ED. In Kansas and Virginia, where ED became a campaign issue, supportive NEA-endorsed Democrats lost to Republicans. In Tennessee, Republican leader Howard Baker won a respectable victory, and Alaskan Ted Stevens got re-elected easily, thus continuing the existing minority leadership team. Republicans picked up two extra seats in the Senate. I counted, overall, a potential net loss of five votes for ED—not bad.

Republican gains in the House were moderate—12 seats. The election meant more trouble for ED there, because in addition, at least 15 of the 41 new Democratic faces fell into the conservative category. There

---

[28] The political party opposite that in control of the White House normally wins bigger in off-year elections.

would be 75 new members in the House: 25 for ED, 25 against, 25 undecided. Democrats would retain their solid control over the body, but generally, the House of Representatives would be younger, slightly more Republican, and definitely more conservative.

The House leadership would not change. Jack Brooks had been re-elected and would remain as House GovOps Chairman. Frank Horton, also re-elected, would continue as Ranking Republican, a plus for ED.

The election results spelled a rougher road ahead, as we expected long ago. But they weren't devastating.

*   *   *

Marilyn met with Pat Gwaltney, her staff, and Terry Straub the day after the elections at the New Executive Office Building to think through preparations for 1979.

The Administration officials had not yet decided whether the President would submit his own bill to Congress in January. Marilyn and NEA encouraged it as a sign of strong presidential backing. Brooks would use Carter's bill; we would use Ribicoff's.

Straub informed Marilyn that the President and his top staff would receive delegations of new members of Congress in December, and ED would be talked up. White House lobbyists were also meeting with key House leaders and with Brooks's staff.

Timing? Marilyn said as far as she knew, Senator Ribicoff would move fast on his bill. She probed Gwaltney and Straub for a reading of how high a priority the White House would attach to ED in 1979. Straub, who was now on Frank Moore's staff, would work constantly on the bill. His higher position meant he could prod the Vice President, the President, and top Administration aides into action more easily. Would ED be mentioned again in the State of the Union address? That was undecided.

Gwaltney had been tightening up on her shop. The increasing conservatism of Congress prompted a change in tactics to a focus on the core issue of the management benefits in separating education from HEW, the cost savings and efficiencies. Gwaltney's analysts looked for the intricate details of how HEW operated, how the money was spent, how regulations moved through the bureaucracy.

Along with the new direction came changes in personnel. Bill Hawley had long since departed and returned to academia. Decker Anstrom left in mid-October to work on the budget side of OMB. Art Sheekey would remain, detailed to corral interest group support. Some professionals from the Office of Education transferred over to fill the vacant slots and help document the management horror statistics.

But the biggest change was that responsibility for political strategy would be housed much higher in the White House strata—an improvement needed the previous summer.

*   *   *

The nation's chief state education officials and their staff invaded the Safari Inn in Scottsdale, Arizona, for their annual convention Monday, November 13. High among the topics for discussion: ED.

"The President's support in unequivocal," Assistant Secretary for Education Mary Berry told the chiefs. "…We will have to broaden the base and convince the public that more people want it than the National Education Association."

The next day, a small group clustered near the hotel pool in the 65° Arizona sun. The confreres: Allan Cohen, executive assistant to the Illinois state superintendent of education, Marilyn Harris, California State Superintendent Wilson Riles, his Washington aide Don White, PRP's Art Sheekey, and Mary Berry's PR person, Connie Stewart.

Their conversation drifted to the reasons why the ED bill had failed that year. They kept coming back to NEA.

The push for ED looked like a total payoff, Carter to NEA. And the giant teacher union had heard it said so much they were simply shrugging it off. But with no big issues to hide behind in 1979, ED would get more exposure. NEA had to get out of the limelight, the group felt.

Scathing attacks on NEA had already begun. That very month, the conservative *Reader's Digest* prominently ran a story, "NEA: A Washington Lobby Run Rampant." It charged NEA's "drive for power" was "a classic study of how special-interest politics can overwhelm the public interest." The self-styled "citizens lobby," Common Cause, hit up NEA's financial contributions to congressmen's campaigns in exchange for support on ED.

If NEA was going to be the only motor behind the bill in 1979, it would not pass, they agreed. The support of other education organizations was being ignored.

What we need is a *real*, working coalition, they decided. It would have to be headed by another education association. NEA should only be one of hundreds of members. All lobbying and PR would have to be supervised and coordinated by this third party. NEA could be a major contributor and participant, but should not try to dominate. That would be a hard undertaking for the powerhouse teacher union, accustomed to leading all other education groups.

But who would run this new coalition? What would it be called? Where would it be located? How would the funding be handled? Would NEA approve? Did NEA have any other choice?

The group-by-the-pool settled on leaving the matter in the hands of Cohen and White, who would feel out NEA leaders back in Washington and go from there.

The independent ED coalition movement took on a life of its own. Some of the state education lobbyists met the following week with NEA Government Relations Director Stan McFarland, who said NEA would not object and would help out. They jumped head-first into making plans for a first meeting.

But many NEA people looked upon the idea with disdain. They were afflicted with the mentality that we can do this by ourselves, and we don't need the headaches of another coalition. They also saw themselves as the real political pros, and doubted seriously that these other lobbyists had enough savvy or clout to head up such a major undertaking. In fact, NEA wanted to be in control of the push for ED. They wanted that bill and the credit for passing it.

Gail Bramblett, who pretty much had gone it alone in 1978, argued within NEA that such a coalition couldn't hurt, at the least. She had worked the issue enough to know the NEA-supports-Carter-gets-ED perception was so pervasive on Capitol Hill and in the press that it could easily bring them to their knees. More and more, she was becoming a believer in the value of coalition politics.

While the debate raged on within NEA, Allan Cohen emerged as the ring leader of the new coalition. The 35-year-old Illinois state education lobbyist began working furiously to line up education groups for an organizational meeting December 6. The coalition would be his baby, and he returned from Arizona full of energy and determination to make it work.

If it had been anyone else, the coalition idea might have collapsed at its inception. But Cohen's personality and style made it easier for NEA to accept. He wasn't over-assertive nor too aggressive, and was careful not to offend or bruise sensitive egos. He laboriously consulted all his key colleagues before making a move—Marilyn, myself, Gail, Stan McFarland, Pat Gwaltney, Don White, and others.

Perhaps Cohen's greatest strength was his indefatigable *energy*. He was willing to invest the time and personal stamina to pull Washington's education community together for this, the biggest fight it would ever have. No one at NEA or anywhere else had been willing to roll up their sleeves and take the initiative. Those close to him knew he possessed good management and organizational skills. In the year ahead, they would be tested to the hilt.

*   *   *

Driving out Route 7 to Reston, Virginia I looked in my rear-view mirror and saw a White House limousine following.

"Look who's behind us," I smiled at Marilyn, sitting beside me in the front seat. She turned her head around and chuckled at the scene: chauffeur at the wheel, Terry Straub talking into the limo telephone, Pat Gwaltney and crew scrunched together in the back seat.

We were all on our way to what someday we would look back on as a landmark in the ED battle—Allan Cohen's first coalition meeting. Allan had purposely chosen the distant, obscure headquarters of the National Association of Secondary School Principals for a number of symbolic reasons. It signified in a small way that the initiative was coming from outside the Capital beltway, and by holding it in a third-party building, no one could construe it as being controlled by the NEA. Lastly, only those most committed to ED would venture so far out of Washington.

The 30 people who gathered at the Wednesday, December 6 conference came from groups including the community and junior colleges, school administrators, university professors, handicapped, ed research, libraries, music educators, school principals, audio visual aids, PTA, students, school boards, and state chiefs. Four NEA lobbyists showed up, somewhat like CIA agents, to monitor everything. This first brainstorming session had been kept largely secret; the press had not been tipped off.

"We're here for a common goal, to get a Department of Education created in the 96th Congress," Allan began. He warned the coalition would not survive if its members bickered over the details of the ED bills.

Ideas and suggestions bounced around the conference room. On timing, everyone agreed we should move early and complete action in 1979. "If you don't get a bill in the first session, the opponents will drag it out and kill the bill," one lobbyist cautioned. Strategically, the "HEW control mentality" should be stressed, along with HEW's fraud and abuse, they agreed.[29] Someone suggested that they "talk Cabinet more than Department—plug the angle that 'your child needs a voice at the White House.'" More talk centered around urging the President, Ribicoff, and Brooks to stay out of turf fights. For several minutes, the conferees tossed around the notion of getting Rosalyn Carter involved, since she had already pushed her husband toward ED and had concerns about education.

The people there later divided up into three smaller legislation, public relations, and outreach.

Gail Bramblett assumed leadership of the legislation subcommittee, retaining control over lobbying. Marilyn participated. They drew up target dates for action in 1979—bills should be introduced in January, hearings held in February, mark-ups sometime in March, and floor consideration in April. Gail divvied up assignments: visit new members of Congress, get readings on present ones, seek out congressional speakers.

In a nearby room, I brainstormed with others on ways to attack our serious public relations problems. The national press would have to be educated, supportive op-ed columns sought, and positive editorials encouraged. To educate the public at large, Don White convinced the group something like a filmstrip should be developed

---

[29] By far, most of all governmental aid—federal, state, local —disbursed for health and welfare programs came from HEW. Agency bureaucrats knew they held the purse strings and thus were affected with a "we're-in-control" mentality. Unfortunately, too often that state of mind seemed to affect HEW decisions and regulations on education, an activity in which the federal government contributed only nine per cent of total funds spent in the U.S.

touting ED's case. We got into a discussion on the upcoming State of the Union address. I argued against any splashy presidential endorsement, believing it didn't mesh with Carter's recent campaign to cut the budget and reduce government. "I disagree," NEA's Jim Green looked me in the eye. "The State of the Union will be the President's most public forum. He'll have all the ears of Congress before him at once. We need him to make that strong statement there to the members." I explained that I was working on a comprehensive press packet to be sent by Ribicoff to the nation's media.

In still another room, NEA's Roz Baker headed up an "outreach" grouping that would work to broaden the base of support for the bill.

Everyone came together once more in mid-afternoon for a wrap-up discussion. How should the coalition be organized? The consensus ruled out any formalized arrangement; no offices or special telephones or expensive budget. It would be an ad-hoc union.

Allan Cohen was appointed head of the coalition without dissent.

*   *   *

Ready to go public, Cohen scheduled a second meeting of his infant coalition for December 20. This time, it was open to any group that wanted to come and join.

On entering that morning the giant conference room in the Hall of the States complex just off the Senate side of Capitol Hill, Marilyn and I were pleasantly surprised. It was jam-packed with more than 100 representatives from as many organizations. *Coalition power.*

We were very impressed. I wondered, though, how many of these people were willing to work, invest time and energy in readying their troops for battle. Many judged that ED was going to pass easily in 1979, and they wanted a seat on-board the chariot of victory. It would not be that easy.

Allan had sown the seeds of a large coalition. The press now knew about it and publicized the early efforts to organize. Everyday, more groups came aboard. Gwaltney and Straub were enthused enough that they began planning for a meeting at the White House for the new coalition. Possibly, the President or Vice President would speak.

The ball was picking up speed.

SEVENTEEN

A New Foundation

Our final campaign. In 1979, it was do or die.

We would have to do everything all over again—redraft and reintroduce Ribicoff's bill, mark it up again, report it to the Senate for floor consideration. The same ritual would be repeated on the House side.

1979 brought with it a new "Congress"—the 96th two-year congressional session in American history. All bills would start from scratch.

One of our biggest concerns the first weeks of January was which senators and representatives would leave or join our Committee and the House Committee. Heavy negotiations and tradeoffs went on behind the scenes in both houses. We ended up with four new senators, two from each party. One of them, Maine Republican William Cohen had pledged in his campaign to oppose the bill, so the vote in our Committee this year would not be unanimous.

On the other side of the Hill, AFT, AFL, and Catholic lobbyists were mapping strategy with conservative groups to stack Brooks's Committee new membership against ED. There would be nine open slots, three Democratic, six Republican. They were ultimately successful—most of the new Republicans had gone on record as opposed to ED and the three Democrats had made no commitments.

At the White House, Terry Straub set up a 30-member "Department of Education Task Force" consisting of top Carter officials from every interested Administration office—personnel, press, legislation, congressional, OMB, PRP, women's and minority issues, Ham Jordan, etc. The group's mission was purely political; lobby the bill through Congress, enlisting the aid of outside groups. Although a junior member of the President's congressional staff, Straub brought to the ED campaign renewed energy at the highest levels of the White House— something that had been sorely missing in 1978.

Allan Cohen had been fine-tuning the shape of his new "Ad Hoc Committee for a Cabinet Department of Education." More associations enlisted, more subcommittee meetings were held.

It would be an out-and-out political fight in 1979. We had already laid the base with research into issues behind ED, past hearings, debate, and turf wars. Eventually, it would come down to a vote for Jimmy Carter and NEA, or for AFT-AFL-Catholics-conservatives and the anti-bureaucracy movement.

If things went our way, hearings, mark-ups, and floor action would be conducted at an accelerated pace.

*   *   *

We wanted Senator Ribicoff's bill ready for reintroduction by the third week of January, when Congress returned. Marilyn and I examined line-by-line the old bill as passed by the Senate in 1978. We did some rewriting.

Lobbyists for state and local groups practically moved into our offices. Most—school boards, state chiefs, governors, state legislators, Education Commission of the States—supported the bill, but warned of strong opposing elements within their organizations. Throughout

January and February, they daily would press Marilyn for language in the new bill protecting state and local control. It wasn't enough to have a special provision *prohibiting* federal control of education; they wanted specific language *defining* the role of state and local governments. Would new precedents or legal interpretations be carved out? Would it restrict the federal government from doing what it was already doing?

Marilyn refereed the negotiations, careful to research the meaning of every word and restrict the state and local language to the "findings and purposes" section, where it would have the least impact. To emphasize our intent, she consented to featuring the new language in a special section there: "Sec. 103, State and Local Responsibilities for Education."

By January 17, our first redraft of Ribicoff's bill had been finished and sent upstairs to the Senate legislative counsel's office for refinements. 99 individually-typed letters went out to senators from Ribicoff inviting cosponsorship. This year, however, we would not go bananas rounding up cosponsors.

*   *   *

Our opponents stepped up their efforts.

The AFT hired Washington lawyer and former U.S. Rep. James O'Hara to lobby full-time against ED in 1979. O'Hara had met with several House Committee members and succeeded in turning some around. The first was Pennsylvania Democrat William Moorhead, whose city of Pittsburgh was one of AFT's top 20 locals. O'Hara also convened a few meetings of lobbyists from other groups, striving to piece together an informal coalition of his own.

AFT teachers flooded House and Senate offices with mail against the bills. AFT officials also began a quiet campaign of courting opposition from American opinion leaders, mostly in the academic and media worlds.

Ivy league colleges' own special interest organization, the Association of American Universities, began working hard against us. Association President Thomas Bartlett and lobbyist Newton Cattell both personally detested ED because of its "potential for further federalizing education." They pressured other higher ed groups to take a stand against ED. Later, the Association of American Colleges released a poll of its members showing 78 per cent opposed, 17 per cent in favor.

A tiny, right-wing group, "National Association of Professional Educators," delivered a statement to our door opposing the bill "based on the fear of big government and big unions."

Marilyn and I had a nice touch-base meeting with the U.S. Catholic Conference's congenial lobbyist, Frank Monihan. We learned there was absolutely no middle ground with the Catholics; they were opposed, period.

Rep. John Erlenborn sent his Illinois constituents in early January a canned column saying, "I fought this proposal in the 95th Congress and expect to lead the opposition to it again in the new Congress.

*   *   *

Monday, January 5, the 96th Congress began business. There were no surprises in elections of leaders and chairmen. Democrats maintained control of the House, Senate, and White House.

Democratic leaders used the interlude to push through procedural changes that would restrict filibusters. The House approved daily gavel-to-gavel television coverage of its floor proceedings.

A boring first month it would be; few bills would be considered because committees were still being organized. But then not much was expected of the 96th Congress. "The 96th Congress: A Mirror to Reflect U.S. Austerity Mood," read a *Washington Post* headline that week. There would be concentration on oversight instead of creating new things, and a determination to hold down the cost of government and fight inflation.

Jimmy Carter picked up on this theme a week later when he delivered his second State of the Union address. Threatened with challenges for the 1980 presidential race by Democrats and Republicans alike, Carter would return to the fiscal conservatism he espoused during the 1976 campaign. The tight Fiscal Year 1980 budget he submitted held down increases for domestic social programs, gave more to defense, and whacked away at the deficit. Observers judged it a neat preemptive strike at Republican issues. There would be few new projects.

"…The challenge to us is to build a new and firmer foundation for the future," Carter said in his speech, "for a sound economy, more effective government, for more political trust…

"We must stop excessive government growth," he told the Congress and people watching TV at home, "and we must control government spending habits." The House chamber burst into loud applause.

"…Now we must make the good programs more effective, and improve or weed out those which are wasteful or unnecessary. With the support of the Congress, we have begun to reorganize and get control of the bureaucracy.

"…This year we must extend major reorganization efforts to education, to economic development, and to the management of our natural resources…".

No applause, not even the words "Department of Education." Asking a new Cabinet agency would have destroyed the theme of the speech. Yet the utterance of "reorganization" and "education" together left an unmistakable inference that ED was on Carter's agenda.

In the lengthy written State of the Union message delivered to Congress two days later, the President was more specific: "I will again propose to the Congress that a Cabinet-level Department of Education be created. This will be a very high priority of this Administration...".

*   *   *

Secret Service agents punched into their computers Social Security numbers of a long line of education lobbyists the next morning. More than 100 were cleared for entry to the Old Executive Office Building fourth-floor auditorium, where Administration heavies would try to whip up their enthusiasm for the battle ahead.

Up on the royal blue curtained stage, Jim McIntyre, Terry Straub, Bert Carp, Richard Pettigrew, Harrison Wellford, Pat Gwaltney, Allan Cohen, and Marilyn took seats at a long conference table facing the audience.

"Senator Ribicoff will introduce his bill today and the number will be 'S.210,'" Marilyn announced to the gathering. "We have scheduled hearings on the bill for February 6, 7, and 8," she continued, the lobbyists scrambling to jot down this important news.

Allan appealed to the lobbyists not to clog the hearings with requests to testify. "We want everything to move as fast as possible."

Marilyn explained the bill would be similar to that passed the previous year, except for some clarification of state and local control language.

Terry Straub briefed the group on some of the things the White House would be doing in the weeks ahead. While he talked, we were distracted by much off-stage activity. Suddenly, several aides appeared in the side rows. Two young Secret Service agents, sporting the telltale ear plugs with wires running into their suit coat pockets, stationed themselves at opposite ends of the stage, eying the audience.

"...And now," said Straub, looking behind him at a side door, "the Vice President of the United States...".

Walter Mondale walked in 30 seconds later to a standing ovation.

"...I have talked to several of my friends on the Hill," Mondale said. "There's a lot of snickering about this proposal. They don't think it's serious. They don't think the educational community is serious about it...They have to hear not only from the President and the rest of us here,...they've got to hear from you!

"I served in the Senate for 12 years and there is nothing that moves a senator or a congressman more than the feeling that he better do something or he won't get by the next election. It's a very, very persuasive argument...

"If you can't do it with the support of this President, and of this government, and with this Congress, you're never going to do it.

"...It is going to be one of the best things we have ever done for the people of this country.

Mondale got another standing ovation, then left. He had succeeded in rousing the crowd.

Not until 4 o'clock that afternoon did we complete all the paperwork and have Senator Ribicoff file his bill with Senate floor clerks. "S.210" had 44 cosponsors.

Marilyn and I began lining up witnesses for the quick, three-day hearing schedule.

*   *   *

Sensing a worsened political situation, Senator Ribicoff went on the offensive. "The Department of Education...will NOT be a national ministry of education," he assured some 200 local school board members at the Hyatt Regency Hotel Sunday, January 27. "Neither Congress nor the American people would stand for that."

The National School Boards Association's traditional support for ED was in jeopardy. In just two months, its annual convention would consider a resolution supporting the bill. Already, three state affiliates—Kansas, Nevada, and Pennsylvania—voted to break with the national body, mostly on the local control issue. More had doubts—Michigan, Texas, and Ohio. We *had* to hang onto their support.

"...Ladies and gentlemen, I served as Secretary of HEW," Ribicoff explained in a passionate voice. "...This Department is so huge it impinges upon the life of every man, woman, and child in this country.

"The Secretary of HEW is putting out a different fire every day, and they're usually in the health or welfare field..."

Ribicoff had their ears. The large banquet room fell silent.

"You are very important for the passage of this bill. I come here today to ask your help and support. You are the people who have the local responsibility, and you realize what it means to have at least someone in the executive branch who is in charge, someone who is a Secretary of Education, someone who will devote all his time and energy to education.

"All I can tell you, if you have 13 commissioners of education in 12 years, you're *never* going to have a policy that is unified and meaningful.

"...I'd like your help, I'd appreciate it. But if I don't have your help, I'm going to do everything I can to pass it in spite of your opposition."

The school board people rose from their seats and applauded warmly. Marilyn and I exchanged approving glances.

*　　*　　*

Marilyn and Pat Gwaltney flew together to Houston that afternoon to win over the education committee of the National Conference of State Legislatures. Gwaltney, entering the second month of a pregnancy, didn't want to travel. But like all the other state-local groups, the state legislators needed stroking too.

Most of the state legislators did not oppose ED; neither did they wholeheartedly endorse it. They were suspicious of the motivations behind it. They feared intrusion by a strong U.S. Secretary of Education upon a delicate area of intergovernmental relations.

Both Gwaltney and Marilyn emphasized the extensive state-local language in the bill already, and indicated their willingness to add more.

At the top of the legislators' list was charging some high-level ED official with responsibility for direct state liaison, specifically the under-secretary of education. Marilyn and Pat practically conceded right then and there.

After the meeting, the state legislatures group started leaning solidly toward backing the bill.

*   *   *

Jack Brooks sat down with the President January 31 in the Oval Office for a one-on-one session. Carter asked the House Chairman's help again this year on ED. Brooks agreed enthusiastically, and told him to send his bill to the Hill quickly.

Waiting for the President somewhere on his desk was the McIntyre decision memo, dated January 25. Carter returned it with his decisions the first day of February.

"This year,…we expect substantial opposition to the Department on the grounds that it will increase bureaucracy and expenditures, be dom-inated by narrow elementary and secondary school interests, and expand federal control over what is primarily a state and local func-tion," the memo told Carter…

Senator Ribicoff's bill should pass "by a wide margin" again in the Senate, the 12-page document predicted. But Jack Brooks "is concerned about the opposition in his Committee…Despite the likelihood of delaying tactics in Committee and on the floor and the general lukewarm interest in the House, we think that the bill will pass, if the Administration demonstrates that it is a high priority," McIntyre told Carter.

"…In order to gain passage, we believe that we must modify our proposal to resemble the Senate-passed Department of Education bill. Senator Ribicoff believes, and so do we, that we should create the Department with a core of education programs largely from HEW and bring in other related programs by reorganization or legislation later. The Vice President, Stu (Eizenstat), and Frank Moore agree that this is the best strategy."

Carter agreed with OMB that Indian education and child nutrition should stay out this year, and that science education should stay in. He reluctantly consented to "leaving open our position" on transferring vocational rehabilitation.

The memo concluded by stating, "We plan to have the Administration bill ready for introduction in the House early in February."

The President's staff had already started recruiting support from civil rights leaders, Catholics (prominent Catholic university presidents), labor (AFL unions to offset AFT), conservatives (businessmen and corporations), and state and local elected officials.

At the top of their list: neutralize higher education. The Association of American Universities executive board breakfasted February 1 in the White House mess, all the while listening to pitches of Jim McIntyre, Stu Eizenstat, and the Vice President. The Ivy-league university presidents were impressed by their arguments, more so that essential education and research funding had been restored in the President's budget. The meeting went so well that AAU President Tom Bartlett left in a huff.

Bert Carp used the same pitch several days later at a luncheon with 500 smaller, independent college leaders. The group would debate that day a policy statement communicating their "increasingly grave misgivings" about ED and their fear of "centralized planning and control of American education." Carp directly asked them for their support: "We want to win, we expect to win, we want your help."

*　　*　　*

Photographers clicked away at the Rev. Jesse Jackson as he sat at the witness table in our hearing room, stroking his moustache and reviewing his prepared statement. The famous, articulate civil rights and education advocate was the perfect star witness at the Committee's first hearing of 1979 and of the new Congress.

"...We are going to make sure this year we get this legislation out on the floor for quick passage so that the House will have ample opportunity," Senator Ribicoff opened the Tuesday, February 6 session. Five other senators sat with him at the dais.

"...Everything worth doing and accomplishing has education as a foundation from which to start," Jackson thundered from the well. "...Education must have the ear of the President and the Congress and only a separate department will assure it.

"...Our children are falling behind in world competition with other nations. It is not because of their genes. It is because of their agenda. Our national agenda does not put education in proper focus. When we are raising a military budget in peacetime, decreasing the educational budget in real dollars, it says something about the character of our leadership and our national priorities.

"...The lack of education increases welfare. The lack of education increases joblessness...It costs more to be without the 'E' than it does to be on the 'W', which almost runs you into 'H'," the black leader punned, eliciting howls of laughter from the crowd.

A hodgepodge of nine groups and individuals followed at the witness table, offering the state and local view. "We do not believe that erosion of local control will occur," the New Jersey school boards association president insisted. The state education chiefs, state boards of education, Mayor of Nashville, and a Nebraska state senator agreed.

But representatives of the Education Commission of the States and the National Governors Association held out, claiming the majority of state-local officials are "uncertain or indifferent and, if pressed, might not come out on the positive side at this time." The price tag: make intergovernmental relations "a core responsibility" of ED, charge the undersecretary with that responsibility, and include strong language either prohibiting outright federal control of education or something meaning the same.

* * *

A heavy snowstorm the next morning paralyzed the city, but at 10 o'clock our hearing went on as scheduled.

A panel of three higher ed reps came forward to the witness table. The teacher colleges and equal-opportunity-in-higher-ed groups endorsed the bill. AAU President Thomas Bartlett didn't.

"A Department of Education offers the possibility of some advantage," Bartlett began his testimony. "It also presents serious risks." He would emphasize the risks.

Bartlett, a middle-aged, balding man pointed out to the Senator having a principal spokesman "assumes that the central focus should be a federal one."

"If I may interrupt," Ribicoff said, "...if $25 billion is being spent in education, there's a legitimate federal role in education...If you don't want any federal input in education, let's cut out any federal contribution altogether and let the states and localities spend all the money. You know the hue and cry that would go up across this nation if you took away that $25 billion."

Bartlett persistently described the "two courses that might be open to us": a simple reorganization within HEW that "presents little long term risk and would cost virtually nothing," or creating an Education Department that "would be a significant and virtually irreversible political decision."

Msgr. Wilfrid Paradis of the Catholic Conference waited in a front-row seat. The elderly priest came forward and delivered another critical statement, similar to last year's. "There is good reason to fear that a new Department of Education will further increase federal interference in both public and private education in areas that rightfully belong to parents and to the local community," he reiterated. Paradis called ED "a policy decision...to make good on a political campaign promise."

"I first put in the Department of Education bill in 1965," Senator Ribicoff commented stiffly when the Monsignor finished. "...The bill we are talking about today is my bill. The bill we had last year was my bill. It wasn't the Administration's bill. The Administration came in and adopted my bill. I understand tomorrow they are going to put in a bill of their own...I have no questions."

The agitated Senator abruptly cracked his gavel, pushed his chair back, got up and stormed out the anteroom door behind him.

*   *   *

Early the next morning, the Vice President and Jim McIntyre marked the send-off of the President's new ED bill to Capitol Hill with a special briefing for the White House press corps.

"...This year we think we're going to have the Department of Education established," Mondale predicted. "...This is the only major industrial democracy in the world that does not have a department or ministry of education."

The OMB director emphasized the new agency would be more manageable, efficient, and coordinated.

Senator Ribicoff introduced the bill on behalf of the President in the Senate, where it would die. Jack Brooks held off three weeks before introducing it in the House so that many cosponsors—72 in all—could be persuaded to sign on.

Minutes later, McIntyre, Harrison Wellford, and Pat Gwaltney hopped a government car for the ride to Capitol Hill. They had a 10:00 a.m. appointment in front of the Senate Governmental Affairs Committee. Our third and final day of ED hearings.

Sitting alongside the three OMB officials were Education Commissioner Ernest Boyer and Assistant Secretary Mary Berry.[30] Secretary Califano again bowed out, sending an endorsing letter almost word-for-word the same as last year's.[31]

The OMB director advocated a provision prohibiting federal control of education and another making the undersecretary responsible for intergovernmental relations.

"The cost of setting up the Department, approximately $10 million during the first full year of operation, will be offset by the savings that result from the elimination of unnecessary overhead and duplicative staff functions in (HEW)," McIntyre claimed. Later in the hearing, he became more specific: between 300 and 400 positions would be eliminated.

The Commissioner admitted his belief in ED was "not a conviction I felt strongly when I assumed the (post) in January 1977." But he said "it would give the Secretary a once-in-a-lifetime opportunity to achieve consolidations and internal (management) improvements." His present set-up in HEW, he granted, was "not efficient" and "indefensible," even though he had been "extremely well supported" by Secretary Califano.

"I am curious," Ribicoff butt in. "How many Cabinet meetings have you attended?"

"Well, I have not attended a Cabinet meeting, Mr. Chairman...," Boyer answered.

---

[31] Top Carter officials' desire that Califano be ordered to work publicly for ED never ceased. In their Feb. 7 "administratively confidential" memo to the President, they recommended he "call Secretary Califano before our Thursday announcement to enlist his active support...His silence could be damaging."

"How many private meetings have you held with the President...?"

"I have not been alone with the President. I have been in several meetings with Secretary Califano dealing with education matters with the President."

"You see, this is the point I make," Ribicoff declared. "Here is education, so important to the future of our country, and the President never sees his Education Commissioner privately...".

Sen. William Cohen closely interrogated the Administration witnesses for the meaning of a separate ED. The Maine Republican could not reconcile in his mind a stronger national focus with local control of education.

"There is already a federal policy concerning education in this country," Berry explained to him.

"What is that federal policy?," he wondered.

"That policy is promoting equal education opportunity for all citizens, and attempting to improve the quality of education in the country for every person who attends an institution of learning. That policy, enacted by the Congress, is administered by the Administration.

"I think the difficulty comes when one fails to distinguish between a federal policy, which we have, and a national policy, which we do not have," Berry clarified. "A national policy would mean that someone in Washington was telling every school system in the country what they were to do, what they were to teach, what the basic education program ought to be in the school.

"We have no such national policy. The establishment of a Department of Education would not affect that one way or the other. The only way there will ever be a national education policy in this country is if the Congress determines to enact one...".

*   *   *

The flood of negative editorials became a torrent after all the news stories prompted by the Mondale-McIntyre briefing.

"Never underestimate the power of a bad idea to generate bad arguments," the *Washington Post* yammered the following Sunday. It featured Mondale's quote about the U.S. being the only nation without a department or ministry. The paper thought local control of education was "a tradition worth holding on to." It predicted ED "will become a gigantic single-minded lobbying outfit. It will be the NEA writ large."

The *Wall Street Journal* February 13 called ED "one of the most inane policy ideas to come down the pike in a long time," and said "it's hard to imagine a less cheering prospect than a unified national education policy set by the NEA."

The *New York Times* suggested "the energies of the White House would be better devoted to the long-overdue reorganization of HEW."

Around the country, newspapers printed editorials faster than we could read them. A samplings

• "...costly bureaucracy..."—Boston *Herald American*

• "...not enough discussion has been heard about whether the general public interest will be well served."—Honolulu *Star Bulletin*.

• "...merely a means for creation of a national education policy..."—San Francisco Examiner

• "...will encourage federal encroachment whether necessary or not..."— Kansas City *Times*

• "...Congress ought to fling it back in the face of the President and the NEA..."—New York *Daily News*

• "...NEA could reasonably expect to enjoy a quantum jump in influence..."—San Diego *Union*.

We fought back. Every newspaper, radio and television station in America received a slick press packet I produced promoting the case for ED—using the Senate Committee logo and the free mailing privilege. White House press operatives set up several briefing sessions for out-of-town editors. And, NEA mailed thousands of "action guides" to its teacher organizers giving instructions on ways of generating favorable publicity.

*   *   *

Marilyn and I had hoped we would be going straight from hearings to mark-up. It was not to be.

Mysteriously, Senator Ribicoff procrastinated in setting the date.

Sensing the need for a cheering session with the Senator, Allan Cohen brought the fourth meeting of his coalition to our hearing room February 28. The enthusiastic, applauding crowd of education lobbyists welcomed Ribicoff warmly, temporarily rejuvenating his spirit for his own bill.

The Senate leadership pressed committees to churn out bills, having received no major bills yet. Byrd's people asked us what was holding up ED.

Finally, Ribicoff caved in and designated Wednesday, March 14.

*   *   *

Wind and heavy rain pelted the tall hearing room windows Wednesday morning. Lobbyists, wearing new, red-white-and-blue buttons exclaiming in bold letters "A DEPARTMENT OF EDUCATION/YES!" filled the audience section well before the 10 o'clock starting time of the mark-up.

A dozen reporters and photographers waited patiently as senators and staff arrived in a steady stream.

In a surprisingly short 15 minutes, a quorum of six senators were present and Ribicoff banged his gavel. Eight other senators would later arrive.

"...My feeling is this bill has had so many days of hearings and so much discussion and so much consideration and we really are presented with few improvements," the Chairman began.

Sen. William Roth proposed more amendments on behalf of the state-local groups. He and Ribicoff, after some public and private negotiating, finally settled on, "The establishment of the Department of Education shall not increase the authority of the federal government over education...". The new language passed unanimously.

Senator Cohen asked to make a statement. "In going through the hearings and listening to the witnesses, I come to the conclusion I must oppose the bill," he said in a low-key tone. Cohen feared that "we haven't really precluded this from becoming an educational policymaking body."

Senator Danforth announced he would vote for the bill, with the understanding that ED would not "be a further reach of the federal government in...decision making at the state and local level." Other senators chimed in and backed him.

Ranking Republican Charles Percy spoke for the bill, citing the "chaos" in HEW.

Going around the table, senators took turns offering not amendments, but instead their praise to Ribicoff.

New York Sen. Jacob Javits, going against the AFT teachers in his state, explained he was "very lukewarm about the Department of Education." But then assured his close friend Abe Ribicoff, "I will vote to report the bill out."

Just one hour after beginning, the Committee was ready to vote. There had been no major amendment.

The chief clerk called the roll. 15 senators voted "aye." Cohen cast the lone dissenting vote.

"President Carter's proposed Department of Education whizzed through the Senate Governmental Affairs Committee yesterday and is expected to get equally breezy treatment on the Senate floor sometime before the April Easter recess," the *Washington Post* reported the next day. "The real battle will be in the House Government Operations Committee, which opens hearings on the issue toward the end of this month."

It was one of the smoothest-running mark-ups ever.

*   *   *

No time for celebration. Marilyn and I strapped ourselves to our typewriters for the next 10 days and slapped together the Committee report on S.210. Essentially, all we had to do was rewrite and revise last year's report.

Savings and costs were given more prominence. We described the 22 "principal" offices and officers dealing with education in HEW, and noted they would be slashed to just 11 reporting to one person—the Secretary of Education—as opposed to three at present. Borrowing from OMB's data, we told how at least 15 offices would be eliminated from the regulations clearance process. OMB's projections of cutting out 450 jobs and saving $100 million more through consolidated computer systems were highlighted.

A new, special section defended the bill against the old federal control litany. "State and local control," the report proclaimed, "…is deeply embedded in the fabric of American society, and cannot be changed through the simple act of giving education Cabinet status at the federal level." It described the "elaborate system of checks and balances" where education, state, and local interests continually monitor and pronounce judgment on federal programs and rules. The report discussed the "hidden danger" in administering education with nationally-focused health and welfare programs.

"The Secretary of Education will be forced to devote more attention to the real needs and problems of states and localities in education, for his constituents will hold most of the control and dollars in education," we wrote. "A new partnership will have to develop...".

*   *   *

Jack Brooks had given the go-ahead for House hearings March 26 and 27. Bill Jones and his team of staff were lining up witnesses.

Resistance mounted in the House. Republicans especially filled the *Congressional Record* daily with statements attacking ED and the political motivations of Jimmy Carter. Early readings of Brooks's Committee were alarming. Only a dozen of the 39 members were counted as solidly for the bill. About 18 were against; the rest undecided.

Many felt if the ED bill reached the floor, it would pass. Brooks's Committee had become the big "if." Proponents and opponents alike agreed the battleground would be the House Committee.

Jim McIntyre and other Carter officials would lead-off at the hearings Monday, March 26. Heading off critics, McIntyre, Bert Carp, and Pat Gwaltney summoned key reporters to the Old Executive Office Building the Friday before for a special preview of their new, improved spiel.

"Just the fact that you create a new department doesn't mean new expenditures," the OMB director told them, pointing to several color-boxed organizational charts of the mess of offices in HEW and the super-clean ED structure after. He pumped the newsmen full of cost-savings figures—personnel eliminated, offices abolished—adding up to "a savings of over $100 million in the long run."

"I don't know anyone who has done a better job than Joe Califano in running HEW over the years," McIntyre said, "but health and welfare so overwhelmingly demand his attention that educational problems are necessarily pushed aside." The quote made the *Washington Post*.

Monday morning, an angry Secretary of HEW phoned Jack Brooks and arranged for the House Chairman to send a brief letter requesting "a list of achievements your Department has accomplished in…education since you became Secretary in early 1977." The incoming Brooks letter got stamped "PRIORITY" over at HEW and a six-page response flew back to Capitol Hill the next day, Tuesday.

The White House staff and Jim McIntyre learned of Califano's orchestration and blew a gasket. Frank Moore spoke to the President about it. Carter pulled out a piece of White House stationery and wrote in his own hand: "To Sec. Califano—I want your active support in the Congress for the Department of Education legislation. J. Carter."

Califano sent back the next day a "personal and confidential" memo to the President. "Since you made your decision," Califano wrote, "I have supported it actively. And I am, of course, prepared to do whatever else you wish." Califano told Carter he disagreed with McIntyre's statement because "it belittles the attention that has been paid to education by me and my colleagues."

* * *

Seven Carter Administration appointees flanked OMB Director McIntyre at the witness table in Brooks's Committee hearing room. Several easels off to one side held the giant, colorful charts explaining the before and after scenarios.

Only standing room was available in the audience that Monday, March 26. A herd of reporters sat around a press table to the far right, below the two-tiered Committee dais.

"The question before the Congress is simply this: How do we most effectively manage more than 150 federal education programs?," McIntyre asked the Representatives. "…Critics have quite understandably chosen to divert attention to (other) factors…".

The Director referred to the chart, littered with boxes and lines illustrating a confused federal structure. The boxes were marked to show how several offices at many different levels did practically the same thing. "The Department of Education will eliminate much of this duplication, including between 350 and 400 positions.... Routine regulations take an average of 519 days to be issued...(ED) will cut this time in half, by eliminating 15 offices from the clearance process."

Offices drawing up the education budget would be cut from 25 to 10, McIntyre asserted. Those involved in developing legislation, cut from 19 to 9. Creating the Department would require "no new funds." $10 million transition costs would be offset by $15-19 million personnel savings. Improved financial management and audit systems could save another $100 million, he said.

The congressmen were impressed. "Very sophisticated...well-thought out," Republican leader Frank Horton praised McIntyre. "I want to commend you for pointing out specific savings."

"That was an excellent statement," Rep. John Erlenborn was moved to say. "...It is so good it almost justifies a poor proposal."

When the laughter died down, Jack Brooks looked over at Erlenborn and cracked, "I thank the gentleman very much." More laughter.

However, Erlenborn would not let McIntyre get away with mere praise. "I have sat in this place and listened to people from your seat make the same sort of statements year after year," he spoke in a deep amplified voice to the OMB director down below. Similar efficiency claims had been made for the Housing, Transportation, and Energy Departments, he insisted "...The proposal before us today...is really little more than a combination of the overseas dependents schools from (DOD) and the present Office of Education."

Chairman Brooks later recessed the first-day hearing. Nearly the entire Congress descended on the White House grounds for the 2:00p.m. ceremony at which Egyptian President Anwar Sadat and Israeli Prime Minister Menachem Begin would sign a treaty of peace.

For Jimmy Carter, it was a moment of great personal triumph. "It will make him look presidential," one senator told reporters.

* * *

A beaming Jack Brooks walked back into his hearing room at 3:30 to a wild, thundering standing ovation and cheers. His fanciers: lobbyists of Alan Cohen's Ad Hoc Committee for a Cabinet Department of Education, some 150 in all. The applause was purposely prolonged and vigorous, as planned in advance.

"...I sense a lot more opposition this year than we year and it was rough then," Brooks spoke to the crowd. Hair on the sides of his head was tasseled from the wind outside. He stood up on the elevated dais floor.

Two main arguments—more bureaucracy and federal control—would be harped on by the opponents, he warned.

"It should be stressed that the bill does not create any additional programs, agencies, or bureaus," he coached the lobbyists. "Everything going into the Department already exists. The programs are operating. The money is being spent already.

"...As for the issue of federal control, that is an emotional one that is hard to respond to. People who raise it just can't—or won't—be convinced that we're not out to take over the schools...

"You just have to keep hammering away, telling about the safeguards we've got in the bill...You won't convince the diehards. But just try to make as much noise as they do and maybe we'll come out even on that one."

* * *

9:30 the next morning, Tuesday, Brooks's second hearing began.

House Education and Labor Committee Chairman Carl Perkins offered his support. National Urban League President Vernon Jordan appeared, as requested by the White House and NEA, to add his endorsement to the bill. White House staff had also been instrumental in persuading Xerox Corp. to send an official who would defend the bill. The huge company owned major facilities in the upstate New York district of ranking Republican Frank Horton.

New York Democrat Sen. Daniel Patrick Moynihan delivered perhaps the most entertaining testimony. The Senator had a reputation for his sometimes verbose and theatrical style of public speaking. "Why are we doing this at all?," he asked. "The answer is this and it is a painful one to present: It is being done for political purposes. It is being done, Mr. Chairman, to win the next election...".

Groans and snickers lifted from the audience. AFT President Al Shanker sat behind Moynihan in the audience, waiting to testify.

"We are now told that we must have a Department of Education by 1980 for the implicit purpose of beefing up the precinct organization of the Democratic Party," Moynihan railed on. "As a Democrat, I would be ashamed to ask a Republican to vote for this bill...".

Brooks had a ready comment. "I am surprised that a man with your political acumen and experience as well as expertise and skill would ever be ashamed of the awareness of political objectives...

"If (the President's) judgment is wrong and it does not turn out to be an improvement, then it will work to his detriment. This is the chance he takes...I think it is perfectly honorable and decent for him to be concerned about 66 million children. I am...".

"Politically, if I were from New York, I would probably go with Mr. Shanker and oppose," commented Rhode Island Democrat Fernand St. Germain.

"I do not think anyone would be defeated or elected on the success or failure of this legislation," St. Germain added. "...In all legislation there is politics involved...".

"...However, I think this is institutionalizing politics in education," Moynihan countered.

Erlenborn thanked Moynihan for his testimony. "It happens that you and I do agree…You finally found a thoughtful member of this Committee."

Politics aside, Moynihan's lengthy written statement documented his assertion that education pervaded the functions of the federal government, and could never be truly consolidated in a single Cabinet department. His line of reasoning: if it's going to be established, throw everything in. Otherwise, leave the "E" in HEW.

A solemn Al Shanker took the witness seat. "…Our clipping service is sending in editorials by the ton…against the separate department…". The AFT President said support was fading away, even among the school boards.

The reason for the bill, he repeated, "was a promise made in a political campaign." But Shanker was quick to add, "there is nothing wrong with that."

Yet this promise contained "a rather broad notion" of what ED would contain. "I would raise this question: If this Department is going to be such a great thing for education of this country, why does everybody that is supposed to be moved over there come before you and demand to be taken out?"

Later that afternoon, Marian Wright Edelman presented a negative statement. The Children's Defense Fund leader had decided to go after killing the whole ED bill, having won on keeping Head Start out of it. "Children's health, education, and social service needs cannot be separated out and still serve the whole child," she said.

"I hope that your opposition will remain unchanged," Erlenborn later told her.

A week after, the subcommittee would hold its last hearing—to hear exclusively voices against the bill. It would be Erlenborn's show.

*   *   *

Marilyn and I worked on the report galleys all afternoon, making a bunch of last-minute changes and substitutions.

We didn't finish until 7:30 that night. Senator Ribicoff had gone home for the day, but Senate clerks let that little detail pass and the report was officially filed.

They knew the Majority Leader wanted that bill on the floor ASAP.

EIGHTEEN

Trouble on the Senate Floor

The "Kamikaze Five" had us worried. Senators Hayakawa, Morgan, Schmitt, Moynihan, and Jepsen were banding together, coming up with all kinds of debris they would toss in our path to final passage on the Senate floor. The danger loomed that Sen. Jesse Helms might also toss us a few of his choice smoke bombs.

Moynihan put up the first road block. "I…must ask your patience, and that of the Committee, as Legislative Counsel works on drafting a complex and rather lengthy amendment," he wrote the Majority Leader March 28—in effect, a "hold" on the bill. We already knew what the New York Democrat had in mind: an amendment transferring *hundreds* of federal programs having even the remotest link to education.

Schmitt's staff was thinking of amendments on DOD schools, making ED an independent agency, and science education. Hayakawa's people sent signals the California Republican was interested in a Department of Education study and in sunsetting the Department. Morgan's L.A. was drawing up an amendment that would prevent the

President from using his reorganization authority to bring programs to ED once established.

The National Right-to-Work Committee was peddling an amendment around the Senate, which conservative Iowa Republican Sen. Roger Jepsen found attractive, giving employees of local schools receiving federal funds the right *not* to affiliate with a union. The anti-union group feared "the NEA will use federal tax money under this bill to install compulsory unionism arrangements in public schools."

As for Jesse Helms, we had to be prepared for any of "his" issues: busing, abortion, prayer, civil rights, sex education...The North Carolina Republican's staff would tell us nothing.

A tight germaneness restriction on the bill would alleviate a lot of worry. But the Majority Leader oftentimes needed that flexibility to nail down the time agreement and prevent a filibuster. So, it was not entirely our decision.

We expected to be called to the floor soon. Allan Cohen's coalition sent out an alert: "We cannot take any votes for granted in the Senate."

Both Marilyn and I filled our calendars of back-to-back appointments with dozens of Senate aides, feeling out undecideds and educating new senators. The last weekend of March, as the world nervously anticipated a possible meltdown at Pennsylvania's Three Miles Island nuclear facility, we toiled just 90 nautical miles south in our Capitol Hill offices, getting ready for the floor.

Senator Byrd, restless about getting *something* substantive to the floor, spoke with Senator Ribicoff Friday, March 30. He wanted to start within the next week or two.

Four days later, at a White House breakfast, Byrd complained to the President that he didn't have enough to fill up the calendar. "Mr. President, unless we take up the (ED) bill next week, we'll have to go out early," he warned. Easter was fast approaching.

Returning to his Senate office a short while later, Byrd had decided to go ahead anyhow. The next day, he set the floor agenda for Thursday,

April 5. "I ask unanimous consent that the Senate proceed to the consideration of Calendar Order No. 54, S.210, a bill to establish a Department of Education..."

The Republicans agreed, so long as the vote on final passage came after the Easter recess.

*   *   *

Thursday morning was breezy and warm. Signs of spring were everywhere around the Capitol grounds—flowers, blossoms, green grass.

At the office, Marilyn and I prepared for the floor. Our files and notebooks were nearly ready. We expected to be called to the floor shortly after noon. By now, we were old hands at this—or so we thought.

We had no time for, nor any interest in, "opponents day" over at Brooks's Committee. John Erlenborn and allies had called in nine individuals to the 9:30 hearing. Brooks graciously presided.

Stanford University President Richard Lyman said ED would be "damaging" to American education. Literacy expert Paul Copperman claimed that ED would "add major costs to American public education."

The Pennsylvania school boards director predicted more local boards across the country would reverse support for the bill.

Brookings Institution senior fellow David Brenneman concluded, "If creating a department does not herald a substantial increase in federal financing of education nor a decisive shift in the purposes for which current expenditures are made, then exactly what purpose is being served?"

Erlenborn enjoyed the testimony. He had praise for them all: "...compelling...on target...eloquent...most perceptive...".

*   *   *

Senator Ribicoff, Marilyn and I were on the Senate floor by 2 o'clock when the presiding officer formally called up the ED bill. We lugged our files to the cramped area behind the small desks in the well.

"I am pleased that the Senate is beginning floor debate today…," Ribicoff stood and read into his microphone. We had written a long, detailed opening statement that went an extra step and rebutted the critics on bureaucratic expansion, federal control, and NEA domination. Ribicoff took the time to read it all.

From the Republican well, Senator Percy engaged Ribicoff in a long colloquy about his stint as HEW Secretary. Ribicoff said he could not remember education ever being discussed at a Cabinet meeting with President John F. Kennedy.

For the first hour, senators made known their views on the bill. Several personally delivered laudatory statements. Senator Roth remarked that S.210 was "a better bill than the one we had last year" because of the improved state-local language. But the antis were always there. "The history we have learned from federal agencies is that whenever there is an opportunity to extend more control, it is taken," warned Senator Cohen. "…Our schools now have so many rules and regulations to cope with that they cannot possibly give full-time attention to the business of teaching," Senator Hayakawa asserted in another of his long, rambling speeches.

As they droned on, Marilyn and I organized our stuff and chatted with Ribicoff, who was relaxed and jovial our first day back on the Senate floor. I looked up to the visitors' galleries and saw hordes of students watching the proceedings. April brings the first rush of annual class trips to the nation's capital.

Ribicoff suggested the absence of a quorum when Hayakawa finally finished. Byrd had returned to the floor with a much-edited piece of paper in hand—a proposed time agreement on the bill. As the clerk called the roll in vain, we all huddled in the center of the Senate floor to look it over—Ribicoff, Marilyn, myself, Byrd, his staff, Senator Stevens, Percy, and Bill Hildenbrand.

It was a hefty agreement: a seven-hour limit on debate of the bill itself and time restrictions on a list of amendments. Byrd mentioned Jesse Helms had two others.

"Well, do we know what Helms wants to do?," Ribicoff quietly asked the group. Neither Byrd nor Stevens knew.

"He's asked for the option of offering amendments that are not in the usual form," Byrd replied.

Marilyn's blood pressure jumped; she sighed in angry frustration. That's exactly what the capricious North Carolina senator wanted—a carte blanche to try blowing away the ED bill with a non-germane amendment on a controversial social issue. And now Byrd, striving to nail down an agreement, wanted to give in to him.

Ribicoff indicated his displeasure at letting Helms do anything. Byrd only nodded his head, communicating silently to Ribicoff it was either take this or face the threat of a filibuster. We could beat back a filibuster, for which the Senate was famous, but it would be messy and draw exaggerated national attention to the bill.

After a few minutes of thrashing it out in the private talk, Ribicoff responded jokingly, "Well, if you're going to get raped, I guess you might as well lay back and enjoy it."

Hildenbrand laughed loudly. Byrd and Stevens smiled. It was Ribicoff's way of giving reluctant consent.

As Byrd asked the presiding officer to rescind the quorum call, Ribicoff, Marilyn and I went back to our seats. Marilyn was panicky. "Isn't there anything we could do?," she whispered to the Senator.

"No, there isn't." Ribicoff began to show his irritation.

"Mr. President, this request has been cleared with Mr. Ribicoff, Mr. Percy, Mr. Stevens, the distinguished assistant Republican leader, with Mr. Helms…and other senators," Byrd spoke into his microphone. He proceeded to spell out the agreement in public.

Marilyn shook her head in her hands, mumbling to me, "This is bad, Bob. This is so bad."

Byrd and Stevens got into an on-the-record discussion about timing. "I am aware that the bill will not pass before the recess," Byrd conceded, but he hoped senators would still call up their amendments.

Suddenly, Senator Helms rushed into the chamber. Byrd asked whether he could call up one of this amendments for a vote that day.

"I think that would be possible," Helms drawled with a nod. "I have some of the stuff still in the typewriter, but...I will be glad to call it up and have a vote on it."

"I thank the Senator from North Carolina," Byrd said. "He is always cooperative and understanding, and his action today is characteristic of his attitude."

Putting it mildly, we were upset. It was bad enough that Helms could offer an amendment that had nothing to do with the subject of the bill. It was worse that shortly he would offer that amendment and we would not know what it was. Seeing Helms's aide Carl Anderson on the floor, Marilyn ran up to him and asked as politely as she could what the amendment would be. Anderson said he didn't know.

We had no statements prepared, nothing to give Ribicoff to argue intelligently against the phantom amendment. Jesse Helms was legendary for this type of behavior, and it earned him many enemies in the Senate.

In the meantime, Helms left to gather his papers. We accepted a minor amendment on rural education. Michigan Democrat Carl Levin gave a speech endorsing the bill.

Helms was back on the floor in minutes, and stood at his desk organizing his materials. Marilyn went up again to Carl Anderson, who sat nearby Helms silent and stiff, and asked for a copy of the amendment. Anderson brushed her off with, "I don't have copies yet."

"The Senator from North Carolina," the presiding officer recognized Helms.

"Mr. President, I have an unprinted amendment which I send to the desk and ask for its immediate consideration."

"The amendment will be stated."

A clerk at the front desk clicked on his mike and read simply, "The Senator from North Carolina proposes an unprinted amendment, numbered 69."

Helms cut him off routinely with, "Mr. President, I ask unanimous consent that further reading of the amendment be dispensed with."

Ribicoff, Marilyn, and I sat in the well, straining our necks around looking across the curved rows of desks in the chamber at Helms, waiting for the solution to the big mystery.

"Mr. President," the 57-year-old right-wing Senator began in his slurred voice, "this morning as we joined with the Chaplain of the Senate in prayer, as we do each day the Senate is in session, I could not avoid the irony that while we in the Senate begin our day's activities by asking God's blessing on our efforts, the Supreme Court has effectively denied this same right and privilege to millions of school children across the nation…The Court has overturned more than 200 years of American custom…"

School prayer. An issue that we knew little about. But to southerners in the "Bible Belt," it was a unifying, emotional issue. Separation of church and state mattered little to fervent southern evangelicals and born-again Christians. Putting prayer back in public schools was high on Jesse Helms's conservative social agenda. He came from a state where many residents didn't distinguish their religion from their politics.

Helms's amendment was simple in conception, but devastating in legal impact. The Supreme Court and U.S. district courts would be prohibited from hearing or ruling on cases relating to "voluntary prayers in public schools and public buildings." On several occasions in the 1960s, the Supreme Court struck down state requirements for school prayer, ruling that daily recital of specific prayers in set-aside time slots in public schools violated the principle of separation of church and state. The

Court's ruling, however, did not forbid a student from silent prayer in public schools during regular school hours. The amendment also raised another thorny issue: did Congress have the right to restrict the Supreme Court's jurisdiction? Would separation of powers between the branches of government be destroyed?

As Helms spoke, we had a flurry of note exchanges with the NEA and Administration lobbyists outside in the Senate Reception Room. They had had little experience too with the prayer issue, but everyone put their heads together quickly to come up with arguments opposing Helms.

Jesse Helms was a smart, cunning man, a near-fanatic about "his" issues. The North Carolina conservative was banking that the element of surprise would give him a victory. He had tried many, many times before.

"They never give up with this," Ribicoff muttered to us as he sat fidgeting with his tie, hardly listening to Helms's statement recounting the Court's history on prayer. "They bring this up year after year and it's always voted down.

"Do you think he'll win?," Marilyn murmured.

"He never has before," Ribicoff assured her.

That made both of us feel better, and we began to relax.

20 minutes passed, and Helms was still ranting on about his amendment. Ribicoff twiddled his thumbs.

"I'll move to table this," he casually informed us.

"...Public schoolchildren are a captive audience," Helms continued talking, gesturing in the air, looking up at the visitors galleries. "They are compelled to attend school. Their right to the free exercise of religion should not be suspended while they are in attendance...".

At last, Helms took a break and Ribicoff rose to state his position. "Mr. President, this is a constitutional question, and challenges the authority of the Supreme Court. It was not considered by the Governmental Affairs Committee, and it is within the jurisdiction completely of the Judiciary Committee. I am against this amendment and I have no further comment."

Our Senator's response was simple and passionless, conveying the image of a floor manager confident of burying a pesky amendment. Ribicoff sat back down, as Helms spoke again for another 10 minutes.

The Republican then put the Senate into a quorum call, and walked over to talk personally with Ribicoff, who stood to receive him. Helms's owlish face smiled; he put his hand on Ribicoff's back. "You're going to move to table?," he asked.

Ribicoff said he would do just that. Helms nodded his O.K., returned to his desk two tiers over, and picked up his microphone.

"I just want the record to show that a vote in favor of tabling the amendment is a vote to kill the amendment," Helms told the still-vacant chamber. "This is a very vital issue…of deep concern to millions of people across this country."

Ribicoff moved to table, and the clerk began calling the roll for a 15-minute recorded vote. I ran out to the Reception Room and told our ED colleagues we needed "yes" votes, so they would accurately coach senators on their way in.

Generally, everyone—even Helms himself—was confident *we* would win. But this was a new Congress and there were 19 new senators, so we couldn't be 100 per cent certain. We nervously watched the voting.

The first 10 minutes, votes trickled in. Robert Byrd walked over to the front desk early on and voted "no"—with Helms—then left. North Dakota Democrat Quentin Burdick stopped by and asked how the teachers wanted him to vote; I said "yes."

The five-minute warning bells rang. Dozens of U.S. senators poured into the chamber. The noise and tension rose.

Recorded in quick succession, the count was perilously close. We'd inch ahead, then Helms would inch ahead. In the last couple of minutes, it stayed about even.

Marilyn and I all at once experienced frightening anxiety.

Teams of senators stood around the well, waiting and watching the outcome. Never before had a vote on school prayer been this close.

Delaware Sen. Joseph Biden rushed down the aisle, raised his hand for recognition. He blessed himself, told us "May God forgive me," and then voted to table Helms's amendment. It was the sole amusing moment.

Helms's face had the look of pleasant shock.

Ribicoff, attempting to keep on his best face, smiled to the senators surrounding him and said, "Well, it looks like he might win."

We were ahead at one point, 45-41. Senators Howard Cannon (D-Nevada) and Dennis DeConcini (D-Arizona) switched from yes to no, making it 43-43.

A tie vote would mean that we'd lose.

Frantically, we tore off to grab staffers of four Committee Democrats who voted with Helms—Chiles, Nunn, Sasser, and David Pryor (D-Arkansas). We pleaded with them, "Get your senator to change his vote—*this will kill the bill!*"

Senator Ribicoff latched on to a few arms, but had no luck. In the noisy chaos on the floor, we were in near-hysteria, begging help from any senator who could sway another in the few seconds remaining.

The piercing sound of the gavel smacking a wood block abruptly stopped the senatorial roar.

"On this vote, the yeas are 43, the nays are 43, and the motion to table is defeated," the officer in the chair announced.

"Mr. President," Helms shouted gleefully for recognition. "I ask for the yeas and nays on the amendment...".

Immediately, the bells were rung for another vote—this one up-or-down on Helms's amendment itself.

Marilyn and I were in tears. Our bill was dying in front of us. We would lose so much support for the ED bill among legislators, civil rights groups, and who knew who else that the bill would die of its own weight. Even Ribicoff would probably vote against his bill if it had a prayer amendment attached to it. The emotions for or against the prayer issue ran that high.

Minutes later, Robert Byrd rushed back to the floor. His, normally expressionless face showed deep concern.

Suddenly, it occurred to me that if he had stuck around and switched his vote at the last moment, we would have barely won. Now the Majority Leader knew what a damn mess we were in, and only he could rescue us from it.

"You've lost this one, Abe," he spoke solemnly in Ribicoff's ear.

"I know," Ribicoff said. "This'll kill the bill."

Byrd nodded. His aides stood around him. In his hand, he had a copy of the Senate calendar with something marked out in red.

"Well, let's try this," Byrd pointed to the booklet. "We've got this bill on the calendar, S.450. It deals with the Supreme Court's jurisdiction. What we could do is lift the Helms amendment off your bill and onto this one…".

Byrd and his people had done some extremely fast brainstorming. There weren't many options for striking an amendment once attached to a bill. It was only through pure luck that S.450 happened, by chance, to be ready for floor consideration, and that it happened to concern the Supreme Court's jurisdiction, which was the real thrust of Helms's amendment.

Byrd's people quickly checked with Judiciary Committee Chairman Ted Kennedy and subcommittee chairman Dennis DeConcini and got their grudging approval, of the strategy. Both were cosponsors of the ED bill, and judged it far more politically beneficial to save that one over the obscure S.450.

The 15 minutes of voting on Helms amendment passed swiftly. We knew we would lose badly on the up-or-down vote, for senators were voting on the issue itself, not on tabling it.

Since Helms's amendment would be passed and put onto the ED bill, the only way out was to reconsider it.

With Byrd coaching him at his side, Ribicoff waited until the last possible moment, then voted "*aye*" on the Helms amendment.

"On this vote, the yeas are 47, the nays are 37, and the amendment is agreed to," the presiding officer announced. School prayer was now officially in our bill.

Ribicoff instantly sought recognition from the chair. "Mr. President, I move to reconsider the vote by which the amendment was agreed to." (By voting on the prevailing side, he could move to reconsider.)

Byrd shouted above the chatter of 70 senators. "Mr. President, I move that the Senate stand in recess, under the order, until 12 o'clock on Monday next."

"The question is on agreeing to the motion that the Senate stand in recess," the officer ruled.

Helms, standing amongst a gathering of Republicans, stared down Byrd with his "why-you-devil" look. "I ask for the yeas and nays, Mr. President." (Senators rarely voted on adjourning.)

The bells rang out. Most senators had stayed on the floor to enjoy the drama.

Republicans lined up behind Helms on his procedural challenge to the Democratic leader, but their effort failed. The Senate voted 55-27 to adjourn until Monday. We left the floor at 6:00 p.m.

Byrd bought us one work day and the weekend to reverse the situation and save our bill.

*   *   *

We hardly slept the next three days. *Crisis time.*

11:00 a.m. the next morning, the ED gang met in the Vice President's office off the Senate floor: Gail Bramblett, Marilyn, myself, White House lobbyists, several Kennedy-Judiciary Committee aides, and Decker Anstrom, who came to help on an emergency basis.

Going down the list of 100 senators, we discussed the votes, the politics, and parceled out assignments. We were especially concerned about the 47 senators who voted for the Helms amendment. NEA would talk to some senators, the White House to others, Kennedy would lean on a few, Marilyn and I would contact more.

Plans were made for the President and Vice President to make calls over the weekend. Staffers gave the President, resting at Camp David, a list with three names: Oklahoma freshman Democrat David Boren, Nevada Democrat Howard Cannon, and Georgia Democrat Herman Talmadge. All voted with Helms. The Vice President, flying to the Midwest on a quick weekend trip, would call 13 other Democrats using an old tactic—phoning from aboard his Air Force jet.

Phone receivers were glued to our ears. Every senator who voted to support us had to be coerced back to the floor Monday afternoon. Senate aides began altering arrangements to fly their senators back early to Washington before the votes.

NEA began lining up religious groups to fight Helms. The Lutherans, Catholics, Presbyterians, Jews, Universalists, and Methodists were asked for their help. At one time or another, each had opposed school prayer in some form.

At the White House Friday morning, the school prayer matter was a hot topic in the President's meeting with out-of-town editors. A Baptist himself, Carter told the journalists, "I think the government ought to stay out of the prayer business."

Marilyn and I visited the Senate parliamentarian's office, where we got an extensive cramming course in Senate rules and procedure. A lot could go wrong, and some slick procedural maneuvering would be necessary Monday. We could expect a slew of roll call votes—putting the prayer amendment on S.450, final passage of S.450, Helms tabling the motion to reconsider, the motion itself, then possibly another vote on removing the amendment from our bill. A filibuster was always a worry.

We worked all weekend, writing the speeches and briefing papers needed to steer Senator Ribicoff through the jungle. The chances for failure at this critical pass were high.

Newspapers across the land flashed the story on front pages: "Senate Votes to Restore Prayers to Classroom."

Throughout the south especially, preachers took to their pulpits Sunday morning, bellowing at their parishioners to write, phone, wire, even journey to Washington—anything to save the sacred Helms amendment.

A "National Advisory Committee to Restore School Prayer" was quickly thrown together and backed with sizable resources of conservative groups. Computerized letters and campaign materials were mailed nationwide. Even my parents received preprinted "petitions" in their Connecticut RFD mailbox, ready for their signature, that could be conveniently mailed to senators and representatives. "We need to get drugs, sex, immorality, and disrespect for laws out of our schools and God back in our schools," the petitions said.

*   *   *

April showers gently washed against our Senate office windows Monday morning, April 9.

Inside, we continued working the phones, cuing our allies to the complicated procedural path we would have to take. Communication was critical; without it, sympathetic senators might vote wrong and flub everything. Senate staffers had trouble following our time-consuming explanations.

The Senate would meet at noon sharp. The prognosis was better. Some borderline Democrats hinted their willingness to buy our strategy: voting to put prayer onto S.450 and off S.210. We had to pick up five senators and hang onto the ones we had.

Back in Washington, the Vice President cleared his schedule; he'd be on hand at the Senate to preside and cast a tie-breaking vote if necessary. He would also pull a few brethren aside for words of wisdom.

The Attorney General talked with a handful of senators, and sent a letter to the Hill criticizing the amendment as "ill-advised matter of constitutional law and public policy."

*   *   *

"…Lead us over the hard road to the lonely garden of decision where life's painful purpose is certified…May we follow the way of faith and duty though it be with a crown of thorns and a cross…"

I stood in the back of the Senate chamber, just seconds after noon, my head bowed, listening to the Senate Chaplain open what would be the most pressure-packed day for us on the floor. No doubt we were hoping for divine guidance as Jesse Helms was.

"…We pray in the name of the selfless Son of God. Amen."

While we organized our files in the well, senators transacted routine morning business.

20 minutes later, Robert Byrd, standing at the desk behind Ribicoff, motioned to the presiding officer. "Mr. President, I move that the Senate proceed to the consideration of Calendar Order No. 42."

"…Mr. President, will the chair call the numbers of these pieces of legislation, so that all senators may understand what we are considering?," Helms intoned.

Byrd's motion first to bring up the Supreme Court bill passed, and so S.450 was officially before the Senate.

"Mr. President, this is an appropriate vehicle for an amendment such as that offered by the distinguished Senator from North Carolina on Thursday to the Department of Education bill," Byrd told the many people on the floor and in the galleries above. "I voted for that amendment, and I voted against tabling it.

"…I am afraid that that amendment, if it stays on the education bill, will endanger the possible future enactment of that legislation.

"…I would hope that the Senator from North Carolina would consider offering such an amendment, and I would hope we could attach it to this bill."

Helms thanked Byrd for his support. "However, some senators are concerned that this is the surest way to kill the prayer amendment…There is some question about whether (House Judiciary Committee) Chairman Rodino…will bury the DeConcini bill so deep that it will require 14 bulldozers just to scratch the surface.

"…Needless to say, I do not want to run that risk, real or imagined. Therefore, I must object to what the Majority Leader proposes."

Byrd pointedly asked if Helms would offer his amendment. Helms said he was "willing to think about it." The Republican conservative rambled on some more about this killing his amendment.

Irritated, Byrd looked straight ahead to the podium, away from Helms. "Mr. President, will the Senator offer his amendment? I hope he will."

"Mr. President, I do not at the moment have a copy of it at hand," Helms replied innocently. "…It may be that I suggest that distinguished Majority Leader submit my amendment."

"All right," Byrd answered tartly. He sent the amendment to the desk. More prayer debate began.

Byrd was taking a big chance, because there was no time agreement on the Supreme Court bill.

Ribicoff, Marilyn, and I remained at our seats in the well, silently watching the proceedings.

"…Mr. President, I, like others, late on Thursday was faced with this issue, virtually without any notice…an amendment which would have a greater impact and assault on the Supreme Court of the United States and its jurisdiction than has taken place in this country over the 200 years of its history," Senator Kennedy roared loudly, emotionally, and red-faced across the chamber. He warned it could lead to Congress establishing a religion in the U.S. and "it is a fact of history...that religions have been more persecuted than protected under democracies."

Sen. Dennis DeConcini, who headed the judicial machinery improvements subcommittee, defended the bill's general purpose which, up to this point, had been noncontroversial. S.450 simply ridded the highest court of the last few areas in which it mandatorily had to review cases. The Supreme Court justices desired the right to pick and choose the cases they would hear.

But the peppery debate centered on prayer. Kennedy and Helms had little respect for each other; they were fighting it out on floor.

"...The Senator from North Carolina has been pleading for hearings for at least five years, and not a syllable of interest has been shown by the distinguished Senator from Massachusetts," Helms charged.

"...I want any senator to name just one child—*one child*—who has been harmed by being exposed to voluntary prayer," Helms railed. "...So we are not bringing down the pillars of justice...".

The tone was so combative that Kennedy and Helms even objected to each other's routine requests, such as rescinding a quorum call.

"I have seen a lot of things in this Senate," Helms remarked, "but I cannot believe that comity is in disarray."

Kennedy predicted if the amendment carried, Congress would start limiting the Court's jurisdiction on other important constitutional rights.

Byrd wanted it all to end and pushed for a vote. New Hampshire Republican conservative Gordon Humphrey began a statement.

"Is the Senator in favor of this amendment?," Byrd asked caustically.

"Yes," Humphrey replied meekly.

"Then why is he filibustering it?," Byrd shouted.

Humphrey went ahead anyhow, leaving the Senate leader stewing.

At last, Helms turned conciliatory, inviting Byrd to make a unanimous consent request setting a time for a vote. Byrd did so.

"I do object," an angry Strom Thurmond surprised everyone.

Helms, horrified, looked over at the South Carolina Republican, motioned and whispered, "No, no."

"Mr. President, I thought the Senate would be recessing tomorrow night, but it does not appear that it will be," Byrd fumed, looking at the ceiling. His threat hit a nerve, and the Republicans agreed to vote by 2:30. "I thank all senators," Byrd said after getting his way. "We may still get out tomorrow evening (for the Easter recess)."

A vote finally came, and the school prayer amendment was attached to S.450, 51-40. Later, the entire bill passed, 61-30. Most liberals, Ribicoff included, voted "no."

The first half of our strategy had been successfully completed. Now, the Senate reverted back to the ED bill and the Helms amendment would have to be removed from it.

Byrd painfully explained to senators that they had passed a bill and had voted for school prayer. He appealed for votes now to lift prayer off S.210.

Ribicoff, the floor manager again, rose to argue the Helms language did not belong on a reorganization bill. He repeated it would kill the ED bill if left on.

Howard Baker popped into the Senate chamber for a surprise backing of Helms. He "enthusiastically" supported ED, but felt "there is no more appropriate place to put statutory language dealing with...prayer."

Helms said he felt overwhelmed. "The President of the United States has been calling senators all day long, beginning, I know, as early as 7:30. The distinguished Vice President is sitting right across the cloakroom. He has been collaring senators here. So there is nobody for me except the people."

"The Majority Leader has neither been collared by the Vice President nor...contacted by the President," Byrd rejoined.

Helms inferred the procedural ploys were unjust. "The Senator from North Carolina…won fair and square." He pledged "to put this amendment on every available piece of legislation coming through the Senate until both the House and the Senate get a chance to vote on it."

Helms moved to table Ribicoff's pending motion to reconsider his amendment. Another roll call vote—the most important to us.

Vice President Mondale assumed the chair. We were on our feet, anxiously monitoring the outcome.

A constant flow of senators recorded their votes. Dozens had planted themselves at their Senate desks, listening to the dramatic debate and watching with fascination Byrd's mastery of Senate rules.

Ribicoff stopped several colleagues as they approached the bench, asking their help. He halted Russell Long. "I can't vote against prayer," Long rudely brushed him off.

To our utter amazement and glee, the votes were going our way. Senators opposing Helms stood with us. Others who helped him last Thursday switched to our side: Byrd, Cannon, Chiles, DeConcini, Magnuson, Nunn, and six others.

15 minutes later, Mondale pronounced the result: 53 against tabling, 41 for.

"The question recurs on the motion to reconsider," the Vice President announced.

Ribicoff struggled to speak through all the topsyturviness following the vote. "Mr. President, this has been a busy day, and I know how strong the feelings are…There should be an opportunity to vote up or down on the Department of Education bill as a basically clean bill…". He asked for a "yes" vote on reconsidering the amendment.

Another roll call vote. Vice President Mondale sat by patiently in case he was needed.

Senators were so royally confused that they couldn't keep all the votes straight in their heads. Marilyn practically had to write the clandestine floor vote instruction sheets herself, because even Byrd's staff was getting befuddled. The three of us—Ribicoff, Marilyn, and I—wore out our vocal cords telling mixed-up senators how to vote.

Mondale slammed his gavel repeatedly, calling order in the packed, boisterous chamber. "On this vote, the yeas are 50, the nays are 43, and the motion to reconsider is agreed to."

The Helms prayer amendment, as attached to the ED bill the previous Thursday, was now again before the Senate for another vote.

With some 60 senators looking on, Byrd said he would move to table the amendment. The *last* thing he wanted was forcing senators to vote directly on the prayer issue again.

Here, Senate rules became tricky. They forbid tabling an amendment twice within three legislative days unless the amendment had been changed in some form by an amendment that was germane to the bill itself. The tidbit of procedure had been passed Friday on to Marilyn and I by the Parliamentarian's staff. Over the weekend, Marilyn, Gail and Decker dreamed up some innocuous amendments for that very purpose.

"Let us have an up-or-down vote and I shall leave this alone," Helms pleaded.

Byrd, however, was no dummy. "...We have already adopted the amendment today...What is the benefit of adding an amendment to a bill that is going to kill the bill?...That is a vain act, it seems to me."

Ribicoff, Marilyn, and I stood nervously in the well. Ribicoff pushed a paper into the hands of a young page. "Mr. President, I send an amendment to the Helms amendment to the desk and ask that it be stated."

Marilyn's little amendment was clever. It required the undersecretary to consult with the secretary of education about recommendations of the Intergovernmental Advisory Council on Education.

"Mr. President, a parliamentary inquiry," Helms shouted to Vice President. He asked if the amendment was in order. Mondale said it was. Helms asked if it was germane. Mondale ruled it was. Ribicoff spoke four vague sentences in support of the amendment. A chorus of senators sought recognition.

"Mr. President, let us understand what is going on here," Helms frowned at his colleagues, as if there was some sinister plot. "...The amendment is simply an effort to have a tabling motion instead of an up-or-down vote," he stressed.

Senators listening to all of this clearly were enjoying themselves. This was some of the best entertainment they'd seen on the Senate floor in years. Liberals delighted in watching Helms squirm.

"...I am going to move to table this amendment," Helms angrily declared. "...I think senators should take a flatfooted stand one way or the other...".

"...How many more times does the Senate have to do the same thing on the same day?," the Majority Leader screeched in frustration. "...So let us be done with it."

More back-and-forth debate. "*Vote! Vote!*," several senators hollered.

Finally, the question was put to a vote, but Helms insisted on another roll call. The bells tolled a fifth time on the same issue.

By this vote, most senators were suffering from total legislative vertigo. "How do I vote now?," many grumbled to us. They couldn't believe they had to vote formally on tabling the meaningless amendment. Jesse Helms earned few friends that day in the world's most exclusive club.

An agitated Senate clobbered Helms's tabling motion, 57-38.

Defeated and dejected, Helms relented and let the tiny amendment pass by voice vote.

"Mr. President, I now move to lay on the table the Helms amendment as amended by the Ribicoff amendment," Byrd addressed the chair.

Helms said he had no detailed response. "I think I know what the outcome is going to be; I have become accustomed to that."

In a closing comment, Byrd told his fellow senators, "I can go back home and tell my constituents I voted to support the prayer amendment, just as the Senator from North Carolina can do."

Senators voted 53-40 to table the amendment.

It took six hours and as many roll call votes, but school prayer had been removed from the ED bill. We bounced back from the grave.

*   * .   *

Completely overshadowed by the prayer war in the Senate, Jack Brooks convened his subcommittee that Monday morning to mark-up and report the President's ED bill to the full House Committee.

Erlenborn lost on his try to carve out the DOD schools. A compromise on the NSF science education transfer was adopted, similar to one passed almost unnoticed by the Senate the same day.

A simple voice vote sent H.R.2444 to the full Committee. It was all over in just 25 minutes.

The big fight would come in a few weeks when Brooks's 39-member Committee would hold its mark-up. At this time, it was much too close to call.

Congress the next day went home for a two-week Easter recess. The Carters would spend nearly the same amount of time in Georgia.

*   *   *

Hurricane-type rains poured down on the Miami convention center Sunday, April 22 as hundreds of American school board members caucused inside.

National-level association execs struggled to convince delegates that NSBA should continue its support for ED. Advance people from the White House lobbied conventioneers.

Lights went out and the delegates viewed the slick filmstrip Allan Cohen's coalition produced. Voices of President Carter, Vice President Mondale, Senator Ribicoff, the PTA president, Rufus Miles, Coretta King, Terrel Bell, and even the deceased Hubert Humphrey wheedled the local education leaders into fighting for ED. "If education's inferior status in Washington is ever to be corrected, it must be done this year," the film summed up. "You are urged to make your congressional contacts now...".

But Pennsylvania, Kansas, Nevada, and Ohio delegations fought back, warning loss of local control. Assisting them, a full-page ad in the school board journal from AFT President Albert Shanker. "While a new and inexperienced department is groping for identity, its attention will inevitably be diverted from the real fights,...budgets and issues...," Shanker suggested.

The climax came Monday. The vote: 105 for the resolution of support, 24 opposed.

ED sponsors in Washington were relieved. The President's OMB director got a warm reception the next day. The band played "Happy Days Are Here Again" upon his introduction as a key speaker.

*   *   *

At the same time in Washington, Al Shanker, Senators Moynihan, Hayakawa and Schmitt, and others staged a press conference in a Senate hearing room to announce the formation of the "Committee Against a Separate Department of Education."

AFT had drawn together more than 60 labor, civil rights, and education leaders into a grouping similar to our old "citizens committee." Most members were university presidents.

But unlike Allan Cohen's growing, energetic coalition, the new AFT effort would be little more than a letterhead operation. We'd already learned that didn't help much when it came time to extract votes.

*   *   *

Congress returned that Monday, April 23.

Robert Byrd and his floor crew decided the Senate would first consider and pass the federal budget resolution, then turn to ED. Byrd announced debate on ED would resume Thursday, April 26.

Jack Brooks and his top Committee staff met and made a tentative decision to set a date for the critical House mark-up: May 2.

NEA and White House lobbyists daily pressured Brooks's Committee members. With little more than a week to go, they still didn't have enough votes. The outcome would hinge on a handful of undecided freshmen.

NEA was bringing to Washington nearly 500 teachers from the 21 states represented on the House Committee. Those and others from various education groups lobbied so hard and so continuously that the Representatives and their staffs found themselves submerged in ED. Cohen's ad hoc coalition always visited congressmen in delegations—usually consisting of a teacher, a school board member, a PTA rep, a school administrator, a professor, a student, and so on. The strategy: project a united front, show the Brooks Committee that the voices against ED were but a few acorns on the great education tree.

On learning of the rapidly-approaching mark-up date, ED coalition leaders made a fast decision to sponsor a full-page advertisement in the *Washington Post* for the day of the Brooks Committee vote. NEA wanted an ad crammed with names and organizations, showing wide bipartisan support. No one else had much power to suggest differently. The teacher union would pick up two-thirds of the expensive tab for the ad—nearly $20,000 to the *Post* plus thousands more to J. Walter Thompson, the advertising agency composing it.

* * *

"You're doing a good job, kids," Senator Ribicoff praised Marilyn and I Thursday morning in his office. We briefed him on the amendments we expected that afternoon.

By 1 o'clock, we were on the Senate floor.

Tall, silver-haired, 52-year-old Senator Daniel Patrick Moynihan was ready with his amendment. He and Ribicoff were old friends who went way back together.

"Mr. President, the purpose of this amendment is to describe what the Department of Education…will look like in five Congresses from now, or 10, in the normal sequence of the workings of government and bureaucracy…," Moynihan soon began speaking from the portable podium on his little desk.

The chamber was deserted, save for the hordes of students that flowed in and out of the visitors galleries.

Pensive and quiet, Ribicoff mumbled to Marilyn and I sitting beside him, "He's tipping his hat to Shanker."

"…We took this list from the catalog of federal education assistance programs," the New York Democrat lectured on. "…We say: Let's put them all in the Department of Education."

Not even Moynihan took his amendment seriously. He just wanted to make a point—AFT's point—that we couldn't claim consolidation in creating ED. The turfers had knocked it all out.

California Senator Hayakawa rose to commend Moynihan.

"…Remember, if you like the Department of Energy, then you will love the Department of Education," Moynihan summed up.

Checker Finn, Moynihan's quick-witted education staffer, walked over with a note: "Our preference is for a voice vote, i.e., no tabling motion, no roll call." They would let it fail quietly. Marilyn nodded her happy acknowledgement.

"...I know that after 40 years of politics, 50 per cent of something is always better than 100 per cent of nothing," Ribicoff rose and responded. "I also know that you can be so doctrinaire in your objectives that not only do you not achieve what you seek, but you lose everything that you are striving for."

Ribicoff said on-the-record he'd like to see many of the programs in Moynihan's amendment transferred, but if he accepted it, "this bill would go down to abysmal defeat."

The presiding officer put the vote to the Senate. "The noes have it and the amendment is not agreed to," he ruled.

Oklahoma Republican Henry Bellmon appeared on the floor and proposed an amendment to transfer Indian education. Ribicoff sympathetically replied it was "a great tragedy" that "we do not have the votes" to make the transfer. He suggested the two of them ask the General Accounting Office to study the issue. Bellmon agreed and withdrew his amendment.

Utah conservative Republican Orrin Hatch offered an amendment restricting ED's rulemaking authority. It required the Secretary of Education to withdraw a regulation if a "majority" of local education "authorities" opposed it in writing within 30 days. Local educators "certainly know better than federal bureaucrats what is necessary and appropriate for their schools," he said.

We couldn't accept it. Senator Ribicoff countered the amendment gave local educators an opportunity "to block implementation of statutes that have been adopted and mandated by Congress." It was unconstitutional.

Ribicoff moved to table the amendment, and a 15-minute roll call vote began. It was surprisingly close: 48 to table, 40 for the amendment.

New Mexico Republican Harrison Schmitt returned with a long floor speech blasting the bill and proposing an amendment blocking the transfer of the DOD overseas schools.

Ribicoff did not take Schmitt's challenge seriously, responding with a short rebuttal. Senators had received a "Dear Colleague" latter from Senators Nunn, Jackson, and Carl Levin (D-MI.) on Armed Services Committee stationery opposing Schmitt's amendment. Letters from the National PTA and Overseas Education Association backed them up.

Schmitt demanded a roll call vote. Ribicoff did not bother to table. The vote was uneventful, except when the elderly, powerful Armed Services Committee Chairman John Stennis stumbled up to Ribicoff and asked what the vote was about. Stennis, strong defender of the Pentagon, had been expected to oppose transfer of any DOD turf. Unprompted, Ribicoff worked over Stennis, telling him why he thought the schools shouldn't "bog down" the military. Stennis, amazingly, voted "no."

Sen. Robert Morgan offered his amendment denying the President the option of using his reorganization authority to transfer programs into ED after its creation. The North Carolina Democrat recounted the torrid turf wars history, and claimed "this amendment is necessary to assure that the will of Congress is not thwarted by executive order." Once established, "attempts to expand (ED) will rapidly follow," he said.

Sen. Ted Stevens pronounced his support for the amendment "because I do not want to see the Indian education programs transferred."

Ribicoff denounced the amendment as "carving out a special exemption" and "setting a dangerous precedent." Since the President's reorganization authority started in 1949, no agencies or departments had been exempted. Our Senator pointed out the obvious: if Congress didn't want a transfer, it could vote down the reorganization plan.

"…Maybe we need an unprecedented measure to prevent an unprecedented Department from growing into a monster…," Morgan retorted. He called for a recorded vote, losing 45-38.

Robert Byrd grabbed a nearby microphone right after the vote. "Mr. President, it will not be possible to complete action on this bill tonight."

Time had flown by. Already it was 6:30 p.m.

The Majority Leader had a list in his hand of the remaining amendments. He mentioned another yet to be offered by Helms. Byrd cajoled several senators into reducing the time needed to debate their amendments.

Byrd announced the Senate would return to the ED bill first thing Monday morning, April 30. He said roll call votes would be held off until after noon so senators could have the morning to return to Washington from their weekend forays. Byrd wanted to "expedite matters on Monday, completing action on the bill."

*   *   *

"...Mr. President, I offer this amendment today because of the incredible change 1 have witnessed in the past year...I am not exaggerating when I say that at least 75 per cent of those who expressed their support for a Department (of Education) in the past have this year come to me to indicate that they no longer feel (it) would have any positive impact on the state of education in this country...".

Pennsylvania Republican Richard Schweiker blared from his desk near the back center of the Senate chamber. The one-time Ronald Reagan running mate opened Monday's debate with his amendment to keep education in HEW and raise it to undersecretary status. Schweiker, however, had to be taken somewhat seriously; he was the new ranking Republican on the Labor and Human Resources Committee. He had voted for ED in 1978.

Schweiker said his amendment (identical to Califano's old proposal) would give education programs "the attention and prestige they deserve, without the increased federal regulation which a separate department would surely bring."

For a fifth day in April, Senator Ribicoff, Marilyn, and I sat scrunched together three levels down in the floor manager's area. It was a little past

10:00 Monday morning, the last day of the month. We would stay until we finished.

"Mr. President,…we examined a number of alternatives…but the first one we ruled out very strongly was any sort of an internal reorganization of HEW," Ribicoff rose and countered.

When the Senator spoke publicly, he elevated and stiffened his voice as if there were no microphone attached to his lapel. He turned and gestured often to the 99 other desks around him.

"…By leaving education in HEW, it would be tantamount to stating that education is integrally tied to health and welfare programs. But in reality, it is not.

"Frankly, to adopt this amendment, for all practical purposes, would mean the defeat of this legislation."

The noon hour arrived and senators were called to the floor for a vote. The amendment failed, 58-26.

Arizona's Senator DeConcini, joined by New Mexico's Pete Domenici, proposed establishing an office and assistant secretary for bilingual education. The two southwestern senators had come under pressure from their large Hispanic populations. Marilyn and I held long talks the previous week with their staffs, urging that they refrain. We built a neat, trim organization for ED and didn't want to spoil it with assistant secretaries for specialized interests.

Throwing sand in the gears, Ribicoff privately told us days earlier he wanted to accept it. The Senator's parents immigrated, and he learned to speak English at public school before his parents spoke it. "Isn't there any way we could compromise with them?," Ribicoff whispered to us in the well as DeConcini addressed the Senate.

After much floor debate, Ribicoff suggested the absence of a quorum, and a big huddle ensued on the Senate floor. One idea surfaced quickly. An "office of minority affairs" already existed in OE. Why not specify that office in the ED bill, assign it a director below the assistant secretary level, and add "bilingual education" to the title? Ribicoff and

DeConcini thought it was a great compromise. Both staffs ran off together to a nearby office outside the Senate floor and worked out the language on a typewriter.

15 minutes later, the compromise passed by voice vote.

We'd been so engrossed in negotiating on bilingual that we didn't notice Jesse Helms had reappeared on the floor. He sent an amendment to the desk and—generously—let us have a copy:

"Purpose: To provide for parental notification and consent before students participate in sex education programs in public elementary and secondary schools."

"Oh wonderful", Marilyn said under her breath the same time a Senate clerk read it aloud to the chamber.

Another of Helms's special issues, sprung on us without prior warning. The conservative senator hoped the element of surprise would work in his favor again.

"...Mr. President, the subject of sex education is not easy to discuss..." Helms drawled into his mike. He ranted on and on about some sex ed film shown to North Carolina public school students and how we were "turning children into sex experts."

His amendment would require schools receiving federal funds first to get written permission from parents before teaching students sex education.

Meanwhile, Robert Byrd rushed to the floor and walked down to Ribicoff. "You might lose on this," the Majority Leader forewarned in a hushed voice.

"*Really?*," Ribicoff asked disbelievingly.

Byrd suggested to Ribicoff it might be better just to accept it.

We thought Byrd had it wrong. This was infinitely more absurd than prayer, and Helms had turned off so many of his colleagues that we couldn't see how he could prevail. Ribicoff told Byrd he had to oppose it.

Marilyn scribbled a note to the White House and NEA lobbyists outside asking their guidance. "DO NOT accept amendment," the response came back. "Up-or-down if you have to."

Helms, continuing his speech, said his amendment sought "to protect the basic right of parents to oversee the education of their children."

"It always amazes me how these conservatives can become so liberal on their issues," I whispered in Marilyn's ear. She had nearly finished a handwritten statement for Ribicoff to rebut Helms.

"...The amendment would try to tell the local school boards what the content of their educational policies should be," Ribicoff argued to the few senators listening in person. "(It) is absolutely contrary to the entire thrust and philosophy of this bill...".

"...All I would have to do is scratch sex education and I could insert nuclear physics, physiology, or almost anything else," Percy agreed.

"...Local control begins with the parents or else the school system will not work," Helms shot back.

Ribicoff allowed an up-or-down vote on the amendment. During the 15-minute roll call, a number of unprintable amendment-related jokes were heard from senators. Helms's latest effort amused them. They didn't take it seriously.

Robert Byrd voted "aye," explaining why he urged that we accept the amendment.

It was good that we didn't. The vote: 73 against Helms, 16 for.

Moments later, Senator Jepsen began spewing out his pack of amendments. One would convert elementary and secondary "special project" programs into a block grant approach that returned the money to states without any federal strings. Ribicoff raised a point of order: the amendment was not germane. The chair agreed.

The Iowa Republican came right back with his "right-to-work" amendment. "We find continually woven into the fabric of NEA activities an attempt to force people to join unions in one form or another," he said on the floor.

Ribicoff again challenged the amendment on germaneness grounds. The presiding officer ruled it did not pertain to the subject of S.210 and dismissed it.

Jepsen appealed the ruling of the chair.

Byrd picked up a microphone and pleaded for senators to uphold the chair. 18 Republicans joined Democrats in voting 68-24 to back the ruling.

Senator Hayakawa, who seldom strayed from the Senate floor during debate on our bill, eagerly called up his sunset amendment. If approved, ED would automatically self-destruct in six years, unless renewed by Congress. "…If it (ED) is successful and truly improves education, then we can renew its lease," the California Republican stressed.

"…It is unnecessary," Ribicoff replied from his desk in the well. He pointed out that 98 per cent of ED's programs already were subject to reauthorization every three to five years. He warned of the danger in terminating a structure but not its programs.

"…Can we not, we might ask, have an experiment with the legislation, with the opportunity to be rid of it?," Senator Moynihan interrupted the debate.

A line of senators pulled up microphones and supplied support to Hayakawa. And then, the roll call vote. As we suspected, it was nip-and-tuck.

Outside the Senate chamber, NEA and White House lobbyists grabbed senators to ask for a "no" vote.

Standing next to Ribicoff, Robert Byrd watched the count. With less than one minute left in the vote, it was 45-45. Marilyn and I ran to a few nearby senators, asking their help in switching if necessary.

At the same time, Hayakawa moved from colleague to colleague on the crowded, noisy floor asking help.

For nearly a full minute after the vote had officially ended, there was a flurry of switches and late votes. Still tied, 47-47, Robert Byrd was the last senator to register a change—from yes to no.

"On this vote, the ayes are 46, the nays are 48, and the amendment is not agreed to," the presiding officer ruled.

"Whew," Marilyn said, wiping her forehead.

Hayakawa, amidst all the after-vote confusion, promptly handed a page another amendment for delivery to the front desk.

A clerk clicked on his mike and began reading. We, our allies outside, and others listened. The new proposal would bar the ED civil rights from enforcing quotas in its anti-discrimination orders. Helms had cosponsored this conservative interpretation of the recent *Bakke* case.

"...With this new Department of Education, I say let us stop this foolishness now...," Hayakawa insisted, gesturing downward with vocal agitation. "They call these plans affirmative action. I call them racial discrimination. The actions taken are really intended to force a reverse bigotry down our throats..."

Ribicoff raised a point of order that the amendment was not germane. The chair agreed.

Hayakawa appealed the ruling of the chair, and senators were called back to the floor for a vote. The Californian lost, 59-32.

We had lost our sense of time. I glanced quickly at the ornate clock in the Senate chamber: 5:45 p.m. After a long opposing speech by Senator Morgan, there came a period of silence.

"The bill is open to further amendment," the chair said.

No response from the senators in the chamber. Ribicoff, Marilyn, and I strained our necks looking around, expecting someone to jump up with another amendment or statement.

"If there be no further amendment," the chair said slowly, "the question is on the engrossment and third reading of the bill...".

"Mr. President, I ask for the yeas and nays on final passage," Ribicoff said.

Before we knew it, the bells were rung for the last vote. Pure joy and relief overcame us. We drew deep breaths.

Everyone knew the bill would pass. "Oh, I pray it's at least 72 again," I told Marilyn. Anything less than the 72 votes cast for the bill in 1978 would be widely interpreted by the media and our opponents as "an erosion of support."

"Are there any senators wishing to vote?," the chair said in banging his gavel 15 minutes later. A clerk then handed him the tally sheet.

"On this vote, the yeas are 72, the nays are 21, and the bill, as amended, is passed."

We were proud. The Senate had sent another strong message to the House.

NINETEEN

A One-Vote Margin

With the bright May Day sun streaming through the tall White House windows, Jimmy Carter and Congress's Democratic leaders sat down to breakfast at 8:00 a.m.

The President congratulated Robert Byrd on the Senate's passage of the Department of Education bill the night before.

He quickly turned to House Speaker Tip O'Neill. "We need your help with Moorhead, Kostmayer, and Fountain…".

*   *   *

In just 26 hours, Brooks's Committee would meet to mark-up Carter's ED bill. Absolutely no one—not Brooks, not NEA, not White House strategists—knew if the bill would pass there. The count was that close.

For the preceding two weeks solid, lobbyists worked every conceivable angle to pressure the 39 Committee members. AFT, AFL, and Catholic lobbyists considered the House Committee their best shot at killing the bill; they were pulling out all the stops. So too were NEA and the White House staff, who knew this one vote could bury the ED concept forever.

By most counts on Tuesday, May 1, it was deadlocked. Some three or four members still had not made up their minds. The situation looked like this:

DEMOCRATS:

•*Jack Brooks*—As the partisanship heated up on the ED issue, the Chairman lost his ability to lean on his Committee members. The arm-twisting would be left mostly to the President and the ed groups. NEA informed him there could be a one-vote margin either way, which made him very uncomfortable. Yet, he would do everything in his power to pass the bill.

•*L.H. Fountain*—This conservative North Carolinian had voted for the bill in Committee in 1978 as a sop to Brooks. However, right-wing groups were urging he switch and his relations with NEA were poor; the two were usually at odds. NEA did not endorse his re-election. When NEA flew three N.C. teachers in to lobby him, he responded that bill was "NEA's excuse for getting its one-third federal funding."

•*Dante Fascell*—Sold solidly on the merits of the issue, although his politics told him to vote no. His Miami teachers were AFT-AFL affiliated. Nevertheless, Fascell would work vigorously for ED.

•*William Moorhead*—Another 1978 yes vote turned against ED. He was the target of major lobbying by Pittsburgh area AFT teachers, AFL laborers, and Catholics. The President and Vice President called to ask his yes vote, but were turned down. "I want to help," he agonized in private discussions with Terry Straub. The Administration helped to spur along a federally-funded transportation project in Pittsburgh in an effort to woo him, but it was not enough.

•*Benjamin Rosenthal*—The New York City congressman, like others, would back the AFT teachers entrenched there.

•*Fernand St. Germain*—Had slightly more NEA than AFT teachers in his Rhode Island district, but was also coming under heavy pressure from Catholics and the AFL. The merits of the issue, plus the personal persuasion of Brooks, would keep him in the yes column.

•*Don Fuqua*—The Floridian would remain unchanged in his support for ED.

•*John Conyers*—A definite no vote. Detroit's AFT teachers got to him. Also, the black Michigan Rep had a falling out with the President over his budget and domestic program. Detroit Mayor Coleman Young had announced his backing for ED, but it would have no effect on this Committee member.

•*Cardiss Collins*—A swing vote. Named recently to head up the Congressional Black Caucus, which had severely criticized the President for his budget, Collins would find it hard to maintain her 1978 support for the bill. Both Shirley Chisholm and John Conyers were good friends and pressuring for a change. However, Chicago's AFT-affiliated teachers were not in line behind the national federation, and did not lean on her. From HEW, Mary Berry was urging that she vote for the bill. Terry Straub considered her the toughest member to win over.

•*John Burton*—In his gruff way, he told NEA lobbyists, "Yeah, I'll vote for your goddamned Department." His California district was split between NEA and AFT.

•*Richard Preyer*—A North Carolinian consistently supporting NEA.

•*Robert Drinan*—The Massachusetts Jesuit priest provided total political and intellectual backing for ED. A thorn in the Catholics side, his liberal politics prompted, in part, the movement within the Church to prohibit priests from seeking elective office.

•*Glenn English*—Represented a both strongly NEA and Catholic Oklahoma district. Would remain solidly in the yes column.

•*Elliott Levitas*—Was stubbornly holding out for a price: support for his amendment extending congressional legislative veto rights to all ED decisions and rules. However, NEA worried the veto might anger civil rights groups because it could be used to block anti-discrimination orders. The Georgian's district was completely NEA. He needed stroking from the Georgian at the White House.

•*David Evans*—A former teacher from an NEA Indiana district, he would back the bill.

•*Toby Moffett*—A reluctant, but committed, Connecticut supporter.

•*Andrew Maguire*—His New Jersey district was heavily Catholic; parishioners there were asking for a no vote. He would side, though, with NEA.

•*Les Aspin*—The Wisconsin Rep would stay with NEA.

•*Henry Waxman*—Solidly opposed, despite his Los Angeles teachers' combined affiliation with both NEA and AFT. Receiving much Catholic and AFL pressure.

•*Floyd Fithian*—Had to contend with numerous Catholics at home in Indiana, but would continue his total support for the bill. He even helped pro-ED forces by talking with other wavering Dems.

•*Peter Kostmayer*—A major Catholic target, the Pennsylvanian had a good working relationship with NEA. He had already committed to vote against the bill, but would mollify NEA by voting its way on amendments.

•*Ted Weiss*—New York City/AFT/no. But not outspoken against ED.

•*Michael Synar*—A youthful Oklahoma freshman whom NEA did not endorse in the 1978 election. However, he was bright, level-headed, realistic, and not disposed to revenge. He would vote yes.

•*Robert Matsui*—NEA opposed the Sacramento, California freshman in the 1978 primary, but like Synar, he was a clear thinker who judged the reorganization of HEW necessary. A yes vote. Bad press erupted from local papers upon learning his decision; NEA arranged for rebuttal letters to the editors.

•*Eugene Atkinson*—The Pennsylvania freshman ran as a conservative Democrat and arrived in Washington opposed to ED. NEA lobbyists met with him several times for several hours. His staff had some former NEA-Pa. people. Jimmy Carter had campaigned for him. Pulling from the opposite direction, the Catholics, state school boards, and AFL-steelworkers. A probable yes vote.

REPUBLICANS:

•*Frank Horton*—The Ranking Minority member had been a fairly consistent supporter of the President, and his backing for ED had been cemented into place by OMB's cost-saving predictions. His only problem with the bill was there weren't enough programs consolidated. NEA had supported the upstate New Yorker through thick and thin.

•*John Erlenborn*—Still the opposition ringleader.

•*John Wydler*—The conservative Long Islander was overjoyed that he finally found an issue on which he could agree with the AFT.

•*Clarence Brown*—An Ohio Republican opinion leader who simply thought ED was a bad idea. Not enthusiastic about any federal involvement in education.

•*Paul McCloskey*—Although impressed with OMB's efficiency figures, the lower-San Francisco area congressman and his staff had an anti-ED mindset. He would press for making education into an independent agency, which NEA could not understand.

•*Thomas Kindness*—At one time inclined to support ED, the Ohioan responded instead to the movement of most Republicans against the bill. He reportedly had ambitions of moving up to a leadership post in the party.

•*Robert Walker*—NEA lobbyists talked often with this conservative, former Pennsylvania teacher, who they pictured as batty and erratic. He was rabidly out to kill ED and "preserve" state-local control.

•*Arlan Stangeland*—NEA had endorsed this Minnesota Rep's opponent in the last two elections. The Vice President used his roots as an excuse to call Stangeland and plug the bill, but it was a lost cause. Definitely, a no vote.

•*Caldwell Butler*—A moderate-conservative Virginia Republican of whom NEA seldom got much cooperation. He knew Pat Gwaltney's family well, but would vote his partisan politics.

•*Lyle Williams*—A swing vote. The Ohio freshman didn't get NEA backing in his predominantly NEA district, but the teachers union was doing everything it could to coax him into voting yes. A major Catholic and AFL target. White House aides learned he might be swayed by approval of an application from a commuter aircraft business in his district to the federal Economic Development Agency for underwriting of the project. The aides pledged a White House check into the application.[32]

•*Jim Jeffries*—A Kansas freshman, new to the ED issue, who would be expected to follow the Republican leadership. A no vote.

•*Olympia Snowe*—A Maine freshwoman, ditto for Jeffries.

•*Wayne Grisham*—A California freshman, ditto for Jeffries.

•*Joel Deckard*—An Indiana freshman, ditto for Jeffries.

*   *   *

On the giant layout easels at J. Walter Thompson's Washington studios, the coalition ad was taking shape Tuesday morning.

A large "H E W" illustration had been sketched at the top, with the "E" being pushed down and distorted by the "H" and "W". Underneath, in large letters, it read: "Too Often, the 'E' Gets Squeezed Out."

Six paragraphs of substantive arguments consumed the top third of the page. "Let's face it, the Department of Health, Education, and Welfare has other things to worry about," they began. "…Only a small amount of HEW's time is spent seeing to the needs of our schools."

---

[32] The "check" was as good as a seal of approval. The application was approved a short while after the House Committee vote, ostensibly on its merits.

Bolder subheadings proclaimed," The federal government should not control education. But it shouldn't ignore it either"; "By cutting some red tape, we can save $100 million"; "Elimination of duplication will mean greatly improved efficiency"; and "Give education the voice it deserves in government."

In the next space down, a dark, protruding phrase: "We urge a yes vote for a Cabinet Department of Education." Under that, a mass of 250 prominent names and 70 organizations scrunched together.

At the bottom of the ad: "Paid for by the Ad Hoc Committee for a Cabinet Department of Education, Allan S. Cohen, Chair."

Page seven in the *Washington Post* had been reserved for Wednesday morning, the day of the House mark-up.

In another advertising agency, an AFT-instigated ad was being composed, a smaller, half-page entry that would, for lack of funds, appear in the less expensive Wednesday *Post* "Business" section.

"WE DO NOT NEED A FEDERAL CABINET-LEVEL DEPARTMENT OF EDUCATION," it read in stark type. "The following individuals are opposed..." It listed some 60 labor and education people, including George Meany, Wilfrid Paradis, and Albert Shanker.

"Committee Against a Separate Department of Education," identified the sponsor.

*   *   *

Around 10 o'clock Tuesday morning, Jack Brooks, Dante Fascell, Elliott Levitas, Frank Moore, Jim McIntyre, and Terry Straub sat in the Cabinet Room at the White House.

The President walked in with a smile. "How we doing on the bill, Jack?"

Without a pause, Brooks motioned next to him. "Ol' Levitas here needs to be talked to."

Brooks was trying to be funny again. Levitas was embarrassed.

"Well, I've some concerns about the new Department," Levitas said shyly.

Carter had come to talk strategy with his top ED defenders. He knew his bill was in a dead heat in Brooks's Committee. With the polls down and the stirrings of the 1980 presidential race already upon him, he couldn't afford to lose this major domestic proposal. The press had built up the House Committee as Carter's main obstacle in his push for ED.

By now, Carter had his pitch down pat, and he delivered it full-force. Only Levitas needed the sweet-talk.

Brooks told Carter of the Committee members who might need a phone call from the Oval Office.

Levitas put in a plug for his legislative veto provision.

Toward the end of the short meeting, Levitas mumbled, "Well, Mr. President, I basically will support the bill." He said it so impassively.

The President was bothered by his Georgian colleague's indifference. As the good-byes were said and the group walked slowly to the door, Carter stared at Levitas and quietly ordered, "Come with me for a minute, Elliott."

The two walked along back to the Oval Office, where Carter did what he did best—a one-to-one workover: We've been friends for a long time...we've been together in the Georgia state government...

When Levitas returned to Capitol Hill, he would become Carter's staunch defender.

*   *   *

Tuesday night, NEA and White House staffers compared predicted vote counts. With Levitas now likely in the yes column, it stood ominously at 18 for the bill, 19 against, two undecided.

The two holdouts: Lyle Williams and Cardiss Collins.

Gail Bramblett and Dale Lestina waited in the reception area for a 6:30 appointment that evening with Lyle Williams. The two NEA lobbyists, still deathly worried that they could lose the bill in the next morning's mark-up, were on their last mission to beg the Ohio Republican's vote.

A veteran NEA lobbyist, Lestina, 42, had been assigned to work the House on the ED bill. He did his job well, with a calm, serious, no-nonsense approach that congressmen respected. His North Dakota upbringing taught him how to be straightforward without offending someone.

Not until almost 7:00 were Gail and Dale ushered into Williams' personal office. The NEA teachers in his Youngstown, Ohio district had been courting his vote with a vengeance, trying to make up for not endorsing him in the election. That, combined with the White House's willingness to move along the EDA underwriting application for the commuter aircraft business in his district, led the lobbyists to hope they might snatch his vote.

"I haven't made up my mind yet," he told the NEA people.

Gail and Dale felt faint. In their shock, they managed to summon up all the reasons—political and substantive, why he should vote for the bill, less than 15 hours from then.

Gail rushed back to her office across town and made some frantic phone calls to the Ohio teachers, who would make more calls to their Congressman's Washington office.

Until Williams actually cast his ballot, nobody knew for sure which side he would come down on.

Cardiss Collins was being tugged by both sides. Nearly all the high-ranking blacks in the Carter Administration had been put onto her. Plus, a few civil rights leaders backing ED, such as Vernon Jordan and Coretta King, had been asked to lean on her. White House aides searched for ways of winning her over, whether through concessions in the budget or else-where. Shirley Chisholm, John Conyers, and elements of the more outspo-ken, anti-Carter forces in the black community urged her opposition.

Terry Straub and Gail Bramblett had a gut feeling Collins would vote for ED, but they would not know for certain until the House Committee clerk asked her vote.

*   *   *

The House Committee hearing room looked busy as a beehive Wednesday morning. The humming roar and tension were reminiscent of a crowded gymnasium before the start of championship playoffs.

Some 30 U.S. representatives talked with staffers, reporters, or other colleagues at the double-deckered dais. While waiting for the mark-up to begin, several read the *Washington Post*. Most had already seen the two pro-and anti-ED ads.

Hundreds of spectators filled the audience seats and packed the aisles. It was a grand reunion of the proud order of federal education lobbyists. Red-white-and-blue "A DEPARTMENT OF EDUCATION / YES!" buttons dotted the crowd. AFT, AFL, and Catholic lobbyists arrived unadorned with campaign-style paraphernalia.

More than a dozen reporters sat cramped around the press table. There were no TV cameras.

The beaming sun rays of a magnificent 70° Washington day battled to permeate the heavy curtains on the long windows behind the upper dais.

Shortly after 10:00, Jack Brooks made his way to his seat, stopping along the way to pat backs of colleagues and make jokes. His bulging eyes were glazed from witnessing the mass of humanity down below.

He sat down in his high-back black leather swivel chair and whacked the gavel at 10:15. In four seconds, the room was quiet, save for the shuffle of paper.

"...Now, I would present, from the subcommittee on legislation and national security, H.R. 2444, to establish a Department of Education," the Chairman began reading from his opening statement.

Behind him, chief counsel Bill Jones and counsels Elmer Henderson and Bob Brink organized their papers. Young and darkly handsome, Brink was a new addition to Brooks's staff, energetically assuming much of the detailed background work on the bill.

"...I recently discussed this legislation with President Carter," Brooks continued. "The President strongly urged passage...".

AFT lobbyist Greg Humphrey sat somberly in the audience. He thought that since Brooks had brought the bill to mark-up, the Chairman had the votes to report it. What he didn't know was that Brooks himself had decided to risk it, not knowing whether he would win or lose.

"...The Department of Education has been widely debated in the press and within this Committee," he read on. "The issues have been clearly stated and vigorously argued...I would urge your support for the bill...".

The Committee began considering amendments.

Republican leader Frank Horton asked the Committee to consider transferring the vocational rehabilitation programs. Brooks spoke against Horton's amendment, on Califano's behalf.

The Chairman called for a voice vote. To the audience, the result sounded divided. "The ayes have it," Brooks ruled, conceding symbolically it wasn't worth the fight.

The Committee agreed to an amendment by Democrat Don Fuqua assigning vocational ed to an assistant secretary, and to another by Cardiss Collins giving the office for civil rights the authority to enter into contracts on its own.

Rep. John Erlenborn moved his amendment to strike the DOD schools transfer. "...I would beg of you," the conservative Republican pleaded. "Don't toy with education for the purpose of getting a bill through. Don't put a Department of Education in the business of operating schools...They will be imposing their decisions and probably using the overseas dependent students as guinea pigs...

"Don't do this. It is not just moving a box on an organization chart."

"What makes you think that the Department of Education would use these kids as guinea pigs?," Cardiss Collins blared into her microphone.

"Because they would be making decisions as to which textbooks to use, what curriculum—". Erlenborn was cut off.

"I really resent that kind of remark, and I don't think the Department of Education is going to do anything like that," Collins said angrily.

In the front row seats, Terry Straub and Pat Gwaltney exchanged smiles. One of their swing votes was transmitting pro-ED signals.

"I find the argument kind of curious that it is okay for the military to control the school system, but it is real bad for the educational system to control (it)," Democrat Dante Fascell observed wryly. "...I think the biggest problem here is turf...I think the military has all (it) can say grace over right now...".

Elliott Levitas chimed in. He noted the schools "are already administered by an agency of the federal government. We are not creating a new federal presence or a new federal intrusion...".

"...I gather you reached a contrary answer about the BIA," Republican Paul McCloskey looked pointedly at Fascell, seven seats away on the dais. "...Is this a political decision...to put Defense in and keep BIA out, or has a conscious decision been made on the merits that DOD schools aren't properly run and the BIA schools are?"

"I don't believe you can take politics out of politics," Fascell retorted in his raspy voice. "I would like to think my judgments are rational."

"...The BIA and the people representing the Indians who have hated each other for 150 years...came to the Committee and hugged and kissed each other and said that all the things they said about each other were not true and they wanted to stay together," Brooks said in another of his comic tirades. The audience chuckled.

"If they want that kind of operation, they can have it. I'm not going to fight it. I didn't have the votes in the Committee.

"This one is a different one," Brooks went on. "In the Defense Department, high priority is not education; it is defense contracts...It is really small potatoes to generals and admirals."

Erlenborn demanded a roll call vote. Six Democrats sided with him, making for a close but unsuccessful try. The amendment failed 21-17.

Republican Robert Walker proposed an amendment requiring that all appointees to the new ED have been a teacher or school administrator prior to their appointment. He rationalized that it would bar special interests from staffing the new Department. His logic was so far-out that the amendment was shelved by a loud "no" voice vote.

Walker tried again with another proposal for an "office for private school education." A chorus of members denounced it as getting the federal government into private education, and it, too, was thrown out by simple voice vote.

Loud sighs could be heard as Walker offered a third amendment—to set up an office for the Indian schools. Walker said he was taking "the same arguments that were used on the DOD schools and was voted for by the Committee."

"Mr. Walker," Brooks replied, "it hurts me to say this, but I agree with you wholeheartedly. I am afraid that between us we don't have the votes."

The clerk called the roll, as Walker requested. The hearing room erupted into nervous laughter and amazed chatter when the count was announced: 15-15. The amendment was barely defeated.

Undaunted, Walker came back with another to transfer the child nutrition/school lunch programs. To leave them out, he argued, was "callous politics of the worst kind."

Many in the audience could hardly believe his antics and stomach his brand of politics.

The nutrition amendment went down to a loud negative voice vote.

Looking up at the clock high on the side wall, Brooks saw it was 12:15 and adjourned for lunch.

*   *   *

Downstairs in the Rayburn Building cafeteria, our large ED team talked over lunch.

"Do you think we've got the votes?"

"Don't know. Looks like Cardiss Collins and Lyle Williams are key. If they go with us, and if we don't have anymore surprises, we'll win."

"God, what if we lose."

"Don't even talk about it."

"Yes, but we really might lose this. It could be all over this afternoon!"

"Look, we'll deal with it when it happens."

"Think positive."

"Oh, I think we've got it."

"Yeah, but I want to know, if we lose, is that *the end?* Will we be able to start over again?"

A tense silence.

"No. That would be the end of the road."

*   *   *

"We are on Title Three." Brooks convened his Committee at 1:40. So far, the panel had made good progress and at this speed would reach a vote that afternoon.

Everyone groaned as Robert Walker sought recognition to offer his fifth amendment. This one *transferred* the Indian schools. "Whereas the Committee (earlier) felt that it would not be a good move to form an office to take care of the BIA programs, I think that, based upon the very close vote, (we) might want to consider transferring the programs…".

This time, Brooks asked for his members' voice votes. "In the opinion of the chair, the ayes have it," he drawled, looking side-to-side. Several demanded a roll call vote.

A confounded audience and Committee listened to the clerk's announcement: "17 yeas and 11 nays."

To the devilish laughter filling the hearing room, Brooks took a moment and smiled from his chair. "17 to 11, the amendment is agreed to."

NEA and White House aides rolled their eyes in disbelief. We didn't know how or whether this would affect the final outcome. I found myself giggling for a few moments.

The Committee moved on quickly to Title Four, and debated at great length an amendment reducing the number of personnel in ED by 450 and restricting hiring of new employees to 50 a year. "We are taking all the fun out of this new Department," Republican Wydler wailed in his Long Island accent. "If we really are going to seriously propose that it is going to have less people,...I have a feeling you are going to see a lot of these buttons down here change from yes to no." It passed by voice vote.

With ease and efficiency, more amendments were quickly disposed of. Levitas's amendment extending legislative veto to all ED functions (except civil rights) passed, bettering the chance that he would vote to report. In a 22-15 decision, the Committee rejected a Walker school prayer amendment.

Three Democrats had opposing statements. Rep. Ben Rosenthal recounted his feelings that it was unwise to spin off a Cabinet department for "a single set of interest groups." Rep. William Moorhead said the bill would promote "economy and efficiency," but worried more about "the dangerous step of centralizing the control over ideas." Rep. L.H. Fountain warned, "We are enacting another monster in the federal government...It is going to grow and grow...".

Finally, Dante Fascell moved that the Committee report the bill to the full House of Representatives.

"A roll call is automatic," Brooks ordered.

The room of perhaps 300 people fell silent. Hearts pounded with anticipation. Some in the audience held hands for support.

The clerk began calling the roll ever so slowly, knowing the sheer importance of the moment.

As members called out their votes, the tension built. Many followed the vote by checking off names on their own lists. Almost every congressman had a Committee list and tallied the vote like a banker counts his thousand-dollar bills.

It was 3:10 p.m., Wednesday, May 2.

The clerk ticked off Democrats' names. Terry Straub and Pat Gwaltney held their breath when the ninth was called for.

"Mrs. Collins?"

"Yes."

Terry beamed from ear to ear and tapped his pen on the paper in his lap.

Five names later: "Mr. Levitas?"

"Yes."

Straub lifted a few inches off his seat in pleasure.

There were no other surprises from the Democrats. Each voted as expected.

The clerk began calling out Republican names. Horton voted yes. All others voted no, until it came to Lyle Williams.

The room was as quiet as outer space.

Williams had been looking up at the ceiling. His face showed a man about to make a painful decision, about which he still wasn't sure.

The millisecond between the clerk's call and his response seemed like a full minute.

"Yes," he said in a forced, loud voice. Then looked immediately down at the dais table top, his face sullen.

Screeches of joy from covered mouths pierced the quiet. A dozen ED proponents couldn't contain themselves. The line of NEA lobbyists slumped in their seats as if just released from a firing squad. Gail Bramblett held her heart and began to smile.

Horton and Williams had been the only two Republicans voting yes. Brooks was last to vote. "Yes."

"The clerk will report," he ordered.

"The vote is 20 yes and 19 no."

*   *   *

"Whatever Lyle Williams wants from now on he gets," one of the jubilant NEA lobbyists proclaimed to the ED gang out in the hallway. Indeed, NEA owed him much.

The ED team ended up at Don White's California State Education Department offices two blocks away. We broke open several bottles of champagne.

"To a Department of Education in 1979," I proposed the toast.

*   *   *

At the *Washington Post*, it was front-page news. "President Carter's department of education squeaked through the House Government Operations Committee yesterday, 20 to 19," the story began. "Although the margin was slight, the victory for the President was substantial. The House Committee was considered the biggest obstacle…".

The *Post* quoted a Carter spokesman: "We have now passed the toughest hurdle…".

The *New York Times* reporter chose a different angle, warning the bill "faced an uncertain fate" for "the fight on the House floor is certain to be a lively one."

TWENTY

A Bitterly Divided House

Attention turned to the full United States House of Representatives. 435 men and women of every political persuasion to cajole, contact, pressure, and lobby. A colossal task.

The bill could have been scheduled on the House floor by the end of May. The Speaker would decide that. But the ED forces needed some time.

Brooks's Committee staff immediately commenced writing the report, and would file it within two weeks. From there, arrangements would be made to bring the bill before the Rules Committee, where there was no guarantee the going would be any easier this year. Missouri Democrat Richard Bolling, who opposed the bill, had become the new Chairman.

The Ad Hoc Committee would go into action. The perception that the bill was only a raw deal between the President and the NEA persisted in the House. The coalition of education organizations had to work to stave off that image. Hundreds of appointments were set up for House members to meet Ad Hoc delegations. Representatives' positions had to be pinned down. It would take weeks before an accurate reading of positions could be had.

ED opponents, having lost their best chance at stopping the bill—Brooks's Committee—were desperate. We could assume they would resort to their old tried-and-true tactic of attaching junky amendments on the House floor in an effort to make the bill unpalatable even to Democrats. They would step up their PR campaign against it.

Did NEA and President Carter have the clout to get it through the House? NEA had many friends there; it also had many enemies. Its friends were hard-pressed to come up with any enthusiasm or passion for the bill. Many thought they could probably get away with opposing ED and still receive NEA's endorsement in the next election by supporting its other goals. NEA, however, began clamping down and passed word to all members a vote for ED would be the biggest factor in their endorsements.

Jimmy Carter's position seesawed. Except for a jump in popularity at the signing of the Mideast peace treaty in late March, his public approval had steadily dropped. Even though the nation was plagued with severe gasoline shortages (and long lines at the pumps), the President's standby gas rationing plan went down to stunning defeat in the House, 264-159. His bill implementing the Panama Canal treaties barely passed a test vote, 200-198. Congress was just not responding to him. Newspaper columnists played up the lack of enthusiasm for the Georgian. "I can't find *anybody* standing up for him," one civil rights leader remarked.

"...Maybe if I was a better politician, I would have gotten these bills through the Congress," Carter told the Democratic National Committee May 25. "...I have done the best I could. I have never backed down. I am going to continue to fight."

Our biggest problem the first days of May was, strangely, *overconfidence.* "With final Senate floor action and passage by the full Government Operations Committee, we are just two steps away from success," Allan Cohen told his troops in a May 7 letter. Days later, the PR subcommittee would meet to talk about "the post-enactment future of the Ad Hoc Committee." And, at a crowded coalition meeting May 14, one ed neophyte boasted to everyone, "We're planning the celebration." NEA's Dale Lestina angrily replied, "Celebrating *what?* We haven't won anything yet. By our counts, we're only 40 votes on the plus side...". Lestina added half again as many were still undecided, and more might renege.

The preceding Thursday, Jack Brooks routinely asked for permission on the House floor to file his ED report before midnight. Republicans objected—a harbinger of the troubles ahead. Word leaked out also that Rules Committee Chairman Bolling was intentionally stalling on allowing the ED bill to come before his clearinghouse panel.

*　　*　　*

That our bill would be a partisan rallying tool in the House became clear that week. Unannounced publicly, the House Republican Policy Committee convened a meeting. Erlenborn pushed for approval of a statement opposing ED. Only 13 of the Committee's 27 members were present. But the Republicans there put the question to a vote: 12-1 to oppose ED.

"Passage of this politically-endorsed, costly presidential payoff is nothing more than raw political expedience, catering and caving in to the powerful education lobbies in Washington," a press release said in spreading the news. "...Republican policy calls for H.R. 2444's resounding defeat."

"There are about three times as many Republicans against as for it," John Rhodes told reporters. The Minority Leader knew the switch from his 1978 position didn't need any public explanation.

*   *   *

The war was on.

"We are sure the separate Department of Education legislation can be stopped," AFT President Albert Shanker told his people by memo May 17. "Against heavy odds, we battled the NEA and the Carter Administration...(and) the fact that one and a half years of extensive pressure only resulted in a 20-19 vote..., leads us to believe that it can be defeated when the full House considers the measure."

Shanker's AFT organization stepped up its campaign of recruiting editorial support, arranging letters-to-editors, asking local school boards in key congressional districts to take stands.

From the *New York Times*, another editorial May 22—"Centralizing Education Is No Reform"—warning that "any day now, it will be up to the House to stop" ED.

From the *Christian Science Monitor* May 14, more of the same: "...the House would help President Carter fulfill a campaign promise...".

From the *Washington Post*, more letters to the editor against the bill.

The Ad Hoc Committee for ED debated how to respond. One idea quickly rejected envisioned a mass demonstration of schoolchildren on the Capitol steps; it would look too manipulative. Generally, flashy media events in Washington were ruled out. Some governors would be asked to author op-ed columns to local and national papers. An effort would be made to entice TV talk shows into airing debates on the topic.

The best strategy was to localize the pressure. Find out which House members were wavering, and target the PR work to their districts. Plans were immediately made to pull together school board members, teachers, students, school principals, and perhaps mayors into single delegations and stage press conferences in home districts declaring support for ED.

*   *   *

"We need higher education support to get over the hump," OMB Director Jim McIntyre appealed to more than 40 higher ed lobbyists who were treated to breakfast in the White House mess May 23. "It would make the difference. We need more than just NEA to pass this bill".

Terry Straub passed out a long list of undecided House members and asked the people to go back to their colleges and drum up support.

The gathering sowed the seeds of the "Higher Education Coalition" that would operate under the auspices of Allan Cohen's Ad Hoc Committee. The university professors' chief lobbyist, Al Sumberg, would head it up. At the same time, 25 college leaders formed their own new group, "State College and University Presidents for a Department of Education."

*   *   *

By Memorial Day week, Jack Brooks, NEA, the ed groups, and the President's staff had all prodded the Speaker's men to move the bill. Tip O'Neill had to nudge Rules Committee Chairman Richard Bolling into setting a meeting on granting a rule for the bill. It would be June 5.

Allan Cohen made plans for establishing "command posts" in the House during the floor debate. More often than not, Brooks's Committee hearing room would be used. Closed circuit TV systems monitoring the House floor would be installed, as would phones and working office facilities nearby. The posts would act as nerve centers for the Ad Hoc Committee, constantly receiving political counts, changes, and trouble spots and coordinating the response. Lobbyists would find it far easier to base themselves in a nearby, discreet House room rather than running between the Hill and downtown offices.

Gail Bramblett and Dale Lestina headed up the lobbying drive. Coalition members by this time had endured a hectic three weeks, meeting personally with almost every House member. Readings still showed far too many soft spots, too many undecideds. The big worry: no enthusiasm. The education groups couldn't find many Reps who would speak out on the floor for the bill.

For the time being, NEA and White House lobbyists concentrated on the Rules Committee. They were anxious not to repeat last year's close-call in the critical gatekeeper panel.

In his office June 2, just three days away from the Rules session, Terry Straub penned in an informal diary his "nervous" thoughts. "I have at this time a growing sense of the importance of the bill politically to the President," he wrote. A House defeat on ED would be devastating to the beleaguered Jimmy Carter.

Gradually, ED advocates sadly realized Brooks's Committee was not the biggest obstacle after all.

*   *   *

Tipped off about the impending Rules and floor action, *Washington Post* editors readied their artillery.

The first shot came in a June 3 editorial, "A Bad Idea." "Some congressmen who have made casual commitments to the Administration or the NEA may find it slightly awkward to back away," the paper said. "But a vote for this regressive, regrettable bill would be much more embarrassing—and impossible to retrieve."

The morning of the Rules Committee meeting, the *Post* tossed out two more bombs. "Education Department's Foes Complain About NEA's Election Gifts in House," headlined a page eight story reporting a conveniently-timed report by the right-wing "Public Service Research Council" that accused NEA of giving money to candidates who favored the bill. "Current members of Congress favoring the Carter bill received $527,522 from the NEA from 1974 through 1978, undecided members got $68,125, while those opposing the bill or leaning against got $98,880," the story said. NEA officials did not dispute the figures, but noted "there's not a blessed thing wrong with legitimate campaign contributions."

In its second salvo, a sequel editorial that same day, "A Bad idea (Cont'd.)", the *Post* said, "it is silly to suggest that this could be pulled off without any growth of the bureaucratic sort."

The paper predicted the 450 positions eliminated in the House bill would be low-ranking personnel.

Opposite the editorial, a Herblock cartoon ridiculed ED.

*   *   *

A line of lobbyists waited in the third-floor Capitol hallway adjacent to the House chamber outside the Rules Committee. Inside, the tiny, elegant hearing room was packed with more lobbyists, members, and staff.

Gray-haired Committee Chairman Richard Bolling presided at the small wood dais with a frown, trying to concentrate on the meeting in spite of all the commotion. The agenda for that Tuesday, June 5 morning had two items: a Social Security disability bill and ED.

Knowing that some key Committee members were away that morning, NEA and White House aides had reached agreement with the Speaker's staff that the Rules vote would be delayed until the afternoon. NEA had asked Connecticut Democrat Rep. Chris Dodd to be their spokesman, but he couldn't return from New England until the afternoon.

The opposition, however, had hidden motives. Chairman Bolling had sent a signal through emissaries to the AFT, AFL, and Catholics that he wanted ED killed somehow. The foursome decided on a simple strategy: schedule the Social Security bill the same day as ED, approve a rule for it, then vote down the rule on ED. The President thus would be handed at least a half victory, and the press would not portray the day's events as a total setback for Jimmy Carter.

The Committee first considered the Social Security bill. Debate turned surprisingly sour. A vote was taken. Amazingly, the Committee rejected the rule for the Social Security bill. Measures dealing with the sacrosanct federal insurance system always had smooth sailing. Shocked and angered, Bolling turned immediately to ED, thereby breaking his agreement with the leadership to hold off until the afternoon. NEA and White House lobbyists bolted into action. They learned from the Speaker's top aide, Gary Hymel, that Bolling had decided to go directly to a vote on the ED rule. NEA was alarmed; their pro-ED spokesman, Chris Dodd, was absent.

As Jack Brooks, Frank Horton, and a string of opposing members testified before the Committee, furious negotiations went on behind-the-scenes. Emergency calls went to the out-of-town members, Dodd and Rep. John Anderson, urgently requesting their immediate return to Washington. White House lobbyists rushed to phone their offices. The President called the Speaker to ask his help in insuring the ED bill got a rule. Carter didn't have to remind O'Neill that he had already botched the Social Security bill. The Speaker called Bolling.

As much as Bolling wanted ED dead, his first loyalty was to the Speaker and the Democratic President. He grudgingly acknowledged that his Committee now had to approve the rule. Bolling backed down, and threw his Committee into a succession of recesses, stalling until enough pro-ED members had arrived. He waited through lunch and into the afternoon.

Meanwhile, more backstage lobbying. Catholic bishops and clergy pressed Chicago Democrat Morgan Murphy and Boston Democrat Joe Moakley for negative votes. AFT lobbyists worked hard Murphy, Florida Democrat Claude Pepper, and Louisiana Democrat Gillis Long.

The Vice President made some calls. He told Morgan Murphy the President had had tough going in the Congress recently, and needed a victory. The Speaker had to lean on his friend Joe Moakley again this year.

Finally, Dodd, Anderson, and a number of other Committee members arrived. NEA had arranged and paid for a helicopter to pick up Anderson, campaigning for President in New England, and ferry him to the nearest airport where he could ride a jet to Washington. Just before entering the Rules Committee room, the Illinois Republican hollered to NEA lobbyist Jim Greene, standing across the hall, "Thanks for the helicopter." Everyone in the crowded corridor stopped and turned to look.

More debate followed. In mid-afternoon, Boiling had his clerk call the roll. The rule, loosely-written and inviting future trouble, was upheld, 9-5.

*   *   *

As it came down to the wire in the House, the hand-to-hand fighting between NEA and AFT escalated.

NEA President John Ryor that same day sent and publicly released a bitter letter to Shanker condemning AFT's alliance on the ED issue with "hard-core anti-employee organizations" such as the Public Service Research Council. It "constitutes nothing less than a betrayal of the entire union movement in the United States," Ryor charged, and "goes beyond the perimeters of reputable dissent and constitutes a sellout of those you claim to represent."

Shanker replied in the same manner three days after that Ryor's letter was a "transparent publicity stunt—a last gasp effort to gain a little attention at a time when your bill is losing some of its support." The AFT president sardonically noted "this is the first evidence I've ever seen of your concern with the labor movement. For over two decades the NEA worked hard to hide the fact that it was a labor union."

*   *   *

ED forces stood by waiting Wednesday, June 6 in their first command post for the signal from the Speaker that Brooks could call up the bill. Stacked neatly on several tables were piles of fact sheets, issue briefs, and boxes of the A DEPARTMENT OF EDUCATION/YES! buttons, which every lobbyist pinned to his clothing.

Not in many years had there been such a spirit of camaraderie among these workers of all the diverse education groups. Teams strolled in and out of the Rayburn Building hearing room, either coming from or going to congressional offices with reports of progress or failure.

Gail Bramblett distributed copies of the latest target vote list. ED lie in peril; supporters were dropping like flies. Gail's list was divided into "leaning right," "leaning wrong," and "undecided." As more reports came in fresh from meetings with these wavering congressmen, more and more of the "leaning rights" and the "undecideds" were being crossed off and placed in the "leaning wrong" column.

Right wing groups, lobbying vigorously, had their vote count that week at 194 for the bill, 182 against, and 58 undecided. The NEA count showed just over 200 for the bill. If all 435 House members were present and voting, ED would need 218 affirmative votes.

The ED crew was fretful; everyone knew that at this late stage, the large number of undecideds spelled certain trouble. Convincing them to vote yes in so hostile and negative an atmosphere would be like walking up Pennsylvania Avenue blindfolded. Lobbying was highly coordinated on both sides. Pro or con educators were hunted in key congressional districts, and then put on to the Reps. Many Catholic bishops placed calls. Local AFT execs were pressed into action. Jimmy

Carter's Cabinet made calls to persuade those House members they had worked with on topics relating to their agencies.

There was still some time left before the final vote, but no knew for sure how much. The first day of House debate would include consideration of the rule first, then hours of the perfunctory opening statements. We knew the Speakers wanted to finish the following week of June 11, or at least before Congress left town for its July 4 recess.

It all depended on how the amendments went. Conservatives wasted no time in filing a ton of amendments—sunset the department, strike the Indian and DOD transfers, attach school prayer, busing, and abortion language, transfer unrelated programs, even reduce ED's budget by the amount of student loan defaults. AFT lobbyist Greg Humphrey and hired hand Jim O'Hara worked closely with people from the American Conservative Union and other right-wing groups to draft meticulously-worded junk amendments that could be ruled germane to the bill. They strove for making it objectionable to liberals and moderates, as well as conservatives.

Education types couldn't understand how AFT would draw up provisions the union had always fought tooth-and-nail. But AFT officials had a clear conscience. They figured if the junk amendments were attached, the bill might be defeated. If the bill passed, the amendments would be dropped in a conference with the Senate.

Terry Straub was briefing the President on these developments every morning. Carter mentioned several times to his advisors that he hoped Fritz Mondale would involve himself more. The deepening controversy and danger warmed up the senior White House staff to an all-out push on the House.

*   *   *

Lobbyists trooped in sunny, 80° weather back to Capitol Hill the next day, Thursday.

At 3:20 in the afternoon, Rep. Chris Dodd stood before the big microphone at the manager's desk on the House floor. "Mr. Speaker, by direction of the Committee on Rules, I call up House Resolution 299 and ask for its immediate consideration."

For the next hour, the House considered the rule governing debate on the bill. It allowed amendments under the five-minute rule, meaning debate would be limited to five minutes on each side. There were no strict limitations on germaneness; rulings would be left to the chair and the House parliamentarian. There was no enforceable limit on how many amendments could be considered.

Marilyn and I sat in Allan Cohen's command post, watching the House floor proceedings on the closed-circuit TV. More than 50 others were there, some taking phone calls, others meeting in small groups to plot more strategy. It reminded me of a busy political campaign office.

On this first day, only statements, not amendments, would be allowed.

Rules Committee Ranking Republican James Quillen rose and spoke on the right side of the huge, oblong House chamber. "It is fair and appropriate...to take the Office of Education out of one of the most bureaucratic departments in government...(This bill) would save the taxpayers money...".

Most Americans are familiar with the House chamber. They see the impressive decorations and layout on TV during the President's State of the Union addresses. The bright American flag hanging vertically behind the rostrum, the Speaker's chair, with the golden phrase IN GOD WE TRUST above. The long, graceful, dark-wood rows of leather-bound seats.

"...I do not know what bill they are talking about," Rep. Ben Rosenthal cackled from one of the two slim wood podiums in front of the marble-topped clerks' desks in the well. "...In my judgment, this is the worst proposal...".

The House proceedings were being televised around the nation, mainly to home cable subscribers. Gavel-to-gavel coverage of the House was still a novelty, having started months earlier. Many Reps played to the cameras, hoping network or local newscasters would splice off a segment for broadcast to home folk.

"...In all of this there is one word that is not mentioned at all," Republican Whip Robert Michel of Illinois blared into the mike. "...That word is 'children.'...They would not be helped." Michel was part of the stream of opponents lined up to speak against the bill—even though technically the rule only was before the House.

Indiana Republican Dan Quayle parodied "this commitment that everyone has made on this bill," quoting other members anonymously, "'Oh yes, I am really not for it, but I committed myself to it. I maybe made that commitment four or five years ago. I committed it to a teacher back home. I committed it to my mother...'".

"All this bill is about is more bureaucracy," Robert Walker yammered to the seemingly indifferent chamber. "...This Department starts out with one-and-a-half employees for every school district in the country...". (He forgot to mention most were overseas teachers.)

"...I have not seen an issue since I have been in this Congress that has less enthusiasm," Kansas Democrat Dan Glickman observed. "...Nobody knows whether it is going to do any good or not. It might...".

To the folks watching at home, and to the many reporters sitting above in the press galleries, the debate was lopsidedly against the bill.

After 50 minutes of listening to this, Jack Brooks stood up and said, "...I urge an affirmative vote on this rule...It is a good rule, it is a good act. We ought to pass the rule now, pass the bill Monday night, and send it down to the President."

The chair called for a voice vote and judged the ayes prevailed. One Rep objected on the grounds that a quorum was not present, putting the House into a 15-minute roll call vote. We knew we were in for repeated roll calls and quorum calls as our opponents did everything they could to bite at our heels.

The 435 House members each carried a coded plastic card, which they inserted into electronic units throughout the chamber and then punched in yes, no, or present buttons. Computers recorded the votes, flashing them simultaneously on both the TV screens and on a giant, lighted board high on the chamber's west wall.

Of course, we had, and we expected, to win the vote on the rule. Many members who had opposed the bill would at least consent to letting the House consider it; there was no political harm in that. A high margin on our side would look good.

We waited anxiously for the 15 minutes to end. The chair announced the vote: 293 for, 73 against.

"Mr. Speaker, I move that the House resolve itself into the Committee of the Whole House on the State of the Union for the consideration of the bill, H.R. 2444...," Jack Brooks read the formal lingo from a small index card. The ED bill was now officially before the House.

Immediately, another point of order was made that a quorum was not present. The stalling tactics would not subside.

With Bill Jones, Elmer Henderson, and Bob Brink at his side, Brooks opened two hours of general debate by reading his statement. He told his colleagues H.R. 2444 was "a bill with only one aim: to improve the management of our federal education program.

"This bill does not create any new education program. It does not set any national education policy. It does not create a new education bureaucracy...

"This is a reorganization that makes sense from every point of view. I urge you to support it," he ended his talk.

"...This is not a spur-of-the-moment proposal, hastily conceived in a political campaign and thrust upon the Congress," Republican floor manager Frank Horton bellowed firmly. "...This is not a partisan issue...This bill would reduce the size of HEW, which in and of itself is a good thing, and I cannot understand why people are opposed to that...".

Horton was repeatedly interrupted by challenging questions of his own Republicans. On the local control issue, Democrat Elliott Levitas stepped in and helped him out. "The language...could not be clearer than it is. It will even be understandable to some of the judges who will have to interpret (it)."

A chain of opponents denunciated the bill, among them:

Connecticut Republican Stewart McKinney—"Mail is running better than two-to-one against."

Arizona Republican Eldon Rudd—"This bill will only institutionalize, centralize, and strengthen that NEA power over federal education policy."

Ohio Republican John Ashbrook—"We have lost sight of the fact that education was once a function of the family."

South Dakota Republican James Abdnor—"My doubts have caused me to change my mind."

Sprinkled in between were only six supportive statements, most bland and repetitive. Illinois Republican Tom Corcoran was one notable exception. "I just disagree with the conclusion reached by my party," he frankly told the House. "...I want our next Republican President to have an executive branch organized along lines that permit management accountability." Elliott Levitas, having become one of ED's most active backers, praised the bill's personnel reduction provisions. "This type of reduction-of-bureaucracy-before-it-gets-started is unprecedented in our history," he said.

Robert Walker returned to berate the ED idea. "It is about programs, more and more programs, bigger and bigger programs...We are going to be spending in the new department $774 million for new paperwork." He got carried away with that statement.

"I would like to know how the gentleman arrives at that figure," Horton inquired sternly.

Walker admitted it was "a rough calculation." He somehow invented an equation multiplying so much paperwork by so many agency officials that didn't make any sense. Horton let it ride.

Then Walker came back with the charge there would be 90 new supergrade (executive) positions in ED. He was wrong, and couldn't explain himself when pressed again by Horton.

The opening debate ran to 6:20 p.m.—late for the House on a Thursday. Brooks and Horton would return to the House floor Monday for the donnybrook over amendments.

*   *   *

The hope within the Speaker's rooms was that the House would work all day Monday, June 11 and finish the bill. Given the pack of amendments and the persistent demands for roll calls and quorum calls, that might have been wishful thinking. The lobbying intensified as final passage came closer.

The White House press operatives exerted great pressure on the *Washington Post* to give equal time to somebody. *Post* editors finally caved in and accepted an op-ed piece by Jim McIntyre. It appeared, timely enough, in Monday morning's edition. McIntyre's column said there were two choices: a new ED or the old HEW. "The Post's failure to develop such a logical assessment is baffling," he commented.

Monday morning, the Vice President met privately with a small group of loyal House Democrats on the Hill to stir up some passion. This bill has come a long way—two years of effort, Mondale told them. This is the final hurdle. It's time to help the President, to stem this growing belief that the Democratic Congress and the President can't get along, he said. The ED bill is politically defensible, a pure reorganization with no new program spending. Mondale stressed there are no religious issues here, regardless of what you may hear from the Catholics. Their position is 40 years old and they've been unwilling to take a fresh look at the merits. Terry Straub handed out lists of undecided Democrats. Mondale appealed for help in talking to them. For floor strategy, follow Jack Brooks, the Vice President smiled and motioned to the Texan who sat off to the side.

* * *

The Chair called on Brooks on the House floor at 12:30, beginning the second day of debate and the first of amendments.

The House didn't even get past the table of contents before there were amendments. John Erlenborn had the first honor: an amendment to change the name to the "Department of Public Education and Youth."

"What he is proposing is an acronym…that would spell D-O-P-E-Y," Rep. Horton responded. "I think it is very frivolous…"

The amendment failed on a voice vote. Unmoved, the Illinois conservative came back with another—making it the "Department of Public Education," or DOPE. He first demanded a division vote, where members present stood to register their vote; he lost 17-39. Then Erlenborn insisted on a roll and quorum call, losing 52-310.

Rep. Paul McCloskey offered his amendment converting ED into an independent agency. "This amendment would cause a very simple change in the bill," he began talking in incredibly understated terms.

"…It is absurd and bizarre to add a new Cabinet officer who will not have a policy advisory capacity to the President." The California Republican admitted there was "no way" the HEW secretary could devote time to education.

Horton rose to remind his colleagues that McCloskey had consistently opposed the bill. "…The gentleman is attempting to set up an Office of Education, using the same personnel, structure, and organization as the Department of Education, but he would call it an Office,"

Horton explained. "My point is that if the gentleman is for one, he ought to be for the other."

"…We do not get federal policymaking, we do not get massive size and complexity to maintain the Office of Education," Erlenborn argued back.

Brooks rose to the microphone in defense of his bill. "An upgraded Office of Education" would not "command direct access" to the President, he said.

McCloskey asked a division vote and lost. Predictably, he demanded another recorded vote. At first, the ED team thought this might be something of a test vote on the bill. But the House buried the amendment, 114-257.

Another long period of general debate ensued. New Jersey Republican Millicent Fenwick explained she renounced her longtime support of ED because of her fear of "a uniform federal policy." Rep. William Goodling (R-Pa.) warned ED could mean "each youngster is going to have to pass some national examination in order to be promoted in grade." Shirley Chisholm begged the body to reject the bill because it would "professionalize education at the expense of the child, the parents, and the lay citizens."

To all of us listening in the command post a block away, this debate got more depressing by the minute. There was little the pro-ED forces could do to change it.

The House eventually moved on to the bill's first title, the findings and purposes.

Robert Walker, who had glued himself to the floor for the bill's consideration, jumped to his feet and sent his amendment to the desk. "This…, is designed to put this department in the business of promoting school prayer," he told the chamber. The amendment inserted a "purpose" of the department "to promote in all public schools…a daily opportunity for prayer."

Some Reps pointed out the incongruity between Walker's anti-federal control beliefs and the amendment. Brooks and Horton made clear the bill was a reorganization measure. "Let us leave the question of prayers in the public schools to the proper forum," Brooks pleaded.

Several members praised Walker. "There is nothing wrong with communal prayer," Illinois conservative Republican Henry Hyde asserted. Others claimed it would be "coercive" on students. "Let us not let the Secretary of Education make regulations about prayer," Levitas implored.

A couple allies persuaded Walker to substitute the word "permit" for "promote." A *purpose* of the Department to *permit* school prayer? It didn't make any sense to us.

The full House proceeded to vote on the amendment. NEA, White House, and Ad Hoc Committee lobbyists stationed at the three main entrances to the House floor frenziedly grabbed as many arms of incoming Reps as they could. They formed a line on both sides of the hallway leading from the subway elevator, each wearing the ED buttons. As members walked by, they motioned thumbs down.

Watching the vote was pure agony. Throughout the 15 minutes, Walker stayed well ahead. True, this language wasn't as bad as Helms's stuff. Yet, it could cause the same amount of trouble.

"Why the hell didn't Brooks make a point of order?" someone wondered aloud back in the command post. Every ten seconds, the TV screen flashed the time remaining and the recent vote count.

Brooks knew he would have lost his germaneness challenge. The findings and purposes was an "inoperative" section of the bill that could say almost anything related to education.

At last, the announcement we hoped wouldn't come: "On this vote, the ayes are 255, the noes 122, and the amendment is agreed to."

The opponents' strategy was working. The ED bill now had a jeopardizing junk amendment adhered to it like a leech. On the floor, the horde of closely-knit conservative Republican ED antagonists smiled broadly and congratulated each other.

Another Republican amendment was proposed to limit ED's budget growth to the consumer price index. Brooks countered that it was unnecessary; Congress could limit spending through the appropriations process. A roll call vote was demanded, and the amendment was barely defeated, 184-187.

Republicans also aimed to tinker with the "Prohibition Against Federal Control" section. Present wording prohibited federal control "except to the extent specifically authorized by law." Their amendment changed "law" to "federal statute", and added that regulations issued by ED would not have "the standing of a federal statute." Their beef had to do with the interpretation of the word "law," which included rules agency decisions, and court orders, in addition to acts of Congress. "Federal statute means us," Rep. John Ashbrook argued. "It does not mean somebody sitting down on Pennsylvania Avenue. It does not mean some court. It means the U.S. Congress."

We feared the amendment would infuriate civil rights groups, since most anti-discrimination enforcement relied on court and agency orders.

The amendment passed by a simple voice vote. Brooks let it go by without comment NEA and White House staffers were galled and roiled.

Ashbrook rebounded with an anti-busing amendment. "I think the Members have gotten the drift," the Ohio Republican said jokingly.

Brooks sure had. He raised a point of order that the busing amendment was not germane.

"Section 103 does contain certain limitations upon...several authorities of the Secretary to control education programs," the chair, Michigan Democrat Lucien Nedzi, spoke. "The amendment is a further restriction...and is germane to Title I, and the chair therefore overrules the point of order."

Brooks shook his head in bewilderment. "I rise in opposition to the amendment..."

ED leaders began panicking. The situation was out-of-control. The chair was not sticking to the script, allowing the junk amendments to be considered and voted on. Frantic calls went back-and-forth between the cloakrooms, the command post, NEA, and the White House. The parliamentarian had made mistakes. Someone—the Speaker or somebody—has got to stop this, now!

The very problem was the Speaker. He had assigned to chair the ED debate a Rep (Nedzi) who opposed the bill. O'Neill was playing both sides of the fence, helping the President by bringing the bill up, helping the AFL and Catholic Church by allowing their strategy a chance to take hold. He would sit back and see how it went; he liked being on the winning side.

Meanwhile, the debate raged on. "Why keep fanning the flames by this kind of amendment?," wondered black Maryland Democrat Parren Mitchell. "Busing does not work, is not successful, is counterproductive, polarizes people...," Henry Hyde declared.

Ashbrook, of course, demanded a recorded vote. They were 15 fearful, hectic minutes. ED lobbyists were desperate to vote down this amendment especially. The civil rights groups all along had been looking for a big excuse to kill the bill.

There was no turning the vote around. The busing amendment passed lopsidedly, 227-135.

Cued by the Speaker and by the White House lobbyists, Jack Brooks pulled the bill off the floor before any more damage was done.

It was 6 o'clock. The day had been disastrous.

*   *   *

The letters began arriving the next morning.

"The ACLU (American Civil Liberties Union), up to this point, has taken no position on...H.R.2444," said one spread throughout the House. "However, in light of the drastic and damaging anti-civil rights amendments recently approved by the House, this legislation has become a mechanism to severely undermine this nation's commitment to civil rights and civil liberties. For this reason, the ACLU now opposes enactment of this legislation."

This latest crisis called for a swift response. Lawyers all over town drew up different interpretations of the junk amendments. Jack Brooks and NEA tried to rationalize that they wouldn't have any real effect, it didn't *mean* anything that ED would *permit* school prayer. And, it didn't *mean* anything that ED was prevented from requiring busing because the Justice Department did that anyhow.

Still, most civil rights groups were upset. NEA and White House staffs rushed to talk with the more supportive ones, calm them down, and hold, at the least, their neutrality.

We Ribicoff people were pulled into action. We would have to make rock-hard assurances that the junk amendments would not be accepted by the Senate conferees in the House-Senate conference committee to work out differences between the two bills (assuming the House bill passed).

Rights groups were warned not to fall into the trap of opposing ED because of the amendments—that's exactly what the conservative Republicans wanted. We begged their trust; the amendments would be dropped later on, or else we would let our bill die.

*   *   *

At noon the next day, Tuesday, June 12, Jack Brooks readied himself at the floor manager's desk. Speaker O'Neill, his imposing body framed by the American flag behind, stood at his elevated central desk.

"The Chair would like to make a statement," O'Neill said firmly in his deep Bostonian voice. "We intend to stay or hope to stay until we finish this bill this evening, regardless of the time." The Speaker wanted this to be over and out of his way.

Robert Walker demanded a vote on just considering the bill. The House voted 362-19 to resume debate. Walker then shouted across the spacious chamber through the roar of a couple hundred Members. "Mr. Chairman, I offer an amendment." The clerk read it, and ED supporters rolled their eyes in disgust. The proposal was his interpretation of the *Bakke* Supreme Court decision, in effect forbidding the setting of quotas to end racial discrimination.

Frank Horton, continually pestered by his fellow Republicans, rose and raised a point of order against the amendment, "Some where we must draw the line as to what is germane in this bill," he railed.

Walker contended his amendment "simply defines material which is already stated in the bill."

The chair, Rep. Nedzi again, issued a ruling. Reading from a paper, he said the bill's findings and purposes were "extremely diverse in character" and "since the pending amendment does not directly address new substantive authorities," it was germane.

NEA and white House lobbyists were enraged. All their scolding the previous night of the parliamentarian and the Speaker's staff was for nothing. Votes on junk amendments were still being allowed.

"…Quotas are by definition discriminatory," a pleased Walker spoke in defense of his amendment. "…I am a proponent of affirmative action programs."

Emotions ran hot. Texas Democrat Henry Gonzalez walked to the well and told the chamber, "The insidiousness of the amendment is compounded by the sponsor's deceptive—I should say hypocritical—presentation of this amendment, disguising it as a quota prohibition."

"I demand that the words be taken down," Walker yelled angrily to the chair.

The Speaker walked up to his chair and ruled that Gonzalez was out-of-order in his personal attack on Walker

Walker demanded a recorded vote. ED advocates watched sadly as he won handily, 277-126.

The bill now had prayer, busing, and anti-quota language in it, making us want to vomit.

Tempers flared momentarily again when John Ashbrook offered an amendment prohibiting the Secretary of Education from spending any money on abortion.

In raising a point of order, Jack Brooks called it "very artfully drawn" but "meaningless."

This time, the Chair sustained Brooks's challenge.

The House finally was able to move on to Title Two, the section establishing ED's structure of offices and principal officers.

John Erlenborn called up his amendment striking the DOD schools office. "The only reason it is in the bill is to make it appear that there is a real reorganization effort underway," he said.

"The Department of Defense's primary mission is not education; it is…military preparedness," Brooks argued. He quoted letters from the European PTSA, National PTA, and Sen. Sam Nunn.

"We have had military commanders tell us they have had to face angry parents concerned about the conditions of the schools…and at the same time they have got their pilots complaining because there are holes in the runway," Michigan Democrat William Ford chipped in.

Paul McCloskey said it would be "ridiculous" to have one chain of command operating the schools and another operating the base. "There are going to be disputes."

The 15-minute recorded vote stayed close throughout. Again, the group of ED lobbyists anchored outside the House chamber doors worked the incoming members, asking no votes.

For a nice change, the vote went our way: 178-230. The 52-vote margin was comfortable, but we knew only too well that Erlenborn would offer another amendment in Title Three to strike the *transfer*.

Robert Garcia (D-N.Y.) proposed adding an "Office of Bilingual Education and Minority Languages Affairs", similar to that in the Senate. It passed, 290-124.

Then, minutes later, Walker demanded another vote on a simple rural ed amendment. It passed 403-3.

More than four hours had gone by, and the opponents had signaled their determination to prolong the battle as long as need be. They wanted more time for civil rights groups to become hostile and make waffling members more uneasy about their vote.

The House spent 40 minutes debating an amendment by California Democrat George Miller that would drop the vocational rehabilitation transfer. Off-the-record, everyone referred to it as "Califano's amendment." Miller and others restated their feeling the voc rehab services were more medical than educational. House Democratic Whip John Brademas, a champion of voc rehab, said there would be "substantial improvement in coordination" if they were merged with ED's handicapped programs. Jack Brooks, interestingly, kept silent. But the handicapped groups had touched enough bases to defeat the amendment, 148-265.

Walker proposed an amendment requiring that major appointees to ED have been a teacher or school administrator, and failed on another roll call 28-374.

A Republican offered another busing amendment, which the chair amazingly ruled nongermane.

The hour of 6 o'clock had passed and the summer sun was setting outside on the Capitol dome. Brooks interrupted the proceedings to announce the House would stay on the bill until 8:00 or 9:00. "We will return tomorrow and from now on stay as long as is necessary," he told his colleagues. "I look forward to the continuation of these wonderful amendments."

Debate stretched 40 minutes on one to create an assistant secretary for private education, which was rejected on voice vote.

Erlenborn submitted an amendment striking some inconsequential language guiding assistant secretaries' assignments. Predictably, he insisted on a recorded vote and quorum call, losing 149-243.

Dan Quayle labeled his amendment dropping five principal officers as "simple" and "conforming." Brooks, though, reminded everyone the bill provided the "blueprints" for ED, "but it does not say where every nail is going and exactly what color paint is going to be used...". Quayle, too, asked a 15-minute formal vote and lost, 170-220.

Tired and bitchy from the day's eight-hour debate on the bill, the House finished up the second title and adjourned at 8:10, Tuesday night.

* * *

ED lobbyists met at 11:00 the next morning in their House command post. The bill would be brought up again that day, Wednesday, June 13 sometime after several appropriations bills had been finished. It was possible the ED bill might reach a vote on final passage later that day or night.

The counts worsened on the hour. More and more congressmen were reconsidering their tentative support because of the junk amendments. New lists were passed out and lobbyists were exhorted to make their contacts.

Work on the counter-strategy was stepped up. Letters would be sent to all House members denouncing the amendments but expressing confidence they would be scrapped in the conference with the Senate. "You can be assured that NSBA will be working diligently to see that the bill emerges from conference without any detracting additions," the school boards group wrote the Reps. The liberal Americans for Democratic Action "deplored" the amendments, and said it would "work hard to defeat (them) in a conference committee."

We were only halfway there. A huge carload of amendments remained to be considered in Title Three, the transfers section, and in Title Four, the "boilerplate" section.

I spent the early afternoon developing a target list for Erlenborn's next DOD schools amendment. I discovered some 40 House members who voted with Erlenborn also were listed as favoring the bill. PTA and overseas teacher lobbyists phoned those offices.

In a morning meeting with the Vice President and his top aides, Terry Straub mentioned, among other things, the upcoming Erlenborn amendment and warned it might be adopted. The biggest problem was that the Defense people were lobbying covertly against it, Straub told the Vice President in his White House office.

Mondale reached over to his phone and picked it up. "Get me Harold Brown." A few minutes later, the phone rang and the Secretary of Defense was on the other end.

"Harold, today there's going to be offered an amendment to the Department of Education bill to delete the transfer of the DOD schools," Mondale said in an unyielding tone. Brown tried to interrupt but Mondale wouldn't let him.

"Now Harold, there are a number of things I want you to do. We'll have a letter drafted up here from you supporting the transfer. We'll send it over to you, and you just go ahead and sign it. I want to get it up there today.

"And," Mondale ordered, "I want to see some brass and some uniforms on the Hill supporting the bill and the President's position on this. Thank you, Harold."

The Secretary of Defense had not been able to say a single word. The Vice President hung up the phone, leaned back in his chair, and puffed his cigar. A smile came over his face; he was real pleased with himself.

Fritz Mondale had got caught up in the spirit of playing hardball. Who are these people (Carter's political appointees) to oppose the President?, he thought.

* * *

While the House debated its appropriation bills Wednesday afternoon, the Congressional Black Caucus quietly met, in part, to discuss the ED bill.

Shirley Chisholm used her heavy influence to urge her black peers to oppose the bill, now laden with anti-civil rights amendments.

NEA, AFT, and the White House knew of the meeting. AFT lobbyists talked with several Caucus members beforehand, asking their backing of Chisholm's move. On behalf of NEA, California Rep. Ronald Dellums took the lead in arguing for neutrality on the bill. NEA and the White House enlisted the help of black leaders Vernon Jordan and Jesse Jackson, who made calls. Mary Berry did the most work, talking with almost every Caucus member. The White House people didn't quell the rumor that Berry or another black might be named the first Secretary of Education.

After heated debate, the Caucus took a vote, deciding not to oppose the bill at that time—contingent upon the success or failure later on of the strategy of dropping the junk amendments in conference.

NEA and White House lobbyists were visibly relieved on hearing the good news just minutes before House debate resumed.

*   *   *

ED was back on the floor at 5 o'clock. The Speaker would hold the bill there until well into Wednesday night.

Health subcommittee chairman Henry Waxman was first up with his amendment to strike the nursing and health student loans.

"This is probably the first of many arguments we are going to hear on Title Three about totally unique programs that need to be withdrawn from the Department of Education," Robert Walker carped from the Republican side. He was right.

Waxman contended the medical student aid programs were "unique" and "part of a national health strategy." Brooks and Horton said they were "purely and simply loan programs" that ought to be consolidated in ED.

Associations representing nursing and medical schools had lobbied the House in favor of Waxman's amendment. NEA and the White House didn't take them seriously, and that showed in the vote: Waxman won, 243-169.

Vermont Republican James Jeffords proposed transferring the Labor-CETA programs. He called moving youth and unemployed into the labor force "one of the most difficult social problems," and claimed "the schools and CETA mostly fight each other."

The House's primary employment expert, California Democrat Augustus Hawkins, criticized the amendment as a "ploy." Everyone understood what he was talking about.

Jeffords asked for a recorded vote. With AFL lobbyists at the doors, the House voted 145-265 against his amendment. CETA would not go to ED.

Next, an amendment to wipe out the NSF science education programs. By a 165-240 vote, they were kept in the bill.

John Erlenborn cleverly persuaded the second-ranking Republican on the Armed Services Committee, Alabama's William Dickinson, to offer his amendment expunging the DOD schools. "We are about to take a well-coordinated, ongoing, successful operation and transfer it over into limbo," he said.

Back in the command post, lobbyists worked phones, urgently advising staffers on the DOD target list to have their Reps vote down the amendment.

Brooks reread his earlier DOD statement. Horton chose this time to read a letter from an overseas teacher, who complained, "The Department of Defense does not understand many of the problems of education, which causes many problems."

In a strategically-correct decision, Erlenborn did not enter the debate. Watchers expected some drama as the votes trickled in.

However, with Tip O'Neill looking on from a front-row seat, the margin stabilized and the amendment fell, 173-225. DOD schools would remain in the bill.

By 9:00 p.m. with members yawning from a long day, the House considered the Indian transfer, which Brooks's Committee nefariously slipped in the bill. Caught off guard, the major national Indian groups had been working diligently in the previous two weeks to drop their programs from ED. Indians worried that should the House pass its bill with BIA in, senators on the conference committee would be too eager to accept the House provision. Neither NEA or the White House bothered to lobby on the issue; it was one vote they would fiendishly sit back and watch. Didn't matter which way it went.

A long line of Indian state Reps spoke for the amendment, including Washington Democrat Thomas Foley who asked his colleagues to apply "the cardinal principle of this bill"—preserving local control—to the Indian transfer.

"I would point out that my youngest daughter—I call her 'my little Indian princess'—is part Chickasaw," Brooks told the busy chamber.[33] "So I have no prejudice whatsoever against Indians. I love them dearly."

"...I do not think anybody in his right mind can say that the Indian education programs to date have been a triumphant success." The Chairman spoke in less colorful and biting tones in asking a no vote. He'd exhausted himself on this one.

---

[33] Ironically, Brooks's wife, Charlotte, had some Indian blood in her ancestry. But neither knew much about the Indian schools before the ED bill surfaced.

The vote was surprisingly close, considering the pro-ED forces lobbied hardly at all: 235-170 for the amendment. Indian ed would definitely not be consolidated in ED.

The debate went on. Outside, on the Capitol steps and in twilight of a clean, clear, 70° night, four men huddled. Greg Humphrey, John Erlenborn, David Obey, and the Speaker's aide, Ari Weiss, talked over Obey's intention to offer a motion to recommit the bill to Brooks's Committee. The House had gone four long days on this bill, and Obey was willing to wager that many would find a chance to end it appealing. Many more amendments remained to be debated and voted.

The Speaker, however, was away at a surprise birthday party for his wife. Weiss urged Obey to hold off at least until the Speaker returned to the Hill, out of respect to him.

Erlenborn, thinking the motion might win, prodded Obey to go ahead with it.

Earlier, Obey had informed Terry Straub of his plans. We've got the votes to beat you, Straub told the Wisconsin Democrat. If you press the motion, you'll lose and set the opponents back. But Straub also banked on the Speaker being present at the time.

Obey decided he would later that night push his recommittal effort, but not until the Speaker returned. He was a man of principle who would not insult the institution.

Word of the impending move spread throughout the Capitol. Lobbyists on both sides cranked phones to warn the 435 members.

Back on the House floor, an effort was made to drop two small law enforcement education programs slated for transfer in the bill from the Justice Department. "This is just another case of let us have a Department of Education but do not put our program in it," Brooks groused. "But you cannot reorganize...if that attitude is going to prevail...". The amendment was rejected, 128-275.

"I thought it might be appropriate to offer an amendment that would put something into it or we may not have anything in the

Department," Rep. William Goodling (R-Pa.) rose immediately after in defense of his amendment to transfer *Head Start*. Goodling opposed ED, so his motives were clear. The amendment would be hitting the House cold. There had been virtually no lobbying on it either by ED advocates or Marian Edelman's troops. Everyone simply assumed it would be slaughtered.

Shirley Chisholm argued blandly against it. Brooks said Head Start was "working satisfactorily now. I would hate to disrupt its operation."

The chair at first put the question to a voice vote. To everyone's surprise, he ruled the *ayes* prevailed.

"Mr. Chairman, *I* demand a recorded vote," Brooks told the chair from his manager's desk three levels into the members' seats. He instantly turned to the laughing Republicans and grinned innocently.

For the first 10 minutes, the votes evened out, giving us a combined vindictively happy and worried feeling. If Head Start were included now, we'd lose all the black and liberal votes. But in the latter five minutes, the noes pulled ahead, fending off the amendment, 179-230. We were amazed at how many yes votes the amendment drew.

It was getting very late, nearing 11:30. Title Three had not yet been completed. Obviously, the House would not finish the bill that night.

Members gazed at Tip O'Neill and David Obey, both of whom were on the floor. Tension mounted throughout the House. A respected Democrat was about to challenge head-on a bill sent up by his Democratic President. With support for the bill dwindling and the Speaker on dubious ground, would the bill be killed then and there?

"Mr. Chairman, I offer a preferential motion," Obey shouted from the aisle. The body, with more than 100 members inside, fell silent. The bespectacled 40-year-old Wisconsin Congressman strode to the podium in the well.

"Mr. Obey moves that the Committee do now rise and report the bill back to the House with the recommendation that the enacting clause be stricken," a clerk read into the microphone.

"Those of you who know me and my record in this House know that I am a friend of education," Obey began. "...I also want to make the point that I have very few AFT people in my district. I have an awful lot of NEA people. So I am not doing this from the standpoint of special interests."

He neglected to mention the strength of the AFL and the Catholics in his northern Wisconsin district.

"I am opposed to this bill because I think if it passes it will significantly weaken the voice of education in this country." Obey made the case that the "giant, progressive" education-labor coalition would be destroyed. Although he acknowledged the bill would give education more visibility, "I would trade visibility for power any time.

"...So, I urge Members, if they are to keep the education community in a powerful position in this country, vote to strike the enacting clause and end this nonsense."

Jack Brooks rose to respond, calling the motion "premature." "Members can vote against the bill if they want to." Brooks yielded to the Speaker, who plodded on over to the podium in the well.

It would be Tip O'Neill's first public utterance on the ED bill. All mouths were shut, all eyes and ears were fixed on the white-haired Irishman. He had a piece of paper in his hand, but he barely referred to it.

"...If we adopt this motion, are we being fair to ourselves?," he boomed to the now-full House chamber. "Are we being fair to the President of the United States who has sent this (bill) to Congress?

"...Sure, people like to say the image of Congress is low, but why is it so low?...We waste all of this time...We are going to give the press a field day, that we wasted some 14 hours.

"There is merit on both sides of the legislation...All I know is that there is opposition as between two labor organizations...I think the President is right.

"Do not let the bill go down this way. Vote your mind, your conscience when you have heard the entire argument. I hope this motion does not prevail and I hope the bill ultimately passes."

The Chamber remained quiet as he hobbled back to the front row benches. It was a powerful, persuasive moment,

As Frank Horton and another member made statement against the motion, the backstage lobbying heated up. Greg Humphrey appeared especially nervous as he wandered around the outside hallways. In face of the Speaker's dramatic midnight appeal, he anticipated a big loss. He began to regret that Obey had decided to go forward with it.

Erlenborn demanded a recorded vote. It was 11:45. Many Democratic opponents, even Shirley Chisholm, voted against recommittal, mostly out of deference to the Speaker. Republicans, by and large, stuck together and voted yes.

The final tally: 146 aye, 266 no.

The House adjourned for the night. Cornered by reporters outside, the Speaker said the body would return to much-delayed appropriations bills. He said the House would get back to ED later, but made no promise when.

*   *   *

"House Kills Assault on Education Dept."

"Education Department Survives Crucial Test"

"House Moves Toward Education Department Vote"

For a change, these were welcome headlines. Yet, they masked the real danger confronting our bill. We could not pin down with any certainty the votes needed to pass it.

The Ad Hoc Committee met Friday morning, June 15 in the Hall of the States. Gail Bramblett and Dale Lestina passed out copies of their latest target list of 31 Republicans and 60 Democrats. Fully one-fourth of the U.S. House of Representatives still had not made up their minds.

"We've got to redouble our efforts," Lestina pleaded passionately to the 75 lobbyists listening. "Sure, we're down in the count, but a sick dog will bite harder."

So far, our counter-strategy of holding off the civil rights groups opposition by promising to strip the junk amendments in conference had been largely successful. But there were leaks in the dam. PRP's Nancy LeaMond told the Ad Hoc coalition top White House officials were trying to calm "agitated" women's groups.

The National Coalition for Women and Girls in Education hovered on the brink of all-out opposition. The group had worked hard over the years to lobby "Title IX" through Congress, preventing sex discrimination in education—sports, curricula, etc. Several of the junk amendments could be used to invalidate Title IX's effectiveness. The women's coalition met Monday morning, June 18 with White House aides and Marilyn, who pledged the conference committee would be rigged so as to jettison the amendments.

A letter from the President's women's advisor, Sarah Weddington, underscored that commitment. "The Vice President is personally making calls and leading the effort to oppose the amendments," she wrote. "Give us a chance to get the amendments removed in the conference committee, as we believe we can, before making a final decision on the bill itself." Weddington tantalized the group with the prospect of appointments to the new Department sympathetic towards women's concerns.

But the women's groups skittishly suspected the Senate conferees would have to accept at least one of the junk amendments to pacify House opponents. They also had a Califano connection: coalition leader Barbara Warden's husband, Richard, was the HEW Secretary's top link to Congress.

Bigwigs called Warden to hold her off. Senator Ribicoff personally phoned her and promised not to let the ED bill become "a Trojan horse." Senators Percy and Javits, whom we found ourselves designating as conferees this early in the game, also vowed their resistance to allowing the amendments.

Tuesday morning, the *Washington Post*, never missing a beat, presented an editorial: "Making A Bad Bill Worse." The paper warned, "Lobbyists for the bill maintain that all the objectionable clauses can be excised in Senate-House conference. They shouldn't count on it." The *Post* called this strategy "a very risky tack."

At 4:30 that afternoon, the coalition sent a telegram to House members. "The...amendments have converted H.R. 2444 into anti-civil rights legislation. The undersigned organizations therefore urge the defeat of the bill." They included the American Association of University Women, League of Women Voters, and National Organization for Women, among 13 others.

*   *   *

The President had been summiting with Soviet President Leonid Brezhnev in Vienna. The two signed a controversial SALT II agreement. Carter flew directly to Capitol Hill Monday night, June 18 from Austria to address a joint, nationally-televised session of Congress in defense of the agreement.

Carter had gone to Vienna as a leader challenged from within and down in the polls. A Gallup survey showed Democrats favoring Ted Kennedy as the next Presidential nominee over Carter, 62-24 per cent. The President stiffened. At a private White House dinner for Democratic congressmen, Carter volunteered, "If Kennedy runs, I'll whip his ass."

He was at rock bottom in his Presidency. The situation called for bold action and toughness. Winning the ED bill became more important to him, Fritz Mondale, and the White House staff.

*   *   *

The President's men pressed the Speaker to reschedule the bill some-time Tuesday, June 19. O'Neill put them off, bumping ED off the calendar to appease the opposition.

Finally, at 4:00 p.m., the Speaker allowed ED to be brought up—for a short while. Brooks and Horton took their stations on the House floor. ED advocates flocked to their command post and the House hallways. But word soon spread the bill wouldn't stay on the floor for long.

The House moved to Title Four, approving by 362-36 a compromise provision on vocational rehabilitation organizational requirements at the state level.

Republicans tried offering another busing/anti-quota amendment. Brooks raised a point of order, and the chair issued a landmark ruling, finding the amendment out-of-order on the grounds that the bill was organizational in nature and amendments going beyond existing law were nongermane. Brooks had said that all along.

Walker popped off an amendment extending the legislative veto to transfers from agencies outside the Office of Education and, borrowing an idea from Senator Hatch, requiring a rule be withdrawn when a majority of school districts disapproved. He lost, 159-243. That was it for Tuesday. Brooks pulled the bill at 5:30 and the House adjourned 15 minutes later.

The Speaker had a fundraiser to go to that night.

*   *   *

"I told the Vice President we need one more legislative day with late-night potential," Terry Straub briefed the Ad Hoc Committee the next morning. "But you should realize there's pressure on Tip O'Neill to get the appropriations bills to the Senate. The Speaker is acutely aware of our desire to move ahead."

When would that one more day come? Senators and Reps looked forward to the oncoming July 4 holiday. Fact-finding trips had been arranged for the following week. The President would travel to the Far East and Sen. Robert Byrd was headed for Moscow, to name a couple.

Congress would thus maintain a sedentary pace the week of June 25, tending only to less controversial matters, then adjourn for a 10-day vacation, returning July 9. ED wouldn't be considered for another two weeks.

The President's men asked the Speaker's staff for a specific date. With one, Reps could be pinned down and strategies finalized. The Speaker *had* to get tough and firm with his unruly House; he had to say flatly, the bill will be passed or defeated on such-and-such a day.

Late Friday afternoon, the Speaker's office called White House and NEA officials. That day would be Wednesday, July 11.

*   *   *

The Secretary of HEW had been touring mainland China. Before leaving June 15, he appointed Marshall Smith acting commissioner of education.

A former Harvard professor, Smith served as an assistant commissioner under U.S. Education Commissioner Ernest Boyer, who would leave his post at the end of June.

Given that the Commissionership would be abolished if ED passed, no outside prominent educator would be interested in the job. So, Califano properly turned to within the existing organization. He had narrowed it down to two men: Smith, or Thomas Minter, a black and deputy commissioner overseeing elementary/secondary programs.

In choosing Smith, the HEW Secretary touched off a hot dispute. Someone tipped off the Congressional Black Caucus. Its new chairman, Parren Mitchell (D-MD.), called White House aides and warned there would be stiff opposition. If this is symbolic of the kinds of appointments to be made in the new Department, then forget it, he said.

At this stage, anybody who wanted anything out of the White House in exchange for support of the ED bill could have gotten it. The Black Caucus's message: appoint Smith acting commissioner and we will fight the bill. Their reason: Smith helped research a 1972 book, "Inequality," that they felt had racist overtones. The book made clear that blacks should be afforded the same educational opportunities as whites, but such an "equalizing...would do very little to make adults more equal."

Word of the appointment spread quickly to civil rights groups. National Urban League staff phoned Marilyn late Friday afternoon, June 22, loudly irate at the appointment and threatening to withdraw their support. At the White House, alarmed aides hurriedly consulted the Vice President for guidance. Mondale wanted to cool it fast. "Tell him (Mitchell) we will...do the right thing," he ordered Terry Straub.

Mondale aide Bert Carp began discussions with both Smith and HEW Undersecretary Hale Champion. The White House wanted Smith to withdraw his name. Champion was livid, feeling the charges of racism against Smith were outrageous and an assault on academic freedom. He and others who knew Smith thought he was the victim of guilt by association. Even White House staffers conceded Smith was no racist.

Champion discussed the situation with Califano, still in China, and with Smith, who had gone to the beach for a mini-vacation. The HEW Undersecretary also met with the Vice President and attempted to change his mind. Mondale wouldn't think of allowing some acting appointment destroy chances for ED's passage. The Vice President ordered Champion to rescind the appointment, and on Tuesday, June 26 he did so—mad as hell.

The plan was to drop Smith quietly, without causing him embarrassment. But reporters for *Education Daily* and Noel Epstein of the *Washington Post*, a personal friend of Smith, heard of the scuffle and front-page stories followed.

The White House took grief from all sides. Several congressmen told Straub, well, if you're going to cave in to the black caucus and other powerful groups that easily on these appointments, then I'm not sure I'm for the bill. But, it showed the civil rights how far out on a limb the Carter-Mondale team would go for them; they felt better about White House pledges to remove the junk amendments in the House bill.

The public fallout stung. In a *Post* editorial, "O, What a Tangled Web," the paper called the affair "a lot of shoddy dealing" for "that about-to-be-hatched bureaucratic turkey, a Department of Education." The *New York Times* ran an editorial, "Education Disgraced," condemning the "smear tactics," and noting, "Shamelessly, Mr. Mondale went to work until Mr. Smith withdrew."

Mary Berry was named acting commissioner for 30 days. Ironically, there would be a single federal education official, if only for a month.

*   *   *

The week of June 25, the White House staff used every power at their disposal and involved every top Carter official to solidify support for ED. Education groups would employ every lobbying and pressure tactic known to the Washington power system.

Support continued to fall at a ghastly rate. The Catholics and the AFL-CIO were pulling out all the stops. In one week, we lost nearly the entire New Jersey congressional delegation, due primarily to Catholic pressure. The Church's school employees and an emerging national network of concerned Catholic parents wrote, called, and visited U.S. Representatives. AFT leaders, particularly from big cities, also made calls to help AFT's Al Shanker.

The Vice President invited Monsignor Paradis and Catholic Conference lobbyists Jim Robinson and Frank Monihan to breakfast in the White House Roosevelt Room. "You people are really serious about this," he marveled at Paradis. Mondale assured the Catholics all

ED appointees would be sympathetic to private schools' needs. He said the Administration would even elevate the head of the new office of nonpublic education to assistant secretary status. Mondale and the White House staff refused to believe there wasn't *something* that would quiet the Catholics. In an after-breakfast hallway tete-a-tete, Mondale pointedly asked Robinson what could be done to turn the bishops around on this issue.

"Our position is firm," Robinson stood up to the Vice President.

"Do you have to be so active?," Mondale wondered.

"Yes, that's what they pay me for," Robinson answered. He handed Mondale a copy of an anti-abortion amendment and said it would be offered to the ED bill on the House floor.

"If we accepted this, would that change your minds?." The Vice President figured he'd get a yes answer.

"No sir, we would still be opposed." Robinson was unmoved.

The Catholics' obstinateness frustrated Mondale, who had been close to them while Minnesota's U.S. senator. Their relations with the Carter Administration had deteriorated, especially over the President's opposition to tuition tax credits.

So, the White House resorted to other tactics. Mondale would lean on New Jersey Governor Brendan Byrne to endorse the bill, or at least talk to the state's 10 Democratic Reps who were under extreme combined Catholic-AFL pressure to vote no. NEA's considerable strength in that key state was not enough to overcome that alliance.

Chicago Democrats secretly told Carter lobbyists that unless some of the Catholic pressure from their heavily-populated and superbly-organized Catholic districts was lifted, they would have to vote no. The White House fought back with (unsuccessful) calls to powerful Chicago Cardinal John Patrick Cody. Also, applications to the Departments of HUD and Commerce for underwriting $90 million in loan guarantees to the "Wisconsin Steel" project in Chicago were speeded up in the hopes of swinging around area Congressmen Morgan Murphy, Frank

Annunzio, John Fary, and Dan Rostenkowski. The project would have created up to 7,000 new jobs.

Organized labor was coming under pressure from AFL leaders not to help NEA. Three unions—AFGE, AFSCME, and UAW—previously gave NEA endorsements of the bill. Terry Straub told the Vice President in a memo that AFL leader Lane Kirkland had been "calling in all the chips" with the groups, and he urged Mondale to call those union presidents to hold their support. In some cases, they used the junk amendments as excuses to withhold support.

White House business liaisons made dozens of contacts, seeking out receptive companies that had plants in key congressional districts. White House press operatives tried stimulating liberal syndicated columnists to produce stories the week of the vote. Plans were under way for small group meetings of wavering Reps with the President and Vice President.

NEA would hold its annual convention in Detroit the first weekend in July, and ED would be played up substantially there. The Vice President would give the keynote speech. There would be much press coverage, and thousands of delegates would be showering the House with cards and letters.

NEA and Allan Cohen's Ad Hoc Committee worked night-and-day coordinating activity in congressional districts for the 10-day July 4 recess. Teachers, school board members, PTA people, and others would be assigned to follow Reps' schedules, catch up with them at fairs, parades, etc. and ask their support for the bill. "This bill will be won or lost in the field," Straub told the Vice President. "We want the Member to have a strong sense of the visibility of this issue in his district."

Jack Brooks sent a letter to liberal House members cutting down the junk amendments as "ineffectual" and "merely restating positions Congress has previously taken." He argued any Member's reservations about the bill because of them were "unjustified and simply give the opponents precisely what they want—no Department of Education."

More than 150 ED teamplayers gathered Wednesday, June 27 for a pep rally in the Victorian-style old library at the Old Executive Office Building next door to the White House. "It's so close," Jim McIntyre told everyone. "Our margin of victory or *defeat* is now 10-15 votes," Terry Straub added. They were deadly serious.

Gail Bramblett and I hailed a cab in front of the White House that Wednesday afternoon for the ride back to Capitol Hill. As we weaved our way through the heavy afternoon Washington traffic, she confided in me some flooring news: "If we had a vote last week, we would have lost." Knowing NEA's vote counts were usually precise, I felt sick to my stomach…

*   *   *

The President arrived back in Washington Monday, July 2. His aides had been writing a possible national television address on the country's energy shortage problems. Domestic problems and the President's standing had gotten so bad that Carter knew he had to do something fast.

He helicoptered up to Camp David for the July 4 holiday. The draft speech would have been another dull Carter speech and didn't really contain any new proposals. The President abruptly canceled it.

Instead, to the astonishment of his countrymen, he began summoning hordes of national leaders to the mountain retreat—members of Congress, his Cabinet, black leaders, businessmen, civic activists, governors, mayors, and many more. Marine choppers busily ferried this stream of visitors to and from Camp David.

There was no explanation for this sudden "domestic summit." Carter, suffering a crisis of leadership, had decided to stop everything and reassess his entire presidency from top to bottom. As the "summit" went on for days, the mystery of what would come of it heightened the drama. Jimmy Carter would have to emerge from the exercise with something truly profound.

Returning visitors said the discussions were freewheeling, touching everything from the future of the republic, energy, and the economy, to blunt criticism of Carter himself and the role of the President. A few told of hearing Carter himself say he had to do a better job as President and fight the general "malaise" the American people were feeling.

The summit would drag on past D-Day for the ED bill, and cast an unwanted shadow over efforts to pass it.

*   *   *

Terry Straub suggested to the Vice President several activities for pushing ED between then and July 11.

The President and Mondale would breakfast with congressional leaders July 10. Straub told Mondale "we must assure adequate discussion" of ED there.

The White House lobbyist had also requested the President's schedulers set up a meeting between Carter and Tip O'Neill, "given the Speaker's reluctance to involve himself."

He also pushed for the President to see undecided Democrats and Republicans, and for Carter to plug the bill at the next Cabinet meeting.

A letter was being drafted from the President to all House Democrats asking their support.

The Governors were meeting in Louisville. Straub coordinated with White House intergovernmental chief Jack Watson a list of governors to be courted on the ED issue.

Straub compiled lists of undecided Reps for senior White House staff and Cabinet members to phone. He told Mondale he'd "continue to feed short lists to you and the President."

Another list concentrating on big-city, Illinois, and New Jersey delegations was given to Mondale to hand over to Joe Califano.

*   *   *

The HEW Secretary had endured an exhausting, three-week trip through China, and wanted to rest a spell in Hawaii on the way back.

The President had also just completed his trip to the Orient and had the same intentions of resting in the Hawaiian sun. White House aides, however, convinced him a luscious vacation while the nation sat in long gas lines would only further irritate the American public. Carter returned home and began his dramatic Camp David summit.

On hearing from aides that Califano would stop over in Hawaii, the President was furious. The ED bill was teetering on the brink of death and the Secretary of HEW was sunning himself. Carter had Mondale call Califano and order him home.

Califano returned to Washington Saturday, July 7. He met with the Vice President Monday morning. The Secretary would later say he detected unusual coolness and detachment from his friend, Fritz Mondale. The Vice President had already put up with the Marshall Smith affair; many White House aides blamed Califano for not fully clearing the appointment there first.

Mondale also knew Califano's days were numbered. For two-and-a-half years, the friction between the Secretary and Carter's closest aides had never ceased. Then, White House lobbyists reported Califano had called many members of the House including those of Italian descent, and urged they vote against the ED bill. At first, Mondale shrugged off the reports, but several Reps confirmed them to him during his telephonic arm-twisting.

Hamilton Jordan was madder than hell. He wanted Califano fired outright. He told Terry Straub to get him the names of those Reps.

Instead, Pat Gwaltney's office drew up a memo documenting Califano's many anti-ED tactics over the years.

The Vice President handed Califano a 25-name list Straub had written. The Secretary called the congressmen, as ordered, but it was all perfunctory on his part. The Reps knew how strongly opposed he was.

But Mondale believed deeply in ED, and friends or not, Califano had committed the cardinal sin of working against it—and directly against the Vice President. With that, Joe Califano had lost his last, and most powerful, defender in the White House.

*　　*　　*

NEA and White House people met secretly early Saturday morning, July 7—just four days before the vote.

"Where do we stand?," Les Francis asked Gail Bramblett.

"If the vote was today, we're down 5-10 votes," Gail replied bluntly.

Terry Straub let out an aghast sigh and slumped in his chair.

"We've got some swing votes," Gail tried to sound positive. She handed out her latest list of 20 or so Reps who needed heavy pressure from the White House.

Indeed, ED's footing was fast collapsing. In the past week alone, 21 supposedly "right" votes slipped over into the "wrong" column, 37 undecideds said they would vote against, and another five "rights" suddenly joined five undecideds.

Only 15 undecideds or "wrongs" had been converted into "rights." NEA leaders were terrified. They pressed their entire government relations crew into action, cashing in every chip the organization had ever accumulated on Capitol Hill. Friendly senators were asked to lobby wavering House colleagues from their states. NEA Washington staff jammed their phone lines with marching orders to local and state affiliates to phone, write, wire, or visit congressmen. Future endorsements were promised, others were taken away. It was time for hardball.

NEA decided to go with another full-page ad in the *Washington Post* on Tuesday, the day before the vote. The creative minds at J. Walter Thompson worked overtime to produce it. The ad would again be credited to the Ad Hoc Committee.

*   *   *

Monday, July 9. The city of Washington returned to its normal routine. Congress came back in session.

The AFT had concluded its annual convention in San Francisco, where teachers were urged repeatedly to send letters to Capitol Hill. Greg Humphrey told many friends that AFT had the votes to kill the bill. That tidbit made its way through channels to ED forces, worrying us that the AFT had perhaps cut some last-minute deals that no one knew about.

Marilyn and I nervously passed the time helping out wherever we could, which wasn't much. We made some preliminary—and hopeful—plans for the conference with the House: the senators we'd want to appoint as conferees, the differences we could accept or reject, etc.

The Camp David summit continued clouded in mystery. The Vice President was there every day. Terry Straub sent up a list of 13 House Democrats for him to call. Straub noted Kansas Democrat Dan Glickman was "getting heat" from his school boards and should be talked to. Indiana Democrat Lee Hamilton needed "a final push" and West Virginia Democrat Harley Staggers "needs a nudge," Straub told Mondale.

House Democratic heavyweight Dan Rostenkowski was giving the Carter crew much trouble. "He's like Jello on this bill," Straub said in his list. The Chicago Rep. "basically doesn't like (the bill) but earlier told the President he would help," Straub wrote. "Reliable reports last week had him bad-mouthing it. He is probably getting Catholic pressure from (Cardinal Cody), needs firming up."

Straub listed other problem Dems: Wisconsin's Bob Kastenmeier (a liberal "offended" by the anti-civil rights amendments), California's Leon Panetta ("might be retrievable"), Pittsburgh's Doug Walgren ("unsure whether we are doing the right thing for education"), upstate N.Y.'s Stan Lundine (would decide "on the merits"), and two other California Reps, Glenn Anderson and George Danielson (both needed "a political touch from you").

The Speaker flew up to Camp David Monday. "He must be persuaded to help us on Wednesday," Straub implored to top Carter lobbyist Frank Moore. "…Ditto for Jim Wright. The President should talk to both of them." Straub wanted five other prominent House Democrats who would meet with Carter at his mountain retreat that day pulled aside by the President for a few words: Phil Sharp of Indiana, Thomas Ashley of Ohio, Richard Gephardt of Missouri, Robert Giaimo of Connecticut, and Pennsylvanian William Moorhead. "The atmosphere will never be better than at Camp David to do this," Straub told Moore.

That night, Straub accompanied another congressional delegation in a huge army green chopper to Camp David. He slipped in a few words on-the-way with Parren Mitchell. The black caucus leader from Baltimore stubbornly resisted White House pleas for support.

*   *   *

Tuesday, July 10. One day to go.

"Our vote count shows that the issue is very close," Les Francis warned the President by memo that morning. "Our most optimistic count shows 220 'for' and 'leaning for', 203 'against' and 'leaning against', and 12 undecided. However, that 220 figure includes only 199 'firm' yes votes and 21 'leaning' yes. The 203 negative votes are, by all accounts, much more firm than those on our side. Furthermore, time has worked to our disadvantage; the delays we have experienced have produced noticeable erosion in our position.

"In short, the outcome is anything but certain.

"...The key to success now rests largely in the hands of the House leadership...It is imperative that you give one final and hard push on this bill...Only a direct appeal from you stands a chance of bringing the Speaker and his top lieutenants into the fray as active proponents of a Department of Education.

"Your appeal should be straightforward and political, to the effect: 'The outcome on the bill is still in doubt. It is a major priority for my Administration. Passage of the bill is important both substantively and politically. I want you to do everything in your power to ensure that Democrats in the House vote (affirmatively).'"

The extraordinarily unreserved memo asked the President to make seven calls immediately:

•*Speaker Tip O'Neill*—"His presence on the floor and active support on Wednesday can shore up and add to our votes among Democrats. The Vice President talked with him on the trip to Camp David last evening, but reported this morning he was anything but enthusiastic."

•*Jim Wright*—"The Majority Leader has not been active at all on this legislation. A personal appeal could produce critical assistance from him."

•*John Brademas*—"Although reluctantly, Brademas has indicated his support..."

•*Dan Rostenkowski*—"...seems to be wavering and may be dissuading Members from voting for the bill. His earlier promise to you must be reaffirmed."

•*Peter Rodino*—"A call from you could 'sew up' Rodino's vote and that, in turn, will influence other Members in the New Jersey delegation..."

•*Phil Burton*—"...needs a boost to reactivate his enthusiasm."

•*Chairman Jack Brooks*—"Your last call should be to Chairman Brooks and the message should be a combination of (1) 'Thanks for all of your help so far'; (2) 'I have talked to Tip, Jim Wright, etc., and asked them to really get in and help'; and (3) 'Is there anything else I or my staff should do?..."

Jimmy Carter got the message and went to work. Orders went out to his appointees in the federal government to help where they could, to barter, cajole, sweet-talk their friends in the House. In these last days before the vote, the Presidency was delivered full-thrust to the ED forces.

The Vice President worked his phone for hours. Terry Straub had him call a New Jersey Democrat, whom he thought could be persuaded with the promise of a high-level federal appointment for his friend. Mondale would also try to reach upstate N.Y. Democrat Matt McHugh, who pulled off the bill at the last minute because he saw "little support beyond NEA" for it, and Ohio Democrat John Seiberling, suddenly fading to the antis. Mondale would also personally see and calm down Michigan Democrat William Ford, upset over the Marshall Smith affair and edgy about the UAW's neutrality.

In that morning's *Washington Post*, congressmen read the NEA-Ad Hoc Committee's clever full-page ad, featuring a confusing organization chart of OE programs darkened with hundreds of lines depicting their relationships to state and local government, institutions, and students.[34] "A few lines to the Congress about the current tangles in HEW," the bold catch-line said at the top.

In the Rayburn House Office Building, the coalition's command post was a busy scene of meetings and phone calling. Lobbyists pried out of

---

[34] NEA officials debated whether to use the 1976 HEW chart in the ad. They knew it had no bearing on the ED debate. The relationships would continue under the new Department. But it looked so messy and the ad agency had come up with such a cute line. NEA decided to solve the problem simply by cutting off the top of the chart that explained it, hoping most people (especially members of Congress) wouldn't remember or understand its true meaning.

hundreds of U.S. Rep's offices their latest positions and whether the member would be present for the vote tomorrow. The information was critical. Lobbying team leaders met in the morning to go over, member-by-member, the vote count one more time. Dozens of NEA teachers were flown in to pressure vacillating Reps.

Meanwhile, Greg Humphrey and his AFT colleagues frantically worked to nail down no votes. They knew they had the momentum, even though they were fighting the power of the White House. Greg was especially frustrated in his battle for the Chicago congressional delegation. His AFT local there was slow to answer to his demands for action. He turned for better assistance to the Catholic Conference, whose Chicago people were well-organized and responsive.

AFL-CIO lobbyists knocked on doors in the House on behalf of AFT. But its member unions' lobbyists were not thorough. One walked up to Gail Bramblett off the House floor and said, "I've just been given a list. It's not our issue. I'm going to lunch."

New target lists were copied and distributed. The battle had come down to about 70 Reps, mostly Democrats, and mainly from the northern industrial and big-city areas.

The antis did not have a tight organization for counting and reporting members' positions. Sometimes they did not follow up, as in the case of Michigan Democrat Charles Diggs, under investigation for ethical misconduct. The AFT and AFL lobbyists stayed away from him. But NEA ignored the Congressman's troubles, figuring as long as he could still vote, they'd lobby him.

Pro-ED lobbyists, however descended upon House offices in waves, every few hours. House staffs were tired of the issue, and constantly being interrupted by ED people angered many of them. It was hard to gauge whether the badgering would pay off or turn off.

The command post/hearing room filled to capacity at 2 o'clock that afternoon for another general Ad Hoc meeting. "It's extremely close," Gail told the crowd in sober tones.

Terry Straub tried to put on a more positive face. "See you all in the Rose Garden real soon," he ended his pep talk.

The group responded to him with awkward silence.

* * *

Wednesday, July 11.

I had waken up many mornings in Washington, D.C., but this day would be the most important to me. The ED bill had passed many an obstacle, sometimes by the skin of its teeth, but this day's would be the hardest.

It would be a hazy, humid, 85° summer day in the nation's capital. I took a moment in my bathrobe to study the distant Capitol dome in the early morning sun from the balcony of my southwest apartment. Through all the stress and emotion inflicted on people who fight daily under it, the Dome stays unchanged—stable, beautiful, peaceful. Life rolls on. America survives.

I tried reading that morning's *Washington Post*, but thoughts kept replaying in my mind: *what if...* What if the bill passed? There would be another battle, reconciling the House and Senate bills and then getting both bodies to vote affirmatively one last time. The slimmer the margin today, the more difficult that would be.

What if the bill died? The thought made my breakfast stomach sour. It would be as if two-and-a-half years of my life didn't exist. The press would romp all over Jimmy Carter at this sensitive time in his term for such a big failure. AFT would come out the only big winner. There was so much at stake for so many people.

A headline at the top of the *Post* editorials stopped me. "One DOE Is Enough."

"Gawd," I sighed aloud. "They just won't stop."

The paper fired off more mortar against the bill, calling ED "a wretched idea." The *Post* had exhausted all its other adjectives.

The House would convene at 10:00 a.m. ED could be called up at any time.

Lobbyists filed into the Ad Hoc command post at 9:00, and got instructions on which Reps to visit one last time. Others picked up phones and completed their attendance checks.

The core group met in a hideaway conference room. Jack Brooks listened to NEA and White House lobbyists assess the floor situation. If all members were present and voting, the count looked like this: 219 for the bill, 216 against. As many as 20 Reps might be absent during the vote. Of these, 10 were members of a delegation traveling abroad (six for ED, four against).

"The longer we wait, the poorer our chances," Dale Lestina cautioned. "Now is the time to pull the trigger."

Jack Brooks, silent throughout the discussion, thought a few moments more then looked up at the small group. "Well, let's go with it," he said solemnly.

The Chairman and his staff contingent left for the House floor. At 10:30 he appeared at the manager's desk and spoke into the microphone. His words brought a hush to the chamber: "Mr. Speaker, I move that the House resolve itself...for the further consideration of the bill H.R. 2444 to establish a Department of Education...".

The House would take up the few remaining amendments to the bill's last three titles and then vote. It would be over in just a couple hours.

Indiana Republican Dan Quayle proposed an amendment arbitrarily increasing the number of personnel to be cut from 450 to 800 and requiring that consultants be counted as full-time personnel.

Brooks called the amendment "pennywise and pound foolish." He pointed out that a consultant hired for only five hours a week would be counted as a full-time employee, which didn't make much sense.

"We need to get a handle on the number of people who we have working for the federal government," Quayle defended himself.

Frank Horton pressed him to justify the 800 figure, but he couldn't satisfactorily.

Members hurried to the House floor and voted on Quayle's amendment. They had to wiggle their way through Capitol corridors packed with lobbyists, most wearing the "A DEPARTMENT OF EDUCATION/YES!" buttons. A team of White House lobbyists stood by, pulling aside Reps here and there for a few words. There were also armies of lobbyists from AFT, AFL, the Catholic Conference, and right-wing groups such as the American Conservative Union.

During the House debate, the Vice President continually phoned members from his White House office. The President phoned several from Camp David.

The House, meanwhile, threw a fit and voted in protest for Quayle's amendment, 263-143.

Backed by the Catholics, Rep. John Ashbrook came to the floor armed with two anti-abortion amendments. Brooks objected to the first with a point of order that it was nongermane. Ashbrook said it was "carefully drafted" and urged its adoption "out of respect for life."

The Catholics had found in the bill a routine, obscure boilerplate provision authorizing the Secretary to provide ED employees facilities at "remote" locations, including "emergency medical services and supplies." The amendment excluded "the performance of abortions except where the life of the mother would be endangered if the fetus were carried to term."

The chair ruled the amendment was germane, and it passed on a simple voice vote.

Ashbrook offered his second, involving another boilerplate section, this one enabling the Secretary to let outside groups and institutions use facilities under ED's custody and control. Ashbrook's amendment would prevent colleges that used mandatory student fees for abortions from using ED facilities. Horton challenged the amendment, but again the chair overruled the point of order.

Ashbrook demanded a recorded vote, knowing his amendment would pass easily and hoping for a wide margin to force the House-Senate conference committee to accept it. The result: 257-149, with two "present" and 26 absent.

It was going to be a terribly difficult conference, we feared. Every conceivable piece of junk had been heaped on the bill—prayer, busing, anti-quotas, abortion.

"If anyone is naive enough to think that the conference committee can effectively take these out, they are absolutely deluding themselves," Ben Rosenthal fussed from the well.

"That is the argument being sold to this Member," Parren Mitchell, a key target, shot back from a mike several rows away.

"...When an amendment carries by over 100 votes,...there is no way (it) will be eliminated from the conference report," Rosenthal reiterated.

"That tilts me a little further in the direction of a 'no' vote on final passage," Mitchell answered with a determined look.

The final vote was not far away. The Ashbrook vote sent lobbyists scurrying back to the phones with new strategies and assignments. It gave the latest attendance count.

The chair moved through Title Four, then Five, and then to the last, Six, which contained the effective date provision.

Tennessee Republican Robin Beard offered the final amendment, to sunset ED in six years. It was defeated on a voice vote.

The outside hallways abutting the floor erupted into a frenzy. With all amendments completed, there were only a few minutes left before the vote. The rush was on to get Reps to the floor for the vote.

Meanwhile, members spent an hour venting out their last thoughts in a mishmash of opposing and supportive statements.

"...My friends, you can rest assured that federal special interests will eventually call all the shots on the educational front...unless we kill this legislation here and now," bellowed North Carolina conservative L.H. Fountain.

Conservative Republican Robert Bauman (MD.), darling of the New Right, rose to utter a sour warning: Jimmy Carter would fall in 1980 and a conservative Republican would take control of the government. "A conservative Secretary of Education will be appointed who will make the NEA wish its pet department had never been born," he spoke caustically. ED would be used to promote basic ed, "free enterprise" ed, "high-discipline" schools, voluntary prayer, voucher systems, and to "enforce local laws against strikes by teachers," Bauman said.

California Democrat Ron Dellums got up on the floor, chanting that he was one of the "few people enthusiastic" about ED. The liberal black Congressman said the House had two alternatives on the "mischievous" amendments. First, kill the bill now. "We have the necessary votes." The other was to send it to conference and hope the amendments were dropped. "If the conference report comes back with these abominable amendments in, I will fight (it) to the last breath," he pledged.

Jack Brooks closed in telling his colleagues they had come to the "moment of decision. So, let us proceed to that decision." He looked tired and apprehensive.

The Speaker had been sitting off to the side on the floor for several minutes. He would not address his House before the vote.

Around the Hill, the delirious furor to pin down votes built to a climax. Gail Bramblett noticed that almost the entire Florida delegation was missing. She tracked them down a block away at the Florida House for a reception. Several calls later from the White House, they charged back across the Capitol plaza for the vote.

The Speaker assumed the chair.

Erlenborn offered a motion to recommit the bill.

The Speaker proceeded to dismiss it in one breath. "The previous question is on the motion to recommit all those in favor say aye all those opposed say no the noes have it and the motion is rejected."

Then O'Neill drew a big gulp of air. "The question is on the passage of the bill."

Buzzers sounded and the House of Representatives' 35th recorded vote on the ED bill began. They would be the most agonizing and strung-out 15 minutes.

The Speaker stayed on the floor during the vote. So did his top aides and the next highest ranking Democrats, Jim Wright and John Brademas. They, along with Jack Brooks and Frank Horton, latched onto arms of entering colleagues, slipping in a final plea for help.

Outside in the hazy Washington sunshine, police held up traffic on Independence Avenue while clusters of U.S. Representatives poured out of the three main House office buildings to walk the block to the Capitol and the House floor.

Lobbyists waited everywhere. There were lobbyists on the House steps, lobbyists in the hallways, lobbyists at the elevators, and more at all entrances to the House floor.

In the command post, many coped with stomachs tied in knots as they eyed the TV screen, flashing every few seconds the latest vote count. First ED was staying ahead, then it wasn't, then it was again. During the middle five-minute period, the votes were in a virtual draw.

The five-minute warning bells sounded, and hundreds of Congressmen trooped into the House chamber, now buzzing with the chatter and excitement of nearly a thousand people inside.

Gail Bramblett stood at the Republican door, so tense she couldn't inhale oxygen. The vote continued ahead for at a time. "It's not going to hold," she cried.

Indeed, on the floor, three dozen members waited patiently to see how the vote was going. Many didn't like the bill, but some had told NEA and the White House they would vote yes if their ballots were the deciding ones.

John Erlenborn, Robert Walker, Robert Bauman, Bob Michel, John Rhodes, and other key Republican opponents grabbed Republican Reps inside, pleading that they not give Jimmy Carter a victory.

The clock ran out. But for several minutes more, the votes still being cast. The tally board read 204-204, then 205-207, 207-207, then 208-207. The votes were still being counted. The fear and tension were akin to being pushed off a 1000-foot cliff.

The Speaker held up announcing the vote as long as he could, until he got a passing count—assuming he could get one.

Democratic leaders saw that Gus Hawkins had voted against the bill They cornered him and pledged the bill would die if the junk amendments weren't entirely removed in the conference committee. The California black caucus member switched his vote to "aye."

Finally, Tip O'Neill banged his gavel as if he were splitting a log. The sharp smack silenced the chamber.

For a few seconds, a clerk adjusted his long white tally sheet. Then, he gave it to the Speaker, who put on his glasses to read it.

Everywhere, in the galleries, in the hallways, on the floor, in the command post, hearts pounded as the Speaker started speaking.

"On this vote, the yeas are 210, the nays are 206, and the bill is passed."

All at once, a shrill roar of screaming enveloped the distinguished body. It came from the galleries and the outside corridors. ED lobbyists hugged each other in large bundles of bodies.

The battle, though, was not over yet.

TWENTY-ONE

Working Out the Differences

Corks popped from champagne bottles and hit the 30-foot ceiling of Brooks's Committee hearing room. Education lobbyists partied all afternoon, celebrating their whisker-thin victory.

Gail Bramblett, high and giddy, temporarily shushed the bash as she read the 416 names of Representatives who voted, and how they voted. For those hard-fought, targeted Reps, "boos" or "hoorays" spewed from the crowd, depending on whose side they came down.

To rousing cheers and applause, Jack Brooks elbowed his way through the throng of ED people up to that dais. "I've seen some close votes in my time, but whew!," he exclaimed, pretending to wipe his forehead. The crowd laughed.

"...Now, we'll have a tough conference ahead," he predicted, bringing the partygoers back to reality. "There are some amendments on the bill that we don't like, but they're not that bad. They don't really mean that much. We may have to keep a few of 'em just to please our friends Erlenborn and Walker...".

Just then, Marilyn thrust her elbow into my side and mumbled through her half-closed mouth, "Oh no." We knew that the junk amendments had to come out entirely, more so now because of the tight House vote.

Brooks left as a big hero. The partying went on.

Back at our Senate Committee office, Dick Wegman surprised Marilyn and I with a small celebration of our own. Senator Ribicoff, exhilarated and joyous, called to congratulate us. "Well, well, it's just like Jonah and the whale," he told me.[35]

Terry Straub walked out to the secluded tennis courts on the south lawn of the White House to give the playing, sweat-soaked Vice President the good news.

Mondale ordered up a small dinner party that night at his upper Northwest mansion for 25 ED lobbyists and wives. While he barbecued steaks, wife Joan treated the privileged guests to a tour of her impressive art collection.

At one point the phone in the garden rang. Mondale answered it. "Hey Jack," he shouted to Brooks. "The President would like to talk with you." Carter called from Camp David with his hearty thanks to the man who carried the heavy ball for him.

It was front-page news across the country. Papers called it "a narrow victory" for President Carter.

---

[35] In the Old Testament, Jonah was swallowed up by a great whale in raging seas, and stayed in the fish's belly three days and three nights. But he didn't lose his faith, praying to the Lord for help, who responded to his pleas and had the whale release Jonah onto dry land.

The *Los Angeles Times* quoted Terry Straub as judging the key to victory was "breaking up what had been a solid bloc of opposition in the New Jersey and Illinois delegations because of heavy Catholic pressure."

Related side-bar stories told how the "well-organized education coalition backing the bill" lobbied the House. "We were all needed when the final crunch came," Allan Cohen told members of his Ad Hoc Committee.

But there were other headlines: "House OKs New Education Dept., But Amendments May Block It," from the *Washington Star*, for example. Reporters focused on the "double-barreled risk" that support for ED could dissolve if the House-Senate conferees either dropped the controversial amendments or retained them.

Days later, John Erlenborn and Ben Rosenthal sent a joint letter to ED opponents. "The bill can still be defeated," they said. "we will not give up. We vow an all-out attempt to kill the conference agreement...".

*   *   *

The next step had us worried.

Conference committees are curious, bizarre, and often unpredictable creatures of a bicameral legislature. The two bodies of Congress, House and Senate, had each passed their own ED bill, but only one could be sent to the President for his signature and enactment into law.

The House could simply vote to approve the Senate's version, which would have been nice. But House members, feeling insulted and out-maneuvered by such a move, would probably reject it. Vice versa, the Senate would in no way accept the House bill with all its junk amendments. So that option was out.

One of the bills could be shuttled back-and-forth for amending until it reached an agreeable state to both chambers, but that involved an open-ended period of time and unlimited votes.

Or, the two bodies could *ask for a conference*, a special panel consisting of senators and representatives who would meet and negotiate a single bill out of the two versions. The compromise bill, or *conference agreement*, would go back to both houses for a final vote.

The road to conference was filled with ruts and potholes. Opponents could tinker with even the *request* for conference, forcing a recorded vote and moving to instruct the conferees to retain certain provisions or reject others.

Of critical importance was which body asked first for conference. Bill Jones called Marilyn at 6:00 p.m. the day of House passage, urging the House ask first. Under the rules, if the House asked first, it would vote on the conference agreement last. Brooks's chief counsel figured the Senate would easily pass the agreement. In doing so first, it would automatically discharge its conferees. The House could then only vote up-or-down, not on sending the compromise back to conference, because technically the committee would no longer exist.

Jones knew the antis would want to use all options: deny the request for conference, instruct the House conferees to retain one of the junk amendments, and later try to send the new bill back to conference, killing it. Erasing the last option might save the bill, because the unenthusiastic House might be tempted to murder ED once and for all by keeping it locked up in conference.

The prospects for a successful conference were shaky. The ED bill contained the most controversial issues conference committees ever dealt with. Whether they would be dropped there depended largely on who served on the special committee, and there were only vague rules for that. Marilyn and I wanted senators who had strong pro-civil rights records to fight the bad amendments. That same day, we decided on Senators Ribicoff, Glenn, Levin, Percy, and Javits. Senators Roth and Nunn wanted to be conferees, but they might have been too inclined to accept the busing and quota amendments. For the House side, Brooks decided to go with the members of his subcommittee, and that posed problems. Three opposed ED (Erlenborn, Stangeland, and Moorhead), and five voted for the prayer, busing, or quota amendments at one time or another.

For every issue, conference committees sail new waters. There are few rules to follow. The principle is they need as much flexibility and leeway to negotiate as possible. Consequently, if the antis succeeded in pushing through a motion to instruct its conferees to keep a junk amendment, the House conferees would not be bound to do so and could ignore the instructions.

One rule had to be observed: the conferees could deal only with the matters in both Senate and House bills. They could not bring in new programs, for example, nor substantially alter principles of both bills. For each side to get what it wanted, tradeoffs would have to be thought up. The art of compromise would be put to the test.

Some mighty fine political reading and judgments would be called for. By dumping the junk amendments, how many votes would we pick up, how many would be lost? Could any of the amendments be kept without damaging our already tenuous position? In the weeks ahead, we would take pains to consult civil rights groups every step of the way. Their reactions would determine our moves; we had to have their neutrality.

"Senator Ribicoff should take the lead and move fast," Gail Bramblett told us. The NEA lobbyist wanted everything done by the end of July. But that notion was laughable. Congress would leave town for the entire month of August. We knew all the tedious negotiations and conference committee meetings, the politicking and writing of the conference report, could not be done in two weeks.

The final votes on ED would not come until sometime in September.

*   *   *

The naivete of some people amazed us. Within days of House passage, jousting began for appointment as the first U.S. Secretary of Education.

Hispanics began their campaign to get former New Mexico Governor Jerry Apodaca named to the post. *The Los Angeles Times* said California State Superintendent of Public Instruction Wilson Riles was "Carter's likely choice." And at the annual PUSH convention in Cleveland, Rev. Jesse Jackson endorsed Mary Berry for the job.

It was no secret that all three were interested. But surprisingly, Wilson Riles took his name out of the running at a press conference the next day in Washington He pointed to the Proposition 13-triggered crisis in his state's public education system as the reason. More likely, the thankless job of building a new Cabinet department for a potentially one-term, weak President no longer appealed to the popular black leader.

All this posturing annoyed us. "We've got enough to worry about just getting the bill through, without worrying about who's going to be Secretary," I complained to a reporter. The quote was printed.

*   *   *

The attention of the nation and the world would be focused on Jimmy Carter Sunday night, July 15. The President would come down from the mountaintop and deliver his long-awaited TV address.

He had spent 10 days in his startling "domestic summit," listening patiently to more than 100 people criticize him and his Presidency. The mysterious exercise built up exaggerated expectations from the American public.

Carter knew this speech would be a turning point for him and his Administration. There were only 15 months before the 1980 election. At least half the American people saw his Presidency as a failure.

Saturday and Sunday, reporters got cursory briefings on the general themes; the President would admit that he had bogged down himself in the internal management of the White House and federal government, that he had not garnered adequate public support for his programs, and that he needed to restore trust between the people and their President.

Sunday night, Carter sat behind his Oval Office desk and gave the nation his cold, icy stare—and one of the most extraordinary Presidential addresses ever.

He read on TV some of the candid assessments of his Camp David visitors. "Mr. President, you're not leading this nation—you're just managing the government," said one. He read into the TV cameras another: "Some of your Cabinet members don't seem loyal. There is not enough discipline among your disciples."

Viewers at home, and especially in Washington, shifted in their chairs as the President spoke. It was generally embarrassing to watch Carter do that to himself, and to his people.

"What I do promise you is that I will lead our fight...and above all, I will act," the President vowed.

Carter turned to chastise the American public for its *malaise* about the country and its future. He said he saw a "crisis of confidence." He also hit up Washington, D.C., believing the nation's capital "has become an island. The gap between our cities and our government has never been so wide."

"...Wherever you have a chance, say something good about our country," the President urged his countrymen.

Carter emerged from the Sunday night spectacle recharged and eager. He was sure he had set himself back on the right track. He would set off the following week for a round of follow-up speeches throughout the country.

Pollsters recorded a 10-point surge in his approval rating after the "malaise" address. Republicans chose to ridicule it. "I don't find people licking their wounds," Sen. Ted Stevens told reporters. "The only one I find licking his wounds is the President."

*   *   *

Jack Brooks was ready to go to the floor Monday morning following the President's speech with his motion asking a conference with the Senate, but he learned that John Erlenborn would object to the normally routine unanimous consent request.

House rules provided one out: committee chairmen could take the request to go to conference back to their committees, get an approving vote, and then the motion would not need unanimous consent on the House floor. Brooks did just that. He pulled his panel together at 9:45 Tuesday morning, July 17. ED groups did some quick checking with Committee members to make sure their votes had not changed. After an 11-minute discussion, the Committee voted 20-17 to send Brooks back to the House floor.

The chair recognized Brooks at 4:30 that afternoon on the floor. "Mr. Speaker, I move that the House insist on its amendments to the Senate bill to establish a Department of Education, and request a conference with the Senate thereon."

Brooks told the House this was "a routine procedural step" that "preserves the rights of the members to vote the conference report up or down when it comes back."

Erlenborn warned his colleagues of the motives to strip the "highly controversial amendments" in conference. "The only way we can protect those as adopted by overwhelming margins in the House is to retain the right to recommit," he argued from the Republican well. He explained the House would lose that right in approving Brooks's motion.

The House voted 263-156 for the motion, formally sending the bill to conference.

Robert Walker stood up immediately and offered a motion to instruct the House conferees to keep his "anti-quota" amendment.

Why that of all the junk amendments? "I picked the amendment that had the biggest vote on the House floor," the Pennsylvania Republican said. (The House had approved the provision, 277-126.)

"The whole idea of a conference…is to try to come up with some compromise, Brooks beseeched his colleagues. "There has to be some give-and-take if we are ever going to get to a final agreement. The effort to instruct conferees works against that hope of compromise. It says to the Senate, 'You give and we take.'" Brooks said he would "do all I can to sustain the House position but…I am not going to stand by and see this conference end in a deadlock."

Walker demanded a recorded vote. The count stayed close throughout as lobbyists pulled aside Members at the House chamber entrances. At last, the House approved Walker's motion, but by the surprisingly slim margin of 214-202.

The Speaker, at Brooks's request, appointed the members of his subcommittee as conferees.

Two hours later, Marilyn and I joined Senator Ribicoff on the Senate floor. He read from a paper, "Mr. President, I move that…the Senate agree to the conference requested by the House…".

"Is there objection?," the chair asked the busy chamber.

"I object," Senator Stevens chirped, sending our hearts our throats. We didn't know for sure whether conservatives might propose their own motion to instruct Senate conferees.

The Senate was left in temporary suspension while Stevens ran out of the chamber to check on a possible Republican motion he'd heard about earlier.

He returned moments later with an apology. "That matter has been taken care of now." He offered no further explanation. Apparently one of his Republicans got cold feet at the last minute.

Ribicoff's motion passed unanimously and the presiding officer appointed, as we requested, Senators Ribicoff, Glenn, Levin, Percy, and Javits as the Senate conferees.

We now had a House-Senate conference committee.

*   *   *

While we were requesting a conference committee to settle the differences between two bills, the President was requesting resignations from 34 top White House aides and Cabinet secretaries in a stunning effort to erase friction between himself and his appointees.

Carter met with his Cabinet and staff in the Cabinet Room at 10:30 Tuesday morning. He announced Ham Jordan would, at long last, be formally named his chief of staff. Then he shocked his crew by asking that they offer their resignations.

As part of his bold new thrust, the President had decided to clean house. Far too many national leaders had told him he could not keep his Cabinet in line with his public positions, and that contributed significantly to his weakness. A cleansing of his Cabinet would, he figured, naturally go hand-in-hand with the new directions promised in his Sunday night "malaise" speech. He would be seen as suddenly grabbing the reins, taking new and strong command over his government.

At the top of his list: the Secretary of Health, Education, and Welfare. The press ran rampant with rumors that Joe Califano would surely be fired.

"Shades of Nixon," Califano told Senator Ribicoff of the Tuesday morning Cabinet meeting in a phone call that afternoon.

"Well, Joe, it looks like they might get rid of you," the Senator counseled. "If I were you, I'd beat 'em to it and resign."

The next day, Wednesday, July 18, Califano talked privately again with Ribicoff and other friends about his predicament. Ribicoff again advised he say, "My resignation is final."

Around 6:00 p.m., the President called Califano to the White House and broke the news to him that he'd accepted the Secretary's resignation.

Strangely, Carter and Califano did not agree on what the President said in that emotional chat. Califano contended Carter told him, "You've been the best Secretary of HEW" and "the problem is friction with the White House staff." Califano also would recall publicly that the President said he had to get his Cabinet in shape for the 1980 election.

Jody Powell, in a bizarre twist, told reporters that Carter had told Califano something entirely different: "You have been a good manager of HEW, but you have failed miserably with the Congress...I must let you go because you do not seem able to support policy once it is made." Powell said Carter cited the national health insurance and Department of Education bills as examples.

The nation learned immediately of the firings. Not only was Califano axed, but also Treasury Secretary Michael Blumenthal and Transportation Secretary Brock Adams. Attorney General Griffin Bell and Energy Secretary James Schlesinger bowed out of their posts.

The Cabinet purge had been done swiftly, mortifying Washington. *The Washington Post* called it a "political Jonestown...You can't tell whether the President is being big and tough or small and mean." To the folks back home watching the hullabaloo on television, Washington appeared in chaos. Reaction to the firings from Capitol Hill was largely acrimonious towards Jimmy Carter. Many liberal senators and representatives were especially angered that Califano had been booted out.

I watched in horror Thursday night the *CBS Evening News* as the sordid story was told. Suddenly, Abe Ribicoff appeared on the screen:

"You can't fault Joe for disloyalty to the President," he said The reporter asked, "Why then was he fired?" After a pregnant pause, Ribicoff replied slowly, "You know, I really haven't the slightest idea."

In my living room, I cupped my red-hot, embarrassed face in my hands. "Oh my God," I moaned to myself. *Califano was fired because of our bill—Ribicoff's bill!* But there, on national TV, was Ribicoff excoriating the President.

Joe Califano had frustrated us at every turn in moving the ED bill the past two years. I should have felt jubilant at his firing, but oddly I had mixed emotions. He was a good man and a good HEW Secretary—yes, probably the best. He simply got carried away in his crusade to keep HEW together.

*   *   *

The aftershocks would continue for weeks.

The President was pictured as serene, satisfied with his Cabinet shake-up. Although only 36 per cent of the public thought it beneficial to the country, analysts were quick to point out the shuffle would indeed strengthen Carter's political position. The event had so shaken the bureaucracy that federal agency executives in political positions would instantly become more loyal to Jimmy Carter and his policies.

Carter picked HUD Secretary Patricia Harris to take Califano's place. We expected she would work hard for the ED bill. Carter's new Cabinet appointments carefully touched the sensitive bases—blacks, women, etc.

In a post-purge story, journalist Carl Rowan reported that in his conversation with Califano, the President "supposedly" accused the HEW Secretary of "inducing the *Washington Post* to editorialize against (ED)."

The comment hit a nerve over at the newspaper's 15th Street offices. The *Post* responded with its most tart editorial on ED ever. "The thing about Washington is that it is even worse than Jimmy Carter and Jody Powell think it is," the piece began. "…We will come clean…there's no point blaming Mr. Califano for our lapse. We are, in fact, hardened criminals, hopeless recidivists and probably—why mince words?—incorrigibles. We have been fighting the creation of a separate Department of Education…since 1953.

"There. We said it. We feel better already. Permit us to continue this cleansing confession…". The editorial said the *Post* had been opposing "this turkey of an idea" with "the regularity of a cuckoo clock" from as far back as 1953 and then again in 1962 when Senator Ribicoff advocated it.

In reality, the *Post* was smarting badly over the sacking of its good friend, Joe Califano. The paper couldn't help itself. Throughout 1977, 1978, and the first half of 1979, it lavished attention and coverage on the HEW Secretary with plentiful front-page stories and overly-large Califano photos. *Post* editors were taking it personally and reacting angrily to news that the firing might have had something to do with their ceaseless opposition to ED. If anything, the July 23 editorial only confirmed the *Post's* close relationship to Califano.

The day after the President dismissed Califano, the Secretary had dinner with *Post* Executive Editor Ben Bradlee and Edward Bennett Williams, his old law partner and one-time *Post* legal counsel.

*   *   *

"…Who serves as head of a department or for how long is a ripple in our country. Who serves as President is a wave…".

Joe Califano uttered those words the Sunday after on ABC's *Issues and Answers* TV program.

"Do you think you were a disloyal member of the President's Cabinet?," asked the ABC interviewer.

"No, I do not…I argued against some proposals…Once (the President) makes the decision, then you go and support the decision. This is what I have done."

The interviewer confronted the HEW Secretary with charges he lobbied against the ED bill.

"That is simply not correct…I was asked to make calls to get congressmen to vote for that Department. I made those calls and indeed, just last week, the Speaker…told me if I had not made those calls and the Vice President had not made calls, it would not have passed the House by four votes…".

* * *

Terry Straub asked Jack Brooks to slow down the rush to conference. Emotions in Congress following the Cabinet shake-up were running too high in support of Califano.

Brooks agreed, but he at least wanted to hold an organizational first meeting of the conference committee before Congress recessed for the hot, sticky month of August. Throughout August, House and Senate staffs would negotiate solutions to minor difference between the two bills and develop a list of the major differences for the special committee to resolve at another meeting sometime in September.

We staffers were already working on prepping for conference. First up for tender negotiation: the side-by-side comparative print of the two bills, the basic conference document. On the left side, S.210, and on the right, H.R.2444. The print would run 200 pages long in aligning similar sections of the two bills for close inspection by the conferees. It took nine days to draft the comparative print and five more for the House and Senate staffs to agree on the placement of the provisions vis-a-vis one another. In some cases, there were political implications in putting certain sections beside others.

Each side had lots of research to do. Marilyn and I spent weeks digging up information on the House provisions, especially the junk amendments—their meaning, precedents, potential effect.

We held a long series of meetings with civil rights groups. "The amendments (in the House bill) should come out entirely. We will not negotiate," said a representative of the Lawyers' Committee on Civil Rights. The groups uniformly put up that hard-line front. "The Hill is a master of compromise. We must be clear that we will not support any kind of tradeoffs," National Urban Coalition leader Carl Holman told a big gathering of rights groups. Marilyn and I sat patiently and listened, pledging to fight with them but not promising success.

"Agreement may be elusive indeed," the *New York Times* proclaimed in a July 28 editorial entitled, "The New D.O.E. May Be D.O.A."

*   *   *

In a sweltering, cramped, third-floor Capitol conference room, the small coterie of senators and representatives bantered for a few minutes, loosening up the awkwardly rigid atmosphere in House-meets-Senate-to-make-a-deal.

"Abe, what's this I hear about you retiring or something like that?," Jack Brooks smiled across the long table.

"Why, I'll miss not working with you like this, Jack," Ribicoff tried to reciprocate. The Senator could never match Brooks's humor.

"If I had as much hair as you do, I'd retire too," Brooks quipped, filling the room with laughter.

Ribicoff had announced he would not seek re-election in 1980, capping a 40-year political career.

Brooks signaled to the stenographer to start.

"I would like to move that Chairman Brooks be named chairman of this conference," Ribicoff began officially. There was no objection.

It was Wednesday, August 1. Brooks had insisted on this first, perfunctory how-do-you-do conference session to get things rolling. The nine Reps sat on one side of the table, the Senators on the opposite facing them. Before each one, the light brown-covered comparative print lie on the table.

Like 99 per cent of all conference meetings, this one assembled in the Capitol, the theory being that both representatives and senators should symbolically and physically meet each other halfway.

"…We have always enjoyed a productive and cooperative attitude, and I trust this will prevail…," Brooks opened his remarks. By naming him chairman of the special committee, the ED forces would retain better procedural control, especially over the House conferees.

"…Year in to year out, we have never had any great difficulties working out the problems," Ribicoff agreed.

"…As is our usual practice, the conference will be open," Brooks continued. "But in instances where the facilities are crowded, we have to control the access…".

Around the perimeter of the small room, 20 staffers, and lobbyists sat listening while guards kept still more waiting in the hallway outside. Few Capitol building conference rooms hold more than 50 people, always restricting the access.

"We would prefer to have none," Brooks cracked to more laughter. Everyone knew he wasn't joking entirely. Senators and Reps would much rather thrash out their differences behind closed doors.

"…I would propose that the conference committee authorize and direct the staffs of the two Committees to get together during the August recess and develop a list of the major differences," Brooks suggested. The congressmen would leave Washington in a couple of days for the whole month.

"…There are numerous other differences, stylistic or technical," Brooks went on. "I would recommend that the staff be directed to work out a suggested resolution of those differences to be presented to the conference committee during our next meeting following the recess."

Ribicoff said it was "an excellent idea" and would save "considerable time."

"We propose that we reconvene the conference committee during the week of September 10," Brooks said. No one had a problem with that.

The meeting was finished in just 10 minutes. "Have a very good August," Ribicoff wished Brooks.

*   *   *

"This is a happy day for our country," Jimmy Carter told a packed East Room audience two days later, Friday. "...It is a time of Thanksgiving among those who look to the Department of Health, Education, and Welfare for a new or sustained chance in life."

Standing behind him were Patricia Harris and Justice Thurgood Marshall, who would swear in the new HEW Secretary.

The President called Harris "a manager with a heart,...bold, strong, outspoken" who had "a superb batting average on the Hill in getting legislation passed."

"We have a crying need to enhance the status of education in our country," Carter continued. "The new Department of Education can provide this role if it is effectively founded in law, adequately staffed by me with the support and nurturing from Secretary Harris."

Later, after taking the oath of office, Harris spoke. "...I want to assure everyone in this room and all others who view or hear this event that I will work tirelessly and resolutely to establish a separate Department of Education...".

Applause filled the huge White House chamber.

*   *   *

Late that afternoon, Marilyn and I secretly met with Bill Jones and Elmer Henderson. The four of us were the chief Senate-House ED staffers.

We relaxed together informally in the elegant, paneled House Reception Room off the House floor. The Capitol corridors were stonily silent and deserted. Congress had fled Washington again.

Away from all the congressmen, and the lobbyists, and the White House aides, and the Republican staffers, we could talk frankly about the course we should follow. The House and Senate Chairmen's people needed to touch bases on their own.

We knew Bill Jones to be tough but honest, always looking out for the best interests of his Chairman. Jones also knew, most often, exactly how Jack Brooks felt and whether there was room for movement in his positions.

Earlier, Jones appeared vaguely cooperative about the strategy of dropping "some" of the junk amendments in his House bill. That was the key to a successful conference. Marilyn and I had to uncover how Brooks really felt, whether he could be convinced to let them all go.

"Well, our count shows we lose a definite 20-25 votes if the civil rights amendments are deleted, and the same if left in," Jones confided to us. His soft voice still had a trace of a Texas accent; it echoed slightly throughout the empty Capitol halls.

"The NEA, White House, and civil rights groups seem to think we lose many more votes if the amendments are left in the bill," Marilyn responded in a subdued, informative tone.

"We've got to get the Administration and NEA to do a complete, accurate count," Jones said. "Before I can go to the Chairman (Brooks), I've got to be able to show him the exact figures—who we lose, who we pick up, who gets mad, who doesn't—if one, or two, or none of the amendments are left in the bill. He may go along with dropping them all. I can't say now."

Elmer Henderson had been patiently debating within himself whether to speak his mind. The middle-aged black lawyer finally did. "I have a vested interest in getting rid of the amendments," he said. "I'm willing to take a chance."

Jones nodded and joined our smiles. He understood only too well the civil rights implications. The critical decision to scrap the junk amendments rested in his and Brooks's laps.

*   *   *

"All right, first page, item one, the official title," House legislative counsel Steve Cope called out.

"We recede," Marilyn blurted, half-seriously.

"No, we insist—*we* recede," Jones laughed.

"Sorry, Bill, we won't give on this one," Marilyn persisted, prompting more laughs.

Both House and Senate bills had the same title: "Department of Education Organization Act." The Senate added "of 1979", the House didn't.

"O.K., you win. The Senate recedes," Jones had the last laugh.

The congressional staff, in its first negotiating session Monday, August 6, had made the first decision in resolving the hundreds of differences between the two bills. Our painstaking bargaining on the "minor" differences would run 15 hours over a three-day period.

Usually, there were nine of us altogether. From the Senate, Marilyn, myself, and Susan McNally. From the House, Bill Jones, Elmer Henderson, Bob Brink, Steve Cope, John Duncan (representing Rep. Frank Horton), and Steve Daniels (representing Rep. John Erlenborn).

We sat around a long table in the spartan conference room within Brooks's Committee's suite of offices, often sending out for lunch and refreshments. We went through the two bills, line-by-line, word-by-word.

If two provisions were essentially similar, Marilyn and I tried always to be the first to recede and give in to the House. We needed to make as many concessions to the House position as we could, because we wanted the House to give up the big game—the junk amendments.

If two provisions had practically the same effect but were worded differently, we often worked to incorporate the gist of both in one, agreeable version.

Sometimes, when the legal meaning was unclear, we left it to the House and Senate legislative counsels, Cope and McNally, to hammer out.

And then there were the obviously "major" differences that the staff knew were beyond their reach to decide: the anti-quota, prayer, busing, abortion, federal control language, etc. These were laid aside temporarily until the formal "memorandum of major differences" would be drawn up for the conference committee itself.

These back-room sessions drove home to me the power of congressional staff. We unelected people were taking two official bills, passed by the U.S. Senate and the U.S. House of Representatives, and reworking their content, out of sight of the public and on what we deemed to be the authority granted us by just nine members—out of 535—of the Congress. Of course, the conference committee could reverse our decisions, but it would be more interested in the controversial major differences. We expected the committee would routinely ratify our negotiated decisions. To be certain, staffers to the other committee members would be asked to sign off on them.

Pat Gwaltney knew our decisions on the "minor" issues would have a big effect on the shape of the new Department, which OMB would be responsible for starting up. She wanted an aide to sit in on our House-Senate staff meetings. Jones and Marilyn refused, angering her. We didn't need an Administration official looking over our shoulders and, in effect, attempt to tell us what we were doing right or wrong. This was a matter between the two houses of Congress.

Often, during these staff sessions, Erlenborn aide Steve Daniels would raise objections to our decisions. Usually we would acknowledge his concerns and politely brush them aside.

Much work remained after the first round: agreeing on the list of major differences, preparing for and arranging the next conference committee meeting, smoothing out a political strategy for saving the ED bill in September.

But with the capital city abandoned for the dog days of August, there was little more we could do for the next two weeks. All the key players went on vacation. Senator Ribicoff was in Connecticut. The Vice President was going to China. The President and his family left for a long voyage down the Mississippi River on a riverboat.

The rest of us made our own plans for leaving town.

Prior to shoving off, the core group talked politics, stepping up the pressure on Bill Jones for effacing the junk amendments.

"We've got to have fall-back positions," Jones insisted to Terry Straub, Marilyn, Gail Bramblett, and myself.

"It's a very dangerous situation," Straub gently rejoined. "You've got to strip them out—just the politics of it."

Later, Jones admitted, "The Chairman will drop the amendments if we have the votes, but he's got to be absolutely sure of that,"

Gail handed Jones a list of 25 Reps who would likely vote against the conference report/agreement if the amendments were left in. "At most, we'd pick up five-to-seven votes if we kept them," she said. Jones scanned the list and nodded quietly.

The Ad Hoc Committee for ED would keep working throughout August. The education groups would each send letters of appreciation to Reps who voted for the bill. Similar letters of praise would be mailed to editors of local newspapers. Plans were made for back-home educators to meet with congressmen in the district, especially at Labor Day picnics, where offsetting AFL pressure was important.

"The Department of Education bill is a 'litmus test' on everyone's list for the 1980 elections," Straub told us. "The conservatives, NEA, AFL, will all use it in their ratings and endorsements. The Members will feel a hard squeeze on this one."

*   *   *

By the end of the month, we had polished off the minor differences memo. On Thursday, August 30 we invited Pat Gwaltney and her crew to the Hill for a briefing on our decisions. The PRP executive, wearing a cool jumper to cover her eight-month pregnant figure, brought along several OMB lawyers and experts to inspect our work.

"The Justice Department feels there is minimal legal impact in the (junk) amendments," she informed us. "The bigger problem is that they will tie things up in a lot of litigation."

"What can we do to get out of this box?," Bill Jones asked her. He wanted Justice to churn out some back-up compromise language in case the amendments couldn't be erased.

"The alternative language route is risky," she said softly.

"Yeah, but I don't like going out on a limb with no bank account," Jones shot back. Brooks's chief counsel was simply not giving up on demanding substitute language, worrying all the ED people.

*   *   *

Labor Day brought Washington back to life. In just two days, Congress would return to consider a fairly busy agenda: energy bills, SALT, 1980 budget, aid to Chrysler, gas rationing, and…ED.

House and Senate staffs turned to the "major differences" list.

Marilyn and I originally concocted a 27-item listing of our own. We had purposely inflated it so the Senate side could recede on more "major" issues, thus giving the House more reason to give up its junk amendments.

But gradually we let many of our major differences be solved in the ongoing staff negotiations. As we whittled away at refining the "minor" list, the remaining items became "major" discrepancies by default. The House and Senate staffs agreed there were *16 major differences* that would have to be decided by the senators and reps:

•*The Walker anti-quota amendment.* Civil rights groups were most offended by this language and demanded it be extracted from the bill. It was the one amendment that could cause the bill's defeat. It was also the only one on which the House had instructed its conferees to stand firm. At least four, perhaps five, of the House conferees might vote to keep it in. We needed five votes to axe it. It appeared Jack Brooks and Bill Jones were willing to support expunging the provision, provided that some sort of compromise language could be found that was acceptable to the House and the civil rights groups. That would be a mountainous task.

• *Walker's school prayer amendment.* We expected to have enough votes among the conferees to delete the provision entirely. By all accounts, that wouldn't cost ED many votes in the House. The prayer groups had not made it a big priority.

• *The federal control of education sections.* The House bill prohibited federal control. The Senate bill stated in weaker terms establishment of ED would not increase federal control. House conferees, the White House, and NEA all pressed Marilyn and I into accepting the prohibition, which they thought vital to retaining support on the House floor. We held off; our price would be removal of the junk amendments. The final resolution probably would include some combination of the two.

The House's section was further complicated by amendments limiting the Education Secretary's authority to those responsibilities *specifically* authorized by *statute*, reducing the legal power of federal regulations, prohibiting busing, and waiving federally mandated organizational requirements for state governments.

Civil rights groups detested the first three. Much of civil rights enforcement case history and precedents had been built on federal regulations, rules, orders, and court orders—all within the body of law but not specifically authorized by a statute. Busing was a particularly sore point. To save the bill, the conferees would have little choice but to drop them all.

The federal requirements for state government organization was strictly a Florida matter. Two Democratic House conferees, Dante Fascell and Don Fuqua, were both from Florida. The orange state had integrated its vocational rehabilitation services within an umbrella human services agency. Federal law, however, required the voc rehab programs to be administered by a separate, outside agency within all the states as a condition for receiving federal funds. Handicapped groups wanted the separate agency rule; Florida officials didn't. The House ED bill had a temporary compromise: Florida could go another eight months after the bill passed with its arrangement.

Presumably, the dispute would be worked out in that time. If both Fascell and Fuqua went along with dropping the junk amendments, the Senate conferees would let the voc rehab waiver stay.

• *Office for Civil Rights additional powers.* The so-called "Rosenthal amendments" in the House bill gave the new OCR power to collect its own data, employ its own employees and enter into contracts. Civil rights groups said retention of these powers was essential for their support. Marilyn and I (and the Senate side) would be privately eager to accept them. But, we would posture and express reservations, mostly as a way of making a high-price trade-off for blotting out the junk amendments.

• *Nursing/health student loans.* The Senate bill transferred them, the House didn't. Senator Kennedy's staff had already asked us to let them slip from the final bill. We and the Administration desired to keep as many programs in ED as possible. But for the small $67 million budget of the loan programs, we were willing to recede, provided it was understood this was part of the price for deleting the junk amendments.

• *Panama Canal Zone College.* In the strange ways of legislation, the ED bill suddenly got caught up in the controversy of returning the canal to Panama. Under the treaties, operation of the small Canal Zone College and elementary-secondary public schools would go to the Defense Department, to be administered with the overseas dependents schools. Of course, the schools would be transferred to ED under our bills. On behalf of Florida State University, which wanted to contract for administering the College, Rep. Fuqua succeeded in attaching an amendment to the House bill simply denying the Education Secretary authority to operate "overseas institutions of higher education." We had planned all along to give in to Fuqua, needing his votes against the junk amendments.

• *NSF science education programs.* The two bills transferred more than $24 million each of the programs, but not the same ones. Between them, two programs overlapped, totaling only about $8 million. To save all the headache, the conference committee would likely just go with the two programs.

• *Migrant education.* Both bills transferred the program, but the House said not until a single office within ED had been established. It was a picayune matter, but gave the Senate side another "major" difference on which to recede to the House for scrapping the junk amendments.

• *Technical employees.* The Senate bill allowed one-third of the research office staff for this category; the House set a limit of 112. The conference committee would probably decide on some middle arbitrary figure in this hardly controversial difference.

• *Personnel limitations.* Both bills provided procedures for putting a cap on bureaucratic growth. The Senate said it would be done in appropriations acts. The House mandated a reduction of 800 personnel (consultants included). We recognized the political need for a specific reduction, but would aim to lower it closer to the original 400 estimate. The House would likely go along with our limitation procedure.

• *Internal reorganization.* Both bills allowed the Secretary of ED to reorganize his new Department, but the Senate stopped at offices created by statute. This was a sensitive issue on the Senate side, and we would have to insist on keeping our language.

• *Legislative veto of ED rules.* House conferee Rep. Levitas had attached a provision extending the legislative veto to cover most ED functions and programs, save for civil rights. Levitas felt strongly about keeping it. The conservative Georgia Democrat's votes against the junk amendments would be hard to attain, but necessary. We had no hope of getting his help if we fought the veto, which the Senate had often opposed as unconstitutional. After some posturing, we would have to swallow hard and take it.

• *Abortion (two major differences).* The abortion amendments had to come out, period. We doubted there would be problems in getting the conference committee to extract them. Marilyn and I called in the major abortion rights organizations for help. The Catholics made a negligible effort to lobby conferees into keeping what they called the "essential" provisions.

• *Annual Report.* The Senate bill required the Secretary, in developing the report of ED's yearly activities, to hold hearings and broaden public participation. The House simply called for a report. We would likely recede, giving us another chit against the junk amendments.

• *Education data collection.* The Senate bill required requests for new forms be cleared through the OMB director. Marilyn and I didn't really care what happened to the section. We did know it would create a germaneness problem on the House floor, and subject the entire conference report to a point of order. We planned to recede.

*   *   *

"The Vice President and Pat Harris will be working on four conference members," Terry Straub told us in the House GovOps conference room Tuesday, September 4. "Fuqua, Moorhead, St. Germain, and Levitas."

"Dale and I met this morning with St. Germain," Gail jumped in. "He's got a problem with prayer and abortion, but he said he'd follow the chairman otherwise and leave a proxy."

With less than two weeks left before the next conference committee meeting, our core political group would come together almost daily to talk strategy. The first readings were coming in on how the House conferees would vote on wiping out the junk amendments. Our attention focused on the House Democrats, whose votes would be key.

"By our latest count, we'll lose 21 (House) members if the amendments are on the bill," Gail informed us. "So far, we haven't seen the antis out lobbying yet."

"Well, after we get through the conference, we need to recanvass the entire House," Straub reminded everyone.

Pat Gwaltney walked in 40 minutes late. "We might be able to live with one abortion amendment," she said.

"And you'd gain all of three votes," Gail retorted with a hint of disgust in her voice.

"Nobody seems to be listening to me, but I'm concerned about at least having in our hands some compromise language for these amendments," Bill Jones said, mildly agitated.

Straub and Gwaltney remained firm: "We don't think it's a good idea."

Wednesday morning, Straub, Gail, Marilyn, and I met again with some 20 civil rights lobbyists at the National Urban Coalition downtown.

"The Administration will discourage any talk of compromise," Straub reassured them.

An ACLU lobbyist pressed Straub and Marilyn: "What if Walker (anti-quota amendment) is not deleted?"

"I'm not going to answer that," Straub fired back. "We want them out—it's politically necessary."

"Yeah, but many members are upset," a National Urban League official spoke across the table. "Compromise is a dangerous possibility."

Urban Coalition staff had begun discussions with the House conferees.

"We're concerned we might lose the Rosenthal amendments in this exercise," the rights official said, looking directly at Marilyn.

"We're open and receptive," she replied cautiously. "We're hopeful we'll accept them. This appears to be an area where the Senate can recede." Marilyn wanted to send positive signals, but she still had to posture her way to making the trade-off.

The civil rights groups agreed to lay low in their lobbying, "We don't want to incite pressure from back home," one said.

*   *   *

That afternoon, NEA lobbyists met with Rep. Don Fuqua. The Congressman's staff told Bill Jones afterwards that Fuqua would back

Brooks in sacking the junk amendments if the Senate side agreed to keep the Panama Canal Zone College provision in the bill.

I later called Fuqua's staff delicately to sound him out. I asked him to fill me in on all the details of Florida State's interest in the College—information I already knew. "I don't find too much interest on this side," I told him. "I think the senators would be willing to accept Mr. Fuqua's amendment. But, we're most interested in obtaining Mr. Fuqua's support for helping us drop the anti-civil rights amendments."

The staffer's breathing indicated excitement at a deal just being cut. "Oh, I think in that case, Mr. Fuqua would be happy to vote against the amendments…".

I hung up the phone and shared the good news with Marilyn. We now had solidly four of the nine House conferees' votes—Brooks, Horton, Fuqua, and Fascell. One more Rep and we were home-free.

*   *   *

"We've got to watch out for filibusters and obstructionist, dilatory tactics on the House floor," Terry Straub warned ED lobbyists at a pep rally in our hearing room Thursday, September 6.

Gail Bramblett passed out a new list targeting 70 House members who voted for final passage, 35 who didn't, and 10 more who were absent back on July 11. The roomful of lobbyists would repeat their round of visits, calls, and letters for the final vote.

The new HEW Secretary had assigned a top aide to help out. "I bring three messages from Secretary Harris," she told the Ad Hoc Committee. "One, the controversial House amendments will come off. Two, the Rosenthal amendments will be accepted. Three, the Department of Education bill will pass."

"You'll find you've got a right arm at HEW now," Straub said.

*   *   *

"I saw the Chairman yesterday morning," Bill Jones opened our Friday, September 7 core group strategy meeting. "He's inclined to get rid of the amendments. 'Vote 'em in or out,' I believe he said."

Sitting around the room: Elmer Henderson, Bob Brink, Marilyn, myself, Dale Lestina, Gail Bramblett, Terry Straub, Pat Gwaltney, and Nancy LeaMond. We smiled at Jones's news. But we knew he was still after compromise language on the quota amendment.

Gail handed out copies of a chart showing House conferees and whether they would vote "right" or "wrong" on the busing, prayer, quota, and abortion amendments. Brooks, Fuqua, Fascell, and Horton all had "Rs", for rights. Levitas had two empty boxes—busing and affirmative action (quotas).

"Jim McIntyre will talk with Levitas on Monday," Gwaltney cut in. "He'll try to make a deal: legislative veto for the amendments."

Pennsylvania Democrat William Moorhead would vote with Brooks on everything except the quota amendment. St. Germain was looking better; he now had "leaning rights" in the prayer and abortion columns. The Rhode Island Democrat, with more high-powered stroking, could become that vital fifth vote.

Republicans Erlenborn and Stangeland, of course, were "wrong" all the way.

Marilyn and I briefed Senator Ribicoff on the situation late Friday afternoon in his office. As we talked, the Senator signed a stack of letters to the other senators and reps on the conference committee transmitting the minor differences memo and announcing the next formal conference committee meeting for 3:00 p.m., Wednesday, September 12.

Ribicoff seemed disinterested in the intricate politics behind removing the junk amendments. We had received to date virtually no guidance from him on the course we were taking. He trusted us to save his bill.

"We'll have to stick it out," he commented simply as we left.

*   *   *

The man on whose strength passage of the ED bill depended so much continued limping along.

Jimmy Carter still trailed Ted Kennedy in Democratic presidential preferences 2-1, the Gallup poll found in early August. His United Nations ambassador, Andrew Young, had to resign in mid-August for holding unauthorized discussions with the Palestine Liberation Organization. The press hopped on the story of a "killer rabbit" swimming toward the President while fishing in a canoe in a Georgia pond. And, his top aide, new chief of staff Hamilton Jordan, became the target of a Justice Department investigation into alleged cocaine use.[36] Inflation was up, unemployment was up, there were some gas shortages around the country.

The *New York Times* reported September 7 on its front page that Senator Kennedy had gotten an O.K. from his family to run for President in 1980. The Kennedy challenge, many predicted, would devastate the Democratic party and severely weaken Jimmy Carter.

*   *   *

---

[36] A year later, Jordan was cleared of any wrongdoing.

Monday morning, September 10, we went down the list of the 16 major differences with Senator Ribicoff, explaining to him the politics and the planned tradeoffs.

"Give them that...no problem...that's fine...you've got to give them that...". The Senator ratified all our strategies.

The two House abortion amendments particularly got his goat. "It's the deterioration of the legislative process," he remarked to the two of us. "There's no respect for committee judgment. It's no fun anymore." Ribicoff was ready for his retirement.

That night, with just two days to conference, we met for three-and-a-half hours with the House staff, reaching agreement on the wording of the major differences memo. It would be sent to the 14 conferees first thing in the morning.

*   *   *

11:30 Tuesday morning, the core strategists met in the House GovOps office to discuss the conference's main sticking point.

"I saw Levitas yesterday," Gail Bramblett reported. "He'll probably be wrong on the quota language."

"Pat Harris talked to Moorhead," Terry Straub added. "He's O.K., except for the Walker quota stuff."

Brooks's chief counsel fidgeted at the end of the table. "I'm really worried that we won't be able to hang on to the 5-4 vote," he told everyone.

Tentatively, the NEA and White House had lined up five House conferees—Brooks, Horton, Fuqua, Fascell, and St. Germain—to vote for dropping the quota amendment altogether.

"And, what's going to happen to us on the floor?," Jones went "We've got instructions on this amendment. That point is going be driven against us over and over.

"We've got to quit thinking of outrightly receding on the only provision that we've got instructions on." Jones's voice was tough and insistent.

The lobbyists doodled quietly, none of them anxious to be the first to respond.

"We've looked at the situation," Dale Lestina attempted to console Jones. "We've found that we'd lose some 30 liberal Democrats if we keep it, not to mention the civil rights groups—"

"Why can't I get anyone to look at compromise language?," Jones broke him off.

"It's a close call, but we've decided we'll take the risk," Lestina reiterated in a pleasant, but tense voice.

Bill Jones's face flushed red. "We need something. Some suggestions or something," he yelled, banging his fist on the table top.

The NEA and White House staffers were shook and speechless. They had hoped Brooks and Jones would stop asking for compromise on the section they had promised the civil rights groups there would be no compromise. Now, with one day to go, they'd have to think up something.

The meeting broke up somberly. "We'll see what we can do," Lestina told Jones as he walked out.

*　　*　　*

All Tuesday afternoon and night, the ED brains went to work. The House provision, as amended by Rep. Walker, said this:

"There is a continuous need to ensure equal access for all Americans to educational opportunities of a high quality and no individual should be denied such education opportunities by rules, regulations, standards, guidelines, and orders which utilize any ratio, quota, or other numerical requirement related to race, creed, color, national origin, or sex."

We knew the most sensitive words were "which utilize any ratio, quota, or other numerical requirement." The Supreme Court's recent decisions in *Bakke* and *Weber* were still being interpreted and studied for their effect on the use of quotas in affirmative action programs.[37] Totally unschooled in this delicate, newly-developing legal area, we could not allow any kind of interpretative language in the ED bill.

We next agreed that if compromise language were written, it would have to track existing law on affirmative action. We would aim to incorporate as much of the Walker language as possible, but neuter it at the same time.

Research into civil rights laws on the books commenced instantly. Leaders of the civil rights groups were called and filled in on the latest development.

Within hours, sketchy agreement evolved on the general thrust of a compromise: take the first phrase of Walker ("There is a continuous need..."), scratch everything from "rules" through "numerical requirement", and somehow reword the rest.

Several variations were produced, but Brooks liked this one the best:

"There is a continuous need to ensure equal access for all Americans to educational opportunities of high quality, and no individual should be denied such educational opportunities because of race, creed, color, national origin, or sex."

---

[37] The Bakke decision struck down the use of racial quotas in higher education, but left open the use of goals and timetables and other tools to increase minority access. Weber allowed private employers to "voluntarily adopt affirmative action plans designed to eliminate conspicuous racial imbalance in traditionally segregated job categories." Thus, Walker's amendment would invite litigation, confusion, delay, and expense. It would interfere with ED's ability to enforce the civil rights laws.

But however phrased, this new language was much closer to existing civil rights acts and was noncontroversial.

*   *   *

Wednesday, September 12. The conference committee was scheduled to meet at 3:00 p.m.

At noon, NEA, Carter, House and Senate staffs met to plot strategy on the Walker-quota compromise. We debated which of the four or five versions we would recommend. Plans were made to clear it through the civil rights groups. Marilyn was asked to make most of the calls, given her friendship with the rights leaders and the Senate's decisive position in the controversy.

Marilyn worked her phone, using several lines at once. ACLU lawyers gave their O.K. Carl Holman grudgingly approved, provided the Senate conferees acceded to the House's Rosenthal amendments. The Children's Defense Fund staff said O.K. Going down the long list, Marilyn encountered some skepticism, but most groups would let it pass. Attorneys for many of the groups said they needed time to study its effect on *Bakke*.

By 1:30, Marilyn and I were briefing staff reps of the four other senators on the conference. Clerks got ready to haul stacks of materials to the Capitol for the committee meeting.

Just before 3 o'clock, Dick Wegman came running back to the office. "We're going to have to cancel," he said gloomily to us. Our staff director explained that Majority Leader Robert Byrd had called an emergency meeting of all Senate committee chairmen to resolve problems in the federal budget resolution. Ribicoff wanted to go there instead. The day's meeting was canceled.

"We could have a rapid conference, maybe even one session, if we can just get Ribicoff to the table," a frustrated Terry Straub told the Vice President. Mondale would speak to our Senator.

*   *   *

At 2 o'clock the next afternoon, the conferees finally met, just a few steps away from the Senate floor, in Room S-207 of the Capitol building. The magnificently paneled and chandeliered room had held countless House-Senate conference committees. It was one of the few rooms in the Capitol large enough to hold 50-75 people.

The five senators and nine representatives shook each other's hands and made pleasant small-talk. In a few minutes, they would split up and form the classic House-Senate face-off around a shiny, oblong wood conference table.

House staff would sit behind the Reps, Senate staff behind the Senators. Surrounding us, an assortment of press, lobbyists, White House staff, and people from the civil rights groups.

Going in to our second, September 13 conference, we managed to construct a rickety consensus amongst the rights groups that our compromise language was tolerable.

"The meeting will come to order," Jack Brooks banged the gavel. The Chairman immediately moved that the minor differences settlements negotiated by the staff be approved en bloc.

"Our staffs have done a superb job," Senator Ribicoff agreed. He sat directly across the table from Brooks.

Rep. John Erlenborn said he thought the "vast majority" were "acceptable," but wondered if members could raise questions about individual differences. He set the stage for fellow Republican Rep. Arlan Stangeland to raise "four minor points."

Brooks looked perturbed.

Stangeland said he didn't agree with the staff's choice of one Senate finding that he thought indicated a preference for greater federal involvement. "I just respectfully request that you look at the House language."

"We did," Brooks shrugged him off. "...Now you had three other matters."

Brooks let Stangeland criticize three other resolutions, each time dismissing them with hardly a comment.

"...Mr. Chairman, I move the adoption of the amendments that have been worked up by the staff," Rep. Frank Horton interjected, sitting beside Brooks.

"Is there objection?," Brooks asked, looking to his right and left. "The Chair hears none. The Senate agrees?"

"I move the Senate conferees agree to the amendments...en bloc," Ribicoff said. "All those in favor?"

A chorus of senatorial ayes answered. The thick listing of minor differences solutions was thus approved.

"Turning to the major differences of the two bills...," Brooks continued.

The atmosphere of the room tensed. We had worked out strategies for reconciling the 16 major differences. Behind the scenes, we had orchestrated who would say what, the tradeoffs, and the votes. But as with any congressional function, even the best choreography could get fouled up by some unexpected last-second move.

The first major difference, Brooks read from his papers, involved the House bill's statement opposing the use of ratios, quotas, and other numerical requirements in affirmative action programs. "There is no comparable provision in the Senate bill," he pointed out to the participants.

Republican Sen. Jacob Javits spoke right up. "I am very strongly opposed...We must reserve the affirmative action idea. This is a very deep social question...The Senate should not recede upon this issue."

Reading from his notebook and from a paper Marilyn had thrust before him, Ribicoff announced, "I do feel I have some substantive language that should bridge this gap."

He read: "'There is a continuing need to ensure equal access for all Americans to educational opportunities of a high quality, and such educational opportunities should not be denied because of race, creed, color, national origin or sex.'"

"I don't think anybody can take exception to this language," he concluded.

"I note, Senator Ribicoff, we in the House were pretty determined in our position," Brooks replied. He pointed out the House had instructed its conferees to keep the amendment in the bill. "I regret we are so adamant at it."

"Certainly I am glad you have alternative language that tracks civil rights legislation. I don't see how anybody can be against unless they really just want to discriminate...", Brooks said.

Erlenborn spoke up, noting the House passed the quota amendment 277-126 and made it the subject of its sole motion to instruct. "If we abandoned (it), we are going against the clearly expressed will of the House...".

"Mr. Chairman, I point out the fact the Senate is just as determined as the House," Javits retorted. The Senate had recently voted 69-32 against similar language on another bill, he revealed. "I don't want to accept an amendment which on its face will invalidate a Supreme Court decision."

Brooks made the point to Javits that his House was "not quite so adamant" when it voted to instruct the conferees (214-202), indicating "a more reasonable attitude."

"To the House conferees, let me say I hope we can adopt this," Brooks said. "I think it is probably a good compromise...".

Rep. Moorhead, in his halting voice, called the new language "a genius solution." We breathed a sigh of relief, knowing that if he approved, it would pass.

Brooks called for a voice vote from the nine House members. Erlenborn promptly insisted on a roll call, The House clerk stood up and called out the names. "The vote is six ayes, three noes," she announced. Only Elliott Levitas, Erlenborn, and Stangeland voted no.

"I move the Senate conferees adopt the language," Javits said.

"All those in favor say aye," Ribicoff called out.

The Senators each muttered "aye."

"It is unanimous," Ribicoff told Brooks.

We'd gotten over our biggest hump.

Brooks turned to the second major difference, the Walker school prayer section.

Senator Ribicoff argued the amendment "causes confusion" and "encourages litigation." He read off a long list of opposing religious groups: Lutherans, Episcopalians, Methodists, Presbyterians, etc.

Horton moved that the House give it up.

Erlenborn reminded his colleagues the amendment had passed 255-122. He charged that receding "would prove the folly of appointed conferees who...don't stand up for the House position, but rather come here to rewrite the bill in the way they wish it had been written by the House."

Horton countered to his fellow Republicans that the will of House on the bill itself—passing only by four votes—was very decisive. "You have to make some balances, it seems to me." Erlenborn demanded another roll call vote of the House conferees.

They decided to toss out the prayer provision, 6-3. This time, Rep. Fernand St. Germain joined with the loyal opposition, Erlenborn and Stangeland.

On to the third difference, the federal control section. So far, so good. Everything was going according to plan.

In directing the committee's attention to a draft compromise, Sen. Charles Percy stated, "We are absolutely united on the fact there will be no infraction on local control of education."

We had agreed to take the House's prohibition against federal control, add the Senate language reaffirming state-local control of education, the Florida-inspired vocational rehabilitation waiver, and throw it all together into one section retitled, "Federal-State Relationships." The compromise called for junking the anti-busing and anti-regulation amendments.

By now, Erlenborn was getting angry at his powerlessness to affect our moves in removing the House junk amendments. "Adoption of this would be a clear violation of the House conferees obligation to try to sustain the House position," he complained. He wanted another call of the roll.

The federal control compromise sailed past the House conferees, 7-2. Erlenborn and Stangeland voted no. The senators agreed to it unanimously.

Next up, the Rosenthal office for civil rights amendments. Ribicoff was supposed to posture and make it look like we were painfully giving in.

"In view of the fact you receded on the last few items, I would recommend to the Senate conferees that we recede to the House," he said simply. And it was done in ten seconds.

The conference committee, moving along at full speed, turned to the nursing and health professions student loans. Again Ribicoff didn't fool around with phony posturing, as we would have liked.

"I understand the House feels very strongly about it," he said, looking at Brooks. "I would recommend to the Senate conferees that we recede to the House." And it was agreed to. The transfer was dropped

Item six, the Canal Zone College (Panama). Rep. Don Fuqua explained the provision he had put in the House bill.

Before much could be said, Brooks cut off discussion and the senators voted, as planned, to accede to the House position.

Checking off the differences, Brooks brought up the NSF science education transfer. Fuqua described a compromise that simply took the small programs transferred by both bills and moved them to ED. "I think everybody is happy," he said. Both sides accepted it without objection.

The House bill's two anti-abortion amendments came up. "Big deal," Senator Javits commented. "It just seems too demeaning." He urged the amendments be removed "as a matter of common decency."

Erlenborn was steaming. He picked up a news clipping from the Los Angeles Times (July 12) and quoted, "...the four chief sponsors of the legislation in the House and Senate had given assurances that the busing, abortion, racial quotas, and prayer amendments would be scrapped in conference."

The Illinois Republican dropped the clipping on the table and looked around the table at the listening senators and reps. "They named four and this is the fourth and it is going," he said. "That was pretty good reporting. They guessed what was going to happen way back then."

Not responding, Brooks immediately put abortion to a voice vote. His House members threw both out, ignoring the two Republicans as if they were empty chairs at the end of the table.

Next, the migrant education office in the House bill. Ribicoff complained it would be "still another highly-specialized office."

"...How strongly do you feel about this?," the Senator pretended to ask.

"We feel pretty keen about it," Brooks replied.

"...Can you go along, Jack and Carl?," Ribicoff asked Senators Javits and Levin.

They both nodded, and the Senate thus let the House keep the provision.

The committee then looked at the technical employees sections. The House limited the number to 112. Ribicoff told Brooks the Administration recommended 184 positions.

"Why don't we make it 175 and let them live on that?," Brooks proposed. There was no objection to his random number.

Following that, a Department-wide personnel limitation compromise was considered. As offered by Ribicoff, it included the House-ordered staff reduction—lowered from 800 to 350—and the Senate annual ceiling procedure. We'd purposely dropped the 800 figure to 350 as a bargaining tactic.

"I have no problem with the compromise, except...I would recommend that we raise the 350 to 500," Horton said. 500 would be 50 more than what OMB had originally estimated could be cut in the reorganization.

"...I am not going to argue this out," Ribicoff answered, "so I will accept it...". Our boss was getting anxious to finish.

By this time, the conferees were no longer even voting formally. It was stretching past 4 o'clock and they knew they could finish that day if they stuck it out.

Without objection, the two sides accepted a compromise on the internal ED reorganization section that rewrote the Senate provision.

Conferees spent several minutes discussing the Levitas legislative veto amendment. Ribicoff pointed out his Committee opposed the use of vetoes. Brooks said they "irritate me just to start with, but a good many members of the House think they are the greatest thing since Scotch tape."

The senators wanted to be sure civil rights were excepted from the congressional vetoes. Levitas said the issue had not yet been decided by the courts.

"Let's have no fuzziness about it," Javits demanded. The patrician New Yorker persuaded Levitas to agree to report language that said current law would not be changed.

"All right, all right, I have heard enough on this," Brooks broke off the members' discussion of the issue. He moved on to the next difference without a vote on vetoes.

Brooks didn't care much for the Senate provision ordering the Secretary of Education to consult the public in writing the annual report to Congress. "We could fill all the hotels up overnight and it is already hard to get a room," he joked.

The senators let it go.

Finally, the 16th and last major difference—the Senate's requirements that ED forms get special clearance through OMB. Percy noted it amended other acts.

"Senator Percy, you are a smart man," Brooks complimented him, and warned ED opponents could raise a point of order against the conference report in the House on grounds of nongermaneness. "If they prevail,…we would have to do this whole thing over."

"I see John smiling," Percy remarked, looking at Erlenborn. "It worries me."

"…It is a danger, and don't think old sweet John wouldn't try and do it," Brooks said with arched eyebrows. The senators anxiously wiped out the provision from their bill. At 4:45, it was all over. Senators and Reps popped up from their seats, hurriedly signed the conference agreement papers, and went home.

"Wow, you staged this so well you ought to do Broadway plays," an amazed journalist commented to me in all the exciting confusion.

Indeed, we emerged from the conference with what we had sought all along: an essentially clean reorganization bill. *A total success.*

But one last step would lift the Department of Education from a paper charter to reality—final Senate and House votes on the single compromise bill just negotiated…or, kill ED altogether.

TWENTY-TWO

The Battle's End

"WE TOLD YOU SO!," Reps. Erlenborn and Stangeland scolded their House colleagues by letter the next day.

"…Almost before the Chairman could shout 'All Aboard,' the train had sped down the tracks…We want to give you a report on how we were railroaded."

The two Republicans ticked off the disposition of the amendments: "local control…gutted, eliminated," "quotas…gutted," "prayer…eliminated," "abortions…eliminated," "busing…eliminated," and so on.

"A House-Senate conference committee approved legislation to establish a Department of Education," the *Wall Street Journal* reported, "but the measure still faces a tough struggle to secure final House approval."

"Some of those who voted in favor of it were conservatives won over by the very amendments deleted yesterday," the *Washington Post* added.

*   *   *

The final, full-steam-ahead push was on. Within two weeks, before the end of September, the Senate and House would vote on our compromise bill. If both approved, the President would have a bill to sign. If one body—the House, in this case—rejected the conference agreement, ED would be dead.

Through tradition, we had the advantage. Rejection of conference reports was rare. But in those few instances, faulty judgments on controversial amendments caused the defeat.

It had been our biggest gamble—dropping the junk amendments to pick up votes. If we miscalculated the outcome, all would be lost.

Time was short. House and Senate staffs zipped along through September's third week finishing off the remaining conference technical requirements—polishing the compromise bill and writing the conference report.

Civil rights groups met with us one more time, desiring to prearrange legislative interpretation of the new affirmative action language. They wanted Ribicoff and Brooks to say the right and the same things on the Senate and House floors. In the conference report, they wanted it stated clearly that the ED bill was not intended to change or affect substantive education policy, existing law, or judicial precedent.

The rights groups still had in their hands the power to sway that vital bloc of 20-30 mostly liberal House members into voting against the conference agreement. We had to listen to them and follow their demands as much as possible.

Lobbyists would blanket the U.S. House of Representatives with their last-gasp press. The American business community mobilized against ED. Groups such as the National Association of Manufacturers and the Chamber of Commerce sent lobbyists to the Hill to fight us. The White House reacted by asking its corporate friends for help, such as Burger King, Xerox, Braniff, and others. The Catholics sent out an alert to their network of bishops, priests, and Catholic schools advising "any effort to defeat this legislation should be focused on the House." AFT officials worked hard to hang onto their opposing votes and gain others.

Rumors of a Senate filibuster cropped up, but we couldn't establish their validity.

"URGENT," topped an appeal from Ad Hoc Committee Chairman Allan Cohen to the education groups. "We expect a vote on final passage to be held in the Senate early next week, with the House to follow within a few days.

"Senators and Representatives are already receiving many letters in opposition to the bill," Cohen warned. "Therefore, it is important that we countermand these efforts by having your organization write letters, send mailgrams, make phone calls and visits. TIME IS LIMITED."

ED lobbyists came together Tuesday, September 18 in our hearing room for a strategy session. Gail Bramblett distributed another target list of 120 House members, reading off each name and parceling out assignments to the various organizations. It included 40 Reps who had voted against the bill in July, but "may still be convinced," the NEA lobbyist said.

Terry Straub drew up his own target list of 46 Democrats and 21 Republicans, broken down into categories of leaning right, undecided, leaning wrong, and wrong but workable. He also busily beseeched other high-ranking White House and Cabinet officials into calling House members they knew well and worked often with.

The President and the Vice President would roll up their sleeves in these last few days and do some of their own gritty lobbying. They could least afford to take the final House vote for granted.

*   *   *

Papers strewn across the table before us, we and the House staff worked in a frenzy Thursday afternoon, September 20 to agree on every word and phrase in the new bill and conference report.

Our goal: file the report that day, before Congress left for the weekend. Then both bodies could take it up the following week.

Senator Ribicoff would file the report in the Senate, Representative Brooks would submit it in the House.

"The Committee of conference on the disagreeing votes of the two Houses...having met, after full and free conference, have agreed to recommend and do recommend to their respective House as follows:," the 64-page report began. First, it set forth the compromise bill. Then it offered a "joint explanatory statement" picking the bill apart section-by-section. For example:

"*Section 1—Short title; table of contents*
The Senate and House provisions are substantially identical. The Senate recedes."

We explained the quota compromise simply: "The substitute language is not intended to change or affect existing law or judicial precedent."

In the instances where the House receded outright on the junk amendments, such as prayer and busing, the report curtly noted, "The House recedes." For abortion, the report said the new Department would "follow the general policy of the United States as specified in other, relevant legislation." Generally, our report passed the buck brilliantly.

* * *

Meanwhile, the House had been debating another conference report on the floor—implementing the Panama Canal treaties. That bill had passed the House in June by only 22 votes. And as with ED, the Panama conference committee stripped several controversial amendments from the House bill.

In a move of defiance that sent shudders through us, the House *rejected* the Panama conference report, 203-192.

The press played up the rejection as "highly unusual" and "almost unprecedented." Our opponents were buoyed by it, seeing a chance for a repeat performance when ED's conference report got considered.

Hours later, a mad Jimmy Carter chewed out 60 moderate-conservative House Democrats he'd invited to the White House for dinner. The President told them to expect retaliation if they voted against his position consistently. "We believe in rewarding our friends and punishing our enemies," he said. In a tough tone, Carter said he'd watch the Members' voting trends on regular computer tallies provided him, and he wouldn't hesitate to hold up grants, White House invitations, jobs, and other favors.

Congressmen quoted the President as saying, "Some of you in Congress haven't supported me at all. I'll be damned if I'll send my wife into your district for a fundraiser."

Terry Straub, who attended the dinner, encouraged Rep. Floyd Fithian to ask the President a question about ED. Halfway through, the Indiana Democrat did so.

Carter came back with an eloquent, 10-minute talk asking the Reps' help. "It's a very high priority," he told his congressional guests.

*　　*　　*

The next day, Friday, the Senate Democratic whip notice was delivered to our office. The Senate would convene at 11:30 Monday morning, it said, and would consider two conference reports—Labor-HEW appropriations and the Department of Education.

The leadership told us to be ready any time Monday. Marilyn and I would work all weekend, writing Senator Ribicoff's statements and floor backgrounders.

Our 32-month battle would end in a few days.

*　　*　　*

MONDAY, SEPTEMBER 24.

A lovely, sunny, 70° day in Washington.

That morning, we put the finishing touches to our papers, constantly checking with the Senate floor staff for updates.

At 12:30, Marilyn and I walked over to Ribicoff's office. We sat down with him and reviewed the conference report materials.

"It's excellent," the Senator complimented us on the main statement. He was calm and collected. The three of us were all too much aware of how incredibly far we had come, how much work we had done. Each had that eerie sense of impending fate, wondering inside ourselves if this week of decision would be a time of joy and accomplishment, or of depression and failure.

"I don't expect any problems," the Senator judged about the afternoon's conference report floor consideration. The rumors of a filibuster had faded, but we would never know for sure until the United States Senate had taken that one last vote.

Ribicoff asked only that we write up a summary list of the major actions taken during the conference committee, which I immediately set about doing back at the office. No time for lunch.

The phone rang at 2:00. "We're on the floor!," a nervously excited Marilyn screamed over the wire.

Moments later, she swung open my door, out of breath and hyper. "C'mon Bob, let's go," she yelled. Seeing that I was still writing the summary, she commanded, "Just finish it up!," and dashed back out the door for the circuitous route through the elevators and the subway to the Capitol.

Frantically, my heart thumping, I managed to bang out the remaining paragraphs. I couldn't think straight nor remember what I had written. I ripped the paper out of the typewriter and ran to the Senate floor.

Jogging breathlessly out of the Capitol elevator, I brushed past several guards and lobbyists hanging around the corridors. Notebooks in hand, I waved briefly to the NEA and White House staff anchored in the Senate Reception Room as I passed through to the cloakrooms.

Once inside the peace and hushed atmosphere of the Senate chamber, I began to breathe deeply and relax. The Senate was in its do-nothing, quorum-call holding mode, waiting for all the principal parties concerning ED to arrive.

Marilyn already was sitting beside Senator Ribicoff in the well. The two chatted merrily. I tiptoed up to them and sat down.

Sen. Daniel Moynihan strolled through the heavy Senate doors and across the floor to Ribicoff, who stood up to greet him with a big smile. "I'm just going to say a few words and leave it at that," he assured our Senator.

At last, Sen. Robert Byrd pulled the Senate out of its quorum call,

Ribicoff stood up to read from his statement, perched on a shiny portable wood podium atop the manager's desk. "Mr. President, I submit a report of the committee of conference on S.210 and ask for its immediate consideration."

"Without objection, the Senate will proceed to the consideration of the conference report," the presiding officer said from his high seat.

Glancing around the chamber, I looked for trouble signs—the presence of arch-conservative senators. There were none, except for Senators Hayakawa and Schmitt, who we knew would simply talk against the report.

Ribicoff chose to read every word of his statement. "Mr. President, after nearly three years of hard work, both the House and the Senate are now ready to complete final action on the bill to separate the "E" from HEW…

"The House, the Senate, and the President all agree that HEW is simply too unmanageable and education too important to continue the present set-up…

"I am pleased to report to my colleagues that the final version agreed upon by House and Senate conferees is an even better bill…". Ribicoff explained both local control provisions were combined, the new structure would be lean and efficient, 500 employees would be eliminated, and the controversial amendments were deleted.

"There are...no changes of any kind in substantive education law policies. In a reorganization, that is the way it should be," he said.

Republican Senator Hayakawa claimed the floor to drone on against the bill. "...Having this new Department is rather like grasping at straws," he said. "...I wish someone would tell me how (it) is going to make our children literate?...".

As he spoke, senators filtered in and off the floor. Several Democrats approached Ribicoff to ask privately how the bill would fare when the House voted in a few days. "It's close," he repeated many times.

Sen. Harrison Schmitt then rose to speak. The New Mexico Republican cautioned, "We are on the road to a major new bureaucracy...I must say how disappointed I am in Congress for not following the will of the American people."

Moynihan trotted over to his desk and addressed the empty Senate. "In the course of getting the Department of Education," he said, "we have brought the Congress to the point where we may have a confrontation with the Supreme Court over judicial review."

He was referring to the Helms school prayer amendment.

"We have come within a hair of adopting provisions having all sorts of peculiar and unwelcome consequences, politicizing education at the highest level," Moynihan continued, referring to the House's junk amendments.

"Finally, we drove from government an honorable young scholar...". The New York Democrat was especially riled over the Marshall Smith fiasco. Smith had been one of his students when he taught college.

Moynihan ended by looking directly at Ribicoff. "He knows I wish this Department well...".

Ribicoff stood up and turned around in a complete circle to search the Senate floor. "Mr. President, to my knowledge," he said slowly to the chair, "there are no further speakers.

"I move the adoption of the conference report."

The presiding officer ordered a call of the roll, and the bells rung out.

As senators streamed on to the floor to cast their votes, Marilyn and I felt a surge of relief pass through our bodies. The vote would be over in 15 minutes, and so too would our official duties on the bill. We knew the conference report would be approved by a wide margin.

Oregon Republican Sen. Mark Hatfield came down the aisle as Senate clerk called out names. He looked over at Ribicoff—to be certain—and made a quizzical motion, "Aye?" Ribicoff nodded.

Hatfield voted "aye."

A bunch of senators crowded around Ribicoff to congratulate him. We noticed that previously supportive Senators Robert Byrd, Orrin Hatch, and Milton Young (R-N.D.) had cast "no" votes. Marilyn went to check with their aides, only to learn their votes were directly related to the dropping of the junk amendments.

The chair banged his gavel. It was 3:30.

"On this vote, the yeas are 69, the nays are 22, and the conference report is agreed to."

The United States Senate had finished with the bill.

*   *   *

TUESDAY, SEPTEMBER 25.

Frank Moore met with the President early in the morning. The White House chief lobbyist briefed Carter on the ED situation and handed him a memo that underlined the need for urgent action.

"With the Department of Education bill on the House floor Wednesday or Thursday of this week and our current count showing us

214-214 with 7 undecideds, it is particularly clear that the role the leadership plays will be crucial," it said.

"Since there was no leadership breakfast this week, I'd like you to call the following and ask their help on the bill: the Speaker, Jim Wright, Dan Rostenkowski.

"Each is key, obviously, with most Democrats, but O'Neill and Rostenkowski particularly within their regions, can be crucial." The Catholics again were furiously lobbying members of the Massachusetts and Chicago delegations.

"As to the Speaker," the memo continued, "you should ask his help and his commitment to move the bill Wednesday afternoon, if possible. The longer we delay the more ground we lose."

Moore also asked the President to call Utah Democratic Rep. Gunn McKay, "who has pulled off this bill because he fears the anti-abortion votes."

The President would do as he was told. He took a one-day trip up to New York City and made several calls to undecided congressmen from aboard Air Force One. He also ordered a no-holds-barred White House effort to secure House passage. In these last days, the White House would once again awaken to an emergency legislative predicament. The power of the Presidency would be employed in every conceivable way.

Terry Straub dispatched memos all around the White House. He asked Hamilton Jordan to call several House Democrats, including California's John Burton to "be sure he gets over to the floor in time to vote this time. We'll win or lose this vote by less than half a dozen," Straub warned Carter's chief of staff. Burton was absent on the last House vote.

Straub had the President's minority affairs advisor call black Reps. "We're pulling out all the stops," he explained to Louis Martin. Carter's special assistant for Hispanic affairs, Esteban Torres, would be touching base with Hispanic Reps. Women's advisor Sarah Weddington would contact women Representatives.

Straub drew up marching orders to the Cabinet. The Attorney General would be calling his friends on the House Judiciary Committee. The Secretary of Agriculture would talk with Reps from farm states. The new HUD Secretary, former New Orleans Mayor Moon Landrieu, would work over wavering members of the Louisiana delegation. The Secretary of Labor was put on to undecided Reps from urban, northern industrial states. HEW Secretary Pat Harris, it seemed, was phoning everyone in the House.

Even Straub's own boss, Frank Moore, got a list of calls to make. "I also think you should call Brooks tomorrow and just prop him up a bit," Straub urged. "He needs to know he's not out there alone."

Lobbyists from NEA, the school boards, PTA, school administrators, and all the other groups in the Ad Hoc Committee for ED covered the House in droves, knocking doors and visiting the 120 target Reps over and over.

Hispanics, thinking Jerry Apodaca would be named the first ED Secretary, helped out.

Civil rights groups made their unenthusiastic calls to friendly House liberals, giving their formal clearance to the compromise bill.

But more than two months had gone by since the House passed the bill. The intense canvassing in the past days showed support had eroded badly. At 5:30 p.m., NEA notified the key players of the latest vote count: 214 wrong, 209 right, 12 undecided.

*　　*　　*

WEDNESDAY, SEPTEMBER 26.
Shortly after 7:00 a.m., Terry Straub, Frank Moore, and Stuart Eizenstat met with the President in the Oval Office. Straub and Moore

gave their gloomy forecast to Carter about the ED bill's prognosis if a vote were taken later that day. Carter listened silently.

"The only opportunity I see involves the Catholic question," Straub told the chief executive. "We could buy a few votes by promising an assistant secretary for nonpublic education."

The President nodded quietly, then reached over his desk and punched his phone buttons. The Vice President came on the other end. Carter explained the situation. "Can you work this out with Terry Straub?," he asked Mondale.

Straub got up and left for Mondale's office. Walking down the west Wing hallway, somebody from one of the intervening offices popped out: the President was calling. Straub picked up the phone.

"Make the deal," Carter said. Apparently, the President and his top aides had decided in the short interval it was worth a chance.

At 9:15, the sun from a warm September day beamed through the windows of the Cabinet Room onto a dozen House Democrats sitting around the huge oval table. They had been invited to meet with the President because most still opposed the bill. Jack Brooks tagged along to lend his presence.

The President walked in, sat down, and wasted no time. The Department of Education is one of my highest priorities, he stressed to them, looking at each Rep. "It's very important to me personally." The conference was successful, producing a clean reorganization bill, he continued. It'll save money and "decrease bureaucracy." It protects local control.

During the President's spiel, Pat Gwaltney plodded in, tired from false labor the night before. Her baby was due any day.

Carter closed with a strong partisan appeal to his fellow Democrats. My. Administration has long sought this bill, he told them, and I need your help.

New York's James Scheuer and New Jersey's Frank Guarini both brought up the lack of a focus on nonpublic education in the bill.

The President responded with a commitment to seek a special assistant secretary.

"Can we get a letter?," Scheuer asked.

The President said O.K., and directed Jim McIntyre to work it out with the Congressman.

The encounter ended in 20 minutes. White House lobbyists were unsure whether any minds had been changed.

Scheuer and Guarini walked with Gwaltney and McIntyre to the OMB director's office, where they spent a few minutes negotiating the content of the President's letter. "You have my personal commitment that (the nonpublic education) office will be continued at the highest level headed by an assistant secretary," it said. "...I appreciate your support for this critical legislation." Carter signed it personally an hour later and White House staff distributed copies to scores of congressmen.

(Returning to his office, Scheuer discovered he had adamant AFT opposition in his district. He would back down from supporting the bill. Guarini's staff, proudly thinking they had extracted something big from the President for the Catholics, phoned Catholic Conference lobbyists with the good news. "We're still opposed," they responded.)

That morning, the vote count was still bad: 208 for the conference report, 215 against, 12 undecided. The situation was getting more desperate by the minute. More arm-twisting had to be done. NEA and White House officials agreed they needed an extra day to nail down votes. The Speaker's office was called and asked to delay bringing up the bill until Thursday.

There would be additional, intense stroking by phone from the White House. The President would call a dozen House members, including New Jersey Democrat Peter Rodino who had been inundated with Catholic pressure. The Vice President stepped up his already considerable effort to woo Democratic Reps.

The Massachusetts and New Jersey delegations comprised most of the problem members. Both states had numerous liberal, Democratic

Reps with heavy Catholic, AFT, and AFL-CIO populations. Sen. Ted Kennedy, we thought, could be of some help in swaying Bay State Reps, but the Carter White House wouldn't think of asking the presidential contender for aid. Marilyn called the Kennedy staff. The Senator agreed a short while later to call several Massachusetts members, but first he would call Abe Ribicoff to let him know he was helping out.

Top White House congressional aides put in a request to the Speaker for him to make a special appearance on the House floor during the conference report debate.

"We're leading by one vote," Gail Bramblett announced at the start of an ED coalition meeting at 11:00 a.m. in the House Committee's hearing room. New readings flowed in to the coalition center on-the-minute as deals were cut and members made their decisions. She handed out her last target list of 50 Reps, most of whom were "leaning wrongs" that needed turning around.

Teams of education lobbyists worked the halls of the House office buildings all day and into the night—as long as anyone was around to listen. They often ran into AFT lobbyist Greg Humphrey, Catholic lobbyist Frank Monihan, and AFL and conservative groups' lobbyists also making the rounds. It was a knock-down, drag-out fight for this, the most important ED vote of them all.

The ED groups' spirits got a lift that afternoon when the House, under extreme pressure from the White House, reversed itself on the Panama conference report, saving the measure 232-188.

Marilyn and I monitored developments in the House all day, sometimes calling senators' offices to ask if they would call their colleagues in the lower body. Our legislative counsel, Susan McNally, tantalized us in telling how she had seen the official red-lined, engraved bill ready for the President's signature. "It's really pretty, on beautiful parchment," she said. A bad House vote and we would never see it.

By nightfall, the White House task force met again to go over the day's gains and losses and persistent question marks. The count had improved slightly, but was still in jeopardy.

The House of Representatives' legislative program recordings told callers the Department of Education conference report would be second on Thursday's agenda.

We had come down to the wire, scared to death it might snap.

*   *   *

THURSDAY, SEPTEMBER 27, 1979.

The most tense, anxious day ever. ED would either be born or killed in the womb.

It would be another beautiful Washington pre-autumn day: sunny, mid-70ºs.

Marilyn and I reminisced on the walk over to the House side at 9:30 that morning. We had endured so much strain and emotion together to see this through. We tried to remain calm.

The Brooks's Committee hearing room was busy. Reports of vote switches were still being recorded and responded to. Lobbyists shuffled constantly in and out. The atmosphere was nervy, but hopeful. At 10 o'clock, the buzzers sounded, and the House of Representatives went into session. The budget resolution came up first. Jack Brooks and his staff stayed in continuous contact with floor schedulers. They expected to called to the floor sometime after noon.

There wasn't much time left. Gail Bramblett put up a doubtful front, telling the troops we had fallen behind again in the count. The wild card would be that bunch of Reps who said they would reluctantly vote "aye" if it meant saving the bill.

White House lobbyists swarmed over the Hill. Virtually anything could be had from the White House for the asking. Florida Democrat William Chappell thought the DOD schools should have their own board of education. After Stu Eizenstat sped a letter to him pledging to pursue it, Chappell said he'd vote yes. Three Reps slipped into the "leaning right" column after they were promised a supply of tickets to the White House reception for Pope John Paul, who would arrive in a week.

Several coalition members returned with reports of seeing priests walking the halls. AFL lobbyists stuck by entrances to the House floor.

The House was in a feisty mood. At 12:30, it passed the budget resolution by only six votes.

The Speaker presided. At 12:40, he recognized Jack Brooks. "Mr. Speaker, I call up the conference report on the Senate bill (S.210) to establish a Department of Education," Brooks hollered from the manager's desk.

ED was on. Lobbyists scurried, knowing the vote would come within an hour, maybe two.

Brooks spent some time justifying the bill he had brought back to his House. It "follows closely" the House-passed version, he said. The same programs would be transferred, there was a prohibition against federal control, the Senate agreed to the House's specific reduction of personnel, and the legislative veto survived, he told his colleagues.

"Now, for what is not in it…". Brooks said the "highly controversial" amendments were out, because "the Senate conferees were adamant in their refusal to accept them."

All in all, the Texan later summed up, "the agreement is a worthy product of the conference procedure."

Republican manager Frank Horton backed Brooks. "…Freed of controversial amendments,…this legislation presents a simple issue. Votes can be cast to bring some organizational sense to the administrative chaos in HEW, or votes can be cast against and thus perpetuate the same inefficient bureaucratic arrangement."

John Erlenborn, as expected, lead the opposition. "We had not too long ago a bill to create a Department of Energy," he reminded the House, "and I heard the same claims then.

"Fool me once, shame on you. Fool me twice, shame on me." Erlenborn predicted the new Department "is going to be establishing policy for education in the United States." A succession of opponents took to the podium to agree with him. By far, the opposition spoke more passionately against ED than the proponents argued for.

Arlan Stangeland said "today is a dark day...We are doing something that the vast majority of the people of this country do not want."

Rep. James Abdnor (R-S.D.) charged, "We do not have a conference report, we have a sell-out. We are selling out the children of this nation."

(During the debate's early stages, news arrived that Pat Gwaltney had just given birth to a baby boy. The coincidental timing astounded us.)

On the floor, Robert Walker waved in his hand a copy of the President's letter to Rep. Guarini promising the nonpublic ed assistant secretary. "The bill has not even cleared Congress and they are already adding high-level, top-echelon bureaucrats," he yelled. His amendments wiped out, Walker proclaimed about the compromise, "It is the Senate bill."

Democrat Ben Rosenthal said he didn't want to "embarrass the President. I would be willing to keep all the teachers in the country happy, but the price is too high."

"We spend our time arguing over a department that nobody can honestly say is absolutely necessary," Republican Whip Robert Michel lamented. "A department that should be called the 'Special Interest Memorial Prize of 1979.'"

Cleveland's black Democrat, Louis Stokes, rose to announce would vote "aye" because the conference committee had dropped the "anti—civil rights measures."

15 other Reps commandeered the microphones to praise or condemn the bill. It seemed to go on and on, fruitlessly. These statements were only staged for the TV cameras; they wouldn't change anyone's mind.

Watching the debate on TV monitors in the House Committee hearing room was agonizing. I couldn't sit still. Finally, I got up and trudged over to the Capitol and up to the House galleries. This may kill me, I thought to myself, but I've got to witness this—especially the vote—in person.

I chatted briefly with the teams of ED lobbyists stationed along the way to intercept Representatives. More than half a dozen NEA lobbyists and top Association officials roamed around the three primary House floor entrances, pulling aside members as often as they could. Terry Straub and other White House congressional people busily held mini-debates with Reps in the hallways.

I entered the crowded galleries to the booming, amplified voice of Republican John Rousselot: "If you like the Department of Energy, you will just love this new Department of Education."

The Majority Leader delivered a positive statement. "I have heard education referred to here today as a special interest," Texan Jim Wright said. "Education is the one quite general interest to this nation of ours."

John Anderson took time out from his presidential campaign to be present for the vote. (He was absent in July.) "Almost any proposal calling for changes in the status quo evokes howls of disapproval and prediction of gloom," he chided his fellow Republicans.

At 2:00, the raving and bitching was over. The Majority Leader grabbed a mike. "Mr. Speaker, I move a call of the House."

The buzzers rang summoning all House members to the floor. It was the set-up for a rare, special talk by the Speaker himself.

During the 10-minute call, the chamber filled. At least 300 congressmen took seats and would stay on the floor to hear their leader and experience the drama of the final vote on a major, hard-fought bill.

As they trickled in, lobbyists tried to get in one last word in the adjacent corridors.

Marilyn walked down the steps in the gallery I sat in. She stooped down and whispered in my ear, "We've got it."

My mouth dropped open. As she turned to find a seat, she smiled and winked. She had been maintaining a vigil with NEA and White House staff outside, so I guessed she knew more than I did about the latest count.

The sharp whack of the chair's gavel silenced the noisy chamber.

"Mr. Speaker, I yield such time as remains to the distinguished and able Speaker of the House," Brooks gestured with a smile.

Tip O'Neill his white hair shining in the bright House lights, walked slowly to the podium in the well. He carried a piece of paper and a somber facial expression.

For a fleeting moment, the near-total silence of the cavernous chamber amazed me.

O'Neill put on his glasses. "...What is the toughest job in government? No question it is that of the President of the United States.

"What is the second toughest job in government? Last week, it was that of the Speaker."

The hundreds of House members laughed loudly. The budget, energy, and Panama bills had taxed the Speaker's abilities.

"But overall," he continued in his deep voice, "it is that of Secretary of Health, Education, and Welfare. How many programs does that Department have?"

A voice from the Republican side hollered out, "Too many." More laughter.

"...Literally thousands of programs," the Speaker went on. "It is unbelievable, the size, and yet in the 45 meetings that the President's Cabinet had last year, the word 'education' was brought up only once.

"Education is the greatest asset this nation has...To retain education in this gigantic bureaucratic structure between health and welfare is to render a disservice to this nation."

Everyone listened attentively to the big man in the center. His appeal was forceful but not emotional.

"…We need a special Department of Education," the Speaker closed. "We are doing it in the best interests of ourselves, of our children and of our nation's educational future.

"I hope that we adopt this conference committee report."

O'Neill took off his glasses and simply walked back to a front-row seat.

"The question is on the conference report," the presiding officer called out.

"On that, I demand the yeas and nays," Erlenborn replied in a nearby mike.

The bells rung. *The final vote.*

My eyes caught a glimpse of the clock—the vote on S.210 began at 2:10 p.m. Immediately, Reps flipped out their electronic voting cards and flocked to the receptacles to register their votes.

Democratic Whip John Brademas stationed himself at the east floor entrance. Brooks and Horton covered the west entrance. Jim Wright and the Speaker worked over members in the center.

For the beginning few minutes, the ayes held a good-sized lead. As the ten-minute point passed, we were still very much ahead.

"Oh, Christ," I said nervously to Susan McNally, sitting beside me. My heart was pounding like a hammer. Every muscle in my body was taught and afire,

The vote board/time clock showed three minutes remaining. It read 215 yea, 185 nay, with 35 left to vote.

From somewhere outside, we could hear cheers.

I tried without success to discern what was happening on the jammed floor below. There were too many figures and faces and it all seemed to be happening so fast.

I did see John Erlenborn run around frantically, latching on to as many colleagues as he could.

The clock read 00:00. So excited I could hardly breathe and comprehend, I watched as the vote suddenly swelled from the 180s all the way up to 200.

"Oh, no!," I prematurely gasped, rising from my seat,

20-25 Reps had held off until the last moment to see how it would go, then they voted—nay.

The Speaker, in the presiding chair, stood, gavel-in-hand, waiting for the House clerks to hand him the final count.

At last, he smacked the gavel hard, many times over. The chamber quieted, and the Speaker spoke firmly but solemnly.

"On this vote, the ayes are 215, the nays are 201, and the conference report is agreed to."

The galleries and the hallways erupted into pandemonium. Crying, screaming, hugging.

Marilyn and I floated to the outside hall and tearfully embraced.

The United States Department of Education had been established.

EPILOGUE

The phones stopped ringing the next day.

Three years of vigorous activity—suddenly, it was over. We were numb and exhausted—emotionally, physically, and intellectually. *The emptiness of victory*. We felt it.

Of course, thankfully, we would have something to show for all our efforts—a new Cabinet department. But the agency existed on paper and would materialize in the form of new stationery and a federal building in Washington with a sign out front.

Marilyn and I felt sorry for our opponents, especially our friends at the AFT, who had little to show for their hard work. The scars from this, the biggest battle in the history of American education, would never disappear.

There were the celebrations. Jack Brooks returned triumphantly to his hearing room where Allan Cohen had unleashed a big party. Marilyn and I tracked down Senator Ribicoff at the Senate Finance Committee and the three of us congratulated each other. "Make sure they don't schedule the signing ceremony on a day when I'm out of town," he ordered. NEA headquarters on 16th Street was in shambles. The entire association staff was treated to champagne. NEA lobbyists reserved a large table at the posh Le Lion D'Or restaurant for a festive dinner with Marilyn, myself, and the PRP staff. The President, decked out in jeans held a little party of his own that night in the Roosevelt Room. Top White House staff, the Vice President, Jack Brooks, and key House members and staff toasted each other with beer, wine, cheese, and dip.

The value of the ED victory to Jimmy Carter revealed itself, by strange coincidence, the next morning when NEA's board of directors kept a long-scheduled appointment with the President in the East Room of the White House. They endorsed him for the 1980 Democratic primaries over Senator Kennedy, the first step toward full-fledged backing in the presidential contest. NEA couldn't stop itself from gloating in victory. Now that they had ED, they didn't care if the whole scene looked like a real, grimy political payoff.

The major newspapers gave final passage prominent, front-page play. "The House yesterday gave President Carter one of the largest legislative victories of his presidency," the *Washington Post* story began. The *New York Times* called it Carter's "first major domestic victory" of the year. Reporters wrote of the "unexpected ease" with which the House passed the conference report. (If they had looked closer, they would have found out our strategy of ridding the junk amendments barely worked—16 Representatives who had voted against the bill in July switched and voted for the conference compromise; 12 who voted for the bill opposed it.) The *Post* quoted a House aide who called the ED effort "as thorough a lobbying job as I've ever seen."

Amusingly, not until the bill passed did the press discover HEW's name would be change to the "Department of Health and Human Services." A string of analytical articles played up the death of the word "welfare."

Editorial comment was subdued. We waited for a decree from the *Washington Post*. It came two days after passage in an editorial entitled, "The Unnecessary Department." The paper said, "A great deal now depends on the person chosen by Mr. Carter to head (it)." Glumly, the Post concluded, "It would best serve the interest of education if this legislation turns out not to make very much difference."

*   *   *

Hundreds of people from the world of education packed the huge, stately East Room of the White House Wednesday morning, October 17. At the back of the room stood several banks of TV lights, cameras, and photographers.

A small stage below the massive central chandelier supported a podium with the Presidential seal and the customary flags. Guards and Secret Service agents were everywhere.

The crowd hushed at the voice of an announcer: "Ladies and gentlemen, the President of the United States."

To thunderous applause, Jimmy Carter entered, a beaming grin on his face. The clapping was prolonged and interspersed with cheers.

Exactly 20 days after the conference report passed, the President would sign the ED bill in a joyous ceremony.

"The first thing I want to do," Carter began, "is to invite into the room the real beneficiaries of the new Department of Education, a group of fourth grade students from Brent Elementary School (in Washington)."

Everyone applauded as some 30 youngsters marched in file to the front. Poor things, they didn't know what they were there for. "Someone just had to do the kids routine," I mumbled into Marilyn's ear. The two of us stood so far back in the mass of people we could hardly see.

"…It is not going to be a panacea which can resolve every problem immediately," the President told the crowd. "But I am determined to make it work. And I am very grateful to all of those who have been instrumental in reaching this goal after I don't know how many years of frustrated efforts.

"Sometimes it didn't look as though we were going to make it." He praised the "superb bipartisan leadership" in the House and Senate.

"…I would like to introduce now to speak for the House Jack Brooks, who is a formidable ally to have in a tough fight."

The room filled with laughter and applause. Brooks, Frank Horton, Abe Ribicoff, Walter Mondale, and Jim McIntyre stood on the stage behind Carter.

"He hates to lose and he rarely does," Carter joked. "…Had it not been for him, we would not have prevailed…I am deeply grateful to Jack." With that, the President turned to Brooks and clapped his hands loudly, spurring the whole audience to do likewise.

Brooks put on his 'aw-shucks expression. "…We weren't always sure we would make this trip," he said, prompting more laughs.

"…Now, I would like to turn to Abe Ribicoff," the President said into his microphone. "He, contrary to Jack Brooks, made an extremely difficult issue look easy." We laughed.

Our Senator recapped how President Kennedy asked him to be HEW Secretary, and he soon realized education was getting shortchanged, and then introduced a bill upon entering the Senate.

"So now it has become a reality," Ribicoff said. "Organization is policy. The policies that we have been adopting can be put into effect." The Senator, the real winner in the endurance race among those on stage, purposely kept his remarks short, sweet, and low-key.

The President called up on stage Atlanta black educator Dr. Benjamin Mays and one of the fourth graders "just to show you how important it is to bridge the generation gap." The move was more an attempt to stage an interesting photo opportunity.

"…And now I would like to sign the bill." The President took out his pens and, with Mays, the child, the Vice President, and congressmen surrounding him, etched his name on the parchment.

Carter exited, smiling, to another standing ovation. Guests were allowed to roam the main two floor of the White House, sipping beverages and eating pastries.

A Marine in full uniform guarded the official red-lined bill as people took turns gazing at it. The National Archives would preserve the Act for posterity.

We would forever preserve the memories.

*   *   *

Public Law 96-88, 20 United States Code 3401, the Department of Education Organization Act.

Section 601, *Effective date*: "The provisions of this Act shall take effect one hundred and eighty days after the first Secretary takes office…".

Before it could lift-off the ground, ED had to have a leader. The struggle to name the first U.S. Secretary of Education would consume four weeks.

The White House personnel office had already done some preliminary snooping around the country. Ironically, a one-time key player in the ED battle headed up the search—Decker Anstrom, once Pat Gwaltney's top assistant.

First, Anstrom drew up a concept of the kind of person who would make the best Secretary—someone who had been above the fray of the battle to establish ED and education politics in general. He and his colleagues wanted to avoid a sharp partisan. They also sought an individual who wasn't beholden to the National Education Association.

The list of candidates grew long the first two weeks of October. First, newspapers reported Jerry Apodaca was the leading contender. Apodaca had lobbied hard for the job, but then a private Oval Office meeting with the President blew his chances. Carter reportedly wasn't very impressed with him, and Apodaca left not as interested or enthused as before.

On October 20, the *Washington Post* ran a story saying Apodaca was out and the search process was "broadening." By this time, names mentioned included Mary Berry, Jesse Jackson, former Florida Gov. Reuben

Askew, Duke University President Terry Sanford, television personality Bill Moyers, civil service head Alan Campbell, former U.S. education commissioner Harold Howe, and several others. Many were listed only for personal ego gratification or to reward them for supporting either ED or the President.

Marilyn and I favored Alan Campbell, whom our Senate Committee had worked closely with and we knew to be an adept manager of bureaucracy. We felt the first Education Secretary would be preoccupied with piecing ED together, a strictly managerial task. Campbell coyly indicated to Dick Wegman that he would appreciate some help in getting the nomination. But Senator Ribicoff refused to involve himself, believing the President had the right and responsibility to pick his own people.

The third week of October, the White House personnel office sent a memo to the President, offering 10 finalists to the President and recommending one specific person.

"Looks like it's going to be Shirley Hufstedler," Gail Bramblett told me by phone Thursday, October 25. NEA, interestingly, kept a respectable distance from the search.

"Shirley *who*?," I asked. Other ED teammates had the same response.

Age 54. A resident of Los Angeles. An accomplished lawyer. California state court system judge, 1961-68. U.S. Court of Appeals judge, 1969-present. Often mentioned as candidate for first female justice of the U.S. Supreme Court.

How or why Hufstedler's name first came up, nobody seems to remember. But she had many friends in Washington, including Deputy Secretary of State Warren Christopher and Defense Secretary Harold Brown. Decker Anstrom was struck by the range of people she knew and their favorable comments about her. He knew she would be a surprise choice, one who would come to Washington with no controversial baggage to speak of, a woman who would bring fresh perspective to the new Department.

The Vice President called to sound her out in a semi-formal way. She said all the right things, indicated her interest, and got an invitation to come to Washington. Hufstedler was ushered the Oval Office Monday morning, October 29. The President liked her, offered her the post, she accepted, and the news broke that night on the national TV newscasts.

The appointment was brilliant because, if for no other reason, it threw our opponents totally off their tracks. The *Washington Post* hailed the announcement in an editorial as "genuine good news." Mrs. Hufstedler, the Post said, "is not part or product of that particular hustling educational bureaucracy whose prospective influence was one of the better reasons for opposing (ED)." The President was praised for not naming a political pawn.

Senate confirmation was swift and easy; it voted 81-2 (Senators Helms and John Tower (R-Texas) opposing) in approval November 30. Hufstedler was sworn in at a White House ceremony December 6.

No longer the top U.S. education official and passed over for the Secretaryship, Mary Berry resigned, effective January 31.

*   *   *

"Department of Education *Transition Team*," secretaries answered phone calls at Pat Gwaltney's PRP offices the day after the House passed the conference report.

The nation had made only 12 Cabinet departments before ED.

No one was really an expert at it. There were no books to follow. The transition process would go a day at a time until finished.

Secretary-designate Hufstedler sat down immediately with top OMB/PRP staff to go over the preliminary plans. OMB would have plenty of say and influence, but Hufstedler caught on quickly and would be no patsy.

Offices scattered at 11 different locations throughout the Washington area had to be pulled together. Nationwide searches would be conducted to find candidates for the 13 top posts. Staffs and offices to be extracted from HEW had to be negotiated with Secretary Patricia Harris. Hufstedler would set up her own "Office of the Secretary" and establish reporting relationships in the new structure. And there were plenty of small details: deciding on the Department's nickname, its seal, flag, signs, stationery, limousine for the Secretary, etc.

Lobbyists and representatives of hundreds of education organizations and interests descended on the small transition staff. The Secretary of Education already was fighting her budget battles with OMB. Literally thousands of people sought jobs, refusing to acknowledge that the bill mandated a cut of 500 positions. Hufstedler and her people were overwhelmed at first.

Progress was slow, touching off howls of criticism from many education groups, especially those ambivalent about ED from the start. The transition through November and December seemed unorganized and confusing. It lacked strong leadership. The prestigious and vital subcabinet slots went unfilled; only four had been named by March 1, 1980.

Gradually, Hufstedler took the reins and acted. She divvied up the transition team into task forces—on space, legal services, personnel, public affairs, finance, management, legislation, and the major program areas. Then she hired early January 1980 a transition chief to bring administrative control to the chaos. The situation turned around.

By April, people had been found for the assistant secretary posts and were going through the Senate confirmation process. Offices had been set up, plans for transfers devised, and Hufstedler aimed to beat the statutory six-month deadline (June 1) with a formal opening sometime in early May.

ED had taken on a life of its own. Shirley Hufstedler had set a mentality—the agency would commence from a clean slate and disassociate itself from its messy political origins. The many proud fathers of ED were ignored and hardly consulted. Allan Cohen volunteered his services and worked almost daily helping to get things moving, but was booted out three months later. Both Marilyn and Gail Bramblett were candidates for assistant secretary, congressional affairs. The post went to former congresswoman Martha Keys. Sam Halperin's name for undersecretary was dropped in favor of former Mass. welfare commissioner Steven Minter, a black. Ironically, Hufstedler hired several ED *opponents* for top positions.

Marilyn and I watched this all happen with melancholic detachment. ED had been our baby for three years, and now it was someone else's entirely. Stoically but with a measure of pain, we eventually accepted our powerlessness to influence the entity we'd created. It hurt even more to brush off the hundreds of groups and job-seekers who approached us for help, thinking we had the ins.

We seldom heard any more from the people we had worked almost daily with in pursuit of the bill. Those lobbyists and officials moved on to other projects, leaving behind their previously close relationships with us.

Washington is an insincere town. Friendships are useful only if they are productive. Once out of power or influence, you are cast off into a twilight zone. We learned that lesson during the transition months. We'd have to make our own, personal transitions.

*   *   *

In hazy, humid sunshine, 1,200 guests filled rows of seats on the south lawn of the White House before an outdoor stage decorated with flags and a giant reproduction of a new postage stamp. "Learning Never Ends," read the stamp's inscription.

It was Wednesday, May 7, 1980—"Salute to Learning Day." The White House grounds were booked for *two* celebrations inaugurating the opening of the United States Department of Education. Jimmy and Rosalyn Carter had invited the nation's most prominent leaders in education, labor, and civil rights to join in the festivities.

The band that afternoon struck up "Hail to the Chief" and the President, his wife, and daughter Amy marched from the south portico to the stage, greeted by warm applause.

"...Because of you, there is today a full-fledged Cabinet-level Department of Education and a chair in the White House, in the Cabinet Room, marked 'Secretary of Education,'" the President praised the crowd.

"...It has been said, victory has a thousand fathers...".

A local grade school chorus sung "America, the Beautiful." The President walked over to the podium—TV cameras recording him—and asked the audience to sing the song again with him and the chorus.

Then, Amy Carter tugged a cord and unfurled ED's official seal—an oak tree superimposed on a radiant sun with an acorn nut below.

Hundreds of the more special guests were invited back to the White House Wednesday night for a unique program of entertainment and refreshments. Rain forced the event to be moved to nearby Constitution Hall, where pianist Byron Janis, opera soloist Robert Merrill, sculptor Louise Nevelson, dancer Arthur Mitchell, poet Richard Wilbur, and country-western singer Loretta Lynn each performed their works and paid tribute to a special teacher in their lives.

Rosalyn Carter followed her husband to the stage after the performances and invited the guests to "come home with us." The first lady and the renowned artists mingled with everyone throughout the executive mansion's main floor, all eating strawberry shortcake and sipping champagne.

The following week, the Department of Health, Education, and Welfare became the Department of Health and Human Services, complete with a new seal and a little ceremony of its own.

Our bill had taken effect. Our Department was fully functioning. In acronym city, it would be known, Secretary Hufstedler decided, as "ED."

*　　*　　*

Some 50 Americans had little to celebrate on the other side of the world—hostages of the Iranian government, imprisoned within the American embassy compound in Teheran.

Their plight—then stretching past six months—captivated the American public's attention. In a presidential election year, Jimmy Carter's standing with the voters fell sharply as the Iranian crisis dragged on. With energetic help of NEA teachers, he had barely managed to beat back the Kennedy challenge. But he would arrive at the summer's Democratic convention in New York without strong, unified support from his party for his renomination.

The Republicans picked arch-conservative Ronald Reagan over moderate George Bush to run against Carter. Reagan would maintain a big lead above underdog Carter in the 1980 race.

ED was an issue in the campaigns, but a minor one. Reagan talked it down more often than Carter boasted about his accomplishment. "An ugly blossom on the academic tree," Reagan called the new Department. The Republican Party platform agreed, "encouraging the elimination of the federal Department of Education."

November 1980 approached. The hostages were still in Iran. President Carter's attempted, bold rescue mission went up in flames on the Iranian desert. The economy worsened. Reagan went into voting day a nearly certain bet to oust the Georgian from the White House.

Tuesday, November 4, Americans voted. Reagan won handily, bringing under his coattails Republican control over the U.S. Senate for the first time in 20 years.

Washington was in shock. The nation had undergone an incredible conservative sweep. Suddenly, every federal program and policy was in jeopardy. "An Education Department under a President Reagan is something we'd have to think twice about," NEA Executive Director Terry Herndon earlier had told reporters. "It might be easier to let the Department go…".

Our new ED, only eight months old, would have to fight for its life.